Sustainability and Poverty Alleviation

DIRECTIONS IN DEVELOPMENT
Environment and Sustainable Development

Sustainability and Poverty Alleviation

Confronting Environmental Threats in Sindh, Pakistan

Ernesto Sánchez-Triana, Santiago Enriquez, Bjorn Larsen,
Peter Webster, and Javaid Afzal
with contributions from Elena Strukova Golub,
Hammad Raza, Mosuf Ali, and P. S. Rajani

WORLD BANK GROUP

Contents

Figures

In memory of Gajanand Pathmanathan

Foreword

Environmental degradation in Sindh severely affects the lives and opportunities of the province's population. In 2009, more than 40,000 people died prematurely in Sindh because of an illness associated with an environmental health risk. This means that almost one of every five deaths that occurred that year in the province was caused by environmental factors. More than half of these deaths occurred among young children, most of them younger than five. Among this vulnerable population group, 3 out of every 10 deaths were associated with an environmental risk. In addition, thousands of people also suffered from illnesses that constrained them from studying, working, or going about their daily lives, resulting in nearly 1.4 million disability-adjusted life years (DALYs).

For Sindh's population, environmental health problems meant not only pain and suffering, but also an economic loss in the form of out-of-pocket medical expenses, lost wages, or time spent caring for sick relatives, among others. Collectively these costs are equivalent to about 10 percent of Sindh's GDP. The environmental problems that caused these impacts are multiple, but primarily include inadequate household water, sanitation, and hygiene; outdoor air pollution in urban areas; household air pollution, primarily in rural areas; noise and accidents caused by road traffic; and exposure to lead.

Loss of natural resources and impacts from natural disasters also represent development challenges for Sindh province. Increased salinity and waterlogging result in loss of agricultural crops. In addition, hydrometeorological hazards recurrently affect Sindh, as illustrated by the devastating effects of the 2010 and 2011 floods, several land-falling tropical cyclones, and the droughts of 1998–2002 and 2009. The annual costs of natural resource losses and natural disasters represent approximately 4–6 percent of Sindh's GDP.

Sindh's environmental problems call for urgent responses. A number of interventions could be carried out to address the categories of environmental degradation that have the highest impacts on Sindh's population. As this book explains, many of those interventions have positive benefit-cost ratios, meaning that every rupee invested in them would result in health and social benefits worth more than one rupee. Interventions to reduce air pollution within households highlight the value of actions to arrest environmental degradation, since the benefits obtained could have a value of more than 20 times the invested amount.

Responding to Sindh's priority environmental problems will also require putting better environmental regulations in place and improving the allocation of people and resources among governmental organizations. The 18th Amendment to the Constitution highlighted the need for Sindh to have its environmental planning and management system in place as early as possible. A fundamental pillar of such a system is the establishment of a formal mechanism to agree on the province's priorities, align resources with responses to such priorities, and monitor and evaluate the results.

Environmental problems in Sindh, as elsewhere, transcend the environment sector. Thus, another critical element to address them is building strong partnerships with other governmental agencies, particularly those with authority over development policies that may result in increased environmental degradation. Other stakeholders, including civil society organizations, academia, the private sector, the media, and representatives of vulnerable groups, also play an irreplaceable role in strengthening environmental governance, providing feedback on the results of implemented interventions, and in general, promoting Sindh's green and inclusive growth.

Sindh faces alarming problems stemming from environmental degradation's adverse effects on the health, quality of life, and livelihoods of the local population. The underlying goal of this book is to facilitate and stimulate further sharing of information regarding those harms, and to provide an interdisciplinary framework for bringing about improved environmental conditions in Sindh.

Paula Caballero
Senior Director
Environment and Natural
    Resources Global Practice
The World Bank

Ede Jorge Ijjasz-Vasquez
Senior Director
Social, Urban, Rural and
    Resilience Global Practice
The World Bank

Acknowledgments

This book is a result of the fruitful collaboration between the government of Sindh, Pakistan, and the World Bank.

This book was prepared by a team led by Ernesto Sánchez-Triana. The core team included Javaid Afzal, Santiago Enriquez, Bjorn Larsen, Peter Webster, and Elena Strukova Golub. The extended team included John Magne Skjelvik, Hammad Raza, Mosuf Ali, Ghazal Dezfuli, Cecilia Belita, Dan Biller, Rahul Kanakia, Marie Florence Elvie, John Pethick, Afzal Mahmood, and Sada Hussain. Peer reviewers Leonard Ortolano (Stanford University), Rafik Fatehali Hirji, Giovanni Ruta, and Yewande Awe provided valuable guidance. Several colleagues also provided helpful advice and detailed contributions, particularly Asif Faiz and Eugenia Marinova. The authors are also thankful for the support of the World Bank management team and the Pakistan Country Office, including Rachid Benmessaoud, Patchamuthu Illangovan, Ede Jorge Ijjasz-Vasquez, Paula Caballero, Bilal Rahil, John Henri Stein, Karin Kemper, Gajanand Pathmanathan, Bernice Van Bronkhorst, Bill Young and Maria Correia. The authors extend their sincere thanks and appreciation to Cecilia Belita, Marie Florence Elvie, Afzal Mahmood, and Sada Hussain for their administrative support.

The government of Sindh, mainly through the Sindh Environmental Protection Agency, provided key feedback during the preparation of the study and participated actively in the production of diverse parts of the book. Special thanks are due to Mr. Mir Hussain Ali and Mr. P. S. Rajani. The government of Sindh established a high-level committee to discuss the findings of this work. It was chaired by the Secretary of the Environment Department, and included representatives from the Pakistan Meteorological Department, the Sindh Environmental Protection Agency, and the Sindh Coastal Development Authority, as well as members from the World Wildlife Fund, Environment Management Consultants, Global Environment Management Systems, SSJD Bioenergy, International Union for the Conservation of Nature Pakistan, Shahri-Citizens for a Better Environment, Bahria University, Cleaner Production Institute, International Development Consultants, Indus Earth Trust, All Pakistan Textile Processing Mills Association, Karachi Urban Transport Corporation, and Korangi Association of Trade and Industry. The authors also acknowledge the important comments provided by the Pakistan

Meteorological Department and the Water and Power Development Authority during the 3rd SAWI Indus Forum Meeting. Discussions with the high-level committee helped to shape the approach and results of this work.

The team is particularly grateful to the Australian, Finnish, Dutch, Norwegian, and UK governments and to the South Asia Water Initiative for their support in funding some of the studies that underpin this book.

About the Authors

Ernesto Sánchez-Triana is a lead environmental specialist for the World Bank. He has worked on projects in Afghanistan, Argentina, Bangladesh, Bhutan, Brazil, India, Mexico, Pakistan, and Peru. Before joining the World Bank in 2002, he worked for the Inter-American Development Bank and served as Director of Environmental Policy at Colombia's National Department of Planning. He has led numerous operations including analytical work on policy options for enhancing the sustainability and inclusiveness of development in Sindh Province, Pakistan, which served as the basis for this book. Ernesto holds two masters of science and a PhD from Stanford University and has authored numerous publications on clean production, environmental economics, energy efficiency, environmental policy, organizational learning, poverty assessment, and green growth.

Santiago Enriquez is an international consultant with more than 15 years of experience in the design, implementation, and evaluation of policies relating to the environment, conservation, and climate change. He has developed analytical work for the World Bank, United States Agency for International Development, and the Inter-American Development Bank on topics that include mainstreaming of environmental and climate change considerations in key economic sectors, institutional and organizational analyses to strengthen environmental management, and policy-based strategic environmental assessments. From 1998 to 2002, he worked at the International Affairs Unit of Mexico's Ministry of Environment and Natural Resources. Santiago holds an MA in public policy from the Harvard Kennedy School.

Bjorn Larsen, is an international development economist and consultant to international and bilateral development agencies, consulting firms, and research institutions with 25 years of professional experience. His primary fields of consulting and research are environmental health and natural resource management from over 50 countries in Asia, Central and South America, Europe, Middle East and North Africa, and Sub-Saharan Africa. Fields of expertise include environmental health risk assessment, health valuation, cost-benefit analysis, poverty-environment linkages, child malnutrition and environment linkages, natural resource degradation and valuation, poverty and natural resources, household survey design and administration, and statistical analysis of household survey data. He has worked extensively on indoor air pollution from solid fuels, urban air pollution, water supply, sanitation and hygiene, and child nutrition and health.

Peter Webster is a professor of Earth and Atmospheric Sciences at the Georgia Institute of Technology and the past president of the American Geophysical Union's Atmospheric Sciences Section. His research concentrates on tropical oceanic and atmospheric dynamics, with emphasis on monsoons and predictability of tropical systems. He has published extensively in peer-reviewed literature, has received many national and international awards, and is a foremost authority on tropical dynamics. In collaboration with USAID, the World Bank, nongovernmental agencies, and national governments, he developed an operational flood-forecasting module for the Ganges and Brahmaputra Rivers, which has been transferred to the Bangladesh Flood Forecasting and Warning Centre. He recently developed an extended forecasting system, discussed in this book, for the entire Indus Delta.

Javaid Afzal is a senior environmental specialist at the World Bank's Islamabad, Pakistan, office. His responsibilities include moving the environment development agenda forward with client government agencies. He also task-manages operations in water resources and the environment, and provides environmental safeguards support for the Bank's South Asia Region. He previously worked at a leading consulting company in Pakistan. He holds a PhD in water resources management from Cranfield University, United Kingdom, and an MSc and BSc in agricultural engineering from the University of Agriculture, Faisalabad, Pakistan. He has also published in a number of peer-reviewed journals on the aforementioned topics.

Abbreviations

ADP	annual development plan
ALRI	acute lower respiratory infection
BCR	benefit-cost ratio
BLL	blood lead level
CBA	cost-benefit analysis
CETP	Common Effluent Treatment Plant
CI	confidence interval
CMORPH	Climate Prediction Center Morphing Technique
CNG	compressed natural gas
COED	cost of environmental degradation
COI	cost of illness
COPD	chronic obstructive pulmonary disease
DALY	disability-adjusted life year
dB(A)	average decibels
DOC	diesel oxidation catalysts
DPF	diesel particulate filters
DRR	disaster risk reduction
EPA	Environmental Protection Agency
EPO	environmental protection order
ET	environmental tribunal
EU	European Union
GDP	gross domestic product
GoS	government of Sindh
HAP	household air pollution
HCV	human capital value
IEE	initial environmental examinations
IPCC	Intergovernmental Panel on Climate Change
IQ	intelligence quotient
IUCN	International Union for the Conservation of Nature

LPG	liquefied petroleum gas
MAF	million acre feet
NDMA	National Disaster Management Authority
NDMF	Natural Disaster Management Framework
NEQS	National Environmental Quality Standards
NICI	noise-induced cognitive impairment
NO_x	nitrous oxides
NPV	net present value
PA	protected area
PAH	polycyclic aromatic hydrocarbon
Pak-EPA	Pakistan Environmental Protection Agency
PDF	probability distribution function
PEPA	Pakistan Environmental Protection Act
PEPO	Pakistan Environmental Protection Ordinance
PM	particulate matter
PM_{10}	fine particulate matter with a diameter of less than 10 microns
$PM_{2.5}$	fine particulate matter with a diameter of less than 2.5 microns
ppm	parts per million
POU	point of use
PRs	Pakistan rupees
RTI	road traffic injuries
SDCC	Social Dimensions of Climate Change
SMART	Self-Monitoring and Reporting program
SUPARCO	Pakistan Space and Upper Atmosphere Research Commission
SWM	solid waste management
VSL	value of statistical life
WHO	World Health Organization
WTP	willingness to pay
YLD	years lost to disease and injuries
YLL	years of life lost to death

Introduction: Responding to Sindh Province's Environmental and Climate Change Priorities

Abstract

Addressing the causes of environmental degradation in Sindh Province is urgent. The conservative estimates presented in this book indicate that the cost of environmental health problems, natural resource degradation, and natural disasters in Sindh is equivalent to 11–19 percent of the province's GDP for 2009 (with a midpoint estimate of 15 percent of GDP). Recognizing the need to develop a systematic approach to address Sindh Province's environmental challenges, the government of Sindh (GoS) and the World Bank collaborated to do the following:

a) create a mechanism for ranking the province's environmental problems;
b) assess the efficiency and cost-effectiveness of alternative interventions identified by GoS to address high-priority environmental problems; and
c) identify the policy reforms, technical assistance, and investments needed to strengthen environmental management and to mainstream social and environmental sustainability considerations into the province's development strategy.

To meet these objectives, the GoS and the World Bank adopted a two-pronged approach of (a) innovative analytical work and (b) facilitating stakeholder engagement to discuss the analytical work's findings and recommendations, as well as to build consensus regarding the measures that the GoS could adopt to address the province's environmental priorities.

Method

From the onset of their collaboration, the GoS and the World Bank agreed that the analytical work would focus on a broad range of issues that would provide a comprehensive assessment of Sindh's sustainable development challenges and assess the linkages between these issues. As a result, the analytical work covered environmental health problems, natural resource degradation challenges, natural disasters, climate change, and a review of the existing institutional and organizational framework.

The findings of the analysis presented in this book are underpinned by interdisciplinary studies based on primary data collected, original modeling, identification of relevant stakeholders, and development of structured and semi-structured interviews. Primary data collection helped to integrate the perspectives and opinions of a wide variety of sectors, while also providing information previously unavailable in Sindh.

The studies on the cost of environmental degradation (COED) presented in this book provide the first attempt to quantify and valuate the negative effects in Sindh of contamination of air, water, and land, focusing on those pollutants with a well-understood and significant direct effect on human welfare. The methods used to estimate the COED and the costs and benefits of environmental and natural resource interventions build on previous efforts completed in the Middle East and North Africa, East Asia, South Asia, and Latin America regions, as well as on a previous assessment completed at the country level in Pakistan. In addition, this book includes the use of new methodologies and scientific findings for categories of environmental degradation that had not been part of previous studies, such as noise.

During the preparation of the analytical work, the GoS indicated the need to address climate-change challenges, particularly by helping to understand better the linkages between climate change, the extreme weather events that frequently affect the province, and sea-level rise. In response to this request, this book discusses available policy options to mitigate the risks of these events.

The analytical work was complemented by institutional and organizational analyses, which assess the GoS's capacity to respond to identified environmental problems. Those analyses are particularly relevant, given the amendments to the Constitution and ensuing institutional changes, including the devolution of responsibilities for environmental management to the provinces.

The consultative process in preparing this work included numerous discussions with government representatives, particularly with the Sindh Environmental Protection Agency (EPA) and the Planning and Development Department. In addition, the GoS established a high-level committee to discuss the policy alternatives with a broad stakeholder base and to build consensus for the adoption, implementation, monitoring, and evaluation of Sindh's environmental management framework, including recommendations to mainstream environmental sustainability into the province's development efforts.

The high-level committee was chaired by the Secretary, Environment Department, and included representatives from the Pakistan Meteorological Department, the Sindh EPA, the Sindh Coastal Development Authority, as well as members from the World Wildlife Fund, Environment Management Consultants, Global Environment Management Systems, SSJD Bioenergy,

International Union for the Conservation of Nature Pakistan, Shahri-CBE, Bahria University, Cleaner Production Institute, International Development Consultants, Indus Earth Trust, All Pakistan Textile Processing Mills Association, Karachi Urban Transport Corporation, and Korangi Association of Trade and Industry.

Contents of This Book

The first seven chapters provide a comprehensive discussion of Sindh Province's environmental and climate change priorities, as well as of different types of interventions that could be adopted to reduce the burden of environmental degradation. After the Introduction, chapter 2 ranks Sindh's priority environmental problems based on their economic and health impacts, while chapter 3 examines the benefits and costs of alternative interventions that could be implemented to address such problems. Chapter 4 assesses priority natural resource degradation challenges and natural disasters in Sindh. Chapter 5 summarizes the findings of the institutional analysis of Sindh's environmental sector, and chapter 6 focuses on the policy options that the GoS might consider adopting to strengthen its environmental management framework. The analytical work's conclusions and outlook are presented in chapter 7.

Chapter 8 includes a more in-depth discussion of the province's environmental health priorities and describes in detail the analytical work completed to valuate the impacts of environmental degradation on human health. Chapter 8 also includes the cost-benefit analyses of targeted interventions that, if adopted, would reduce premature deaths and illnesses caused by inadequate water supply, sanitation, and hygiene; outdoor air pollution in urban areas; and household air pollution. Following chapter 8 are 12 appendixes, each covering a different element of the analyses undertaken to estimate the current health and nutritional status of Sindh's population, the levels of key pollutants and their impacts on health, and the extent of natural resource degradation in Sindh.

Chapters 1–7 will likely be of interest to a broad audience, including policy makers, environmental and climate change practitioners and academics, civil society organizations, and those interested in general in the linkages between environmental degradation, climate change, and sustainable development. Chapter 8 and the appendixes are likely to appeal to those interested in the use of economic tools to inform the development of public policies targeting priority problems caused by pollution and depletion of natural resources.

The assessment of environmental health effects and their economic costs presented in this book was undertaken in early 2012. Assessment methodologies have undergone several major developments since then, as reflected in the Global Burden of Disease 2010 Project, released in December 2012. Applying these latest developments to Sindh indicates that mortality from the environmental risk factors assessed in the book was around 45,000 instead of 40,000 in 2009. Applying these newer methodologies would also yield different results in terms of the mortality caused by some of the risk factors. Specifically, mortality would be 140 percent higher from household air pollution and 33 percent higher from outdoor air pollution. In contrast, mortality from inadequate water supply, sanitation, and hygiene could be 35 percent lower than estimated in this book. Based on these revised estimates, the average cost of environmental health risks would be equivalent to 1.9 percent of GDP (instead of 0.9 percent) for household air pollution, 1.7 percent (instead of 1.4 percent) for outdoor air pollution, and 2.2 percent (instead of 3.3 percent) for inadequate water supply, sanitation and hygiene. The cost of lead (Pb) exposure, traffic accidents and urban traffic noise remains the same, at 2.5 percent, 1.15 percent and 0.7 percent, respectively. It is important to note that these revised results do not change the main findings and conclusions in this book. In fact, they underscore the need for urgent action to address Sindh's priority environmental problems.

CHAPTER 2

Sindh Province's Priority Environmental Problems[1]

Abstract

The costs of premature deaths and illnesses caused by environmental health risks are equivalent to 10 percent of Sindh's GDP. More than 40,000 people died in Sindh in 2009 from environmental health risks. Nearly half of the deaths were from inadequate household water, sanitation, and hygiene; nearly one-quarter were from outdoor air pollution in urban areas; and more than one-quarter from household air pollution, road traffic noise, and road traffic accidents. About 55 percent of total deaths were among children (mostly children younger than five years of age) and 45 percent were among adults.[2] Deaths from the environmental risk factors represent 18 percent of all deaths in Sindh, and deaths among children younger than five represent 30 percent of all under-five child mortality. The environmental health risks are also causing millions of cases of illness, injuries, and children with reduced intelligence. Inadequate water supply, sanitation, and hygiene are the province's most pressing environmental problem, followed by air pollution and lead exposure. Road traffic noise and accidents also have substantial costs, particularly in urban areas.

Introduction

One main objective of the World Bank's assistance was to support the government of Sindh in ranking the province's environmental problems. To this end, analytical work was completed to estimate the costs of environmental degradation (COED), particularly for problems associated with environmental health risks, natural resource degradation, and natural disasters.

The methods used to estimate the costs and benefits of the different categories of environmental degradation relied on available data at the provincial and national levels. Estimation of the risks for different stakeholders was based on available data and on the household characteristics that could be extracted from them. For example, because household air pollution occurs within home dwellings, its impacts for different households can be more easily evaluated. Other categories of environmental degradation—such as outdoor air pollution, traffic accidents, or exposure to lead—occur in areas where the differentiation of effects across different stakeholder groups cannot be measured using the available resources and data.

In addition to monetary values, estimates also reflect the effect of environmental degradation on disability-adjusted life years (DALYs), an internationally accepted measure of years of healthy life as a result of diseases caused by environment degradation or other causes.

This chapter consists of nine sections. The first presents an overall ranking of environmental health risks in Sindh. Each of the assessed problems is then discussed in a subsequent section: inadequate water supply, sanitation, and hygiene; outdoor air pollution in urban areas; lead exposure; road traffic accidents; road traffic noise in urban areas; and household air pollution. The final section presents this chapter's conclusions.

Ranking of Environmental Problems in Sindh Province

Even under conservative assumptions, the COED in Sindh is equivalent to between 11 and 19 percent of the province's gross domestic product (GDP) for 2009 (with a midpoint estimate of 15 percent of GDP).[3] The most important environmental problems are those affecting human health, which have an annual cost in the range of PRs 261–486 billion in 2009, with a midpoint estimate of PRs 372 billion. This cost is equivalent to 7–13 percent of Sindh's estimated GDP in 2009, with a midpoint estimate of 10 percent.[4] Among these problems, inadequate water supply, sanitation, and hygiene has the highest cost; air pollution, both in urban areas and within households, is another pressing challenge. The problems associated with degradation of natural resources and losses from floods and other natural disasters have a cost equal to 5.3 percent of Sindh's GDP (see table 2.1 and figure 2.1).[5]

Environmental health hazards result in premature deaths and welfare loss as a result of illness. The analysis estimated that 40,000 people died prematurely in 2009 in Sindh from major environmental health hazards (figure 2.2). Nearly half of these premature deaths were caused by inadequate household water, sanitation, and hygiene; nearly one-quarter were from outdoor air pollution in urban areas (chiefly in Karachi); and the remainder by household air pollution, road traffic noise, and road traffic accidents. Young children, mainly those younger than five years of age, are particularly vulnerable to environmental health risks. About 55 percent of total deaths were among children, and most of these were caused by diarrheal diseases, respiratory infections, and other infectious diseases.

Environmental health risks are also the cause of millions of cases of illness, injuries, and cognitive impairments in Sindh. There were an estimated 37.5 million cases of diarrheal disease in 2009 as a result of inadequate water supply, sanitation, and hygiene; diarrheal infections in early childhood are a major contributor to poor nutritional status that leads to children's being underweight or stunted.

Table 2.1 Annual Cost of Environmental Degradation in Sindh Province, Pakistan

Percentage of GDP

	Low	Midpoint	High
Environmental health			
Inadequate water supply, sanitation, and hygiene	2.88	3.32	3.77
Lead exposure	1.56	2.54	3.52
Outdoor air pollution	0.81	1.42	2.03
Road traffic accidents	0.68	1.15	1.62
Household air pollution	0.69	0.92	1.15
Road traffic noise	0.40	0.67	0.99
Subtotal	7.02	10.01	13.08
Natural resources			
Agricultural losses resulting from salinity and waterlogging	1.60	2.40	3.10
Losses from natural disaster	1.70	1.70	1.70
Loss of mangroves	0.30	0.70	1.00
Loss of productive land from seawater intrusion	0.30	0.40	0.40
Loss of fisheries	0.10	0.10	0.10
Subtotal	4.00	5.30	6.30
Total	**11.0**	**15.3**	**19.4**

Figure 2.1 Annual Cost of Environmental Degradation in Sindh Province, Midpoint Estimate, 2009

Percentage of GDP

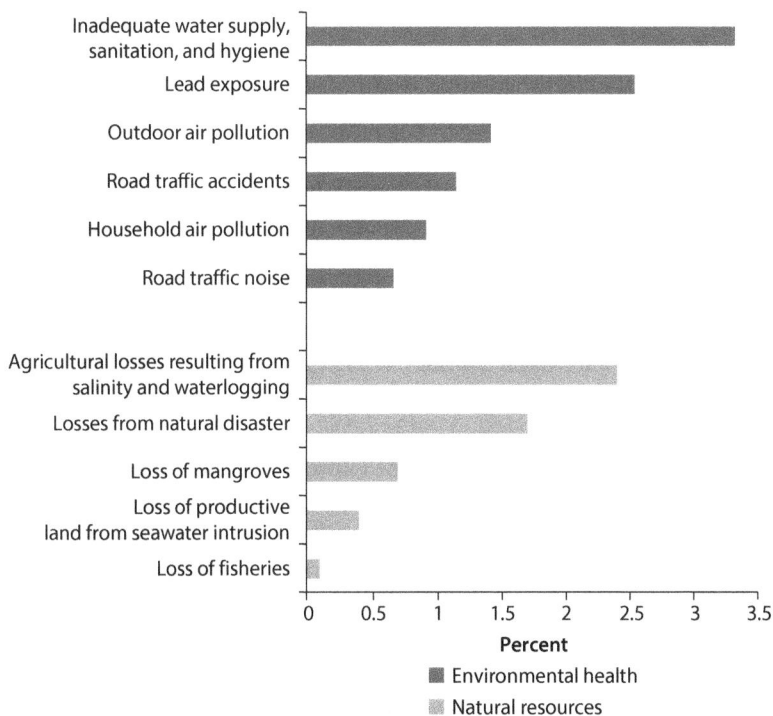

In Karachi, nearly 90 percent of sewage wastewater is discharged untreated into the environment, while in rural areas, half the flush toilets discharge directly into the nearby environment, with no septic tank or hygienic pit.

The second environmental problem, in terms of its costs, is caused by exposure of children to lead, which represents 25 percent of the total cost of health effects. Available evidence indicates that lead levels in children's blood have declined substantially in the last two decades in Pakistan, largely as a result of banning lead in gasoline. Nevertheless, lead in the blood of children in Sindh's urban and rural area seems to remain at levels that damage their neuropsychological development, causing impaired intelligence, among other effects.

Sindh is a highly urbanized province; in 2007, about 47 percent of the population lived in urban areas and 53 percent in rural areas (GoP 2009). Several of the province's top environmental problems affect primarily the urban population, particularly those living in Karachi, which was home to 13 million out of the 17 million people living in cities with a population greater than 100,000 inhabitants in 2009 (World Gazetteer 2011).[11] Environmental problems that predominantly affect the urban population include outdoor air pollution, road accidents, and traffic noise.

Outdoor air pollution is the third major environmental health risk factor in Sindh. In addition to its high economic cost, equivalent to more than 1.4 percent of the province's GDP, it results in more than nine thousand premature deaths in Sindh, principally among adults, and more than 200,000 DALYs. These are the consequences of high concentrations of fine particulate matter ($PM_{2.5}$) in urban areas, which are five to nine times higher than the levels recommended by recent World Health Organization (WHO) guidelines.

Road accidents are the fourth largest factor contributing to poor environmental health in Sindh. In addition to their role in causing fatalities, injuries, pain, and suffering, road accidents generate significant economic costs, representing 1.15 percent of the provincial GDP.

On the basis of scientific evidence, excessive and loud noise exposure is considered an increasingly important public health concern. Most of the population in Sindh's cities is exposed to levels of road traffic noise that cause health effects and impaired well-being, that is, noise levels greater than 45–55 decibels (dBs). A recently published noise map for Karachi indicates that as much as two-thirds to three-fourths of the population in the city is exposed to a weekly average noise level greater than 70 dB (Mehdi and others 2011).

Household air pollution is a severe environmental problem with higher incidence among rural households. More than 90 percent of rural households and about 15 percent of urban households in Sindh use wood/biomass fuels for cooking. The use of these fuels in the household environment causes air pollution levels that often are several times higher than outdoor air pollution in urban areas and cause substantial adverse health effects, particularly among adult women and young children, who tend to spend more time in household environments. The use of these fuels in unimproved stoves with no venting of smoke results in especially high exposure to damaging concentrations of air pollutants.

Limited available information indicates that more than 40 percent of rural households in Sindh cook outdoors but that this does not eliminate exposure to smoke and the associated health effects.

Natural resource degradation and natural disasters are also among the most severe challenges in Sindh. Their economic costs represent 4–6 percent of the provincial GDP, with a midpoint estimate of 5.1 percent. Although the major element of natural resource losses is degradation of agricultural land (representing 2.4 percent of GDP), all components of natural resource degradation in Sindh are interrelated. In most cases, these stem from the reduction of water flows in the Indus River resulting from inadequate management practices in the entire watershed. For example, soil salinity is partly caused by the reduction in the inflow of freshwater to the Indus River delta, reduction of soil deposition, delta seawater inundation, and decline in mangrove forests. This, in turn, results in a reduction of marine fishery populations. Excessive regulation of the river flow is an indirect reason for water shortages, waterlogging, increased sedimentation of the riverbed in the middle part of the river, and floods.

The following sections discuss in more detail Sindh's most pressing environmental problems.

Inadequate Water Supply, Sanitation, and Hygiene

The most important environmental health hazard stems from a lack of access to safe drinking water and from poor sanitation and hygiene. The main factors associated with this high environmental health risk are limited household water supply coverage, distance to the drinking water source, poor household water quality, limited treatment of drinking water at the point of use, limited access to sanitation facilities, and lack of hygiene. Each of these factors and the resulting environmental effects are subsequently discussed.

Coverage of Household Water Supply

In 2006–07, about 91 percent of the population in Sindh had drinking water from improved water sources (table 2.2).[12] Within urban areas, towns had the highest population coverage and major cities, the lowest. While the percentage of the population with improved drinking water sources was almost the same in both urban and rural areas, the type of drinking water sources differed significantly between these areas. In major cities, more than 80 percent of the population had piped drinking water supply into a dwelling or to a yard/plot; in small cities, towns, and rural areas, the predominant drinking water source was a hand pump. Predominant unimproved water sources included tanker trucks in major cities, carts with small tanks and tanker trucks in small cities, other (unspecified) sources in towns, and open, unprotected water sources (rivers, dams, lakes, ponds, and so forth) in rural areas.

Young children's access to improved water sources and type of drinking water source in rural and urban areas was very similar to that of the rest of Sindh's population. However, only 23 percent of children younger than five years old

Table 2.2 Drinking Water Sources, 2006–07
Percentage of population

	Major cities	Small cities	Towns	Urban	Rural	Total
Improved drinking water sources						
Piped into dwelling	77.2	19.2	36.7	60.5	3.9	31.6
Piped to yard/plot	4.1	0.8	2.5	3.2	0.5	1.8
Public tap/standpipe	1.7	2.0	0.0	1.6	0.5	1.1
Tube well or borehole	1.5	21.6	19.9	7.6	7.1	7.3
Hand pump	1.5	47.7	38.7	15.2	73.0	44.7
Protected well	0.6	1.9	0.0	0.9	4.6	2.8
Rainwater	0.0	0.0	0.0	0.0	0.4	0.2
Bottled water	3.5	0.0	0.5	2.5	0.0	1.2
Total	**90.1**	**93.2**	**98.4**	**91.4**	**89.9**	**90.6**
Unimproved drinking water sources						
Unprotected well	0.0	0.0	0.0	0.0	2.5	1.3
Rivers, dams, lakes, and ponds	0.0	0.9	0.0	0.2	6.8	3.6
Tanker truck	8.5	1.6	0.0	6.3	0.2	3.2
Cart with small tank	1.3	3.6	0.0	1.7	0.5	1.1
Other	0.2	0.7	1.6	0.4	0.2	0.3
Total	**9.9**	**6.8**	**1.6**	**8.6**	**10.1**	**9.4**

had piped drinking water supply, compared with 32 percent of the total population, and 54 percent had drinking water from a water source with hand pump, against 45 percent of the total population. These differences are due to a larger share of children younger than five years of age living in rural areas and in small cities and towns in Sindh.

High coverage rates mask problems in actual water availability. In Karachi, the piped water system supplies around 675 million gallons per day to service a population of 12.6 million, including industry and the commercial sector (KWSB 2011)[13] Distribution losses are estimated at 35–50 percent, rendering barely 90 liters per capita per day for domestic users. Some areas are supplied less than 45 liters per capita per day with supply only a few hours per day, and sometimes only a few days a week. More than 10 percent of households rely on water from tanker trucks, costing several U.S. dollars per cubic meter (ADB 2005).

Distance to Household Drinking Water Supply

Distance from household dwelling to water source is an important dimension of water supply. Longer distance compromises quantity of water available in the dwelling. It may also reduce convenience and thus quality of personal and domestic hygiene practices, including regular and frequent hand washing. In addition, if drinking water is stored inadequately and for longer periods, it may be contaminated, for example by repeated withdrawals from open tanks or buckets.

About 73 percent of the population in Sindh has a drinking water source on their premises and the remaining 27 percent of the population has to spend an average of 18–19 minutes on a roundtrip to their drinking water source

Table 2.3 Population with Drinking Water Source on Premises and Distance to Household Drinking Water Source, 2006–07
Percent

	On premises			Time to drinking water source (minutes, roundtrip)[a]		
	Urban	*Rural*	*Total*	*Urban*	*Rural*	*Total*
Piped into dwelling	100	100	100	n.a.	n.a.	n.a.
Piped to yard/plot	100	100	100	n.a.	n.a.	n.a.
Public tap/standpipe	23	15	21	59	21	49
Tube well or borehole	95	79	87	5	5	5
Hand pump	73	64	66	6	8	8
Protected well	11	14	13	22	51	47
Rainwater	n.a.	68	68	n.a.	19	19
Bottled water	77	n.a.	77	2	n.a.	2
Unprotected well	n.a.	0	0	n.a.	57	57
Rivers, dams, lakes, and ponds	0	7	7	57	28	29
Tanker truck	37	52	37	18	39	19
Cart with small tank	43	0	33	14	37	19
Other	55	0	37	6	60	24
Total	**88**	**58**	**73**	**18**	**19**	**19**

Note: n.a. = not applicable. a. Average time for the population without drinking water source on premises.

(table 2.3). There are, however, noticeable differences in water availability throughout the province: 88 percent in urban areas, compared with 58 percent in rural areas. For the 21 percent of the rural population that got their water from tube well or borehole, protected and unprotected shallow wells, or open, unprotected water sources, the average roundtrip to such water source could take up to 38 minutes. In the case of the 18 percent of the urban population of individuals who relied on public taps or standpipes, tube wells or boreholes, protected and unprotected shallow wells, tanker trucks, and carts with small tanks, their average roundtrip was 24 minutes long.

Quality of Household Water Supply

Household water quality is a major contributor to illnesses and premature deaths in Sindh. A technical assessment survey was carried out under the Provision of Safe Drinking Water Project of 2006, covering all of the 1,247 piped water supply schemes serving 11.7 million people in Sindh (PCRWR 2010a).[14] The survey found that 58 percent of the schemes, serving 5.5 million people, were not functioning at the time of the survey. About 75 percent of the nonfunctioning schemes were temporarily closed and 25 percent were permanently closed. About 28 percent of the functioning schemes used groundwater sources, 71 percent used surface water sources, and 1 percent used both sources. On average, the functioning schemes supplied water five hours per day. Six percent supplied water less than one hour per day, 30 percent for 1–3 hours per day,

Table 2.4 Drinking Water Quality in Other Locations

Location	Percentage of samples containing coliform	Source
Thatta, Badin, and Thar districts in southern Sindh	77–96	Memon and others (2011)
Ground water samples from hand pumps in Rohri city	25	
Ground water stored in containers in households in Rohri city	100	Shar and others (2010)
Municipal water in households in Rohri city	100	
Rural households in Hyderabad	23	
Rural households in Karachi	76	PCRWR (2010b)
Rural households in Sukkur	16	

28 percent for 3–5 hours per day, 26 percent for 5–10 hours per day, 4 percent for 10–15 hours per day, and only 6 percent for 15–24 hours per day.

In functioning schemes, 95 percent of source water was unsafe for drinking, of which 91 percent was microbiologically unsafe (total coliform) and 23 percent was chemically unsafe, based on WHO guidelines and drinking water quality standards of Pakistan. The analysis of water samples collected in households revealed that 98 percent was unsafe for drinking, of which 97 percent were microbiologically unsafe and 22 percent were chemically unsafe.

The poor quality of water for human consumption in Sindh is corroborated by several additional studies that document the widespread existence of coliform bacteria in various locations throughout the province (table 2.4). Recent studies have also found elevated levels of chemicals and metals in water supply in various locations in Sindh, including chromium, lead, and arsenic, in violation of drinking water quality standards (Haq and others 2009; Junejo n.d.; Memon and others 2011; PCRWR 2010a, 2010b). Lead in drinking water is discussed in the section on lead exposure.

Point of Use Treatment of Household Drinking Water

Despite pervasive drinking water quality problems, only 15 percent of households in Sindh treat drinking water using appropriate methods. Boiling is the most common of these methods, ranging from 2 percent in rural areas to 39 percent in major cities (NIPS/Macro 2008). In contrast, more than 65 percent of households do so in Cambodia, the Lao People's Democratic Republic, and Vietnam (Rosa and Clasen 2010). There are substantial differences in rates of drinking water treatment in urban and rural areas. About 44 percent treat their drinking water in major cities, mostly by boiling it. In contrast, in rural areas, only 6 percent treat their water, chiefly by straining it through a cloth, which does not make it safe for drinking.

Rates of treatment also vary substantially by type of drinking water source. About 32 percent of the population uses piped water supply for drinking and 45 percent of this population treats their water prior to drinking (table 2.5).

Table 2.5 Household Treatment of Drinking Water in Sindh Province, 2006–07
Percent

	Any treatment	Boiling	Bleach/ chlorine	Straining through cloth	Water filter	Solar disinfection	Stand and settle	Other
Major cities	44.0	30.0	4.6	7.3	4.4	0.0	0.0	0.1
Small cities	8.0	3.5	0.3	4.0	0.3	0.0	0.9	0.0
Towns	16.0	4.6	10.0	5.1	1.9	2.0	0.0	0.0
Urban	33.0	22.0	4.0	6.3	3.2	0.2	0.2	0.1
Rural	6.0	0.7	0.6	4.1	0.2	0.0	0.9	0.3
Piped into dwelling	45.0	28.0	6.0	9.0	5.0	0.3	0.0	0.1
Piped to yard/plot	35.0	32.0	0.0	1.1	2.0	0.0	0.0	0.0
Public tap/standpipe	32.0	6.0	4.0	29.0	0.0	0.0	4.0	0.0
Tube well or borehole	3.0	2.0	0.0	0.5	0.0	0.0	0.8	0.0
Hand pump	2.0	0.5	0.0	0.8	0.0	0.0	0.0	0.3
Protected well	22.0	6.0	0.0	14.0	0.0	0.0	6.0	0.4
Rainwater	0.0	0.0	0.0	0.0	0.0	0.0	0.0	0.0
Bottled water	33.0	27.0	6.0	0.0	0.0	0.0	0.0	0.0
Unprotected well	34.0	0.0	0.0	34.0	0.0	0.0	0.0	0.0
Rivers, dams, lakes, and ponds	24.0	3.0	6.0	14.0	0.9	0.0	2.0	0.0
Tanker truck	29.0	22.0	4.0	4.0	0.0	0.0	0.0	0.0
Cart with small tank	9.0	0.0	0.0	9.0	0.0	0.0	0.0	0.0
Other	9.0	9.0	0.0	0.0	0.0	0.0	0.0	0.0
Total	**20.0**	**11.0**	**2.3**	**5.0**	**1.7**	**0.1**	**0.4**	**0.2**

Note: The figures add up to more than 100 percent because some of the population practice more than one treatment method.

On the other hand, 45 percent of the population (and 54 percent of children under five years) rely on drinking water from a hand-pumped source, but only 2 percent of this population treats the water prior to drinking.

Household Sanitation and Hygiene

Sanitation coverage remains limited throughout Sindh province. According to 2006–07 data, nearly 51 percent of the population had access to a toilet. However, a number of these facilities are shared between households, and are thus categorized as unimproved facilities by WHO/UNICEF. About 26 percent of the population had access to unimproved toilets, and 29 percent practiced open defecation because of lack of access to a toilet. In major cities, 90 percent of the population had access to an improved, nonshared toilet facility, but more than 50 percent of the rural population did not have access to a toilet facility, although this figure was reported to be substantially lower in 2008/09 (GoP 2010).[15] Because the proportion of children is higher in rural areas, only 36 percent of children younger than five years of age lived in households with access to an improved, nonshared facility.

The lack of adequate drainage is another factor contributing to environmental health risks. Flush toilets are the most common type of sanitation facility among households, even in rural Sindh, but 37 percent of these toilets in small cities,

Table 2.6 Type of Household Sanitation, 2006–07
Percent

	Major cities	Small cities	Towns	Urban	Rural	Total
Improved sanitation						
Flush to sewer system	94.6	36.9	49.0	77.5	7.8	42.0
Flush to septic tank	1.1	5.4	10.4	2.8	6.3	4.6
Ventilated improved pit	0.0	3.6	0.3	0.9	0.7	0.8
Pit latrine with slab	2.7	4.0	0.0	2.8	3.7	3.3
Total improved, shared/ nonshared	**98.4**	**49.8**	**59.6**	**84.1**	**18.5**	**50.6**
Total improved, nonshared	**90.0**	**41.9**	**55.1**	**76.1**	**15.4**	**45.1**
Unimproved sanitation						
Improved but shared facility	8.5	7.9	4.5	8.0	3.1	5.5
Flush to somewhere else	0.5	9.1	13.0	3.5	7.1	5.3
Flush, don't know where	0.4	15.3	7.0	4.4	5.5	5.0
Pit latrine without slab	0.1	4.0	5.0	1.4	10.4	6.0
Bucket toilet	0.3	1.8	5.1	1.0	2.7	1.8
Hanging toilet/latrine	0.0	12.4	0.5	3.0	2.6	2.8
No facility/bush/field	0.3	7.6	9.8	2.8	53.2	28.5
Total unimproved	**10.0**	**58.1**	**44.9**	**23.9**	**84.6**	**54.9**

25 percent in towns, and 47 percent in rural areas have unsanitary drainage flowing directly into the nearby environment, with no sewer, septic tank or pit (NIPS/ Macro 2008). The situation is also worrisome in urban areas. For example, the sewerage networks in many parts of Karachi suffer from poor connectivity and broken and undersized sections; much wastewater is consequently discharged to the drainage system for storm water (ADB 2005). Nearly 90 percent of sewage wastewater is discharged untreated into the environment (KWSB 2011).

Limited information is available on household and community hygiene practices and conditions in Sindh. Two studies in Karachi assessed the effectiveness of hand washing with soap on diarrheal illness and respiratory infections (pneumonia) among children (Luby and others 2004, 2005). The studies found that diarrheal incidence and pneumonia in children living in households that received hand-washing promotion and soap were 53 percent and 50 percent lower, respectively, than in households in a control group (see table 2.6).

Health Effects of Inadequate Water Supply, Sanitation, and Hygiene

Inadequate drinking water, sanitation, and hygiene caused more than 19,500 deaths in Sindh in 2009 (table 2.7).[16] About 17,200 deaths were among children younger than five years of age, including 88 percent of all diarrheal disease mortality, 29 percent of all acute lower respiratory infections (ALRI) mortality and 35 percent of all other infectious disease mortality in this age group.[17] This represents 23 percent of total under-five child mortality in the province. About 60 percent of deaths were diarrheal mortality and 40 percent was caused by the

Table 2.7 Estimated Annual Child Mortality from Inadequate Water Supply, Sanitation, and Hygiene in Sindh, 2009

	Annual mortality among children younger than five years old	Attributable fraction from inadequate WSH (%)	Annual mortality from inadequate WSH	DALYs (YLL) from inadequate WSH
Diarrheal diseases	11,771	88	10,359	352,198
Acute lower respiratory infections	13,358	34	3,868	131,506
Measles	44	29	13	429
Malaria	n.e.	n.e.	n.e.	n.e.
Other infectious diseases	8,541	35	2,979	101,283
Other causes	39,942	0	0	0
Total	**73,656**	**23**	**17,218**	**585,416**

Note: n.e. = not estimated; DALYs = daily-adjusted life years; WSH = water, sanitation, and hygiene; YLL = years of life lost.

effect of diarrhea on child nutritional status and the consequent increase in mortality from infectious diseases.[18] These environmental problems also caused an additional 15 million cases of diarrheal disease among children younger than old and 20 million cases among the population five years of age or older. These health effects are equivalent to an annual loss of 640,000 DALYs, of which more than 90 percent are among children younger than five years of age.[19]

Diarrheal infections affect young children's growth. Research studies have typically found that these infections cause 20–50 percent of impaired weight gains in children younger than five years of age and affect height gains perhaps to a somewhat lesser extent.[20] A significant share of young children is underweight in Sindh.[21] Underweight children face higher risks of infectious disease and mortality. Fishman and others (2004) reported that a severely underweight child is 5–12 times more likely to die from respiratory infections, diarrheal illness, measles, or malaria than a nonunderweight child is. Even a mildly underweight child is reported to be twice as likely to die from these illnesses than a nonunderweight child is.

Economic Effects of Inadequate Water Supply, Sanitation, and Hygiene

On the basis of the aforementioned number of premature deaths and cases of diarrhea, the study estimates that the midpoint annual cost of the effects of inadequate water supply, sanitation, and hygiene is PRs 123 billion, which is equivalent to 3.3 percent of Sindh's GDP in 2009. The total cost, the share of morbidity and mortality, and the share of the effects among young children vary, depending on the valuation technique applied (tables 2.8 and 2.9).[22]

The annual cost of diarrheal morbidity in Sindh is estimated at PRs 24.1 billion based on the cost-of-illness (COI) approach (table 2.10). This corresponds to the "low" estimate of cost in the previous tables. No survey data on treatment of diarrhea among the population five or more years of age is available, and is here assumed to be 60 percent of treatment rates of children younger than five years old.[23] The economic cost of medical treatment is estimated at PRs 700 per case. Ill individuals and caretakers of ill children also incur time losses from seeking

Table 2.8 Estimated Annual Cost of Inadequate Water Supply, Sanitation, and Hygiene, 2009

Billion PRs

	Low	Midpoint	High
Children younger than five years of age			
Premature mortality	79.5	79.5	79.5
Morbidity	12.6	18.8	25.1
Population 5+ years			
Premature mortality	3.0	7.4	11.8
Morbidity	11.5	17.2	23.0
Total annual cost	106.5	123.0	139.4
Total annual cost (% of GDP in 2009)	2.88	3.32	3.77

Note: "Low" reflects valuation of health effects using human capital value for mortality and cost of illness for morbidity. "High" reflects using human capital value for child mortality, value of a statistical life for adult mortality, and willingness to pay for morbidity.

Table 2.9 Distribution of Annual Cost by Health Effects and Population Groups in Sindh Province, 2009

Percent

	Low	Midpoint	High
By health effects			
Mortality	77	71	65
Morbidity	23	29	35
By population groups			
Children younger than five years of age	86	80	75
Population 5+ years	14	20	25

Note: "Low" reflects valuation of health effects using human capital value for mortality and cost of illness for morbidity. "High" reflects using human capital value for child mortality, value of a statistical life for adult mortality, and willingness to pay for morbidity.

treatment and from being prevented from conducting daily activities during illness. The cost of these time losses is estimated at a rate of 50 percent of hourly income.[24] This cost is applied to both income-earning and non–income-earning adults, recognizing the value of non–income-earning work in the household.

The estimated cost of inadequate water, sanitation, and hygiene presented here does not include the effects of diarrheal infections on child stunting and cognitive development, or the associated impacts on education and lifetime earnings. Several longitudinal research studies have recently been undertaken that document the effect of early childhood stunting on education outcomes, which in turn, reduce lifetime income (Psacharopoulos and Patrinos 2004).[25] The World Bank (2008) estimated the annual cost of these effects from WSH-related diarrheal infections at 3.8 percent of GDP in Ghana and 4.7 percent of GDP in Pakistan.[26] The cost may be of similar magnitude in Sindh in light of the high prevalence of child stunting. Accounting for these effects on education and lifetime earnings would likely bring the estimated annual cost of inadequate water supply, sanitation, and hygiene to 7–8 percent of GDP in Sindh province.

Table 2.10 Estimated Annual Cost of Diarrheal Morbidity, 2009

	Children younger than five years of age	Population five years of age and older
Annual cases attributable to water, sanitation, and hygiene	15,254,855	19,548,814
Percentage of cases treated by medical provider (PDHS 2006–07)[a]	66.2	39.7
Percentage of cases treated by medical provider (PSLM 2008–09)[b]	95.0	57.0
Percentage of cases treated by medical provider (weighted average)	75.8	45.5
Estimated number of cases treated	11,563,180	8,890,801
Economic cost of medical treatment (PRs per case treated)	700	700
Time spent on medical treatment (hours per case)	3	3
Time lost to illness (hours per case per day)[c]	2	2
Value of time (PRs per hour)	29.4	29.4
Total cost of medical treatment (million PRs)	8,094	6,224
Total cost of time losses resulting from illness (million PRs)	4,472	5,275
Total cost of diarrheal morbidity (million PRs)	12,567	11,499
Cost per case of diarrhea (PRs)	824	588

Note: a. See NIPS/Macro (2008). b. See GoP (2010). c. An average case of diarrhea is assumed to have a duration of 4 days.

Outdoor Air Pollution in Urban Areas

Outdoor air pollution is the second major environmental health risk factor in Sindh (figures 2.2 and 2.3). In general, cities in Pakistan are infamous for their low quality of life. As a case in point, Karachi ranked 135 out of 140 in the world's urban livability index (based on stability, healthcare, culture and environment, education, and infrastructure) from the Economist Intelligence Unit (2010).

The severe impacts of air pollution (and poor livability ranking) of Sindh's cities are the result of high concentrations of PM, especially that with a diameter of less than 2.5 microns ($PM_{2.5}$). Urbanization and motorization largely explain Sindh's worsening air quality. As the number of registered vehicles increases in Pakistan, so does the level of air pollution in urban areas, particularly in metropolitan regions such as Karachi, where they emit a large share of various pollutants, including PM, sulfur dioxide (SO_2), and nitrous oxides (NO_x), which contribute to respiratory ailments. The following sections discuss ambient air quality and exposed population in Sindh, as well as the health and economic effects of outdoor air pollution.

Ambient Air Quality and Exposed Population

The analysis focused on ambient air concentrations of PM, especially $PM_{2.5}$, because it is the outdoor air pollutant globally associated with the largest health effects, including significant increases in cardiovascular and pulmonary diseases that may result in death or permanent incapacitation (WHO 2004). In Karachi,

Figure 2.5 Estimate of Annual Average PM$_{2.5}$ Ambient Air Concentrations in Karachi, 2006–09

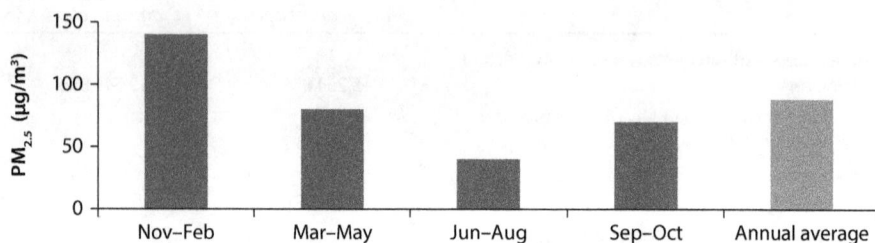

annual average PM$_{2.5}$ ambient air concentrations are estimated at 88 micrograms per cubic meter (μg/m^3) (figure 2.5), and in the range of 55–88 μg/m^3 in other cities with a population greater than 100,000 inhabitants. These concentrations exceed the guidelines of WHO, which recently reduced the recommended limits to an annual average ambient concentration of 10 μg/m^3 of PM$_{2.5}$ and 20 μg/m^3 of PM$_{10}$ in response to increased evidence of health effects at very low concentrations of PM.

To estimate annual average ambient air concentrations of PM$_{2.5}$ in Karachi, the analysis used four sources of PM monitoring data: (a) Mansha and others (2011) report PM$_{2.5}$ concentrations at a residential site in Karachi for the period January 2006 to January 2008; (b) Ghauri (2008) reports PM$_{2.5}$ and PM$_{1.0}$ concentrations at the Pakistan Space and Upper Atmosphere Research Commission (SUPARCO) in Karachi from September 2007 to June 2008; (c) the Sindh Environmental Protection Agency (Sindh EPA) (2010) reports PM$_{2.5}$ concentrations during periods of the year from February 2008 to April 2009; and (d) Alam and others (2011) report PM$_{2.5}$ concentrations at M. A. Jinnah Road, at SUPARCO, and at Sea View site for April–May 2010. Overall, the four sources report PM$_{2.5}$ concentrations in the range of 120–180 μg/m^3 from November to February, substantially lower concentrations during other months of the year, and 30–50 μg/m^3 during June–August.[27] This suggests that annual average PM$_{2.5}$ concentrations in Karachi are about 88 μg/m^3. Annual PM$_{10}$ concentrations may thus be about 183 μg/m^3.[28]

Karachi consists administratively of 18 towns and several cantonments. The total area of Karachi is 3,600 km^2 and had an estimated population of 15.1 million in 2005 (CDGK 2007).[29] About 12.8 million of the population lived in 15 of the towns with an area of 365 km^2 and an average population density of 35,000 people per km^2.[30] This makes Karachi one of the megacities with the highest population density in the world. A very large number of people are therefore exposed to every ton of air pollution emitted in the city.

Seasonal variability and the contribution to ambient PM concentrations of emissions originating from a specific location in the city are influenced by wind conditions, rainfall patterns, and other climatic factors. The wind in Karachi is predominantly from the southwest and west-southwest from March to October, and east-northeast and north-northeast from November to February. Wind speed is generally highest during May to August and lowest during October to February.

Table 2.11 Populations and Estimates of Annual Average Particulate Matter Concentrations in Cities in Sindh Province, 2009

Cities	PM_{10} ($\mu g/m^3$)	$PM_{2.5}$ ($\mu g/m^3$)	Population (millions) 2009
Hyderabad	170	82	1.54
Sukkur	125	60	0.48
Larkana	124	60	0.44
Mirpur Kas	136	65	0.24
Nawabshah	123	59	0.26
Jacobabad	125	60	0.19
Shikarpur	115	55	0.17
Tando Adam	115	55	0.14
Khaipur	114	55	0.14
Dadu, Tando Allah Yar, and Khandh Kot[a]	115	55	0.38
Total			**4.0**

Source: PM_{10} concentrations are World Bank modeling estimates for 2004. $PM_{2.5}$ is 48 percent of PM_{10} in Karachi, based on Alam and others (2011). Population is for 2009, based on estimates reported by World Gazetteer (2011).

Note: a. World Bank does not report PM_{10} for these cities. Therefore, PM_{10} concentrations are assumed to be the same as the model estimates for Shikarpur, Tando Adam, and Khajpur.

Rain falls predominantly during July to September. These wind and rainfall patterns are likely important factors in explaining why $PM_{2.5}$ ambient concentrations in Karachi are 3–4 times higher during November to February than during June to August.

In addition, an estimated 4 million people lived in 12 other cities with a population of more than 100,000 in 2009 (table 2.11). This estimate reflects an annual average population growth of 3 percent since the population census in 1998 and is thus likely an understatement of the entire urban areas of the cities. World Bank modeling estimates of annual average PM_{10} concentrations were applied to these cities, given that monitoring data of PM_{10} or $PM_{2.5}$ are not available for them.[31]

Health Effects of High PM Concentrations

High concentrations of fine PM in urban areas are a major cause of premature death. The COED estimated that $PM_{2.5}$ concentrations cause more than 9,000 premature deaths each year, representing 20 percent of ALRI mortality among children younger than five years of age, and 24 percent of cardiopulmonary mortality and 41 percent of lung cancer mortality among adults 30 or more years of age in these cities. About 12 percent of the deaths are among children younger than five years of age and 88 percent are among adults. Nearly 80 percent of the deaths are in Karachi (table 2.12).[32]

Premature mortality caused by high PM concentrations can also be measured in years of life lost (YLL). The analytical work estimated that nearly 97,000 years of life were lost annually in Sindh because of outdoor air pollution (table 2.13).[33] In addition, more than 106,000 years are lost to disease every year; 38 percent of lost years are among children younger than five years of age, and 62 percent are among adults.

Table 2.12 Estimated Annual Mortality from Particulate Matter Ambient Concentrations in Cities in Sindh Province, 2009

Mortality	ALRI	Cardiopulmonary	Lung cancer	Total
Population group	Children <5 years of age	Population 30+ years of age	Population 30+ years of age	
Total deaths from PM	1,059	7,752	216	9,026
Karachi (% of total)	81	78	78	79

Note: ALRI = acute lower respiratory illness.

Table 2.13 Years of Life Lost as a Result of Mortality from Particulate Matter Ambient Concentrations in Cities in Sindh Province, 2009

	Population group	YLL per premature death	Total YLL
ALRI mortality	Children <5 years of age	35	37,051
Cardiopulmonary mortality	Population 30+ years of age	7.5	58,137
Lung cancer mortality	Population 30+ years of age	7.5	1,617
Total			**96,806**

Note: ALRI = acute lower respiratory illness.

In addition to premature mortality, high concentrations of fine PM are also responsible for increased illness. This study estimated that PM causes 59 percent of CB cases in Sindh's cities with population of more than 100,000 inhabitants, or a total of nearly 185,000 cases, and close to 33,000 hospital admissions, more than 645,000 emergency room visits (ERV), more than 1.6 million cases of lower respiratory illness in children, more than 100 million restricted activity days (RAD), and more than 300 million respiratory symptoms (RS) annually.[34] Around 80 percent of these effects are localized in Karachi (see table 2.14).

These health effects represent more than 106,000 YLL to disease each year, of which the large majority is among the adult population (table 2.15). Thus in total, more than 213,000 years of life is lost each year as a result of PM exposure in the cities in Sindh with more than 100,000 inhabitants.

Economic Effects of High PM Concentrations

On the basis of the aforementioned data, this study estimated that the cost of health effects caused by outdoor air pollution in Sindhi cities with a population greater than 100,000 is PRs 30–75 billion per year in 2009, with a midpoint estimate of PRs 53 billion (table 2.16). This cost is equivalent to about 0.8–2.0 percent of Sindh's GDP in 2009, with a midpoint estimate of 1.4 percent of the province's GDP. Nearly 80 percent of this cost is from PM pollution in Karachi.[35]

Mortality accounts for 50–60 percent and morbidity for 40–50 percent of estimated cost (table 2.17). The large range in the cost of mortality reflects the use of the human capital value (HCV) for adults in the "low" end and value of a statistical life (VSL) for adults in the "high" estimate. In the case of morbidity, the study used the COI approach to calculate the "low" estimate and willingness to pay (WTP) for the "high" estimate.

Table 2.14 Estimated Annual Cases of Morbidity from Particulate Matter Ambient Concentrations in Cities in Sindh Province, 2009

	Chronic bronchitis	Hospital admissions	Emergency room visits	Restricted activity days	Lower respiratory illness in children	Respiratory symptoms
Karachi	145,185	26,686	523,498	81,838,293	1,353,000	260,459,264
Hyderabad	16,877	2,957	58,003	9,067,520	149,910	28,858,368
Sukkur	4,533	662	12,994	2,031,360	33,584	6,465,024
Larkana	4,138	602	11,808	1,845,888	30,517	5,874,739
Mirpur Kas	2,368	363	7,118	1,112,832	18,398	3,541,709
Nawabshah	2,434	353	6,916	1,081,184	17,875	3,440,986
Jacobabad	1,794	262	5,143	804,080	13,294	2,559,072
Shikarpur	1,534	214	4,202	656,880	10,860	2,090,592
Tando Adam	1,263	176	3,460	540,960	8,943	1,721,664
Khaipur	1,257	175	3,427	535,808	8,858	1,705,267
Dadu Tando, Allah Yar, and Khandh Kot	3,429	479	9,392	1,468,320	24,275	4,673,088
Total	**184,814**	**32,929**	**645,963**	**100,983,125**	**1,669,514**	**321,389,773**
Karachi (% of total)	**79**	**81**	**81**	**81**	**81**	**81**

Table 2.15 Years Lost to Disease from Particulate Matter Outdoor Air Pollution Exposure in Sindh Province, 2009

Health end point	Population group (years)	YLD/10,000 cases	Total YLD
Chronic bronchitis	Adults 15+	2,000	36,963
Hospital admissions	All ages	160	527
Emergency room visits	All ages	45	2,907
Restricted activity days	Adults 15+	3	30,295
Lower respiratory illness in children	Children <15	70	11,687
Respiratory symptoms	Adults 15+	0.75	24,104
Total			**106,482**

Note: YLD = years lost to disease and injuries.

Table 2.16 Estimated Annual Cost of Health Effects of Outdoor Particulate Matter Air Pollution in Sindh Province, 2009

	Low	Midpoint	High
ALRI mortality (children <5 years)	4.9	4.9	4.9
Cardiopulmonary mortality (adults)	9.9	24.4	38.9
Lung cancer mortality (adults)	0.3	0.7	1.1
Chronic bronchitis	2.2	3.3	4.5
Hospital admissions	0.4	0.6	0.8
Emergency room visits	1.1	1.7	2.2
Restricted activity days	4.4	6.7	8.9
Lower respiratory illness in children	3.4	5.1	6.7
Respiratory symptoms	3.5	5.3	7.1
Annual cost (billion PRs)	**30.1**	**52.6**	**75.1**
Annual cost (% of GDP)	**0.81**	**1.42**	**2.03**

Note: In cities with population of more than 100,000. ALRI = acute lower respiratory infection.

Sustainability and Poverty Alleviation • http://dx.doi.org/10.1596/978-1-4648-0452-6

Table 2.17 Cost of Mortality and Morbidity from Outdoor Particulate Matter Air Pollution in Sindh Province, 2009

	Low		Midpoint		High	
	Billion PRs	%	Billion PRs	%	Billion PRs	%
Mortality	15.0	50	30.0	57	44.9	60
Morbidity	15.1	50	22.7	43	30.2	40

Note: In cities with population of more than 100,000.

Table 2.18 Estimated Annual Cost of Illness, 2009

	Unit cost (PRs)	CB	HAD	ERV	LRI	RAD	RS
Hospitalization	1,500 per day	225	9,000				
Doctor visits	700 per visit	700			700		
Emergency visits	1,000 per visit	150		1,000			
Time losses (50% of urban wage rates)	352 per day	900	3,523	705	1,321	44	11
Reduced work productivity[a]	10,076 per year	10,076					
Cost-of-illness per case (PRs)		**12,051**	**12,523**	**1,705**	**2,021**	**44**	**11**

Note: a. Ten percent of annual income, with annual income adjusted for nonworking adult population (50%). CB = chronic bronchitis; HAD = hospital admission; ERV = emergency room visits; LRI = lower respiratory illness; RAD = restricted activity days; RS = respiratory symptoms.

The estimated cost per case of illness used in the aforementioned calculations is presented in table 2.18. The annual cost of a case of CB assumes that annually 1.5 percent of individuals with this illness have a 10-day hospitalization, 15 percent have an emergency visit to the doctor, and all of these individuals have one visit to the doctor per year. Time losses are estimated at 2.6 days per person per year. In addition, the study assumes CB causes a 10 percent reduction in work productivity. A hospital admission (HAD) is assumed to have duration of 6 days and result in 10 days of time losses. An ERV is associated with two days of time losses. Lower respiratory illness in children is assumed to result in a time loss (caretaking by adult) of two hours per day for 15 days. RAD and RS are assumed to result in a time loss of 1 hour and 0.25 hours, respectively, per case. Time losses are valued at 50 percent of an average urban wage rate of PRs 705 per day. The urban wage rate or income is 1.5 times higher than the average wage rate or income in Sindh, according to FBS (2009).

Lead Exposure

Lead exposure is another source of critical environmental health risks in Sindh. Young children are particularly vulnerable to lead exposure. Studies have documented neuropsychological impacts in children (for example, impaired intelligence and increased incidence of mild mental retardation) at blood lead levels (BLL) below 10 micrograms of lead per deciliter of blood (μg/dL)

(Canfield and others 2003; Jusko and others 2008; Lanphear and others 2005; Surkan and others 2007). None of these studies has identified a threshold below which BLLs have no impact on children's intelligence. Higher BLLs may result in other effects; anemia and gastrointestinal symptoms in children generally occur at BLLs greater than 60 µg/dL (Fewtrell and others 2003).

The analysis focused on the effects of lead exposure on IQ losses in children younger than five years of age because very few children in Sindh are likely to have BBL greater than 60 µg/dL today.[36] Exposure to lead has also many health effects in adults, including increased blood pressure, cardiovascular disease, and reproductive effects (Fewtrell and others 2003). However, these effects were not estimated as part of this analysis because recent data on BLL in adults in Pakistan are even scarcer than for children. The following sections discuss current blood levels in children younger than five years of age and the consequent neuropsychological and economic effects.

Blood Lead Levels in Children under Five Years

Currently, sources of lead exposure in Sindh include industry and workshops, dust and soil, food and fish, drinking water, housing materials, paint, cosmetics (for example, surma[37]), utensils, children's toys, and other materials and articles containing or being contaminated by lead. Lead levels in children's blood in Karachi have declined substantially in the past two decades as a result of the removal of lead from gasoline, possibly from more than 35 µg/dL in the late 1980s to around 15 µg/dL in 2000 (Kadir and others 2008). Recent data on children's BLL in Sindh and Pakistan are scarce.

A study of children younger than five years of age in Karachi in 2000 found an average BLL of 12 µg/dL among children in a rural community 50 km from Karachi and 16.5 µg/dL among children in the inner city of Karachi with high traffic density (Rahbar and others 2002). The highest average BLL (21.6 µg/dL) was found among children in an island community outside Karachi (Baba Island). The study identified some of the sources of lead contributing to the elevated BLLs, such as lead in house dust, food, and drinking water.

No published studies have assessed BLLs in representative samples of children younger than five years of age in Pakistan after the phaseout of lead in gasoline. The findings of recent studies of BLL in children in Pakistan are summarized in table 2.19.

On the basis of data in Khan, Ansari, and Khan (2011) and Ahmad and others (2009), it may be suspected that mean BLL in children younger than five years of age is 7 µg/dL in urban areas and 5 µg/dL in rural areas of Sindh, that is, half of BLLs in 2000. The percentage of children with BLL greater than 10 µg/dL may be approximately 20 percent in urban areas and 10 percent in rural areas. Applying a lognormal distribution of BLL (Fewtrell and others 2003), an estimated 13 percent of children younger than five years old in Sindh have a BLL greater than 10 µg/dL (figure 2.6).[38]

Drinking water in Sindh appears to be a major source of lead exposure. In a study of 18 districts of Karachi in 2007–08, lead concentrations exceeded the

Table 2.19 Blood Lead Levels in Children in Pakistan, 2009 and 2011

	Khan, Ansari, and Khan (2011)	Khan, Ansari, and Khan (2011)	Ahmad and others (2009)
Age	Children 1–6 years	Children 1–6 years	Children <4 years
Area	Punjab province	Punjab province	City of Lahore
Location	Near industry	30 km from industry	Near auto and battery-repair shops
Sample size	123	123	106
Mean BLL (µg/dL)	9.0	6.5	10.9
Standard deviation	4.5	2.7	5.3
BLL >10 µg/dL (%)	31	11	52

Note: BLL = blood lead level.

Figure 2.6 Suspected Blood Lead Levels in Children Younger than Five Years Old in Sindh Province

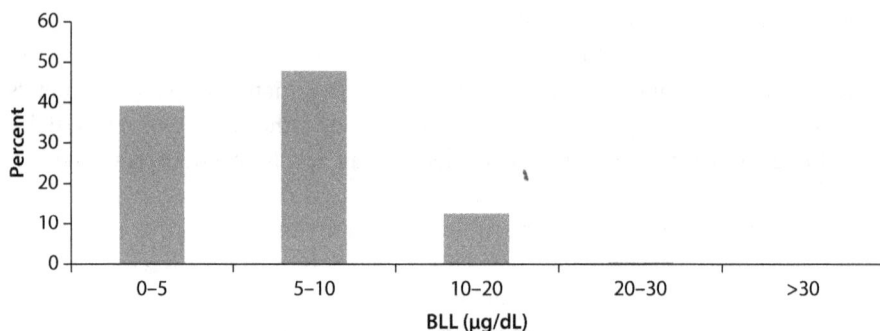

WHO guideline limit of 10 microgram per liter of water (µg/L) in 89 percent of the sampled sources. The average lead concentration was 77 µg/L in drinking water originating from surface sources and 146 µg/L in groundwater sources (Ul-Haq and others 2011). In a study of groundwater quality throughout Sindh province (excluding Karachi), 54 percent of samples contained lead concentrations above 10 µg/L and 23 percent of the samples, more than 50 µg/L. The highest measured concentration was 111 µg/L (Junejo n.d.).[39] On the basis of these studies, this book estimates that lead in drinking water results in an average BLL of 3–4 µg/dL among children younger than five years of age in Sindh and may be responsible for more than 50 percent of suspected BLLs among these children (figure 2.7).

On the basis of the model and the lead concentrations measured in drinking water in Sindh, it is estimated that lead in drinking water results in an average BLL of 3–4 µg/dL among children younger than five years of age in Sindh. This one source of lead exposure may therefore be responsible for more than 50 percent of suspected BLLs among these children (that is, 7 µg/dL in urban and 5 µg/dL in rural children).

Traditional cosmetics (that is, surma) may be another potentially important source of lead exposure. Lead concentration in surma is often very high

(>65 percent). Rahbar and others (2002) report that 13 percent of children have surma applied to their eyes at least twice a week in Karachi. Studies in other countries have found that application of surma on children, or use of surma by their mothers, increases children's BLL by several μg/dL (Rahbar and others 2002). Children's ornaments and jewelry often also contain lead to which children are exposed (Toxic Link 2010).

Studies have also found relationships between BLLs in children and their nutritional status. Anemia, or low iron levels, is associated with higher BLLs; iron supplementation or iron fortification of food given to anemic children have been found to reduce their BLLs. More than 60 percent of children younger than five years old in Pakistan are anemic according to preliminary findings from the National Nutrition Survey (Aga Khan University and others 2011).

Neuropsychological Effects of Lead Exposure in Young Children

Recent international literature has not identified a BLL threshold under which there are not impacts on children's IQ. Several recent studies have documented neuropsychological effects in terms of IQ losses in children younger than five years of age with BLL less than 10 μg/dL (table 2.20).[40] Most of these have

Figure 2.7 Estimated Blood Lead Level in Children 2–5 Years Old in Relation to Lead in Drinking Water in Sindh Province, 2007–08

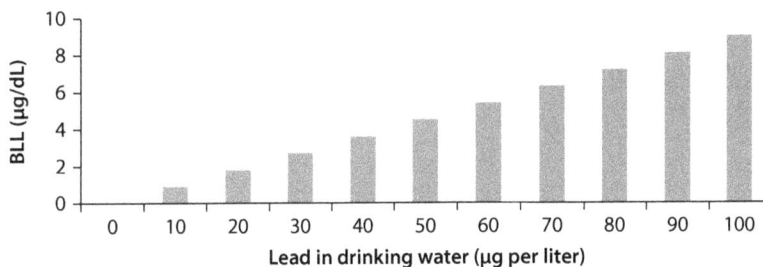

Table 2.20 Recent Studies Assessing the Effect of Blood Lead Level Less than 10 μg/dL on Children's IQ Score in Pakistan

	Lanphear and others (2005)	Jusko and others (2008)	Surkan and others (2007)	Canfield and others (2003)
Type of study	Longitudinal cohort (7 pooled studies)	Longitudinal cohort	Cross-sectional	Longitudinal cohort
Age of children	<1 to 5–10 years	0.5–6 years	6–10 years	6 months–5 years
Mean BLL (μg/dL)				
Concurrent	9.7	5.0	2.2	5.8
Lifetime	12.4	7.2	—	7.4
Peak	18.0	11.4	—	11.1
Number of children	1,333	174	408	172
Children with BLL <10 μg/dL	244 (peak)	94 (peak)	408 (concurrent)	101 (peak)

Note: — = not available.

Sustainability and Poverty Alleviation • http://dx.doi.org/10.1596/978-1-4648-0452-6

followed children from infancy to 5–10 years of age, with regular measurement of BLLs and IQ testing at 5–10 years of age. According to these studies, impairment of a child's intelligence associated with a BLL of about 10 µg/dL is in the range of 4–7 IQ points (table 2.21).

On the basis of the reviewed literature, this study estimated the loss of IQ points associated with different BLLs, assuming various thresholds above which lead causes neuropsychological effects in children. If the threshold were 2.0 µg/dL, a child 5–7 years of age with a BLL of 10 µg/dL would have lost 4.4 IQ points as a result of lead exposure during the first five years of her life; a child with BLL of 20 µg/dL, 6.2 IQ points. If the threshold were 1.0 µg/dL, it would imply an additional loss of 1.8 IQ points (figure 2.8) (Canfield and others 2003; Jusko and others 2008; Lanphear and others 2005; Surkan and others 2007).

Thus, this analysis estimates that lead exposure results in an annual loss of 2–3.7 million of IQ points in children in Sindh.[41] The total annual losses of IQ points among children younger than five years of age add to 1.2–2.7 million

Table 2.21 Effect of Blood Lead Level Less than 10 µg/dL on Children's IQ Score in Pakistan

	BLL	Concurrent BLL	Lifetime BLL	Peak BLL
		IQ-point loss (total)		
Lanphear and others (2005)	from 2.4 to 10 µg/dL	3.9	—	—
Jusko and others (2008)	from <5 to 5–9.9 µg/dL	3.7	4.9	5.6
Surkan and others (2007)	from 1–2 to 5–10 µg/dL	6.0	—	—
Canfield and others (2003)	from 1 to 10 µg/dL	—	7.4	—

Note: — = not available.

Figure 2.8 Loss of IQ Points in Early Childhood in Relation to Lower Threshold Levels in Pakistan

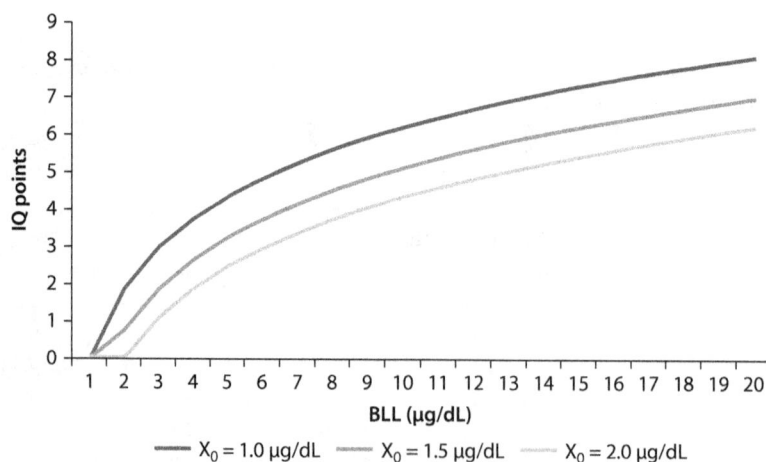

Note: X_0 means the threshold under which there are no impacts on children's IQ.

with a midpoint estimate of 2.0 million, if a threshold of value of 2.0 μg/dL is applied (table 2.22).[42] If the threshold value is lower (1.0–1.5 μg/dL), the midpoint estimate of annual losses of IQ points is 2.7–3.7 million.

Economic Costs of Lead Exposure in Sindh Province

An individual's lifetime income is associated with the individual's IQ score, among other factors. Salkever (1995) and Schwartz (1994) found that a decline of one IQ point is associated with a 1.3–2.0 percent decline in lifetime income.[43] In this study, the present value of future lifetime income of a child younger than five years is estimated at PRs 4.8 million, based on a real annual future income growth of 2 percent, assuming that real income in the long run grows at a rate close to the growth rate of GDP per capita, which grew in Pakistan at 2 percent per year from 1990 to 2009, and 2.3 percent per year from 1970 to 2009 (World Bank 2011).

The cost of a lost IQ point is estimated at PRs 47,000, which is the product of income loss per lost IQ point and the percentage of children that may be expected to participate in the labor force. Expected labor force participation is assumed to remain at its current level. With an estimated annual loss of 1.2–2.7 million IQ points among children younger than five years of age in Sindh, the estimated annual cost is PRs 58–130 billion, with a midpoint estimate of PRs 94 billion. This is equivalent to 1.6–3.5 percent of Sindh's estimated GDP in 2009, with a midpoint estimate of 2.5 percent of GDP (table 2.23).

Table 2.22 Estimated Annual Losses of IQ Points among Children Younger than Five Years Old in Sindh Province, 2009

BLL (μg/dL)	Low (β = 1.66)	Midpoint (β = 2.7)	High (β = 3.74)
<10	1,021,902	1,662,130	2,302,357
10–20	196,705	319,942	443,179
>20	1,702	2,768	3,835
Total	1,220,309	1,984,840	2,749,371

Table 2.23 Estimated Annual Cost of IQ Losses among Children Younger than Five Years Old in Sindh Province, 2009

	Low	Midpoint	High
Present value of future lifetime income (15–64 years) (PRs)	4,824,922	4,824,922	4,824,922
Lifetime income loss per IQ point lost (% of lifetime income)	1.66	1.66	1.66
Labor force participation rate (15–64 years) (%)	59.05	59.05	59.05
Cost per lost IQ point (PRs)	47,372	47,372	47,372
IQ points lost per year	1,220,309	1,984,840	2,749,371
Total cost (million PRs)	**57,808**	**94,025**	**130,243**
Cost, % of GDP, 2009	**1.56**	**2.54**	**3.52**

Sustainability and Poverty Alleviation • http://dx.doi.org/10.1596/978-1-4648-0452-6

Road Traffic Accidents

Road traffic accidents are the fourth largest contributing factor to poor environmental health in Sindh. Pakistan ranks among the most hazardous countries in the world in terms of road safety. Road crashes occur periodically as trucks come into conflict with other vehicles (for example, two-wheelers, three-wheelers, and carts), as well as with pedestrians. In Karachi, pedestrians and motorcyclists represented 43 percent and 32 percent of accident fatalities, respectively (Ahmed 2007). The analytical work assessed road accident statistics in Sindh and based on them, estimated the number of fatalities, permanent disabilities, and serious and minor injuries, as well as the associated economic costs.

Data on Road Accidents

Figures on road accidents in Pakistan and Sindh vary widely. Official statistics, as reported to and recorded by the police, indicate there are about 1,000–1,100 fatalities and 1,100–1,300 injuries in Sindh per year (FBS 2011). Other sources provide significantly higher figures. A road traffic injuries (RTI) surveillance project, involving several institutions in Pakistan, identified around 1,000 deaths and 33,000 injuries per year in Karachi alone during 2006–09 (Shamim and others 2011). Using data from 2008, Lateef (2010) indicated that road traffic fatalities are at least twice as high as official statistics from police records. According to the National Road Safety Secretariat of Pakistan, data from 21 hospitals in 112 districts in Pakistan 19 percent of district hospitals) indicate that fatalities and serious injuries are 320 per 100,000 population. The first national injury survey of Pakistan in 1997 found that RTI (serious and minor) were 1,370–1,650 per 100,000 people (Ghaffar, Hyder, and Masud 2004). Fatmi and others (2007) report a similar rate of 1,380–2,020 injuries per 100,000 people five years and older from road traffic/streets that required medical advice or treatment (analysis of the National Health Survey 1990–94). Fatmi and others (2007) also reported that 9.1 percent of injuries requiring medical advice or treatment from road traffic/streets in Pakistan resulted in some form of handicap.

The aforementioned studies indicate that injuries from road traffic accidents in Karachi increased substantially from 1994 to 2006–09, but that the death rate per 100,000 people declined by about 20–40 percent and the injury rate by 15 percent (table 2.24). Such a comparison must, however, be done with caution because the methodologies of the studies differ and the incidence rates are

Table 2.24 Annual Incidence of Deaths and Injuries from Road Traffic Accidents in Karachi, 2006–09 (per 100,000 Population)

	1994	2008	Annually, 2006–09
Death rate	9.7	7.6	5.7
Injuries	218	—	184

Sources: Lateef 2010; Razzak and Luby 1998; Shamim and others 2011.
Note: — = not available.

Figure 2.9 Age Distribution of Road Traffic Accident Fatalities and Injuries, Karachi, September 2006 to September 2008

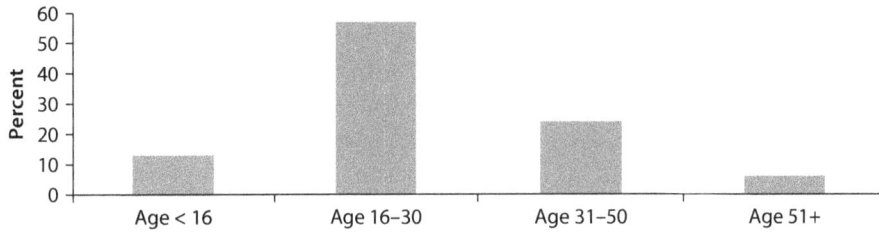

Source: Results from the RTI surveillance project in Karachi. See http://www.toyota-indus.com/concern/roatinju.asp.

Figure 2.10 Vehicle Distribution of Road Traffic Accident Fatalities and Injuries, Karachi, September 2006 to September 2008

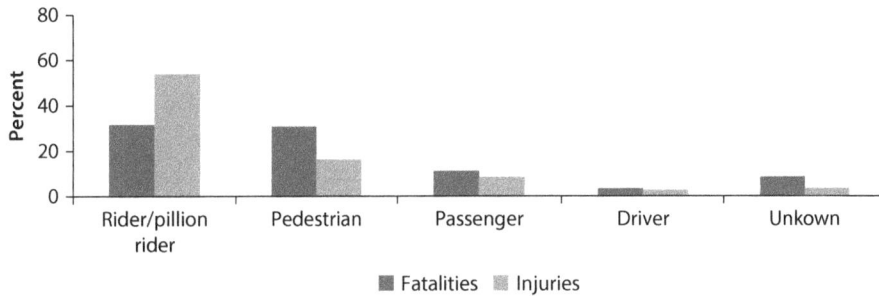

Source: Results from the RTI surveillance project in Karachi. See http://www.toyota-indus.com/concern/roatinju.asp.

influenced by the assumed population of Karachi. The assumed population of Karachi was about 10 million in 1994, and 18 million in 2006–09.

Most of those affected by a road accident were men and part of the working population. About 90 percent of injuries and deaths from road traffic accidents in Karachi were among males in 1994, as well as during the period between September 2006 and September 2009. More than half of deaths and injuries were among 16–30 year olds and about 80 percent of deaths and injuries were between 16 and 60 years of age (figure 2.9). More than 70 percent of fatalities and 80 percent of serious injuries were among pedestrians and riders/pillion riders of two-wheelers (figure 2.10).

Health Effects of Road Accidents in Sindh Province

On the basis of the aforementioned studies, this assessment applies a road transport injury rate of 185–320 per 100,000 population in Sindh, with the lower bound reflecting the incidence rate found in the RTI surveillance project in Karachi.

Many RTIs result in permanent disability with lifetime consequences on ability to work and perform normal daily activities. Fatmi and others (2007) report that 9.1 percent of injuries requiring medical advice or treatment (serious and relatively minor) from road traffic/streets in Pakistan ended with some form of handicap, based on an analysis of the National Health Survey of Pakistan (PNHS) (1990–94). Studies in the Philippines and Japan report a relatively lower percentage (De Leon, Cal, and Sigua 2005; Ono and others 2004). However, a large portion of people with head injuries suffered permanent neurological or brain damage (ETSC 2007). In Pakistan, about 9 percent of RTIs involve head injury (Tahir 2011), meaning that about 4 percent of injured people from road accidents in Pakistan may sustain permanent neurological or brain damage. In addition, road accidents also result in permanent disability from spine injuries, lost limbs, and other types of injuries. For Sindh province, a disability rate of three times the fatality rate is applied, which is 6–8 percent of serious injuries and 1.1 percent of serious and minor injuries. This disability rate is substantially lower than the rate of handicap reported by Fatmi and others (2007) from Pakistan in 1990–94, but is intended to reflect a severity of disability that on average impairs work capacity by 50 percent.

On the basis of the aforementioned fatality, disability, and injury rates, this study estimates that there were 1,800–2,200 deaths, 5,400–6,600 cases of permanent disabilities, 59,000–105,000 other serious injuries, and 423,000–474,000 minor injuries in Sindh in 2009 (table 2.25).[44] These fatalities and injuries represent around 113,000 DALYs (table 2.26).[45] More than

Table 2.25 Estimated Fatalities and Injuries from Road Traffic Accidents in Sindh Province, 2009

	Low	Midpoint	High
Sindh population (million people)	35.67	35.67	35.67
Annual incidence (per 100,000 people)			
Road traffic injuries (serious)	185	253	320
Road traffic injuries (serious and minor)	1,370	1,500	1,650
Annual cases			
Fatalities	1,800	2,000	2,200
Permanent disabilities	5,400	6,000	6,600
Road traffic injuries (serious)	58,787	82,064	105,340
Road traffic injuries (minor)	422,676	444,969	474,396

Table 2.26 Estimated DALYs from Road Traffic Accidents in Sindh Province, 2009

	DALYs/case	Low	Midpoint	High
Fatalities	30	54,000	60,000	66,000
Permanent disabilities	7.5	40,500	45,000	49,500
Road traffic injuries (serious)	0.082	4,832	6,745	8,658
Road traffic injuries (minor)	0.0034	1,448	1,524	1,625
Total		100,779	113,269	125,783

50 percent of these lost years are from mortality and more than 45 percent from morbidity.

Economic Cost of Road Accidents in Sindh Province

On the basis of the aforementioned number of deaths and injuries, this study estimates that the cost of health effects of road traffic accidents in Sindh is PRs 25–60 billion per year in 2009, with a midpoint estimate of PRs 43 billion (table 2.27). This cost is equivalent to about 0.7–1.6 percent of Sindh's GDP in 2009, with a midpoint estimate of 1.15 percent of GDP. Other costs, including material damage costs (vehicles, structures, and so forth) and administrative costs (police work associated with accidents) are difficult to quantify because of data limitations.[46]

Fatalities account for 21 percent of the midpoint cost estimate, permanent disability for 55 percent, other serious injuries for 18 percent, and minor injuries for 6 percent (table 2.28). The range in unit cost of mortality reflects the use of HCV for adults as a "low" estimate and VSL for adults as a "high" estimate.[47] In the case of morbidity, COI was used to estimate the "low" value and WTP for the "high" estimate.

Table 2.29 presents the estimated cost per case of injury. About 90 percent of injured persons are males, implying that almost all injured adults are in the workforce. The average wage rate is therefore applied for adults to estimate the cost of days lost for injured persons. Half of average wage is applied for children younger than 16 years of age (that is, to about 13 percent of accident victims) as children receive care giving by adults, most of which are not in the workforce. Road traffic accidents occur disproportionately in urban areas, so urban and rural wage rates are weighted by two-thirds and one-third, respectively (see Fatmi and others 2007).[48]

Table 2.27 Estimated Annual Cost of Road Traffic Accidents in Sindh Province, 2009

	Low	Midpoint	High
Fatalities	6.8	9.0	11.2
Health—permanent disability	13.6	23.4	33.2
Health—serious injuries	3.4	7.7	12.0
Health—minor injuries	1.5	2.5	3.4
Annual cost (billion PRs)	**25.2**	**42.6**	**59.9**
Annual cost (% of GDP)	**0.68**	**1.15**	**1.62**

Table 2.28 Cost of Mortality, Morbidity, and Material Damage from Road Traffic Accidents in Sindh Province, 2009

	Low		Midpoint		High	
	Billion PRs	Distribution of cost (%)	Billion PRs	Distribution of cost (%)	Billion PRs	Distribution of cost (%)
Mortality	6.8	27	9.0	21	11.2	19
Morbidity	18.5	73	33.6	79	48.6	81

Table 2.29 Estimated Cost of Road Traffic Accident Injury in Sindh Province, 2009

	Minor injury	Serious injury	Permanent disability
Days lost for the injured person	5	60	n.a.
Weighted average wage rate (PRs per day)	530	530	n.a.
Days of care giving	1	10	26 (per year)
Cost of time for care giving (PRs per day)	283	283	283
Hospitalization (days)	0	15	15
Cost of hospitalization (PRs per day)	n.a.	1,500	1,500
Doctor visit (PRs)	700	n.a.	n.a.
Total medical treatment cost (PRs)	700	22,500	22,500
Total cost of days lost for injured persons (PRs)	2,648	31,778	2,271,658
Total cost of care giving (PRs)	283	2,832	217,279
Total cost-of-illness (injury) per case (PRs)	3,631	57,111	2,511,437

Note: n.a. = not applicable.

The cost of time for care giving at home is half the weighted wage rate, because many caregivers are not in the workforce. Hospitalization for a serious injury is assumed to have a duration of 15 days (see De Leon, Cal, and Sigua 2005).

About 90 percent of the estimated cost of permanent disability is days lost to disability. The study assumes that permanent disability on average impairs work capacity by 50 percent, and thus, its cost is estimated as half of the HCV, where the HCV is calculated based on the weighted average urban and rural income. The study also assumes that a person with permanent disability requires an average of a half day of care giving per week. The present value of care giving over the lifetime of the disabled person is calculated in the same fashion as the HCV.

Road Traffic Noise in Urban Areas

The recognition of noise as a serious health hazard, as opposed to simply a nuisance, is a recent development. The health effects of excessive and loud noise exposure are now considered to be an increasingly important public health concern. Besides its harmful effects on the ears, noise can cause sleep disturbances, interfere with speech, and cause cardiovascular disorders. Excessive noise levels can also temporarily or permanently damage ears, and lead to an increase in aggressive behavior and other psychiatric problems.

Analysis by WHO (2011) confirms that long-term chronic noise exposure augments the risk of increased blood pressure, metabolic dysfunction, hypertension, and cardiovascular disorders, and thus, ischemic heart disease (IHD). According to WHO (2011), based in a study in Europe, noise above a threshold level of 55 average decibels (dB[A]) causes cardiovascular disease and cognitive impairment in children, while sleep disturbance and annoyance are caused above a threshold of 45 dB(A). Sørensen and others (2011) find that noise exposure increases the risk of cerebrovascular disease (stroke): A 10 dB(A) higher level of traffic noise was associated with 1.14 times higher risk of stroke in all age groups, and 1.27 times higher risk among 64 year olds or older.

There are no national standards for determining noise limits for residential, industrial, and commercial areas, or silence zones in Pakistan. The National Environmental Quality Standards (NEQS) for Motor Vehicle Exhaust and Noise apply only to noise generated from motor vehicles, and there are no standards for noise emanating from other key mobile sources, including trains, airplanes, airports, or industrial/construction activities. To estimate the health effects of road traffic noise, this study reviewed data on noise levels in Sindh and estimated the associated health effects and economic costs.

Exposure to High Noise Levels in Sindh'sise Urban Areas

Most of the population in larger cities in Sindh is exposed to road traffic noise at levels causing health effects and impaired well-being (that is, at levels greater than 45–55 dB(A). Khan and others (2010) found that the average morning to evening noise level along M. A. Jinnah Road and Shahrah-e-Faisal Road in Karachi was 95 dB(A), and the average noise level at a residential site with no major traffic was 60 dB(A). Zubair and Siddiqui (2011) found that the average noise level in the afternoon was 78–87 dB(A) around two large road intersections in Gulshan-e-Iqbal town of Karachi. A recently published noise map for Karachi indicates that as much as two-thirds to three-fourths of the population in the city is exposed to a weekly average noise level greater than 70 dB(A) during the morning, daytime, and evening.

Health Effects of Noise Pollution in Sindh Province's Urban Areas

The study estimated the health effects of excessive noise levels in cities in Sindh with a population greater than 100,000. To this end, the study adopted recent methodological developments from WHO (2011) and a large study of cerebrovascular disease (stroke) mortality from noise in Europe (Sørensen and others 2011), which were combined with the aforementioned noise map of Karachi and adjusted maps for other cities in Sindh.

Table 2.30 presents estimates of population exposure to road traffic noise in Karachi and other large cities in Sindh in 2009. The high estimates for Karachi are based on the work of Mehdi and others (2011). To account for the potential risk that these estimates may overstate population noise exposure levels, the analytical work developed low and medium estimates reflecting lower noise exposure levels, with 55–67.5 percent of the population exposed to a weekly average noise level greater than 70 dB(A). Because noise levels are likely to be lower in smaller cities, the medium and high estimates for these cities reflect the low and medium population distribution noise exposure levels in Karachi. To estimate the health effects of night time noise (that is, sleep disturbance) and 24-hour noise, the study assumed nighttime and 24-hour noise levels of 10 dB(A) and 5 dB(A) lower, respectively, than the levels in table 2.30.

The study found that road traffic noise is the cause of 12–16 percent of IHD mortality and 14–18 percent of cerebrovascular (CBV) mortality in Sindhi cities with more than 100,000 inhabitants. In addition, 31–43 percent of children (6–15 years of age) have NICI; 10–13 percent of the population is highly sleep disturbed (HSD); and 16–21 percent of the population is highly annoyed (HA) because of noise in these cities. This means that 3,100 people die prematurely as a result of noise exposure each year in Sindh, 1.6 million children have NICI, 2 million people are HSD, and 3 million people are HA by noise (table 2.31). These health effects are equivalent to an annual loss of 235,000 DALYs (table 2.32).[49] About 90 percent of the DALYs are due to NICI, HSD, and HA, and 10 percent are due to mortality.

Table 2.30 Estimated Population Exposure to Road Traffic Noise in Cities in Sindh Province, 2009 (6:30 am–12 am)

dB(A)	Applied midpoint	Population distribution, Karachi (%)			Population distribution, other cities 100K+ (%)		
		Low	Medium	High	Low	Medium	High
<55	55	10	5	0	15	10	5
55–59	57	10	7.5	5	12.5	10	7.5
60–64	62	10	7.5	5	12.5	10	7.5
65–69	67	15	12.5	10	17.5	15	12.5
70–74	72	30	35	40	25	30	35
75–79	77	25	30	35	18	25	30
80+	80	0	2.5	5	0	0	2.5
Population-weighted dB(A)		68.3	70.4	72.4	66.3	68.3	70.4

Table 2.31 Estimated Annual Health Effects of Road Traffic-Noise Exposure in Cities in Sindh Province, 2009

Health end points	Low	Medium	High
IHD mortality	1,661	1,956	2,235
CBV mortality	1,012	1,146	1,277
Children with NICI	1,360,864	1,610,206	1,865,991
HSD people	1,722,554	1,972,533	2,225,453
HA people	2,656,873	3,085,743	3,522,217

Note: IHD = ischemic heart disease; CBV = cerebrovascular; NICI = noise-induced cognitive impairment; HSD = highly sleep disturbed; HA = highly annoyed.

Table 2.32 Estimated DALYs Lost Annually as a Result of Road Traffic Noise in Cities in Sindh Province, 2009

Health end points	DALYs per case	Low	Medium	High
IHD mortality	7.5[a]	12,456	14,668	16,762
CBV mortality	7.5[a]	7,588	8,598	9,574
Children with NICI	0.006[b]	8,165	9,661	11,196
HSD people	0.07[b]	120,579	138,077	155,782
HA people	0.02[b]	53,137	61,715	70,444
Total		201,926	232,719	263,758

Note: DALY = disability-adjusted life year; IHD = ischemic heart disease; CBV = cerebrovascular; NICI = noise-induced cognitive impairment; HSD = highly sleep disturbed; HA = highly annoyed.
a. Estimated based on age at death from IHD and CBV in Pakistan.
b. WHO 2011.

Economic Costs of Noise Pollution in Sindh Province's Urban Areas

The cost of health effects from road traffic noise in Sindhi cities with a population greater than 100,000 is estimated at PRs 15–37 billion per year in 2009, with a midpoint estimate of PRs 25 billion (table 2.33). This cost is equivalent to about 0.4–1.0 percent of Sindh's GDP in 2009, with a midpoint estimate of 0.7 percent of GDP. The majority of this cost is due to noise pollution in Karachi. The cost includes IHD and CBV mortality, NICI in children, effects on HSD people, and an estimate of WTP for avoiding noise among people exposed to excessive levels of noise (≥45 dB[A]).[50,51] Mortality accounts for 40 percent and morbidity for 60 percent of the midpoint estimate of cost (table 2.34). The large range in cost of mortality mainly reflects the use of HCV for adults in the "low" estimate of cost and VSL for adults in the "high" estimate.

Children's learning, reading comprehension, memory, and attention are affected by noise exposure (WHO 2011), thus affecting their overall educational performance. This study assumes that a child with NICI throughout the child's primary and secondary education will have a lifetime income that is 0.6 percent lower than for a child without NICI (equivalent to the disability weight assigned in [WHO 2011]). The annual cost of NICI is therefore PRs 3,427, assuming on average 10 years of schooling.[52]

Table 2.33 Estimated Annual Cost of Health Effects of Road Traffic Noise, 2009

Health end points	Low	Midpoint	High
IHD mortality	2.1	6.2	11.2
CBV mortality	1.3	3.6	6.4
Children with NICI	4.7	5.5	6.4
HSD people	2.7	4.9	7.5
People exposed to noise ≥45 dB(A)	4.1	4.6	5.1
Annual cost (billion PRs)	**14.8**	**24.7**	**36.6**
Annual cost (% of GDP)	**0.40**	**0.67**	**0.99**

Note: IHD = ischemic heart disease; CBV = cerebrovascular; NICI = noise-induced cognitive impairment; HSD = highly sleep disturbed.

Table 2.34 Cost of Mortality and Morbidity from Road Traffic Noise, 2009

	Low	Midpoint	High
Billion PRs			
Mortality	3.4	9.8	17.6
Morbidity	11.4	14.9	19.0
Mortality and morbidity (%)			
Mortality	23	40	48
Morbidity	77	60	52

Note: In cities with population of more than 100,000.

Table 2.35 Estimated Annual Cost of High Sleep Disturbance per Person

	Low	High	Source
Lost workdays per year (absenteeism)	1.3	3.5	Maca, Melichar, and Scancy (2008)
Reduced on-work productivity (%)	2	4	Assumption
Urban wage per day (PRs) in 2009	705	705	FBS (2009)
Cost of lost work days per working person (PRs)	916	2,466	FBS (2009)
Cost of reduced on-work productivity (PRs)	4,030	8,061	FBS (2009)
Cost per working person (PRs)	4,946	10,527	FBS (2009)
Cost per nonworking person (PRs)	458	1,233	Half of wages or income
Labor force urban Sindh (% of those 15+ years old)	43.5	43.5	FBS (2010)
Weighted average cost per person (PRs) 15+ year olds	**2,410**	**5,276**	

Sleep disturbance is one of the most common complaints of people exposed to noise. Studies have shown that noise negatively affects quality of sleep, daytime performance and cognitive function (WHO 2011). This study assumes that HSD people lose 2–4 percent in on-work productivity, based on Maca, Melichar, and Scancy (2008). These productivity impacts are valued at the average urban wage rate for individuals who are 15 or more years of age and are working. For those who are not in the labor force, the cost is estimated as a loss of 1.3–3.5 days valued at half the urban wage rate, as most of these individuals perform household and childcare work that is valuable for the household. Thus, on average, the cost of noise exposure per HSD person is estimated at PRs 2,410–5,276 per year (table 2.35). This amount is applied to the HSD people who are 15 or more years of age as an estimate of the cost of sleep disturbance from noise. However, this cost estimate does not include the cost of less severe sleep disturbance from noise.

Household Air Pollution

About 52 percent of households in Sindh use solid fuels (wood, biomass, and charcoal) for cooking. More than 90 percent of rural households used them, compared with 15 percent in urban households GoP (2010) (see figure 2.11). Combustion of these fuels generates fine particulates (smoke) and other pollutants that are harmful to human health. Pollution levels within households are often several times higher than outdoor air pollution in urban areas in Sindh. $PM_{2.5}$ concentrations from use of solid fuels in cooking and living areas are often in the hundreds of µg/m^3 (Siddiqui and others 2009). Adult women and young children are particularly exposed to these pollutants, as they tend to spend more time in household environments. The following sections discuss the fuel types used by households in Sindh, their place of cooking, and the associated health and economic effects.

Household Fuel Types and Place of Cooking

Natural gas is the most predominant modern fuel used for cooking in Sindh according to the PDHS 2006–07 (NIPS/Macro 2008). Less than 0.5 percent of

Figure 2.11 Household Fuels Used for Cooking in Sindh Province, 2008–09

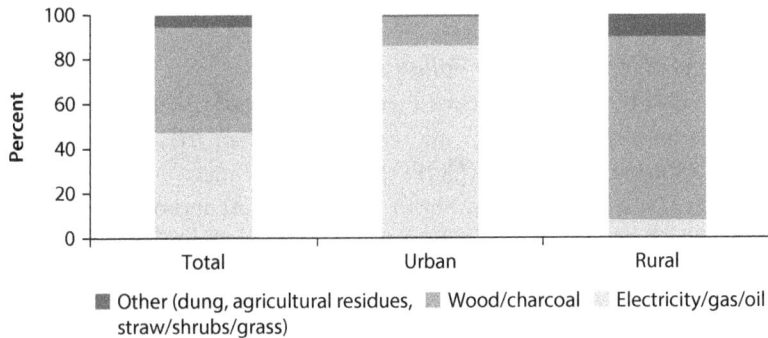

Other (dung, agricultural residues,   Wood/charcoal   Electricity/gas/oil
straw/shrubs/grass)

Source: PSLM 2008–09 (GoP 2010).

Figure 2.12 Cooking Fuel, by Household Living Standard in Sindh Province, 2006–07

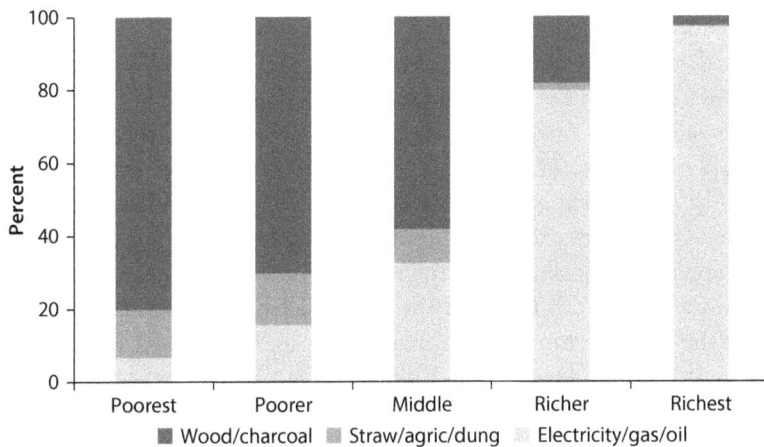

Wood/charcoal   Straw/agric/dung   Electricity/gas/oil

Source: Produced from the PDHS 2006–07 (NIPS/Macro 2008).
Note: Household living standard is measured by a household asset index.

households use charcoal; 7.5 percent of rural households use biogas, compared to less than 1 percent of rural households in Punjab and Khyber Pakhtunkhwa, and 4.5 percent of rural households in Baluchistan.

Solid fuel use varies greatly by household living standard (figure 2.12). Households in the two richest living standard quintiles are the predominant users of modern fuels (electricity, gas, and oil). In contrast, 93 percent of the households in the poorest quintile and 68 percent in the middle quintile use wood/charcoal and straw/agricultural residues/dung.

Very little information is available on household place of cooking. Sindhu (2006) reports that 48 percent of households in Pakistan cooks outdoors, varying from 29 percent in urban areas to 56 percent in rural areas. This suggests that 43 percent of households in Sindh cooks outdoors, based on the province's urban-rural population shares reported in the Pakistan Demographic Survey (PDS) 2007 (GoP 2009).

Health Effects of Household Air Pollution

Combustion of solid fuels is associated with an increased risk of several infections and diseases, including ALRI in children younger than five years, and chronic obstructive pulmonary disease (COPD), CB, lung cancer, and tuberculosis in adult women (Desai, Mehta, and Smith 2004; Dherani and others 2008; Kurmi and others 2010; Po and others 2011; and Smith and others 2004).[53] Ezzati and Kammen (2001, 2002) also document elevated risks of ALRI in adult women and acute upper respiratory infections (AURI) in children and adult women. Studies of health effects of outdoor ambient pollution have found that exposure to PM increases the risk of cardiovascular mortality (Pope and others 2002). In addition, a recent study in Guatemala found that cooking with wood on open fire compared to cooking with wood using an improved chimney stove is associated with higher systolic blood pressure among adult women, which is correlated with an increased risk of cardiovascular disease and mortality (Lawes and others 2004; McCracken and others 2007).

Increased risks from the use of solid fuels are generally compared to those from the use of liquid fuels (for example, LPG, biogas, and kerosene). On the basis of the aforementioned references, the study developed relative risks ratios associated with the use of wood and other biomass fuels for cooking in Sindh (table 2.36).[54] These relative risks are applied to children younger than five years of age and adult women in households using these fuels. The relative risk of COPD is applied to mortality, and the relative risk of CB is applied to morbidity because more data on CB morbidity are available than on COPD morbidity.

Out of the 52 percent of the population in Sindh that used wood and other biomass as primary cooking fuel in 2008–09, about 57 percent cooked primarily indoors and 43 percent outdoors.[55] Cooking outdoors reduces but does not eliminate exposure to air pollution from use of solid fuels, as it often implies the

Table 2.36 Relative Risks of Health Effects from Cooking with Wood and Other Biomass Fuels, 2009

Health outcome	Relative risk ratios
Children <5 years	2.0
Acute lower respiratory infections	
Acute upper respiratory infections	2.0
Women ≥30 years	2.8
Chronic obstructive pulmonary disease	
Chronic bronchitis	2.4
Ischemic heart disease	1.19
Cerebrovascular disease	1.26
Hypertensive heart disease	1.51
Other cardiovascular disease	1.12
Lung cancer	1.5

use of a simple shelter from rain and wind that captures and retains a portion of the emissions. In addition, outdoor cooking may result in community effects and in smoke entering into the dwellings. Available studies from South Asia suggest an exposure ventilation factor of 0.5 from outdoor versus indoor cooking, with reductions in health effects of a similar order of magnitude (Balakrishnan and others 2002, 2004).

The use of wood/biomass fuels for cooking indoors and outdoors in Sindh is estimated to cause 6,158 premature deaths each year, of which 53 percent are children younger than five years of age and 47 percent adult women (table 2.37). These deaths represent 25 percent of ALRI mortality among young children, and 7 percent of all deaths among women 30 or more years of age (43 percent of COPD mortality, 8 percent of cardiovascular mortality, and 17 percent of lung cancer mortality). These deaths represent 139,000 YLL per year, of which about 80 percent are among children younger than five years of age.[56] The use of these fuels is also estimated to be the cause of CB among 146,000 women, and of 3.2 million annual cases of respiratory infections among children younger than five years of age. These health effects are equivalent to an annual loss of 180,000 DALYs.

Household use of solid fuels also resulted in more than 3.3 million cases of illnesses in 2009, including ALRI, AURI, and CB; these represented a loss of about 41,400 DALYs (table 2.38).[57]

The burden of household air pollution falls disproportionally on women, children, and vulnerable groups, as underscored by the figures presented in this section. These findings are consistent with the existing literature that highlights the different associations of environmental health hazards on males and females. Many studies find stronger effects among females than males; however, what remains unclear is whether the observed impacts are attributed mainly

Table 2.37 Estimated Annual Mortality from Household Use of Wood and Biomass for Cooking in Sindh Province, 2009

Health outcome	Population group	Annual baseline mortality	Attributable fraction from use of solid fuels (%)	Annual mortality from use of solid fuels	DALYs (YLL) from use of solid fuels
ALRI	Children younger than 5 years old	13,347	25	3,279	111,474
COPD	Women age 30+ years	3,310	43	1,408	12,673
Ischemic heart disease	Women age 30+ years	10,150	7	736	8,093
Cerebrovascular disease	Women age 30+ years	5,918	10	572	5,146
Hypertensive heart disease	Women age 30+ years	363	17	63	692
Other cardiovascular disease	Women age 30+ years	1,014	5	48	572
Lung cancer	Women age 30+ years	310	17	53	581
Total		**34,412**	**20**	**6,158**	**139,232**

Note: Mortality from AURI is minimal and not presented here. DALY = disability-adjusted life year; YLL = years of life lost to death; ALRI = acute lower respiratory infection; COPD = chronic obstructive pulmonary disease.

Table 2.38 Estimated Annual Cases of Morbidity from Household Use of Wood and Biomass for Cooking in Sindh Province, 2009

Health outcome	Population group	Annual baseline cases	Attributable fraction from use of solid fuels (%)	Annual cases from use of solid fuels	DALYs from use of solid fuels
ALRI	Children younger than 5 years old	5,178,631	29	1,509,255	10,791
AURI	Children younger than 5 years old	5,842,558	29	1,702,750	1,396
CB	Women age 30+ years	399,681	37	146,050	29,210
Total		**11,420,870**	**29**	**3,358,055**	**41,397**

Note: DALY = disability-adjusted life year; ALRI = acute lower respiratory infection; AURI = acute upper respiratory infection; CB = chronic bronchitis.

to biological differences between men and women, cultural differences (for example, women primarily work in the kitchen), or to some interplay of the two factors (Clougherty 2010). However, women and children clearly spend the majority of their time doing household chores, and thus suffer from high levels of RS, including lung cancer and mortality, among others.[58] Incorporating aspects of gender into the environmental health paradigm should be a key component in the overall strategy for reducing environmental degradation in Sindh. As a particular short-term strategy that can be implemented, stove replacements have effectively decreased exposures and improved women's health in household settings, as discussed in chapter 3.[59]

Economic Costs of Household Air Pollution

As indicated in the previous section, more than 6,000 individuals died prematurely and nearly 3.4 million cases of illness occurred because of household air pollution caused by the use of solid fuels for cooking in Sindh in 2009. The annual cost of these health effects is estimated at PRs 25–43 billion, with a midpoint estimate of PRs 34 billion. This cost is equivalent to 0.7–1.2 percent of Sindh's estimated GDP in 2009 (table 2.39). The cost associated with mortality is more than twice the cost of morbidity; 60–81 percent of the cost is from health effects among children younger than five years of age (table 2.40).[60]

Annual cost of acute respiratory and CB morbidity in Sindh is estimated at about PRs 6.6 billion based on the COI approach (tables 2.41 and 2.42). This corresponds to the "low" cost estimates in the previous tables. As documented by the PDHS (2006–07) (see NIPS/Macro 2008), a very high share of cases of acute respiratory infections is medically treated in Sindh. The economic cost of medical treatment is estimated at PRs 700 per case. Ill individuals and caretakers of ill children also incur time losses from seeking treatment and from being prevented from conducting daily activities during illness. The cost of these time losses is estimated at a rate of 50 percent of hourly income.[61] This cost is applied to both income-earning and non–income-earning adults, recognizing the value of non–income-earning work in the household.

Table 2.39 Estimated Annual Cost of Household Air Pollution from Use of Solid Fuels in Sindh Province in 2009

billion PRs

	Low	Midpoint	High
Children younger than five years of age			
Premature mortality	15.1	15.1	15.1
Morbidity	5.3	8.0	10.7
Adult women			
Premature mortality	3.7	9.1	14.5
Morbidity	1.2	1.8	2.5
Total annual cost	25.4	34.0	42.7
Total annual cost (% of GDP in 2009)	0.69	0.92	1.15

Note: "Low" reflects valuation of health effects using HCV for mortality and COI for morbidity. "High" reflects using HCV for child mortality, VSL for adult mortality, and WTP for morbidity. HCV = human capital value; COI = cost of illness; VSL = value of statistical life; WTP = willingness to pay.

Table 2.40 Distribution of Annual Cost by Health Effects and Population Groups, 2009

percent

	Low	Midpoint	High
By health effects			
Mortality	74	71	69
Morbidity	26	29	31
By population groups			
Children younger than five years of age	81	68	60
Adult women	19	32	40

Note: "Low" reflects valuation of health effects using HCV for mortality and COI for morbidity. "High" reflects using HCV for child mortality, VSL for adult mortality, and WTP for morbidity. HCV = human capital value; COI = cost of illness; VSL = value of statistical life; WTP = willingness to pay.

Table 2.41 Estimated Annual Cost of Acute Respiratory Morbidity in Sindh Province, 2009

	Children younger than five years of age	
	ALRI	AURI
Annual cases attributable to air pollution from solid fuels	1,509,255	1,702,750
Cases treated by medical provider (%)	78	78
Economic cost of medical treatment (PRs per case treated)	700	700
Time spent on medical treatment (hours per case)	3	3
Time lost to illness (hours per case per day)[a]	2	2
Value of time (PRs per hour)	29.4	29.4
Total cost of medical treatment (million PRs)	**824**	**930**
Total cost of time losses resulting from illness (million PRs)	**2,762**	**817**
Total cost of respiratory morbidity (million PRs)	**3,586**	**1,747**
Cost per case of morbidity (PRs)	**2,376**	**1,026**

Note: a. An average case of ALRI and AURI is assumed to have duration of 30 and 7 days, respectively. ALRI = acute lower respiratory illness; AURI = acute upper respiratory illness.

Sustainability and Poverty Alleviation • http://dx.doi.org/10.1596/978-1-4648-0452-6

Table 2.42 Estimated Annual Cost of Chronic Bronchitis in Sindh Province, 2009

Annual cases of CB from use of solid fuels (women 30+ years of age)	146,050
Persons with CB being hospitalized per year (%)[a]	1.5
Average length of hospitalization (days)	10
Average number of doctor visits per person with CB per year[a]	1
Persons with CB with an emergency visit to a health facility per year[a]	15
Estimated lost workdays per year per person with CB associated with medical treatment	2.6
Reduction in work productivity resulting from CB (%)	10
Economic cost of hospitalization (PRs per stay)	15,000
Economic cost of emergency visit to health facility (PRs)	1,000
Economic cost of doctor visit (PRs)	700
Value of time lost to illness (PRs per hour)	29.4
Value of lost productivity (PRs per year)[b]	6,617
Total cost of annual cases of CB from use of solid fuels (million PRs)	**1,226**
Cost per case of CB (PRs)	**8,392**

Note: a. Niederman and others 1999; and Schulman and others 2001. b. 10% of annual average income, with annual income adjusted for nonworking adult population (50%). CB = chronic bronchitis.

The cost of CB morbidity is difficult to estimate. This study assumes that women with CB in Sindh have the same rates of medical treatment as those in high-income countries (Niederman and others 1999; Schulman, Ronca & Bucuvalas, Inc. 2001). CB is a progressively debilitating illness and it is therefore assumed that work productivity is reduced by an average of 10 percent over the duration of the disease. Table 2.41 presents the estimated annual cost of acute respiratory morbidity in Sindh, and table 2.42 presents the estimated annual cost of CB morbidity in Sindh.

Conclusions

Environmental health risks cause a significant number of preventable premature deaths and illnesses in Sindh (tables 2.43 and 2.44). Nearly 1.4 million DALYs were lost in Sindh in 2009 as a result of environmental health risk factors, out of which almost 1 million were from premature mortality and more than 0.4 million from illnesses and injuries.[62] Almost 60 percent of these DALYs were lost among children younger than five years of age and are caused by inadequate water supply, sanitation, and hygiene, and by household air pollution.[63] Outdoor air pollution and road traffic noise affect mainly adults, representing close to two-thirds of DALYs lost among this population group.

The health effects from the environmental risk factors can be monetized using standard valuation techniques in order to provide an economic perspective of the magnitude of these effects. This study estimated the annual cost of the environmental health effects in Sindh at PRs 371 billion, which is equivalent to 10 percent of the province's GDP (table 2.45).[64]

These costs are distributed unevenly throughout the province. Inadequate water supply, sanitation, and hygiene, and exposure to lead affect both urban and

Table 2.43 Attributable Fraction of Deaths from Environmental Risk Factors in Sindh Province, 2009

Environmental risk factor	Population group affected	Geographic area	Deaths caused by environmental risk factor (in population group in geographic area)
Water, sanitation, and hygiene	Children younger than five years of age	Sindh province	88% of diarrheal mortality 29% of respiratory infections mortality 35% of other infectious disease mortality
	Adults	Sindh province	88% of diarrheal mortality
Outdoor air pollution	Children younger than five years of age	Cities >100,000 population	20% of respiratory infections mortality
	Adults (30+ years of age)	Cities >100,000 population	23% of cardiopulmonary and lung cancer mortality
Household air pollution	Children younger than five years of age	Sindh province	25% of respiratory infections mortality
	Adult women (30+ years of age)	Sindh province	14% of COPD, cardiovascular disease, and lung cancer mortality
Road traffic noise	Adults	Cities >100,000 population	15% of IHD and cerebrovascular disease mortality
Road traffic accidents	Children and adults (80% among 16–50-year-olds)	Sindh province	6% of all deaths among 16–50-year-olds
Lead exposure	Adults	Sindh province	Not estimated

Table 2.44 Midpoint Estimates of Morbidity and Injuries from Environmental Risk Factors in Sindh Province, 2009

Environmental risk factor	Population group affected	Morbidity and injuries resulting from environmental risk factor
Inadequate water, sanitation, and hygiene	Children younger than five years of age	15.3 million cases of diarrheal disease
	Population five years of age and older	22.2 million cases of diarrheal disease
Outdoor air pollution	Children younger than 15 years of age	1.7 million cases of lower respiratory infections
	Adults	185,000 people with chronic bronchitis; 100 million restricted activity days; 321 million respiratory symptoms
	All age groups	33,000 hospitalizations; 645,000 emergency room visits
Household air pollution	Children younger than five years of age	1.5 million cases of acute lower respiratory infections; 1.7 million cases of acute upper respiratory infections
	Adult women (30+ years of age)	146,000 women with chronic bronchitis
Road traffic noise	Children	1.6 million children with noise-induced cognitive impairment
	Adults	2.0 million people with high sleep disturbance; 3.1 million people experiencing high level of annoyance
Road traffic accidents	Children and adults	6,000 permanent disabilities; 82,000 serious injuries; 445,000 minor injuries
Lead exposure	Children younger than five years of age	2 million lost IQ points

Sustainability and Poverty Alleviation • http://dx.doi.org/10.1596/978-1-4648-0452-6

Table 2.45 Estimated Annual Cost of Environmental Health Effects in Sindh Province, 2009

percentage of GDP

Environmental risk factor	Low	Midpoint	High
Inadequate water, sanitation, and hygiene	2.88	3.32	3.77
Lead exposure	1.56	2.54	3.52
Outdoor air pollution	0.81	1.42	2.03
Road traffic accidents	0.68	1.15	1.62
Household air pollution	0.69	0.92	1.15
Road traffic noise	0.40	0.67	0.99
Total	**7.02**	**10.02**	**13.08**

rural populations. Road traffic accidents occur more in urban than in rural areas. Outdoor air pollution and road traffic noise mainly affect the urban population and especially Karachi, where a third of the population of Sindh resides. Household air pollution from use of wood/biomass fuels for cooking mainly affects the rural population.

Given the significant premature deaths, illnesses, and economic costs caused by inadequate water supply, sanitation, and hygiene, as well as outdoor air pollution, these two categories of environmental degradation should be at the top of GoS's environmental agenda. Lead exposure should also be tackled urgently, as it results in irreversible effects, including impaired intelligence in children, which have significant and lifelong consequences.

Responding to Sindh's most pressing environmental problems will require a major overhaul of the province's environmental management and institutional framework. The country's environmental management framework relies on environmental impact analysis and the ill-enforced NEQS to improve environmental conditions. However, the severity of environmental degradation speaks to the ineffectiveness of these mechanisms and the need to develop other instruments. Moreover, environmental agencies' capabilities are low. They still need to adopt deep reforms to set up mechanisms for priority setting, efficient resource allocation, and adequate monitoring, evaluation and social learning, as well as mechanisms for enhancing accountability for environmental management. This has to be done while also adapting to the post–18th Amendment context, as discussed in chapter 5.

Notes

1. See appendix A for an in-depth discussion of the cost of environmental health risks in Sindh.

2. These estimates do not include deaths from exposure to lead among adults. Lead has been found to increase blood pressure, which in turn increases the risk of cardiovascular disease and mortality (Fewtrell and others 2003).

3. The analysis of the COED indicates the categories of environmental degradation that are causing the most significant costs. The government of Sindh requested and

the World Bank agreed to use COED as the basis for identifying environmental priorities. The use of economic valuation to rank priorities is the state-of-the-art methodology adopted by the World Bank for this type of work (World Bank 2005, 2011). This book also discusses in the following sections the benefit-cost ratio of different interventions that could be carried out to address the costs of key categories of environmental degradation. While the COED and benefit-cost analysis offer a number of advantages, including a sound basis for estimating the severity of different categories of environmental degradation and prioritizing responses to them, the analytical work recognizes that this approach is not exempt from limitations, including (a) the difficulty of incorporating the cost of management; and (b) the methodology does not say much about what would be the "residual" COED after the interventions have been implemented. In addition to the COED, the World Bank conducted a household survey and had meetings with stakeholders in the high-level committee created by the GoS to discuss the findings of the analytical work. The feedback obtained through these channels complemented the COED and helped to validate its findings with the perceptions of different stakeholders.

4. "Low" cost estimate is based on the human capital value (HCV) for child and adult mortality and the cost-of-illness (COI) for morbidity and injuries. "High" cost estimate is based on the HCV for child mortality, value of statistical life (VSL) for adult mortality, and willingness-to-pay (WTP) to avoid illness or injury.

5. The assessment of environmental health effects and their economic costs presented in this book was undertaken in early 2012. Assessment methodologies have undergone several major developments since then, as reflected in the Global Burden of Disease 2010 Project, released in December 2012. Applying these latest developments to Sindh indicates that mortality from the environmental risk factors assessed in the book was around 45,000 instead of 40,000 in 2009. Applying these newer methodologies would also yield different results in terms of the mortality caused by some of the risk factors. Specifically, mortality would be 140 percent higher from household air pollution and 33 percent higher from outdoor air pollution. In contrast, mortality from inadequate water supply, sanitation and hygiene could be 35 percent lower than estimated in this book. Based on these revised estimates, the average cost of environmental health risks would be equivalent to 1.9 percent of GDP (instead of 0.9 percent) for household air pollution, 1.7 percent (instead of 1.4 percent) for outdoor air pollution, and 2.2 percent (instead of 3.3 percent) for inadequate water supply, sanitation and hygiene. The cost of lead (Pb) exposure, traffic accidents and urban traffic noise remains the same, at 2.5 percent, 1.15 percent and 0.7 percent, respectively. It is important to note that these revised results do not change the main findings and conclusions in this book. In fact, they underscore the need for urgent action to address Sindh's priority environmental problems.

6. Intelligence quotient (IQ) is a score on standardized tests designed to assess intelligence. When IQ tests are devised, the mean score within an age group is set to 100 and the standard deviation generally to 15.

7. The estimated health effects of environmental risks in Sindh do not include intestinal parasite infestations; arsenic in groundwater; other diseases related to water, sanitation, and hygiene; the effect of repeated diarrheal infections on child nutrition (cognitive development and stunting) and consequent impacts on lifetime income; cardiovascular morbidity from household air pollution; health effects among adult males from household air pollution; and health effects of lead among adults. In this respect, the estimates of health effects and their social cost are conservative.

8. DALYs are calculated using WHO methodology with age weighting, and a discount rate of 3 percent.

9. IQ losses from lead exposure have not been calculated as DALYs.

10. DALYs among children may be underestimated, as sleep disturbance and annoyance from road traffic noise is only estimated for adults.

11. These estimates are projections from the population census in 1998, and are not necessarily consistent with the population estimates reported in GoP (2009). Other estimates place the population in Karachi at even higher levels—around 16–17 million.

12. The Pakistan Social and Living Standards Measurement Survey (PSLM) 2008–09 (GoP 2010) indicates that a similar percentage of the population has an improved drinking water source, although the data are not categorized by improved and unimproved water sources (GoP 2010).

13. Imperial gallons (1 imperial gallon = 4.546 liters).

14. Surveys of Karachi and Hyderabad cities were planned separately.

15. The Pakistan Social and Living Standards Measurement Survey (PSLM) 2008–09 (GoP 2010) reports that 20 percent of rural households were without a toilet facility, a figure substantially lower than reported by the PDHS two years earlier. It is, however, unlikely that more than 30 percent of the rural population in Sindh obtained a toilet facility in two years.

16. These estimates include diarrheal mortality in children and adults; child mortality from poor nutritional status caused by inadequate water supply, sanitation, and hygiene; and diarrheal morbidity. However, they do not include intestinal parasite infestations, other diseases such as typhoid, health effects of arsenic contamination of drinking water, and respiratory infections from poor hand washing practices, which were not estimated because of data constraints.

17. ALRI and other infectious disease mortality associated with inadequate drinking water, sanitation, and hygiene stems from the effect of diarrhea on nutritional status and consequent increase in mortality risk in early childhood (Fewtrell and others 2007; Fishman and others 2004).

18. Years of life lost (YLL) are estimated according to WHO's calculation of disability-adjusted life years (DALYs) using age weighting and a discount rate of 3 percent.

19. YLL are estimated according to WHO's calculation of DALYs using age weighting and a discount rate of 3 percent.

20. Bangladesh (Bairagi and others 1987; Becker, Black, and Brown 1991; Black, Brown, and Becker 1984); Brazil (Guerrant and others 1983; Moore and others 2000); Colombia (Lutter and others 1989); the Gambia (Rowland, Cole, and Whitehead 1977); Guatemala (Martorell and others 1975); Guinea-Bissau (Molbak and others 1997); Indonesia (Kolsteren, Kusin, and Kardjati 1997); Mexico (Condon-Paoloni and others 1977); Pakistan (Fikree and others 2000); Peru (Checkley and others 1997, 2003); the Philippines (Adair and others 1993); Sudan (Zumrawi, Dimond, and Waterflow 1987); and Tanzania (Villamor and others 2004).

21. Prevalence rates from the National Nutrition Survey (NNS) (2011) were not published at the time of this book.

22. Assessment methodologies have undergone several major developments since the assessment presented in this book was undertaken. Applying these latest developments to Sindh, mortality caused by inadequate water supply, sanitation and hygiene

could be 35 percent lower than estimated in this book. Based on these revised estimates, the average cost of inadequate water supply, sanitation and hygiene would be around 2.2 percent (instead of 3.3 percent) of GDP.

23. Treatment rates usually decline with a child's age. For example, treatment rate among 4-year-olds is 78 percent of the rate among children from birth to age 4 years, according to the PDHS (2006–07) (see NIPS/Macro 2008).

24. Hourly income is estimated at PRs 58.7 on the basis of an annual income per worker of PRs 134,345 in 2009 (appendix G).

25. See, for example, Grantham-McGregor and others (2007) regarding Brazil; Behrman and others (2006), and Maluccio and others (2006) regarding Guatemala; Walker and others (2005) regarding Jamaica; Alderman and others (2001) regarding Pakistan; Daniels and Adair (2004), and Glewwe and others (2001) regarding the Philippines; and Alderman, Hoddinott , and Kinsey (2006) regarding Zimbabwe.

26. These annual costs reflect a discounting of losses in lifetime earnings at 3 percent per year (rate of time preference, which reflects the relatively higher utility that is obtained from consuming a good at an earlier date compared with consuming it at a later date). At a discount rate of 5 percent, the annual cost is 1.9 percent and 2.3 percent of GDP in Ghana and Pakistan, respectively.

27. The contribution to ambient PM concentrations of emissions originating from a specific location in the city is influenced by wind conditions, rainfall patterns, and other climatic factors. The wind in Karachi is predominantly from the southwest and the west-southwest from March to October, and from the east-northeast and north-northeast from November to February. Wind speed is generally highest during May to August and lowest during October to February. Rain falls predominantly during July to September. These wind and rainfall patterns are likely important factors in explaining why $PM_{2.5}$ ambient concentrations in Karachi are 3–4 times higher during November to February than during June to August.

28. Alam and others (2011) report a $PM_{2.5}/PM_{10}$ ratio of 0.48 from monitoring at SUPARCO and M.A. Jinnah Road in 2010. SUPARCO reported PM_{10} concentrations 194 µg/m^3 in Karachi in 2004.

29. The area of Karachi is 2,950 km^2 without the Kirther National Park Area in Gadap.

30. Excluding Gadap, Kemari, Bin Qasim, and the cantonments of Clifton, Korangi Creek, Faisal, Malir, and Manora.

31. See WHO (2004) for a description of the model and data applied for estimation of annual average PM_{10} concentrations in cities in the world with a population of more than 100,000.

32. Mortality is estimated based on Ostro (2004), and Pope and others (2002, 2009).

33. Estimates follow the methodology of WHO using age weighting and a 3 percent discount rate.

34. Morbidity is estimated based on Abbey and others (1995) and Ostro (1994).

35. Assessment methodologies have undergone several major developments since the assessment presented in this book was undertaken. Applying these latest developments to Sindh, mortality caused by outdoor air pollution could be 33 percent higher than estimated in this book. Based on these revised estimates, the average cost of outdoor air pollution would be around 1.7 percent (instead of 1.4 percent) of GDP.

36. An exception is a study in a low-income urban area in eastern Karachi that found an average BLL of 11.7 µg/dL among adults 18–60 years of age (Yakub and Iqbal 2010).

37. http://www.fda.gov/Cosmetics/ProductandIngredientSafety/ProductInformation/ucm137250.htm.

38. The standard deviation (SD) of BLLs applied in the distribution function is the value that gives a distribution with 20 percent of urban children having a BLL >10 μg/dL and 10 percent of rural children having a BLL >10 μg/dL. About 63 percent of children younger than five years of age in Sindh live in rural areas and 37 percent live in urban areas (GoP 2009).

39. The study is undated, but published in 2005 or more recently. The study does not state the year of the groundwater sampling.

40. IQ losses associated with BLLs >10 μg/dL have been established long ago.

41. Based on the log-linear central estimate of effects of BLLs in the meta-analysis by Lanphear and others (2005).

42. Annual loss of IQ points is calculated as Δ IQ/5 by assuming that the children's IQ points are lost in the first five years of life.

43. The high bound reflects the estimated loss in income for males and females in Salkever (1995), weighted by the labor force participation rates of males and females in Sindh province reported by FBS (2010). The low and high bounds do not include the effect of IQ on the rate of participation in the labor force.

44. Sindh's population is estimated at 35.7 million in 2009, based on the population reported in the Pakistan Demographic Survey 2007 (PDS 2007) of GoP (2009).

45. Estimates of DALYs from mortality and permanent disability follow the methodology of WHO using age weighting and a 3 percent discount rate. The disability weight (DW) applied to permanent disability is 0.25. DW applied to serious and minor injuries is 0.5 and 0.25, with duration of 60 and 5 days, respectively.

46. Ahmed (2007) at the National Road Safety Secretariat reports an estimated cost of road accidents in Pakistan at 1.5 percent of GDP in 2006.

47. About 13 percent of road traffic accident fatalities were among children younger than 16 years of age.

48. Average wage rate or income per person per working day in Sindh is estimated at PRs 470 in 2009 (see appendix G). Wage or income per person working in urban areas is about 2.4 times higher than in rural areas of Sindh (FBS 2009). Thus, average urban and rural wage or income is PRs 705 and PRs 290, respectively, per day.

49. Estimates of DALY resulting from mortality follow the methodology of WHO using age weighting and a 3 percent discount rate.

50. The section on health effects of noise included an estimate of the number of highly annoyed (HA) people from exposure to excessive noise. The estimate of the cost of noise, however, includes the cost to all people exposed to excessive noise.

51. Navrud (2002) reports that studies in Europe found that individuals' median WTP to avoid road traffic noise is nearly a25 per dB per household per year (2001-a). Adjusting to 2009-a, and transferring the value to Sindh using an income elasticity of one, the study estimates a WTP of PRs 84 per dB per household per year.

52. The cost is annualized over 10 years (years of schooling).

53. CB is a subset of COPD.

54. Tuberculosis and acute respiratory infections in adult women are not included, as the evidence is somewhat weaker than for the other health effects.

55. Based on Sindhu (2006).

56. YLL are estimated according to WHO's calculation of DALYs using age weighting and a discount rate of 3 percent.

57. Cases of cardiovascular disease and lung cancer are not estimated because of data constraints. DALYs are estimated according to WHO's calculation.

58. See Behera (1997); Behera and Balamugesh (2005); and Lopez and others (2006), as cited in Clougherty (2010).

59. See Khushk and others (2005) and McCracken and others (2007), as cited in Clougherty (2010).

60. Assessment methodologies have undergone several major developments since the assessment presented in this book was undertaken. Applying these latest developments to Sindh, mortality caused by household air pollution could be 140 percent higher than estimated in this book. Based on these revised estimates, the average cost of household air pollution would be around 1.9 percent (instead of 0.9 percent) of GDP.

61. Hourly income is estimated at PRs 58.7, based on an annual income per worker of PRs 134,345 in 2009.

62. IQ losses from lead exposure have not been calculated as DALYs.

63. DALYs among children may be underestimated, as sleep disturbance and annoyance from road traffic noise is only estimated for adults.

64. "Low" cost estimate is based on the HCV for child and adult mortality and the COI for morbidity and injuries. "High" cost estimate is based on the HCV for child mortality, VSL for adult mortality, and WTP to avoid illness or injury.

Bibliography

Abbey, D., M. Lebowitz, P. Mills, and F. Petersen. 1995. "Long-Term Ambient Concentrations of Particulates and Oxidants and Development of Chronic Disease in a Cohort of Nonsmoking California Residents." *Inhalation Toxicology* 7: 19–34.

Adair, L., B. M. Popkin, J. VanDerslice, J. Akin, D. Guilkey, R. Black, J. Briscoe, and W. Flieger. 1993. "Growth Dynamics during the First Two Years of Life: A Prospective Study in the Philippines." *European Journal of Clinical Nutrition* 47 (1): 42–51.

ADB (Asian Development Bank). 2005. *Karachi Mega Cities Preparation Project*. Final Report, Vol. 1, TA 4578-Pakistan.

ADB (Asian Development Bank) and World Bank. 2010. *Pakistan Floods 2010: Preliminary Damage and Needs Assessment*. Washington, DC: World Bank.

Aga Khan University Pakistan, Pakistan Medical Research Council, and Nutrition Wing of Pakistan's Ministry of Health. 2011. *National Nutrition Survey*. Islamabad. https://pak.humanitarianresponse.info/system/files/documents/files/Pakistan_NNS_Version%20 27.7.June%202012.pdf.

Ahmad, T., A. Mumtaz, D. Ahmad, and N. Rashid. 2009. "Lead Exposure in Children Living Around the Automobile and Battery Repair Workshops." *Biomedica* 25: 128–32.

Ahmed, A. 2007. *Road Safety in Pakistan*. The National Road Safety Secretariat, Ministry of Communications.

Alam, K., T. Blaschke, P. Madl, A. Mukhtar, M. Hussain, T. Trautmann, and S. Rahman. 2011. "Aerosol Size Distribution and Mass Concentration Measurements in Various Cities of Pakistan." *Journal of Environmental Monitoring* 13: 1944–52.

Alderman, H., J. Behrman, V. Lavy, and R. Menon. 2001. "Child Health and School Enrollment: a Longitudinal Analysis." *The Journal of Human Resources* 36 (1): 185–205.

Alderman, H., J. Hoddinott, and B. Kinsey. 2006. "Long-Term Consequences of Early Childhood Malnutrition." *Oxford Economic Papers* 58: 450–74.

Bairagi, R., M. K. Chowdhury, Y. J. Kim, G. T. Curlin, and R. H. Gray. 1987. "The Association between Malnutrition and Diarrhoea in Rural Bangladesh." *International Journal of Epidemiology* 16 (3): 477–81.

Balakrishnan, K., S. Sambandam, P. Ramaswamy, S. Mehta, and K. Smith. 2004. "Exposure Assessment for Respirable Particulates Associated with Household Fuel Use in Rural Districts of Andhra Pradesh, India." *Journal of Exposure Analysis and Environmental Epidemiology* 14: S14–25.

Balakrishnan, K., S. Sankar, J. Parikh, R. Padmavathi, K. Srividya, V. Venugopal, S. Prasad, and V. L. Pandey. 2002. "Daily Average Exposures to Respirable Particulate Matter from Combustion of Biomass Fuels in Rural Households of Southern India." *Environmental Health Perspectives* 110 (11): 1069–75.

Becker, S., R. E. Black, and K. H. Brown. 1991. "Relative Effects of Diarrhea, Fever and Dietary Energy Intake on Weight Gain in Rural Bangladeshi Children." *American Journal of Clinical Nutrition* 53: 1499–503.

Behera, D. 1997. "An Analysis of Effect of Common Domestic Fuels on Respiratory Function." *Indian Journal of Chest Disease and Allied Sciences* 39: 235–43.

Behera, D., and T. Balamugesh. 2005. "Indoor Air Pollution as a Risk Factor for Lung Cancer in Women." *Journal of the Association of Physicians of India* 53: 190–92.

Behrman, J. R., J. Hoddinott, J. A. Maluccio, J. F. Hoddinott, J. A. Maluccio, E. Soler-Hampejsek, and E. L. Behrman. 2006. "What Determines Adult Cognitive Skills? Impacts of Pre-School, Schooling and Post-Schooling Experiences in Guatemala." PSC Working Paper Series, Population Studies Center, University of Pennsylvania, Philadelphia, PA.

Black, R. E., K. H. Brown, and S. Becker. 1984. "Effects of Diarrhea Associated with Specific Enteropathogens on the Growth of Children in Rural Bangladesh." *Pediatrics* 73: 799–805.

Canfield, R. L., C. R. Henderson, D. A. Cory-Slechta, C. Cox, T. A. Jusko, and B. P. Lanphear. 2003. "Intellectual Impairment in Children with Blood Lead Concentrations below 10 μg per Deciliter." *New England Journal of Medicine* 348 (16): 1517–26.

CDGK (City District Government Karachi). 2007. *Karachi Strategic Development Plan 2020.* Master Plan Group of Offices, Karachi, Pakistan.

Checkley, W., L. D. Epstein, R. H. Gilman, L. M. Cabrera, and R. E. Black. 2003. "Effects of Acute Diarrhea on Linear Growth in Peruvian Children." *American Journal of Epidemiology* 157: 166–75.

Checkley, W., R. H. Gilman, L. D. Epstein, M. Suarez, J. F. Diaz, L. Cabrera, R. E. Black, and C. R. Sterling. 1997. "Asymptomatic and Symptomatic Cryptosporidiosis: Their Acute Effect on Weight Gain in Peruvian Children." *American Journal of Epidemiology* 145: 156–63.

Clougherty, J. E. 2010. "A Growing Role for Gender Analysis in Air Pollution Epidemiology." *Environmental Health Perspectives* 118 (2): 167–76. http://www.ncbi .nlm.nih.gov/pmc/articles/PMC2831913.

Condon-Paoloni, D., J. Cravioto, F. E. Johnston, E. R. De Licardie, and T. O. Scholl. 1977. "Morbidity and Growth of Infants and Young Children in a Rural Mexican Village." *American Journal of Public Health* 67: 651–56.

Daniels, M., and L. Adair. 2004. "Growth in Young Filipino Children Predicts Schooling Trajectories through High School." *Journal of Nutrition* 134: 1439–46.

De Leon, M. R. M., P. C. Cal, and R. G. Sigua. 2005. "Estimation of Socio-Economic Cost of Road Accidents in Metro Manila." *Journal of the Eastern Asia Society for Transportation Studies* 6: 3183–98.

Desai, M. A., S. Mehta, and K. Smith. 2004. "Indoor Smoke from Solid Fuels: Assessing the Environmental Burden of Disease at National and Local Levels." Environmental Burden of Disease Series 4, World Health Organization.

Dherani, M., D. Pope, M. Mascarenhas, K. Smith, M. Weber, and N. Bruce. 2008. "Indoor Air Pollution from Unprocessed Solid Fuel Use and Pneumonia Risk in Children Aged under Five Years: A Systematic Review and Meta-Analysis." *Bulletin of the World Health Organization* 86: 390–98.

Economist Intelligence Unit. 2010. "Livability and Ranking Overview. Worldwide Cost of Living Survey." http://store.eiu.com/product/475217632.html.

ETSC (European Transport Safety Council). 2007. *Social and Economic Consequences of Road Traffic Injury in Europe.* Brussels: ETSC.

Ezzati, M., and D. Kammen. 2001. "Quantifying the Effects of Exposure to Indoor Air Pollution from Biomass Combustion on Acute Respiratory Infections in Developing Countries." *Environmental Health Perspectives* 109 (5): 481–88.

———. 2002. "The Health Impacts of Exposure to Indoor Air Pollution from Solid Fuels in Developing Countries: Knowledge, Gaps, and Data Needs." *Environmental Health Perspectives* 110 (11): 1057–68.

Fatmi, Z., W. C. Hadden, J. A. Razzak, H. I. Qureshi, A. A. Hyder, and G. Pappas. 2007. "Incidence, Pattern and Severity of Reported Unintentional Injuries in Pakistan for Persons Five Years and Older. Results of the National Health Survey of Pakistan 1990–94." *BMC Public Health* 7: 152–58.

FBS (Federal Bureau of Statistics). 2009. *Household Integrated Economic Survey 2007–08.* Islamabad: Federal Bureau of Statistics.

———. 2010. *Labor Force Survey 2008–09.* Islamabad: Federal Bureau of Statistics.

———. 2011. *Pakistan Statistical Yearbook 2011.* Islamabad: Federal Bureau of Statistics.

Fewtrell, L., R. Kaufmann, and A. Prüss-Üstün. 2003. "Lead: Assessing the Environmental Burden of Disease at National and Local Levels." Environmental Burden of Disease Series 2, World Health Organization, Geneva.

Fewtrell, L., A. Prüss-Üstün, R. Bos, F. Gore, and J. Bartram. 2007. "Water, Sanitation and Hygiene: Quantifying the Health Impact at National and Local Levels in Countries with Incomplete Water Supply and Sanitation Coverage." Environmental Burden of Disease Series 15, World Health Organization, Geneva.

Fikree, F. F., M. H. Rahbar, and H. W. Berendes. 2000. "Risk Factors for Stunting and Wasting at Age Six, Twelve and Twenty-Four Months for Squatter Children of Karachi." *Journal of Pakistan Medical Association* 50 (10): 341–48.

Fishman, M. S., L. E. Caulfield, M. De Onis, M. Blossner, A. A. Hyder, L. Mullany, and R. E. Black. 2004. "Childhood and Maternal Underweight." In *Comparative*

Quantification of Health Risks—Global and Regional Burden of Disease Attributable to Selected Major Risk Factors, Vol. 1, edited by M. Ezzati, A. D. Lopez, A. Rodgers, and C. J. L. Murray. Geneva: World Health Organization.

Ghaffar, A., A. Hyder, and T. Masud. 2004. "The Burden of Road Traffic Injuries in Developing Countries: The 1st National Injury Survey of Pakistan." *Public Health* 118 (3): 211–17.

Ghauri, B. 2008. "Satellite Data Applications in Atmospheric Monitoring, SUPARCO." PowerPoint presentation, Graz, Austria.

Glewwe, P., H. G. Jacoby, and E. M. King. 2001. "Early Childhood Nutrition and Academic Achievement: A Longitudinal Analysis." *Journal of Public Economics* 81: 345–68.

GoP (Government of Pakistan). 2009. "Pakistan Demographic Survey 2007." Pakistan Bureau of Statistics, Government of Pakistan, Pakistan.

———. 2010. "Pakistan Social and Living Standards Measurement Survey (PSLM) 2008–09." Statistics Division, Government of Pakistan, Pakistan.

Grantham -McGregor, S., Y. B. Cheung, S. Cueto, P. Glewwe, L. Richter, B. Strupp, and the International Child Development Steering Group. 2007. "Development Potential in the First 5 Years for Children in Developing Countries." *Lancet* 369: 60–70.

Guerrant, R. L., L. V. Kirchhoff, D. S. Shields, M. K. Nations, J. Leslie, M. A. de Sousa, J. G. Araujo, L. L. Correia, K. T. Sauer, K. E. McClelland, F. L. Trowbridge, and J. M. Hughes. 1983. "Prospective Study of Diarrheal Illnesses in Northeastern Brazil: Patterns of Disease, Nutritional Impact, Etiologies, and Risk Factors." *The Journal of Infectious Diseases* 148 (6): 986–97.

Haq, N-ul., M. A. Arain, Z. Haque, N. Badar, and N. Mugha. 2009. "Drinking Water Contamination by Chromium and Lead in Industrial Lands of Karachi." *Journal of Pakistan Medical Association* 59 (5): 270–74.

Junejo, S. A. n.d. *Groundwater Quality in Sindh*. Indus Institute for Research and Education (IIRE), Hyderabad, Pakistan.

Jusko, T. A., C. R. Henderson, B. P. Lanphear, D. A. Cory-Slechta, P. J. Parsons, and R. L. Canfield. 2008. "Blood Lead Concentrations <10 μg/dL and Child Intelligence at 6 Years of Age." *Environmental Health Perspectives* 116 (2): 243–48.

Kadir, M. M., N. Z. Janjua, S. Kristensen, Z. Fatmi, and N. Sathiakumar. 2008. "Status of Children's Blood Lead Levels in Pakistan: Implications for Research and Policy." *Public Health* 122 (7): 708–15.

Khan, D. A., W. M. Ansari, and F. A. Khan. 2011. "Synergistic Effects of Iron Deficiency and Lead Exposure on Blood Lead Levels in Children." *World Journal of Pediatrics* 7 (2): 150–54.

Khan, M. W., M. A. Memon, M. N. Khan, and M. M. Khan. 2010. "Traffic Noise Pollution in Karachi, Pakistan." *Journal of Liaquat University of Medical and Health Sciences* 9 (3): 114–20.

Khushk, W. A. R., Z. Fatmi, F. White, and M. M. Kadir. 2005. "Health and Social Impacts of Improved Stoves on Rural Women: A Pilot Intervention in Sindh, Pakistan." *Indoor Air* 15: 311–16.

Kolsteren, P. W., J. A. Kusin, and S. Kardjati. 1997. "Morbidity and Growth Performance of Infants in Madura, Indonesia." *Annals Tropical Pediatrics* 17 (3): 201–08.

Kurmi, O. P., S. Semple, P. Simkhada, W. C. Smith, and J. G. Ayres. 2010. "COPD and Chronic Bronchitis Risk of Indoor Air Pollution from Solid Fuel: A Systematic Review and Meta-Analysis." *Thorax* 65: 221–28.

KWSB (Karachi Water Supply and Sewerage Board). 2011. http://www.kwsb.gos.pk.

Lanphear, B. P., R. Hornung, J. Khoury, K. Yolton, P. Baghurst, D. C. Bellinger, R. L. Canfield, K. N. Dietrich, R. Bornschein, T. Greene, S. J. Rothenberg, H. L. Needleman, L. Schnaas, G. Wasserman, J. Graziano, and R. Roberts. 2005. "Low-Level Environmental Lead Exposure and Children's Intellectual Functions: An International Pooled Analysis." *Environmental Health Perspectives* 113 (7): 894–99.

Lateef, M. U. 2010. "Estimation of Fatalities due to Road Traffic Crashes in Karachi, Pakistan, Using Capture-Recapture Method." *Asia-Pacific Journal of Public Health* 22 (3): 332–41.

Lawes, C. M. M., S. Vander Hoorn, M. R. Law, P. Elliott, S. MacMahon, and A. Rodgers. 2004. "High Blood Pressure." In *Comparative Quantification of Health Risks: Global and Regional Burden of Disease Attributable to Selected Major Risk Factors*, edited by M. Ezzati, A. D. Lopez, A. Rodgers, and C. J. L. Murray. Geneva: World Health Organization.

Lopez, A. D., C. D. Mathers, M. Ezzati, D. T. Jamison, and C. J. L. Murray. 2006. *Global Burden of Disease and Risk Factors*. Washington, DC: World Bank.

Luby, S., M. Agboatwalla, D. Feikin, J. Painter, M. S. Ward Billheimer, A. Altaf, and R. Hoekstra. 2005. "Effect of Hand Washing on Child Health: A Randomised Controlled Trial." *Lancet* 366: 225–33.

Luby, S., M. Agboatwalla, J. Painter, A. Altaf, W. L. Billheimer, and R. Hoekstra. 2004. "Effect of Intensive Hand-Washing Promotion on Childhood Diarrhea in High-Risk Communities in Pakistan: A Randomised Controlled Trial." *Journal of the American Medical Association* 291 (21): 2547–54.

Lutter, C. K., J. O. Mora, J. P. Habicht, K. M. Rasmussen, D. S. Robson, S. G. Sellers, C. M. Super, and M. G. Herrera. 1989. "Nutritional Supplementation: Effects on Child Stunting Because of Diarrhea." *American Journal of Clinical Nutrition* 50 (1): 1–8.

Maca, V., J. Melichar, and M. Scancy. 2008. "Literature Review of Theoretical Issues and Empirical Estimation of Health End-Point Unit Values: Noise Case Study." HEIMTSA Noise Valuation Review. http://www.heimtsa.eu/.

Maluccio, J., J. Hoddinott, J. Behrman, R. Martorell, A. R. Quisumbing, and A. D. Stein. 2006. "The Impact of an Experimental Nutrition Intervention in Childhood on Education among Guatemalan Adults." IFPRI, FCND Discussion Paper 2007, Washington, DC.

Mansha, M., B. Ghauri, S. Rahman, and A. Amman. 2011. "Characterization and Source Apportionment of Ambient Air Particulate Matter ($PM_{2.5}$) in Karachi." *Science of the Total Environment* 425: 176–83.

Martorell, R., J. P. Habicht, C. Yarbrough, A. Loehtig, R. E. Klein, and K. A. Western. 1975. "Acute Morbidity and Physical Growth in Rural Guatemalan Children." *Pediatrics* 129: 1296–301.

McCracken, J. P., K. R. Smith, A. Díaz, M. A. Mittleman, and J. Schwartz. 2007. "Chimney Stove Intervention to Reduce Long-term Wood Smoke Exposure Lowers Blood Pressure among Guatemalan Women." *Environmental Health Perspectives* 115 (7): 996–1001.

Mehdi, M. R., M. Kim, J. C. Seong, and M. H. Arsalan. 2011. "Spatio-Temporal Patterns of Road Traffic Noise Pollution in Karachi, Pakistan." *Environment International* 37 (1): 97–104.

Memon, M., M. S. Somro, M. S. Akhtar, and K. S. Memon. 2011. "Drinking Water Quality Assessment in Southern Sindh (Pakistan)." *Environmental Monitoring and Assessment* 177: 39–50.

Molbak, K., M. Andersen, P. Aaby, N. Hojlyng, M. Jakobsen, M. Sodemann, and A. P. da Silva. 1997. "Cryptosporidium Infection in Infancy as a Cause of Malnutrition: A Community Study from Guinea-Bissau, West Africa." *American Journal of Clinical Nutrition* 65 (1): 149–52.

Moore, S. R., A. A. Lima, J. B. Schorling, M. S. Barboza, A. M. Soares, and R. L. Guerrant. 2000. "Changes over Time in the Epidemiology of Diarrhea and Malnutrition among Children in an Urban Brazilian Shantytown, 1989 to 1996." *International Journal of Infectious Diseases* 4 (4): 179–86.

Navrud, S. 2002. *State of the Art on Economic Valuation of Noise.* Final Report to the European Commission, DG Environment. Ståle Navrud, Department of Economics and Social Sciences, Agricultural University of Norway.

Niederman, M., J. S. McCombs, A. N. Unger, A. Kumar, and R. Popovian. 1999. "Treatment Cost of Acute Exacerbations of Chronic Bronchitis." *Clinical Therapy* 21 (3): 576–91.

NIPS (National Institute of Population Studies)/Macro. 2008. "Pakistan Demographic and Health Survey 2006–07." National Institute of Population Studies, Pakistan, and Macro International Inc., Islamabad, Pakistan.

Ono, K., S. Nagano, K. Miyoda, and N. Kiuchi. 2004. "The Significance of 'Permanent Disabilities Database' Caused by Automobile Collisions in Japan." Proceedings of the 2004 IRCOBI Conference on the Biomechanics of Impact.

Ostro, B. 1994. "Estimating the Health Effects of Air Pollution: A Method with an Application to Jakarta." Policy Research Working Paper Series 1301, World Bank, Washington, DC.

———. 2004. *Outdoor Air Pollution: Assessing the Environmental Burden of Disease at National and Local Levels.* Environmental Burden of Disease Series 5, World Health Organization, Geneva, Switzerland.

PCRWR (Pakistan Council of Research in Water Resources). 2010a. *Technical Assessment Survey Report of Water Supply Schemes in Sindh Province.* Prepared by M. A. Tahir, M. K. Marri, and F. ul Hassan. PCRWR, Ministry of Science and Technology, Pakistan.

———. 2010b. *Water Quality Status in Rural Areas of Pakistan.* Prepared by M. A. Tahir, H. Rasheed, and S. Imran. PCRWR, Ministry of Science and Technology, Pakistan.

Po, J. Y. T., J. M. FitzGerald, and C. Carlsten. 2011. "Respiratory Disease Associated with Solid Biomass Fuel Exposure in Rural Women and Children: Systematic Review and Meta-analysis." *Thorax* 66: 232–39.

Pope, C. A., III, R. T. Burnett, D. Krewski, M. Jerrett, Y. Shi, E. E. Calle, and M. J. Thun. 2009. "Cardiovascular Mortality and Exposure to Airborne Fine Particulate Matter and Cigarette Smoke: Shape of the Exposure-Response Relationship." *Circulation* 120: 941–48.

Pope, C. A., III, R. T. Burnett, M. J. Thun, E. Calle, D. Krewski, K. Ito, and G. Thurston. 2002. "Lung Cancer, Cardiopulmonary Mortality, and Long-term Exposure to Fine Particulate Air Pollution." *Journal of the American Medical Association* 287: 1132–41.

Psacharopoulos, G., and A. Patrinos. 2004. "Returns to Investment in Education: A Further Update." *Education Economics* 12 (2): 111–34.

Rahbar, M. H., F. White, M. Agboatwalla, S. Hozhabri, and S. Luby. 2002. "Factors Associated with Elevated Blood Lead Concentrations in Children in Karachi, Pakistan." *WHO Bulletin* 80 (10): 769–75.

Razzak, J. A., and S. P. Luby. 1998. "Estimating Deaths and Injuries Due to Road Traffic Accidents in Karachi, Pakistan, through the Capture-Recapture Method." *International Journal of Epidemiology* 27 (5): 866–70.

Rosa, G., and T. Clasen. 2010. "Estimating the Scope of Household Water Treatment in Low- and Medium-Income Countries." *The American Journal of Tropical Medicine and Hygiene* 82 (2): 289–300.

Rowland, M. G., T. Cole, and R. G. Whitehead. 1977. "A Quantitative Study into the Role of Infection in Determining Nutritional Status in Gambian Village Children." *British Journal of Nutrition* 37: 441–50.

Salkever, D. S. 1995. "Updated Estimates of Earnings Benefits from Reduced Exposure of Children to Environmental Lead." *Environmental Research* 70: 1–6.

Schulman, Ronca & Bucuvalas, Inc. 2001. *Confronting COPD in North America and Europe: A Survey of Patients and Doctors in Eight Countries.*

Schwartz, J. 1994. "Societal Benefits of Reducing Lead Exposure." *Environmental Research* 66: 105–12.

Shamim, M. S., J. A. Razzak, R. Jooma, and U. R. Khan. 2011. "Initial Results of Pakistan's First Road Traffic Injury Surveillance Project." *International Journal of Injury Control and Safety Promotion* 18 (3): 213–17.

Shar, A. H., Y. F. Kazi, N. A. Kanhar, I. H. Soomro, S. M. Zia, and P. B. Ghumro. 2010. "Drinking Water Quality in Rohri City, Sindh, Pakistan." *African Journal of Biotechnology* 9 (42): 7102–07.

Siddiqui, A. R., K. Lee, D. Bennett, X. Yang, K. H. Brown, Z. A. Bhutta, and E. B. Gold. 2009. "Indoor Carbon Monoxide and $PM_{2.5}$ Concentrations by Cooking Fuels in Pakistan." *Indoor Air* 19: 75–82.

Sindh EPA. 2010. "Daily $PM_{2.5}$ Data Collected from Air Quality Monitoring Network." Karachi, Pakistan. Unpublished.

Sindhu, A. S. 2006. "Indoor Air Pollution: The Case of Pakistan. Rural Development Policy Institute (RDPI), Pakistan." Presentation at the South Asia Regional Workshop on Indoor Air Pollution, Health and Household Energy, Kathmandu, February 26–27.

Smith, K., S. Mehta, and M. Feuz. 2004. "Indoor Air Pollution from Household Use of Solid Fuels." In *Comparative Quantification of Health Risks: Global and Regional Burden of Disease Attributable to Selected Major Risk Factors*, edited by M. Ezzati. Geneva: World Health Organization.

Sørensen, M., M. Hvidberg, Z. J. Andersen, R. B. Nordsborg, K. G. Lillelund, J. Jakobsen, A. Tjønneland, K. Overvad, and O. Raaschou-Nielsen. 2011. "Road Traffic Noise and Stroke: A Prospective Cohort Study." *European Heart Journal* 32 (6): 737–44.

Surkan, P. J., A. Zhang, F. Trachtenberg, D. B. Daniel, S. McKinlay, and D. C. Bellinger. 2007. "Neuropsychological Function in Children with Blood Lead Levels <10 µg/dL." *Neurotoxicology* 28 (6): 1170–77.

Tahir, M. N. 2011. "Road Traffic Accidents—A Major Urban Health Challenge." Presented at the Pakistan Urban Forum 2011, Lahore, Pakistan, March 3.

Toxic Link. 2010. "Toxic Trinkets: An Investigation of Lead in Children's Jewelry in India." Toxic Link. New Delhi, India.

Ul-Haq, N., M. A. Arain, N. Badar, M. Rasheed, and Z. Haque. 2011. "Drinking Water: A Major Source of Lead Exposure in Karachi, Pakistan." *Eastern Mediterranean Health Journal* 17 (11): 882–86.

Villamor, E., M. R. Fataki, J. R. Bosch, R. L. Mbise, and W. W. Fawzi. 2004. "Human Immunodeficiency Virus Infection, Diarrheal Disease and Sociodemographic Predictors of Child Growth." *Acta Paediatrica* 93 (3): 372–79.

Walker, S. P., S. M. Chang, C. A. Powell, and S. M. Grantham-McGregor. 2005. "Effects of Early Childhood Psychosocial Stimulation and Nutritional Supplementation on Cognition and Education in Growth-Stunted Jamaican Children: Prospective Cohort Study." *Lancet* 366: 1804–07.

WHO (World Health Organization). 2004. *Comparative Quantification of Health Risks: Global and Regional Burden of Disease Attributable to Selected Major Risk Factors.* Geneva: WHO.

————. 2011. *Burden of Disease from Environmental Noise: Quantification of Healthy Life Years Lost in Europe.* WHO Regional Office for Europe. Copenhagen: WHO.

World Bank. 2005. *Integrating Environmental Considerations in Policy Formulation Lessons from Policy-Based SEA Experience.* Environment Department Report 32783. Washington, DC: World Bank. http://siteresources.worldbank.org/INTUNITFESSD /Resources/integratingenvironmental.pdf.

————. 2006. *Pakistan Strategic Country Environmental Assessment.* Report 36946-PK. Washington, DC: World Bank.

————. 2008. *Environmental Health and Child Survival: Epidemiology, Economics, Experiences.* Washington, DC: World Bank.

————. 2011. *Policy Options for Air Quality Management in Pakistan.* Report submitted to the Government of Pakistan. Washington, DC: World Bank.

World Gazetteer. 2011. *Population Data and Statistics.* www.world-gazetteer.com.

Yakub, M., and M. P. Iqbal. 2010. "Association of Blood Lead (Pb) and Plasma Homocysteine: A Cross-Sectional Survey in Karachi, Pakistan." *PLoS One* 5 (7): e11706.

Zubair, A., and S. N. Siddiqui. 2011. "Status of Noise Pollution–A Case Study of Gulshan-e-Iqbal Town, Karachi." *Indus Journal of Management and Social Sciences* 5 (2): 100–05.

Zumrawi, F. Y., H. Dimond, and J. C. Waterflow. 1987. "Effects of Infection on Growth in Sudanese Children." *Human Nutrition and Clinical Nutrition* 41: 453–61.

CHAPTER 3

Benefits and Costs of Environmental Health Interventions

Abstract

Environmental health hazards in Sindh result in premature deaths and welfare loss as a result of illness, with a cost that is equivalent to 10 percent of the province's GDP. An estimated 40,000 people died prematurely in 2009 in Sindh from these hazards. A number of interventions are available to mitigate much of these health effects. A benefit-cost analysis was conducted on a set of such interventions to estimate the monetary value of the health and social benefits realized by implementing a project, compared with the amount it costs to execute the project. The results of the analysis support the identification of interventions that could be implemented in the short, medium, and long term to address the negative health effects of inadequate water supply, sanitation, and hygiene; outdoor air pollution; and household air pollution in rural areas. For most of the interventions assessed, the expected health and social benefits would be significantly higher than the associated costs.

Introduction

The economic analysis used in chapter 2 to estimate the costs of environmental degradation revealed that inadequate water supply, sanitation, and hygiene is the main cause of environmental health hazards in Sindh, followed by outdoor air pollution, road traffic accidents, household air pollution (HAP), and road traffic noise. The order of severity for each category can help inform priority setting in the environmental agenda of the government of Sindh (GoS), particularly given the significant premature deaths, illnesses, and economic costs caused by the first two categories of environmental degradation.

Environmental conditions negatively affect the health of a large share of Sindh's population, but there are interventions available to mitigate much of these health effects. This book provides an assessment of monetized benefits and costs of several interventions to mitigate some of the aforementioned environmental health effects. Short-term recommendations are chosen based on the highest benefit-cost ratio (BCR), which is the present value of benefits divided by the present value of costs of an intervention evaluated over the useful life of the intervention, that is, over the time period or number of years that the intervention is expected to provide benefits. In other words, implementing interventions with a BCR larger than 1 ensures that, for each rupee spent on selected interventions, the Sindh population receives health and social benefits with a value of more than one rupee.

Interventions often entail public and private costs. Public costs may include the costs of programs promoting behavioral change (for example, adoption of improved stoves, hand washing, household treatment of drinking water, and total sanitation programs), costs of improvements in public transportation, enforcement of pollution regulations, or subsidies for services or hardware (for example, water tariffs, toilet facilities). Private costs may include increased vehicle fuel cost or increased cost of vehicles, industrial pollution abatement, household purchases (for example, stoves, soap) and time use associated with behavioral change (time spent on hand washing or household treatment of drinking water). A cost-benefit analysis (CBA) should include both public and private costs to reflect the social or economic viability of interventions.

The assessed interventions in this study in no way represent a complete plan of action against environmental health risks in Sindh—the estimated benefits and costs are orders of magnitudes rather than precise point values. The assessment, therefore, serves as an illustration and first round of identification of interventions, many of which have potentially high social and environmental rates of return.[1] A next stage would be to improve and expand the number of interventions assessed, and undertake a similar assessment for other environmental health risks (for example, children's exposure to lead, urban noise, and traffic accidents). In addition, this book recognizes that institutional constraints would affect the implementation of selected interventions and that existing incentives could debar pursuit of the proper interventions. Chapters 5 and 6 of this book discuss these issues. This chapter proceeds as follows: the next section discusses interventions to improve drinking water supply, sanitation, and hygiene. The third section presents the analysis of interventions to improve outdoor air quality in Sindh's urban areas, and particularly, in Karachi. The fourth summarizes the results of the analysis of interventions to control HAP in Sindh's rural areas; and the fifth and last presents the chapter's conclusions.

Improving Drinking Water Supply, Sanitation, and Hygiene

As discussed in chapter 2, inadequate water supply, sanitation, and hygiene result in adverse health impacts valued at PRs 123 billion per year. To address these environmental health risks, this section assesses the following interventions: (a) upgrading and rehabilitation of the existing water supplies in Karachi and other urban areas to provide improved water quality, increased water quantity, and reliable, continuous water supply; (b) provision of improved water supply on household premises in rural areas for those who currently do not have it; (c) promotion of household point-of-use (POU) treatment of drinking water; (d) improvement of existing sewerage networks and sewage collection in Karachi, and connection of households to sewerage networks in smaller cities and towns; (e) provision of improved toilets to households without a toilet, with an unimproved toilet, or where a toilet is shared with other households; and (f) promotion of improved hand-washing practices with soap for health protection.

In this study, promotion of household POU treatment of drinking water and hand washing with soap are assessed for young children and the rest of the population separately for two primary reasons: (a) these interventions can be targeted at specific individuals, for example, at mothers with young children for the protection of these children's health; and (b) young children are at higher risk of disease and mortality caused by inadequate water supply, sanitation, and hygiene than most older population groups. The POU drinking water treatment method assessed is boiling of water, the most common in Sindh.

The CBA studies generally evaluate both health and nonhealth benefits of interventions. Health benefits from water supply, sanitation, and hygiene interventions consist mainly of reduced incidence of diarrheal illness and mortality. The main nonhealth benefit is time savings from improved access to water supply and sanitation facilities. Some of the studies include potential improvements in child nutritional status and associated health benefits from reduced diarrheal illness based on Fewtrell and others (2007), Larsen (2007), and World Bank (2008). However, none of the CBA studies of hand-washing promotion includes potential reductions in respiratory infections from improved hand washing, which is likely to represent a significant underestimation of the benefits of hand-washing programs. Such programs have been found to substantially reduce pneumonia in Pakistan (Luby and others 2005), and to generally reduce respiratory infections in developed countries (Rabie and Curtis 2006). Table 3.1 summarizes the benefits and costs of such interventions, including those that are quantified and those that are not.

The expected reduction in diarrheal disease and mortality varies by interventions. Water-supply interventions would result in estimated reductions of 20–25 percent; sanitation interventions, 15–35 percent; household POU treatment of drinking water, 30 percent; and hand washing with soap, 40 percent. These levels were obtained from literature review and meta-analytic studies of the international evidence bearing on the effectiveness of interventions in reducing diarrheal illness (table 3.2) and were applied in the CBA. Other expected nonhealth benefits include (a) increases in water quantity from the water-supply interventions (20–50 liters per person per day); and (b) water collection time savings of 18–19 minutes for households that currently do not have a water supply on premises and 3–5 minutes per person per day for those currently sharing a toilet facility with other households or practicing open defecation.

Total health and nonhealth benefits are estimated in the range of PRs 1,300–1,780 per person, per year (PRs 8,000–11,000 per household) for the water-supply interventions and PRs 800–1,730 per person per year (PRs 5,000–11,000

Table 3.1 Benefits and Costs of Assessed Water-Supply Interventions

Intervention	Benefits quantified	Public costs quantified	Private costs quantified	Benefits and costs not quantified
Improved water supply	Health improvements; reduced time spent on water collection; increased household water quantity; reduction in network water losses	Cost of infrastructure and maintenance and cost of water production and delivery, if subsidized	Cost of infrastructure and maintenance, if partially or fully born by the household; cost of water if charged for	Reduced fatigue and physical ailments from water collection; increased convenience, well-being, and status from (for example) piped water supply to dwelling; increased possibilities for improved hygiene (cleaning with water)
Household treatment of drinking water	Health improvements	Promotion program; and cost of water, if subsidized	Cost of treating water, and time used for water treatment	Air pollution from fuels used for boiling water
Improved sanitation	Health improvements; reduced time spent on accessing place of urination or defecation	Cost of infrastructure and maintenance, if subsidized	Cost of infrastructure and maintenance, if partially or fully born by the household	Increased convenience, well-being, and status from better toilets or not having to resort to open defecation; community benefits of a cleaner environment; reduced prevalence of intestinal parasite infestation
Hand washing with soap	Health improvements	Promotion program	Purchase of soap, incremental water consumption, and time used for hand washing	Personal well-being and status

Table 3.2 Reduction in Diarrheal Disease from Water-Supply, Sanitation, and Hygiene Interventions[a]

Intervention	Intervention effectiveness (% reduction in diarrheal disease)	Applied in this study
Improved water supply	25% (Fewtrell and others 2005) 21% (point-of-use) (Waddington and Snilstveit 2009)	20–25%
Water quality improvement (point-of-use treatment)	35% mainly chlorination and disinfection (Fewtrell and others 2005) 29% chlorination (Arnold and Colford 2007) 40–60% chlorination or filtration (Clasen and others 2007)[b] 44% mainly chlorination, filtration, or disinfection (Waddington and Snilstveit 2009)	30%
Improved sanitation	32% (Fewtrell and others 2005) 36% (Cairncross and others 2010) 31% sewer (Waddington and Snilstveit 2009) 35% toilet (Waddington and Snilstveit 2009)	15–35%
Hand washing with soap	44% (Fewtrell and others 2005) 47% (Curtis and Cairncross 2003) 48% (Cairncross and others 2010) 32% LMIC, 39% HIC (Ejemot and others 2009) 37% (Waddington and Snilstveit 2009)	40%

Note: POUT = point-of-use treatment; LMIC = Low- and middle-income countries; HIC = high-income countries.
a. Summary of review and meta-analysis studies.
b. Studies reporting rate ratio or risk ratio.

per household) for the sanitation interventions. Annual health benefits of household POU treatment of drinking water and hand washing with soap are calculated in the range of PRs 7,200–9,600 per child younger than five years of age and PRs 270–360 per person five or more years of age.[2] The large difference in benefits is because of the dissimilar rates of diarrheal disease incidence and diarrheal fatality of these two population age groups.

The capital cost of interventions is estimated at PRs 1,600–3,000 per person (PRs 10,000–19,000 per household) for the water-supply interventions and PRs 1,600–1,900 per person (PRs 10,000–12,000 per household) for the sanitation interventions. The annualized intervention cost is PRs 270–500 per person for the water-supply interventions and PRs 290–320 per person for the sanitation interventions, including operations and maintenance costs.

The annualized cost of household POU treatment of drinking water is estimated at PRs 630–2,700 per person and annualized cost of hand washing with soap, at PRs 1,380–3,200 per person. These estimates include both private and public costs. Private costs consist of boiling water, water used for these practices, cost of soap, and cost of time required for these practices. Public costs consist of promotion programs to encourage households to adopt POU treatment and improved hand-washing practices with soap. The large range in cost is associated with household response rates (percentage of households adopting the practices) per rupee spent on promotion and the number of years that the households continue the practices.

The benefits per rupee spent (that is, BCR) on the water-supply interventions are estimated at PRs 3.5–5.8. This indicates that each of these interventions provides a very high rate of return (figure 3.1). The largest benefits derived from all water-supply interventions are health improvements, followed by increased water quantity expected from improvement of Karachi's piped water supply and provision of improved water supply on household premises in rural areas. Time savings benefits are also substantial for households currently without water supply on premises. The three interventions with the highest

Figure 3.1 Benefit-Cost Ratios of Water-Supply Interventions in Sindh Province

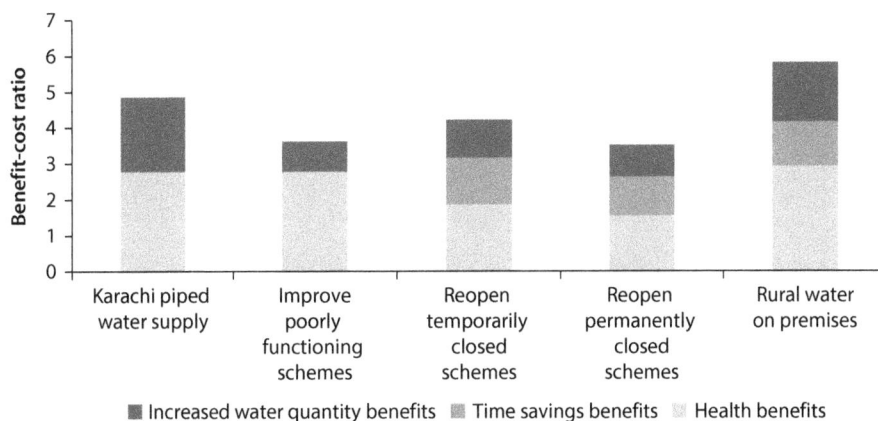

Legend: ■ Increased water quantity benefits ▨ Time savings benefits ░ Health benefits

BCR for improving water supply are improving Karachi piped water supply, reopening temporarily closed schemes, and providing water supplies on premise to rural households.

The benefits per rupee spent on the sanitation interventions are estimated at PRs 2.5–5.8 (figure 3.2). These are quite similar to the BCRs for the water-supply interventions. The highest benefits per rupee spent are estimated to result from household access to a nonshared improved toilet for those households currently without a toilet or sharing one with other households. Calculated benefits per rupee spent on sewerage improvements in Karachi and other cities and towns are lower than for the other sanitation interventions, but substantially higher than the corresponding costs. In addition, proper sewage collection and wastewater treatment provide additional environmental and water resources benefits that are not included in this assessment.

Benefits per rupee spent on household POU treatment of drinking water are estimated to be in the range of PRs 4–10, and in the case of improved hand washing with soap, PRs 4–6.5 (figure 3.3). These BCRs pertain to protection of young children's health by targeting promotion programs at mothers or caretakers of young children. The benefits per rupee spent depend on how many households adopt these practices because of the promotion programs. "High program cost" reflects low adoption rates, while "low program cost" reflects high adoption rates. These costs influence intervention costs per household and thus BCRs. Nevertheless, this book finds that these interventions are likely to provide the highest benefits per rupee spent on water, sanitation, and hygiene improvements. Therefore, promotion of improved hand washing with soap should be a component of a strategy to protect health against environmental health risks, as should promotion of household POU treatment of drinking water until safe drinking water can be provided through a piped water supply or other sources of water supply to all households in Sindh. Benefits per rupee spent on POU treatment and improved hand washing with soap to protect adults' health are comparatively low, at only PRs 0.2–0.5, because of much lower disease incidence and fatality rates among this population group.

Figure 3.2 Benefit-Cost Ratios of Sanitation Interventions in Sindh Province

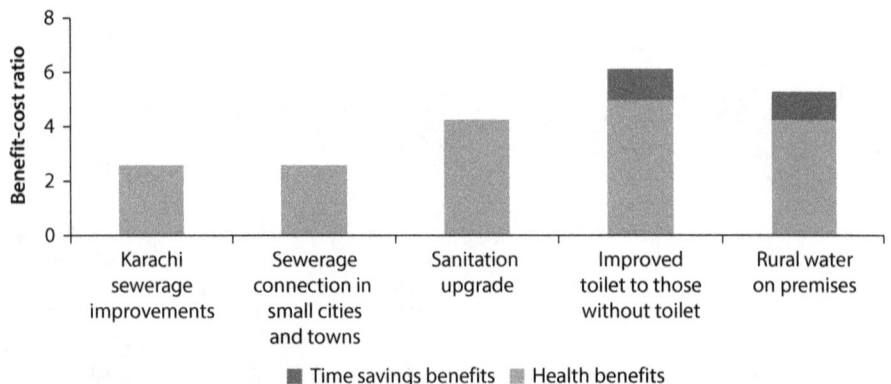

■ Time savings benefits ■ Health benefits

Figure 3.3 Benefit-Cost Ratios of Point-of-Use Treatment of Drinking Water and Improved Hand Washing with Soap to Protect Young Children's Health in Sindh Province

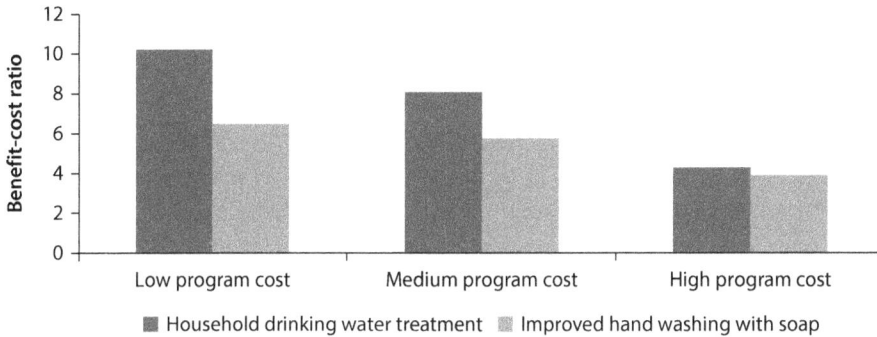

Table 3.3 Recommended Water-Supply and Sanitation Interventions

Timeframe	Category	Interventions
Short term	Water supply	Expand Karachi piped water supply Reopen temporarily closed schemes Provide rural water on premises
	Sanitation	Improve toilets for those without toilets Improve toilets for those currently sharing a toilet Upgrade sanitation Promotion of improved hand washing with soap and point-of-use treatment of water campaign programs
Medium and long term	Water supply	Reopen permanently closed schemes Improve poorly functioning schemes
	Sanitation	Improve Karachi sewerage system

On the basis of the analysis presented in this section, this book recommends undertaking in the short term the seven water supply and sanitation assessed interventions with the highest BCR, and implementing three additional interventions in the medium term to long term (table 3.3).

Improving Outdoor Air Quality

The analysis presented in this book estimated that outdoor air pollution in Sindh causes adverse environmental health problems that result in costs equivalent to more than 1.4 percent of the provincial GDP (chapter 2). The analysis focused on ambient air concentrations of particulate matter, especially fine particulate matter with a diameter of less than 2.5 microns ($PM_{2.5}$), because it is the outdoor air pollutant globally associated with the largest health effects. Nearly 80 percent of the health effects caused by particulate matter in Sindhi cities with a population greater than 100,000 inhabitants occur in Karachi. Therefore, the assessment of benefits and costs of interventions to improve PM air quality in this book focuses on Karachi.

Identifiable source-specific PM emissions in Karachi are estimated at 20,000–28,000 tons of fine particulate matter with a diameter of less than 10 microns (PM_{10}) per year, of which 16,000–22,000 tons are $PM_{2.5}$. About 70–80 percent of these emissions are estimated to end up in the urban air shed of Karachi, that is, 15,000–19,000 tons of PM_{10}, of which 13,000–16,000 tons are $PM_{2.5}$ (table 3.4). The remaining emissions drift away from the city, depending on such factors as location of emission source and wind conditions. With the addition of secondary particulates (sulfates and nitrates)[3] and PM from areawide sources, total annual PM_{10} that causes the PM ambient concentrations in the urban air shed of Karachi is estimated at 43,000–51,000 tons, of which 21,000–25,000 tons are $PM_{2.5}$. The secondary particulates are formed in the atmosphere from sulfur dioxide and nitrogen oxide emissions originating from fuel combustion and industrial processes. The areawide sources of PM include natural dust carried by the wind from outside the city, resuspended road dust, dust from the construction sector, agricultural residue burning, and salt particles from the sea.

The research underlying this book yields the following estimates regarding the sources of ambient $PM_{2.5}$ concentrations in Karachi:

- 24–28 percent is from road vehicles
- 23–24 percent is from areawide sources
- 19–20 percent is from industry
- 12–13 percent is secondary particulates (sulfates and nitrates)
- 8–14 percent is from burning of solid waste in the city
- 4–5 percent is from domestic use of wood/biomass
- 2.3–2.8 percent is from oil and natural gas consumption by power plants and the domestic/public/commercial sectors.

Around two-thirds of PM emissions from road vehicles is estimated to be from diesel trucks, diesel buses and minibuses, and light-duty diesel vehicles. About one-third, however, appears to be from motorcycles and rickshaws, which almost exclusively have highly polluting two-stroke engines. A major source of PM emissions from industry appears to be ferrous metal sources (steel mills, foundries, and scrap smelters).[4]

Table 3.4 Estimated Particulate Matter Emissions in Karachi, 2009

	Urban air shed PM_{10}		Urban air shed $PM_{2.5}$	
	Low	High	Low	High
Source-specific emissions	15.2	19.4	13.1	15.8
Secondary particulates (sulfates, nitrates)	2.7	3.2	2.6	3.0
PM from areawide sources[a]	25.1	28.5	5.0	5.7
Total	**43.0**	**51.1**	**20.7**	**24.6**

a. Includes natural dust, sea particles, construction dust, resuspended road dust, and agricultural residue burning.

An aggressive implementation of well-targeted interventions could possibly improve ambient air quality ($PM_{2.5}$) in Karachi by 40–50 percent over the next 10–15 years. Reducing PM emissions from road vehicles will be an essential component, as road vehicles are the principal sources of $PM_{2.5}$ in the city. This book assesses the following interventions: (a) reducing sulfur in diesel and fuel oil; (b) retrofitting in-use diesel vehicles with PM emission control technology; (c) converting diesel-fueled minibuses and vans to compressed natural gas (CNG), (d) controlling PM emissions from motorcycles; and (e) converting three-wheelers (rickshaws) to CNG. These interventions would not only reduce PM emissions, but low-sulfur fuels would also reduce secondary particulates by reducing sulfur dioxide emissions. Government plans to expand further the use of CNG buses will also reduce PM emissions, but add to nitrates. Thus, vehicles converted to CNG should be equipped with three-way catalytic converters to reduce nitrogen oxide emissions that contribute to secondary particles. Other potential interventions that should be assessed in further studies include curtailing burning of solid waste in the city (with consideration to the informal recycling industry), PM emission control from ferrous metal sources and other industrial sources, improved street cleaning, and control of construction dust.

The health benefits per ton of PM_{10} emission reductions are on average estimated at PRs 0.5–1.2 million (US\$6,200–15,500).[5] Benefits of PM emission reductions are highest for emissions from road vehicles; oil and gas consumption in the domestic, public, and commercial sectors; and domestic use of wood/ biomass. This is because almost all of the emissions from these sources end up in the urban air shed and the emissions have a very high $PM_{2.5}$ fraction, thus high mortality reduction benefits. The source-specific benefits are applied when assessing the benefits and costs of a specific intervention. However, reducing PM_{10} emissions from a source with low benefits per ton of emissions might still have high benefits relative to costs if the cost of intervention is relatively low.

The world is rapidly moving towards the use of diesel with low sulfur content in transportation, as well as in other sectors. Low-sulfur diesel reduces PM emissions from combustion and allows installation of very effective PM emission control technology on diesel vehicles. The European Union (EU) implemented a maximum allowable sulfur content of 500 parts per million (ppm) (0.05 percent) in diesel in 1996, 350 ppm in 2000, 50 ppm in 2005, and 10 ppm in 2009. Many developing countries, including in Asia, have already implemented 500-ppm sulfur diesel standards (for example, India, Malaysia, the Philippines, Thailand, and Vietnam). Some developing countries have introduced 350-ppm or 50-ppm sulfur diesel in some metropolitan areas (for example, China and India), and some are in the process of introducing or have established timetables for 50-ppm sulfur diesel (for example, Malaysia, the Philippines, Thailand, and Vietnam) (UNEP 2011).

Sulfur in diesel is being reduced to 500 ppm in Pakistan, but no confirmed timetable has been established for 50-ppm sulfur diesel. This book estimates that the health benefits of using 500-ppm diesel in road transport amounts to at least US\$2.3–3.5 per barrel of diesel for light diesel vehicles and large diesel buses and trucks used primarily within Karachi. Lowering the sulfur content further to 50 ppm would provide additional health benefits of US\$3.0–4.6 per barrel.[6] This compares to an approximate cost of US\$1.5–2.5 per barrel for lowering the sulfur content to 500 ppm, and US\$2–3 per barrel for lowering sulfur from 500 to 50 ppm. Thus the midpoint estimated health benefits per dollar spent (that is, BCR) on cleaner diesel are in the range of about US\$1.1–1.2 for light duty diesel vehicles and US\$1.7–1.8 for large buses and trucks for both 500-ppm and 50-ppm diesel (figure 3.4).[7]

Fuel oil in Pakistan generally has a sulfur content that averages around 3 percent, but some fuel oil with 1 percent sulfur is being imported. PM emission rates from combustion of fuel oil are greatly influenced by the sulfur content. Reducing sulfur from 3 percent to 1 percent is estimated in this book to have health benefits of US\$35–47 per ton of fuel oil. The additional cost of low-sulfur fuel oil in international markets fluctuates and has recently been around US\$50 per ton. Thus, use of low-sulfur fuel oil in Karachi should be targeted at users within the city, where all PM emissions contribute to ambient concentrations and health benefits are highest. However, low-sulfur fuel oil has additional health benefits that this book does not assess; such benefits include reduced sulfur dioxide emissions and associated lower secondary particulates formation.

More stringent PM emission standards and control options can be implemented for diesel vehicles once low-sulfur diesel is available. EURO standards can be mandated on new diesel vehicles (and secondhand imports), and PM control technologies can effectively be installed on in-use diesel vehicles, such as diesel oxidation catalysts (DOC) and diesel particulate filters (DPF).

DOCs require a maximum of 500-ppm sulfur in diesel, and DPFs require a maximum of 50 ppm to function effectively. A DOC generally reduces PM emissions by 20–30 percent, while a DPF reduces PM by more than 85 percent. Even five to six years ago, DOCs had already been installed on more than 50 million diesel passenger vehicles, and on more than 1.5 million buses and trucks worldwide. All new on-road diesel vehicles in the United States and Canada are equipped with a high-efficiency DPF, and all new diesel cars

Figure 3.4 Benefit-Cost Ratios of Low-Sulfur Fuels in Karachi

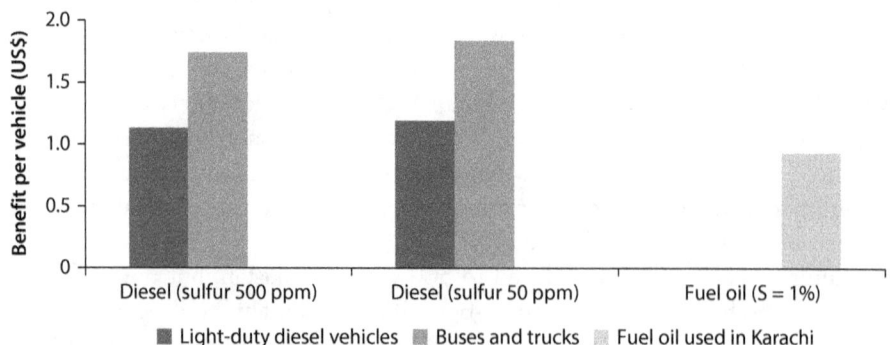

Note: Midpoint estimate of incremental cost of low-sulfur fuels.

and vans in the EU have been equipped with DPF since 2009. About five or six years ago, more than 200,000 heavy-duty vehicles had already been retrofitted with DPF. DOCs and DPFs have also been used for retrofitting buses and trucks in many countries (for example, India and Thailand) and locations on a wider scale or in demonstration projects.

Potential candidates for retrofitting with a DOC, or with a DPF when 50-ppm sulfur diesel becomes available, are the high-usage commercial diesel vehicles on the roads of Karachi today and primarily used within the city. This book estimates the annual health benefits from each retrofitted vehicle to be in the range of US$95–568 for a DOC and US$216–1,295 for a DPF, depending on the vehicle's type and annual usage (table 3.5).

Retrofitting EURO 1 or pre-EURO 1 diesel vehicles with a DOC generally reduces PM emissions by 20–30 percent, although reductions of as much as 20–50 percent have been reported. A DOC costs US$1,000–2,000 and a DPF as much as US$6,000–10,000. The expected number of years that the vehicle will continue to be in use and years that the devices will be effective are therefore an important consideration. The midpoint estimate of benefits per rupee spent on retrofitting in-use diesel vehicles with a DOC, once 500-ppm diesel is available, is PRs 1–1.3 for large buses and trucks used within the city, but less than its cost for minibuses and light duty vans (figure 3.5).[8] Estimated health

Table 3.5 Estimated Health Benefits of Retrofitting Diesel Vehicles with Particulate Matter Control Technology in Karachi

US$ per vehicle

	Vehicle usage			
	Diesel oxidation catalyst (DOC)		Diesel particulate filter (DPF)	
	35,000 km/year	70,000 km/year	35,000 km/year	70,000 km/year
Heavy-duty trucks	284	568	647	1,295
Large buses	208	417	475	949
Minibuses	133	265	302	604
Light-duty vans	95	189	216	432

Figure 3.5 Benefit-Cost Ratios of Retrofitting In-Use Diesel Vehicles with DOC in Karachi

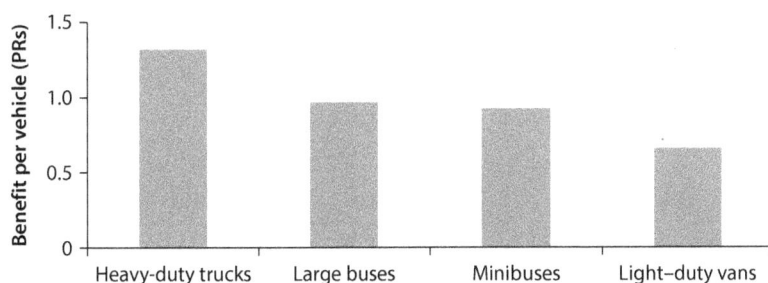

Note: Seven years of useful life of DOC; 50,000 km/year vehicle usage.

benefits of a DPF are currently lower than the cost for all classes of diesel vehicles, but should be reassessed once 50-ppm sulfur diesel is available in the future.

Given the relatively high cost of DOCs per unit of PM emission reduction, alternative options can be considered for in-use diesel-fueled minibuses and light duty vans. One of these is the conversion to CNG, which almost entirely removes PM emissions. This book estimates the health benefits of CNG conversion to be in the range of US$455–1,288 per vehicle per year, depending on the vehicle's type and annual usage (table 3.6).

Conversion of such vehicles to CNG in Pakistan is reported to cost in the range of PRs 150,000–200,000 per vehicle, or US$1,900–2,550, at 2009 exchange rates. Applying a cost of PRs 200,000, the midpoint estimate of health benefits per dollar spent (BCR) on conversion to CNG are US$1.7 for minibuses and US$1.2 for light-duty vans (figure 3.6).[9] The BCRs for vans are somewhat lower than for minibuses because of a difference in estimated PM emissions per kilometer of vehicle use.

Two-stroke rickshaws are also a large source of PM emissions and urban noise. Conversion to a four-stroke engine using CNG is reported to cost around PRs 40,000–60,000 in Pakistan. At a cost of PRs 60,000, the midpoint estimate of health benefits is two times the conversion cost (figure 3.6).

Table 3.6 Estimated Health Benefits of Conversion to Compressed Natural Gas in Karachi
US$ per vehicle

	Vehicle usage	
	35,000 km/year	*70,000 km/year*
Minibuses	644	1,288
Light-duty vans	455	909

Figure 3.6 Benefit-Cost Ratios of CNG Conversion of Diesel Vehicles, Rickshaws, and Motorcycles in Karachi

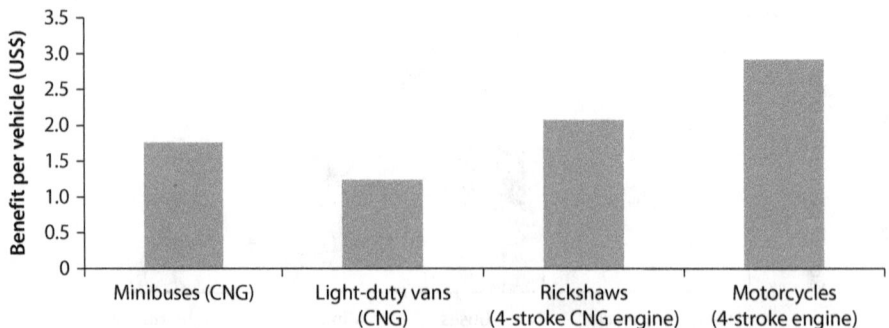

Note: Seven years of useful life of CNG conversions, and 50,000 km/year usage of minibuses and light-duty vans.

Two-stroke motorcycles tend to have high PM emissions per ton of gasoline consumption. They also contribute greatly to urban noise. Many countries are therefore limiting or banning the use of two-stroke motorcycles. In comparison, four-stroke motorcycles emit substantially less PM, are more fuel efficient, and cause substantially less noise. The additional cost of a four-stoke motorcycle engine is approximately US$50, but varies with engine size. At this cost, and for a two-stroke motorcycle emitting 0.25 grams of PM per kilometer, the health benefits of switching to a four-stroke motorcycle are around US$2.9 per dollar of additional engine cost (figure 3.6). If fuel savings are considered, the BCR is as high as 4.2.

In summary, based on the benefit-cost analysis, this book recommends the following interventions for outdoor air pollution:

- Moving to 500-ppm sulfur in diesel in Pakistan, because it will result in health benefits that are larger than the additional fuel cost
- Establishing a timetable for moving to 50-ppm sulfur in diesel (as many other Asian countries have done) in the long term
- Continuing the cost-effective conversion of diesel-fueled minibuses and city delivery vans to CNG and installing DOC on existing large buses and trucks used in the city
- Introducing new CNG full-size buses, which is also cost-effective, as DPF cannot be used with 500-ppm sulfur in diesel
- Introducing low-sulfur fuel oil (1 percent sulfur) to major users located in Karachi
- Converting existing two-stroke rickshaws to four-stroke CNG engines
- If CNG supply is a constraint, preference for CNG conversion should be given to diesel minibuses, commercial light duty diesel vans, and rickshaws, rather than to gasoline cars
- Implementing and enforcing a ban on new two-stroke motorcycles and rickshaws and exploring options to control PM emissions from in-use two-stroke motorcycles
- In the long term, requiring that CNG vehicles conform with EU emissions standards (as stringently as possible) and progressively moving to higher EU standards for gasoline vehicles, in order to reduce, for example, NOx emissions, which contribute to secondary particulates.

Additional short- and medium-term interventions can include the following:

- Effectively enforcing a ban on solid waste burning in the city and finding solutions to the issue of recycling so that trucks stop selling/dumping waste at unofficial sites where waste is burned to separate out recyclable materials
- Moving any existing brick kilns, metal foundries, and scrap smelters out of the city and considering wind directions and future urban development when deciding on acceptable locations
- Improving street cleaning to reduce resuspension of road dust and implementing measures to reduce construction dust

Table 3.7 Recommended Outdoor Air Pollution Interventions in Sindh Province

Timeframe	Intervention
Short term	Enforcement of 500-ppm sulfur content in diesel
	Introduce low-sulfur fuel oil (1% sulfur) to major users located in the city
	Convert existing two-stroke rickshaws to four-stroke CNG
	Install diesel oxidation catalysts (DOC) on existing large buses and trucks used in the city
	Continue introducing new CNG full-size buses
Medium and long term	Reduce sulfur in diesel to 50 ppm
	Continue introducing new CNG to full-size buses and light duty vans
	Mandate EU standards on new diesel vehicles and secondhand imports
	Install PM control technologies on in-use diesel vehicles, such as DOC and diesel particulate filters (DPF)

- Controlling emissions from large point sources (ensuring that existing control equipment is operating properly and installing new where nonexistent), but assessing on a case-by-case basis in light of population exposure, location, and wind directions.

The government is already pursuing many of these actions—such as conversion of rickshaws, banning two-stroke vehicles, selectively using low-sulfur fuel oil, and banning waste burning in the city—to various degrees. The analysis in this book provides support for these actions and highlights additional ones. Table 3.7 summarizes the recommended interventions that could be implemented to reduce the health effects of outdoor air pollution in Sindh.

Controlling Household Air Pollution

As explained in chapter 2, use of solid fuels for cooking generates smoke and other pollutants that affect human health. In addition to causing pain and suffering, HAP results in costs that are equivalent to 0.92 of Sindh's GDP. This environmental health risk occurs predominantly in rural areas, where the vast majority of households rely on solid fuels. Thus, interventions to control HAP are assessed for rural households. Most of the wood/biomass stoves used in these areas are unimproved stoves (that is, with low fuel efficiency and no control of smoke, which is emitted directly into the immediate environment). Evaluation of benefits and costs of HAP control focuses here on replacing such unimproved stoves with improved wood/biomass stoves or with liquefied petroleum gas (LPG) stoves. LPG stoves (or, alternatively, CNG) are chosen for evaluation here, since central natural gas supply is unlikely to be available any time soon to most rural households.

Improved wood/biomass stoves and LPG stoves provide a cleaner burning that creates less smoke and health effects than unimproved ones or cooking over an open fire. Improved stoves are also more fuel-efficient and often reduce time required for cooking. This book estimates that replacing an unimproved stove with an improved wood/biomass stove would result in benefits that include a reduction of health effects of HAP by 50 percent, a 40 percent increase in fuel efficiency, and a reduction in cooking time of 20 minutes per household per day. Switching from such an improved wood/biomass stove to LPG would eliminate the remaining 50 percent of health effects of HAP from solid fuels, result in another 60 percent in wood/biomass fuel savings relative to an unimproved stove, and reduce cooking time by another 20 minutes per household per day. Switching directly from an unimproved wood/biomass stove to LPG would remove 100 percent of the health effects of HAP from solid fuels, reduce wood/biomass fuel use by 100 percent, and reduce cooking time by 40 minutes per household per day. In a pilot study conducted in Sindh in 2002, women reported that improved cooking stoves produced less smoke and had beneficial impacts on their health (Khushk and others 2005).

These interventions are estimated to provide annual health, fuel savings, and time savings benefits in the range of PRs 12,000–24,000 per household that currently cook indoors with wood/biomass fuels, and PRs 8,000–17,000 for households currently cooking outdoors with wood/biomass fuels.[10] Annualized cost per household of an improved wood/biomass stove is estimated at PRs 544 and the annualized cost of using an LPG stove for cooking is estimated at somewhat more than PRs 10,000. These estimates include costs of a promotion program to encourage households to adopt the interventions.

Benefits per rupee spent on switching from an unimproved to an improved wood/biomass stove are on average estimated at more than PRs 20 for households cooking indoors and nearly PRs 15 for households cooking outdoors (figure 3.7). Estimated benefits per rupee spent on switching to LPG from unimproved wood/biomass stoves are on average PRs 2.4 for households cooking indoors and PRs 1.4 for households cooking outdoors (figure 3.8). For households switching from improved wood/biomass stoves to LPG, benefits per rupee spent are on average estimated at PRs 1.2 for households cooking indoors and PRs 0.8 for households cooking outdoors. About 60–65 percent of total benefits of these interventions would be

Figure 3.7 Benefit-Cost Ratios for Use of Improved Wood/Biomass Stoves among Rural Households in Sindh Province

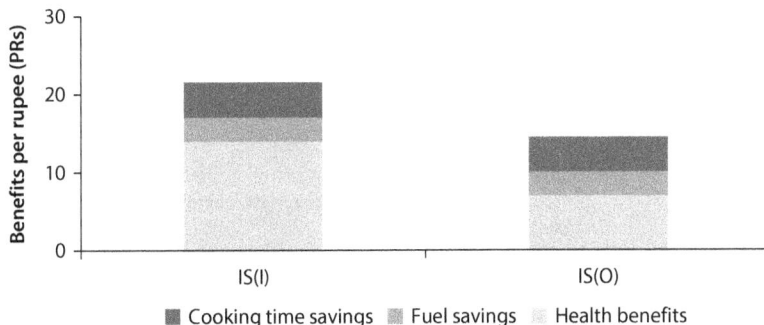

■ Cooking time savings   ▓ Fuel savings   ░ Health benefits

Note: IS = improved wood/biomass stove. I = indoor cooking. O = outdoor cooking.

among households cooking indoors and 45–50 percent for those cooking outdoors. The value of time savings is somewhat larger than the value of wood/biomass fuel savings for the improved stove intervention and for switching to LPG from an unimproved stove.

The benefit-cost assessment indicates that promotion of household adoption of improved wood/biomass stoves should receive high priority, even among households that cook outdoors. This is especially important given that more than 50 percent of households use wood and other biomass fuels for cooking in Sindh. Various improved stoves can be piloted to identify household preferences and assess likelihood of adoption. Promotion programs can educate households of the benefits, as well as emphasize the potential social status that cleanliness and use of more sophisticated technology can bring about. LPG stoves can also be promoted. Because of the high cost of LPG fuel in today's markets, however, these stoves are likely to be adopted only by households that place a high value on time savings and by wealthier households that can afford LPG. Table 3.8 summarizes the interventions that are recommended to reduce the health effects of household air pollution, based on the CBA presented in this section.

Figure 3.8 Benefit-Cost Ratios for Use of LPG Stoves among Rural Households in Sindh Province

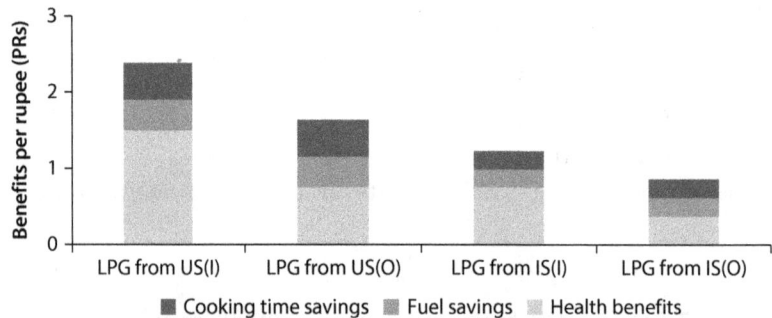

Note: LPG = liquefied petroleum gas. US = unimproved wood/biomass stove. IS = improved wood/biomass stove. I = indoor cooking. O = outdoor cooking.

Table 3.8 Recommended Household Air Pollution Interventions in Sindh Province

Timeframe	Interventions
Short term	Introduce improved wood/biomass stoves to rural households
	Introduce liquefied petroleum gas stoves to unimproved wood/biomass stoves for indoor cooking
Medium and long term	Introduce liquefied petroleum gas stoves to improved wood/biomass stoves for indoor cooking

Conclusions

This chapter presented the findings of a CBA conducted on a set of possible interventions to address the health and social impacts of inadequate water supply, sanitation, and hygiene; outdoor air pollution; and HAP in rural areas. The analysis found that the benefits resulting from the interventions would significantly exceed the associated costs.

The assessed interventions do not represent a complete plan of action or the entire range of options to mitigate environmental health risks in Sindh. However, the assessment serves as an illustration and first round of identification of interventions, many of which have potentially high social and environmental rates of return. Similar analyses should be completed to identify options to mitigate other significant environmental health risks in Sindh, including lead exposure, road traffic accidents, and road traffic noise.

On the basis of the benefit-cost analysis presented in this chapter, the following interventions are recommended to address Sindh's environmental health priority problems (table 3.9).

Table 3.9 Summary of Recommended Interventions to Address Top Environmental Health Hazards in Sindh Province

Timeframe	Category	Interventions
Short term	Water supply	Expand Karachi piped water supply Reopen temporarily closed schemes Provide rural water on premises
	Sanitation	Improve toilets for those without toilets Improve toilets for those currently sharing a toilet Upgrade sanitation Promote improved hand washing with soap and point of use treatment of water campaign programs
	Outdoor air pollution	Enforce 500-pm sulfur content in diesel Introduce low-sulfur fuel oil (1% sulfur) to major users located in the city Convert existing two-stroke rickshaws to four-stroke CNG Install diesel oxidation catalysts (DOC) on existing large buses and trucks used in the city Continue introducing new CNG full-size buses
	Household air pollution	Introduce improved wood/biomass stoves to rural households Introduce liquefied petroleum gas stoves to unimproved wood/biomass stoves for indoor cooking
Medium and long term	Water supply	Reopen permanently closed schemes Improve poorly functioning schemes
	Sanitation	Improve Karachi sewerage system
	Outdoor air pollution	Reduce sulfur in diesel to 50 ppm Continue introducing new cleaner natural gas to full-size buses and light-duty vans Mandate EU standards on new diesel vehicles and secondhand imports Install PM control technologies on in-use diesel vehicles, such as diesel oxidation catalysts and diesel particulate filters
	Household air pollution	Introduce liquefied petroleum gas stoves to improved wood/biomass stoves for indoor cooking

Notes

1. See appendix A for an in-depth discussion of the benefit-cost analysis of interventions presented in this chapter.

2. Health benefits are valued using the techniques described in chapter 2. Nonhealth benefits are valued as follows: time savings are valued at 50 percent of wage rates and water quantity benefits are valued at PRs 40 per cubic meter.

3. Tons of secondary particulates are estimated based on Mansha and others (2011).

4. Estimated PM source attribution is based on seasonal wind directions and speeds, emission source locations, sector-specific emission coefficients and emission inventories, and ambient PM size distributions.

5. The lower bound reflects valuation of mortality risk using the human capital approach. The upper bound reflects valuation of morality risk using a value of statistical life (VSL). The upper bound is applied in the benefit-cost analysis (CBA) in this book.

6. Health benefits are estimated based on an expected 20 percent reduction in vehicle particulate emissions ($PM_{2.5}$) by reducing sulfur to 500 ppm, and a 33 percent additional reduction by reducing sulfur from 500 to 50 ppm (ADB 2005; Blumberg, Walsh, and Pera 2003; UNEP 2006).

7. Nearly 90 percent of premature mortality from PM pollution in Karachi is among adults. These individuals may be losing around 10 years of life as a result of PM pollution. The book estimates the social cost of premature mortality using two values, the HCV and the VSL. These two methodologies provide vastly different cost estimates. In the assessment of benefits and costs of PM control interventions, the VSL is applied because this value is more likely than the HCV to be closer to the actual value that individuals place on a reduction in the risk of death.

8. A cost of a DOC of US$1,500 was applied for heavy-duty trucks and large buses, and a cost of US$1,000 for minibuses and light-duty vans. A discount rate of 10 percent was applied to annualize the cost of the DOC.

9. A discount rate of 10 percent was applied to annualize the cost of conversion to CNG.

10. Health benefits for a household cooking outdoors are half of the health benefits for a household cooking indoors. Monetized health benefits are an average of the range of estimates provided in this book. Wood/biomass fuel savings are estimated based on household fuel expenditure data. Time savings are estimated by valuing time at 50 percent of the average rural wage rate.

Bibliography

ADB (Asian Development Bank). 2005. *Karachi Mega Cities Preparation Project*. Final Report. Vol. 1. TA 4578-Pakistan. August. http://www.adb.org/sites/default/files/project-document/69115/38405-pak-dpta.pdf.

Arnold, B., and J. M. Colford. 2007. "Treating Water with Chlorine at Point-of-Use to Improve Water Quality and Reduce Child Diarrhea in Developing Countries: A Systematic Review and Meta-analysis." *American Journal of Tropical Medicine and Hygiene* 76 (2): 354–64.

Blumberg, K., M. Walsh, and C. Pera. 2003. *Low-sulfur Gasoline and Diesel: The Key to Lower Vehicle Emissions*. Washington, DC: International Council on Clean Transportation (ICCT), http://www.unep.org/pcfv/PDF/PubLowSulfurPaper.pdf.

Cairncross, S., C. Hunt, S. Boisson, K. Bostoen, V. Curtis, I. C. H. Fung, and W. P. Smith. 2010. "Water, Sanitation and Hygiene for Preventing Diarrhoea." *International Journal of Epidemiology* 39: i193–i205.

Clasen, T., W.-P. Schmidt, T. Rabie, I. Roberts, and S. Cairncross. 2007. "Interventions to Improve Water Quality for Preventing Diarrhoea: Systematic Review and Meta-analysis." *British Medical Journal* 334: 782–91.

Curtis, V., and S. Cairncross. 2003. "Effect of Washing Hands with Soap on Diarrhoea Risk in the Community: A Systematic Review." *Lancet Infectious Diseases* 3: 275–81.

Ejemot, R. I., J. E. Ehiri, M. M. Meremikwu, and J. A. Critchley. 2009. "Handwashing for Preventing Diarrhea (Review)." *Cochrane Library* 3. http://onlinelibrary.wiley.com /doi/10.1002/14651858.CD004265.pub2/pdf.

Fewtrell, L., R. B. Kaufmann, D. Kay, W. Enanoria, L. Haller, and J. M. Colford. 2005. "Water, Sanitation and Hygiene Interventions to Reduce Diarrhea in Less Developed Countries: A Systematic Review and Meta-analysis." *Lancet Infectious Diseases* 5: 42–52.

Fewtrell, L., A. Prüss-Üstün, R. Bos, F. Gore, and J. Bartram. 2007. "Water, Sanitation and Hygiene: Quantifying the Health Impact at National and Local Levels in Countries with Incomplete Water Supply and Sanitation Coverage." Environmental Burden of Disease Series 15, Geneva, World Health Organization.

Khushk, W. A., Z. Fatmi, F. White, and M. M. Kadir. 2005. "Health and Social Impacts of Improved Stoves on Rural Women: A Pilot Intervention in Sindh, Pakistan." *Indoor Air* 15: 311–16.

Larsen, B. 2007. "Cost of Environmental Health Risk in Children under Five Years of Age: Accounting for Malnutrition in Ghana and Pakistan." Background Report Prepared for the World Bank. Environment Department, World Bank, Washington, DC.

Luby, S., M. Agboatwalla, D. Feikin, J. Painter, M. S. Ward Billheimer, A. Altaf, and R. Hoekstra. 2005. "Effect of Hand Washing on Child Health: A Randomised Controlled Trial." *Lancet* 366: 225–33.

Mansha, M., B. Ghauri, S. Rahman, and A. Amman. 2011. "Characterization and Source Apportionment of Ambient Air Particulate Matter (PM2.5) in Karachi." *Science of the Total Environment* 425: 176–83.

Rabie, T., and V. Curtis. 2006. "Handwashing and Risk of Respiratory Infections: A Quantitative Systematic Review." *Tropical Medicine and International Health* 11 (3): 258–67.

UNEP (United Nations Environment Programme). 2006. "Opening the Door to Cleaner Vehicles in Developing and Transition Countries: The Role of Lower Sulphur Fuels." UNEP Partnership for Clean Fuels and Vehicles. Nairobi.

———. 2011. *Asia-Pacific 50-ppm Diesel Sulphur Matrix*. UNEP.

Waddington, H., and B. Snilstveit. 2009. "Effectiveness and Sustainability of Water, Sanitation, and Hygiene Interventions in Combating Diarrhoea." *Journal of Development Effectiveness* 1 (3): 295–335.

World Bank. 2008. *Environmental Health and Child Survival: Epidemiology, Economics, Experiences*. Washington, DC: World Bank.

CHAPTER 4

Natural Resource Degradation in Sindh Province[1]

Abstract

The annual cost of natural resource losses and natural disasters is calculated to be equivalent to 4–6 percent of Sindh's estimated GDP. Agricultural crop losses resulting from salinity and waterlogging contribute about 46 percent of the total annual cost, natural disasters about 33 percent, and the rest is the result of different categories of natural resource depletion. A cost-benefit analysis (CBA) was conducted on six potential interventions that could be implemented to mitigate these costs: (a) emergency management; (b) capacity building in water resource management of hydrological resources; (c) rehabilitation of existing water supply systems, including irrigation and small-scale drainage; (d) agricultural extension; (e) reforestation; and (f) sustainable fisheries management. Given the substantial uncertainties associated with the implementation of each intervention, the analysis also included a real options methodology to evaluate irreversible decisions with uncertain future results. On the basis of the analysis, this chapter recommends implementing the agricultural extension and water supply systems rehabilitation interventions with the highest priority.

Over the past several years, Pakistan has been struck by several major hydrometeorological hazards, including the catastrophic floods of 2010, the 2011 floods in Sindh, several land-falling tropical cyclones (TCs), and the recent droughts of 1998–2002 and 2009. The impacts of these hazards have been devastating. Given the significant negative effects of natural disasters—particularly floods and droughts—on the development of Pakistan, and particularly of Sindh, this chapter discusses the results of an assessment on prospects for mitigating the adverse impacts of such hazards through improved extended-range forecasts of rainfall, stream flow, and TCs. The study found that coupling a prediction system to a hazard warning system could result in the successful evacuation of regions that face storm surge peril.

Introduction

Natural resource degradation poses significant challenges in Sindh, where roughly 50 percent of population lives in rural areas and depends on these resources. Moreover, Sindh holds nearly one-quarter of Pakistan's population, and the province's population is projected to double in the next 25 years; it is likely that demographic growth will constitute a major pressure on natural resources. While continued economic growth and urbanization are expected to reduce poverty, they are also likely to exacerbate the province's environmental challenges, as difficult livelihood conditions and current natural resource management practices create high dependence and pressure on local natural resources, especially in the Indus River delta, that result in increased degradation.

The quality and quantity of natural resources have important linkages with mortality, morbidity, and livelihood outcomes. Natural resources degradation is a particular concern in a region such as Sindh, in which the majority of the population is engaged in agriculture-related activities, a sector that suffers severely from natural climatic hazards, including flooding. Agricultural productivity is further threatened by depleting soil fertility; the coastal wetlands of Sindh are deprived of water and losing their productivity potential. A fragile and degrading resource base has impacts on poverty levels. Moreover, Pakistan is heavily reliant and dependent on the Indus River for its surface water, making the country more vulnerable to water pollution and the consequences of basin degradation than its neighbors.

The next section discusses the main natural resource degradation and natural disasters challenges in Sindh, including estimates of the economic costs of these phenomena. The following sections describe key challenges in further detail. These are loss of productive land due to sweater intrusion; agricultural losses resulting from salinity and waterlogging; loss of mangroves; loss of fisheries; and losses from natural disasters. We then present the results of the benefit-cost analysis of potential interventions that could be implemented to reduce losses from natural resources degradation and natural disasters in Sindh. Given the concern of the government of Sindh about the province's vulnerability to extreme weather events and climate change, we then assess sea-level rise in the Indus Watershed. Then, we focus on the prediction of floods and droughts in Pakistan. The last section presents the chapter's conclusions.

Main Natural Resource Degradation and Natural Disaster Challenges in Sindh Province

According to the study of the cost of environmental degradation in Pakistan by the World Bank (World Bank 2006), the major categories of natural resource degradation in Sindh are similar to those in the other provinces. They include (a) Indus River delta degradation and loss of productive agricultural lands resulting from reduction of river flows and siltation; (b) irrigation-related land degradation, in particular secondary salinity, waterlogging, and irrigation-related soil erosion; (c) reduction of mangroves and related loss of biodiversity; (d) marine fishery reduction; and (e) other forms of natural resources degradation as a result of natural disasters, soil contamination, and other factors.

Although the major element of natural resource losses in Sindh is degradation of agricultural lands, it is important to mention that all components of natural resource degradation in Sindh are interrelated and causal links often work in both directions, thus aggravating the economic costs of degradation. For example, soil salinity is in part caused by the reduction in the inflow of freshwater to the Indus River delta, reduction of soil deposition, delta seawater inundation, and decline in mangrove forests. This, in turn, results in the reduction of marine fishery populations. Moreover, excessive regulation of river flows is an indirect reason for water shortages, waterlogging, increased sedimentation of the riverbed in the middle part of the river, and floods. It is very difficult to quantify these relations because of insufficient data. However, the analysis conducted under this study allowed the estimation of direct losses of natural resources and natural disasters, particularly in relation to the following categories: (a) loss of productive land resulting from seawater intrusion; (b) agricultural losses resulting from salinity and waterlogging; (c) loss of mangroves; (d) loss of fisheries; and (e) damages from natural disasters (floods).

The costs of loss of productive land resulting from seawater intrusion in the Indus River Delta are estimated based on reduction in net profit margins on affected lands. For agricultural losses, the cost is estimated based on the effects of salinity and waterlogging on crop yields. Annual losses of mangroves are highly uncertain and are calculated from secondary data sources. Their annual cost is estimated as the net present value of the benefits provided by mangroves. Loss of fisheries was estimated as the annual decline in profit associated with an average marine fish catch loss. Damages from natural disasters are estimated using probabilistic modeling of floods during a 10-year period. The cost of these natural resource losses and natural disasters is calculated to be equivalent to 4–6 percent of Sindh's estimated GDP for 2010, with a midpoint estimate of 5.1 percent (table 4.1; figure 4.1). Agricultural crop losses resulting from salinity and waterlogging contribute about 46 percent of the total annual cost, natural

Table 4.1 Estimated Annual Cost of Natural Resources Degradation and Natural Disasters in Sindh Province, 2010
Percentage of GDP

	Low	*Midpoint*[a]	*High*
Loss of productive land resulting from seawater intrusion	0.3	0.4	0.4
Agricultural losses resulting from salinity and waterlogging	1.6	2.4	3.1
Loss of mangroves	0.3	0.7	1.0
Loss of fisheries	<0.1	<0.1	<0.1
Losses from natural disasters (floods)	1.7	1.7	1.7
Total losses	3.9	5.1	6.2

Note: a. Rounded to nearest tenth of a percent.

Figure 4.1 Midpoint Estimate of Annual Cost of Natural Resources Degradation in Sindh Province, 2010

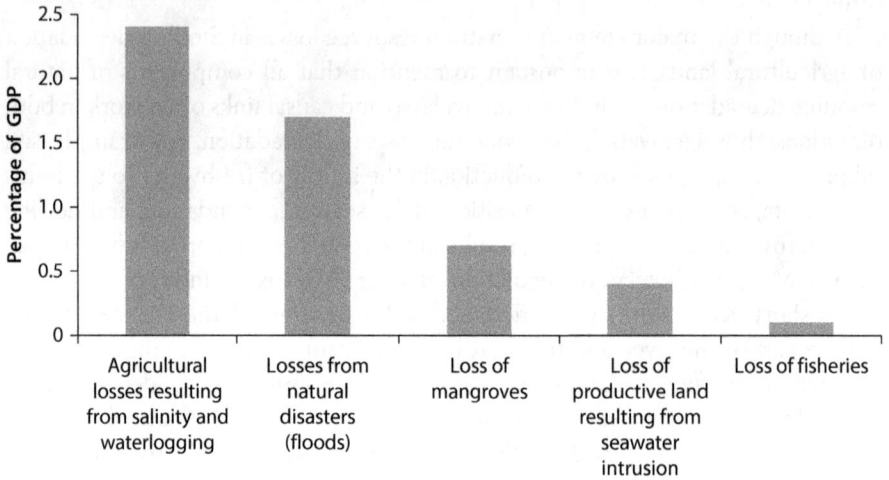

Figure 4.2 Composition of Estimated Annual Cost of Natural Resource Degradation in Sindh Province, 2010
Percent

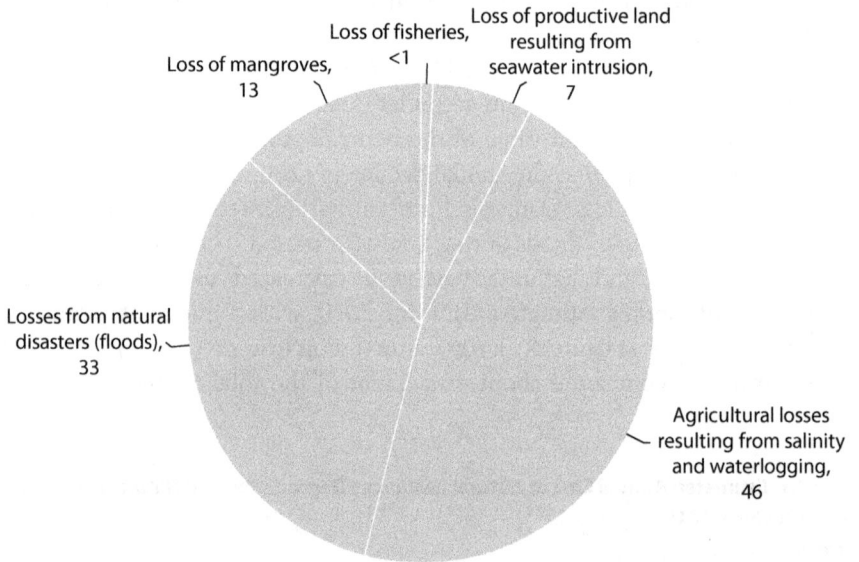

disasters about 33 percent, and the rest is the result of different categories of natural resource depletion (figure 4.2).

Inadequate water resource management is at the core of natural resource losses in Sindh. The situation originates from overregulation of the Indus River water flow. Beginning in the late 1850s, more than 70 percent of the average annual flow of the Indus River and its tributaries has been stored in reservoirs and diverted from the river by barrages used for irrigated agriculture. In the past

55 years, 19 barrages and 43 canal systems with 48 off-takes on the Indus River System in Pakistan created one of the largest water regulation systems for irrigation in the world, comprising about 14 million hectares of land. The Indus Water Accord of 1991 for the Indus River estimated a total water availability of 114.35 million acre feet (MAF)[2] below rim stations, with 55.95 MAF allocated for Punjab, 48.76 MAF for Sindh, 5.78 MAF for Khyber Pakhtunkhwa, and 3.87 MAF for Baluchistan. Ten MAF of downstream water flow was allocated for discharge to the sea. However, these allocations were not implemented. Instead, downstream water flow discharges have been close to zero. Over the next two decades, the projected water shortage in the Indus River is estimated to be 23–25 MAF. Because outflows have been near zero, seawater intrusion into the active delta and the Indus River has increased, reaching about 65 kilometers (km) upstream (at least up to the Thatta-Sujawal).

The Indus Water Accord launched an ecological crisis in the Indus River Delta. Inadequate water flow results in loss of valuable sediments that increase soil nutritional status; drastic increase of waterlogging and salinity resulting from seawater intrusion; soil erosion; and mangrove forest reduction together with extinction of wildlife, including fish and shrimps. A comprehensive study of the ecological consequences of outflow reduction was never conducted. However, some information on the negative impacts is published in various reports, including those by IUCN Pakistan and World Wildlife Fund Pakistan.

Loss of Productive Land Resulting from Seawater Intrusion

The rising sea level of the Indus River Delta has encroached on agricultural croplands in the coastal region and inundated them. Vast cropped areas in the districts of Thatta and Badin are often under seawater or eroded as a result of sea currents, where seawater intrusion has badly affected 39 percent of the total agricultural cropland. Fully destroyed and partially affected areas constitute about 11 percent of cultivated lands in Sindh.

The main crops cultivated in Sindh are wheat, rice and cotton, with a weighted average gross margin of PRs 61,000 per hectare (table 4.2). If about 50 percent of cultivated land is fallow, crop intensity is on average 1.17 in Thatta and Badin, and average crop margins are as in Sindh, then the loss of these agricultural lands amounts to a cost of PRs 15–21 billion, or about 0.3–0.4 percent of Sindh's GDP annually.

Table 4.2 Crop Mix and Estimated Profit per Hectare in Sindh Province, 2010

Crop	Share in crop mix (%)	Gross margin per hectare (PRs)
Wheat	34	67,000
Rice	21	88,000
Cotton	21	23,000
Weighted average	n.a.	61,000

Note: n.a. = not applicable.

Sustainability and Poverty Alleviation • http://dx.doi.org/10.1596/978-1-4648-0452-6

Agricultural Losses Resulting from Salinity and Waterlogging

Water salinity has long been a problem in Sindh. Agriculture relies mostly on surface water from the Indus River basin because most groundwater is saline. At the same time, surface water is becoming scarce in the downstream Indus River. People are therefore forced to spend resources trying to ensure a sufficient water flow. The irrigation system built in the Sindh Province more than 80 years ago is deteriorating. Briscoe and Qamar (2005) report that substantial parts of the main irrigation canal leak and that a substantial amount of water never reaches the crop zone. In addition, some water is wasted for irrigation purposes as it mixes with the saline groundwater. This waste of irrigation water is causing waterlogging in head command areas, as well as water deprivation at the far end of the canals. Salinity and waterlogging are still important problems for farmers in Sindh. Although the recent construction of the Left Bank Outfall Drain Project benefited three districts of Sindh—Nawabshah (now Shaheed Benazir Bhutto), Sanghar, and Mirpurkhas—it altered the natural drainage in the Indus River delta, contributed to rising water tables, and resulted in waterlogging and increased salinity.

Annual agricultural losses in these areas are estimated using the difference between potential[3] crop yields in Pakistan and actual crop yields in the six districts most affected by salinity and waterlogging. The Sindh Department of Agriculture reports farm gate prices of paddy rice and cotton lint at PRs 40,000 per ton, wheat at about PRs 21,000 per ton, and sugar cane at about PRs 325,000 per ton. At these prices, the cost of crop yield losses resulting from waterlogging and salinity is estimated at PRs 16–60 billion per year (table 4.3). This estimate is conservative as it does not include the effects of waterlogging and salinity on all crops and only includes cultivation in the six most affected districts in Sindh.

Annual losses from unused degraded croplands can also be included in the estimate of the economic cost of waterlogging and salinity, by applying crop production profit margins (table 4.3). There are about 2 million hectares of fallow lands in Sindh. Assuming that 40–60 percent of these lands are out of use because of salinity and waterlogging, the total cost of these phenomena is in the range of PRs 66–99 billion per year.

Table 4.3 Annual Costs of Agricultural Crop Yield Losses as a Result of Waterlogging and Salinity in Sindh Province, 2010

billion PRs

Crop	Low	Midpoint	High
Rice	7	9	10
Wheat	4	11	16
Sugar cane	3	7	12
Cotton	1	12	22
Total	**16**	**38**	**60**

Note: Rounded to nearest billion.

On the basis of estimated crop yield losses, the total annual cost of waterlogging and salinity in Sindh is estimated at about PRs 82–160 billion or 1.6–3.1 percent of Sindh's GDP in 2010. Although salinity in Sindh has been reduced in the past several years, data on total irrigated area still demonstrate an unreliable supply of water that is highly dependable on weather variability.

Loss of Mangroves

Mangroves covered more than 160,000–280,000 hectares in the 1980s (IUCN Pakistan 2005). A later assessment reported a drastic reduction of mangroves in Pakistan, down to about 87,000 hectares; furthermore, the remaining mangroves are being degraded at an estimated rate of 3,200–8,000 hectares of mangroves per year over the past 25 years. With more than a 10-fold reduction of silt deposits (at about 30 million tons annually) the mangrove forests will degrade further because of loss of nutrients and silt from the freshwater outflow, salinity increase in the water resulting from seawater intrusion, and rising sea levels. Another reason for mangrove losses is overharvesting of fuel wood and timber. Mangrove forest losses have adversely affected fishery and shellfish production, mainly because mangroves serve as fish and shrimp nurseries. Loss of mangroves reduces the income of local populations that heavily depend on them. In terms of environmental services, mangrove losses increase the risk of tidal surge damage for all coastal areas, including Karachi.

The direct fishing value of mangroves in the Indus River delta is estimated at about US$1,290 per hectare per year, and the value of habitat provision at about US$650–1,200 per hectare per year.[4] Annual fuel wood extraction per hectare of mangroves is around 0.22 tons per hectare and fodder in the form of mangrove leaf extraction is about 0.26 tons per hectare. That adds a value of about US$10 per hectare of mangroves per year, which is consistent with other estimates of nontimber values per hectare of forest in Pakistan (FAO 2005). Therefore, the total estimated economic value of mangroves is US$1,950–2,600 per hectare per year, with a present value (PV) of US$65,000–$86,000 per hectare over the life of the mangroves (using a social discount rate of 3 percent). On the basis of the value per hectare of mangroves and the number of hectares degraded annually, this study estimates that the annual cost of annual mangrove losses in Sindh is approximately PRs 15–51 billion, or 0.3–1.1 percent of Sindh's GDP in 2010.

Loss of Fisheries

The Indus River delta is getting drier and saltier as it receives minimal amounts of fresh water. Limited inflow of water into the delta area is causing the depletion of fish along the coast of Sindh. Fish stock decreased by 50 percent between 1993 and 1999. Many sweet water fish species have died or are close to extinction. In this chapter, loss of fisheries is estimated based on marine fishery losses. The total marine fish catch in Sindh declined from around 270,000 tons in 2003, to a little more than 200,000 tons in 2007 (figure 4.3), which is 25 percent. The decline in

Figure 4.3 Total Catch of Major Marine Fish Types in Sindh Province, 2003–07

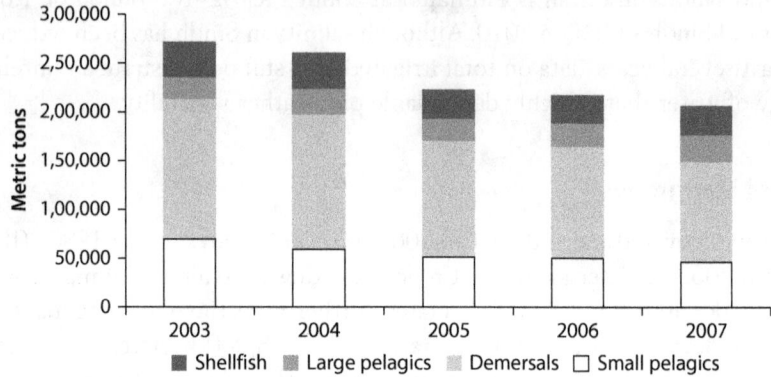

Shellfish   Large pelagics   Demersals   Small pelagics

Figure 4.4 Marine Fish Catch per Unit of Effort in Sindh Province, 1999–2007

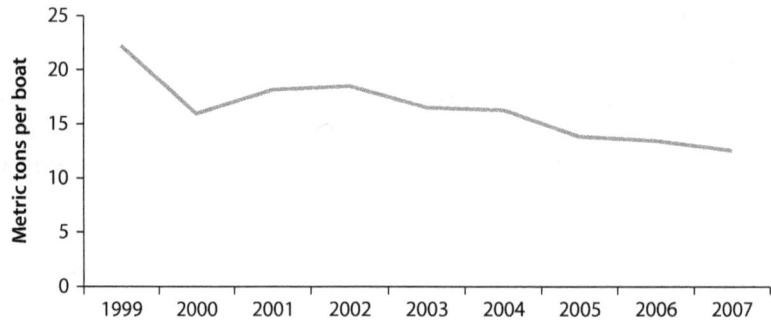

the past 10 years was nearly 40 percent. While the marine fishing fleet increased by about 10 percent from 1999 to 2007, a rough estimate suggests that average fish catch per boat declined by as much as 45 percent over this period (figure 4.4). Average annual marine fish catch reduction is in the range 10,000–20,000 tons (estimates from this study and ANZDEC [2005]).

Arby and Rasheed (2010) suggest that average marine fish prices were about PRs 16 per kg in 2008. At present, marine fish prices may increase up to four times. Fishery profits are 64 percent of gross revenue. The estimated annual cost of declines in marine fish catch was equivalent to about 0.01 percent of Sindh's GDP in 2010. These losses are important for the local population that is engaged in fishing.

Losses from Natural Disasters (Floods)

Sindh is almost flat and located at the bottom of the Indus River basin; the water of the Indus River and its tributaries passes through it. High floods have occurred 16 times since 1940. The flood in 2010 claimed lives of more than 400 people, damaged about 1 million houses, and displaced 1.5 million people. ADB and the World Bank estimated that the total cost of the flood in Sindh was the highest among the provinces of Pakistan and reached about PRs 250 billion in direct costs and PRs 120 billion in indirect costs.[5] This represents about 7.2 percent of Sindh's GDP. The major component of the cost of flood damage was destruction of crops, which comprised more than 50 percent of the total damage cost (table 4.4).

A historic flood could be described as a catastrophic event with a relatively low annual probability of occurrence. Therefore, a conventional expected value approach may not be the best to characterize the actual cost of risks attributed to this event. Although historic flood events happen relatively rarely and it may take several years for the next record-breaker to occur, other high-magnitude flood events happen regularly enough. This is confirmed by the recent sequential high-magnitude floods of 2010 and 2011. On the basis of flood data for the past 35 years, this study applied a probabilistic model that takes into account the random frequency of flood events in Sindh and the probabilistic distribution of severity and exposure to these to estimate the expected annual cost of floods. The risk adjusted cost of floods was calculated as a hedonic price of an insurance premium that could be paid as a contribution to a hypothetical recovery fund. The annual average contribution to the recovery fund should be at least PRs 90 billion or 1.7 percent of Sindh's GDP. This amount was calculated assuming a confidence in adequate funds for a successful recovery with a probability of at least 90 percent.

There is also a high risk of droughts in Sindh, when available water resources are significantly less than those required for reliable water supply, based on current irrigation practices. Climatic change exacerbates weather variability and further increases the risk of droughts, while also increasing the frequency and severity of floods. Transition to water-efficient technologies will provide reliability of

Table 4.4 Components of Damage from Floods and Rains in Sindh Province, 1976–2011

Component	1976	1977	1979	1992	1994	1995	2002	2003	2007	2010	2011
Number of lives lost	99	280	72	232	218	172	—	519	127	414	233
People affected (million)	3,000	0.300	0.552	—	0.690	1.025	1.400	4.100	0.753	7.274	6
Area affected (million acres)	3.400	0.320	3.935	—	—	1.423	—	—	0.575	7.238	5.938
Cropped area affected (million acres)	—	—	2.062	—	2.745	0.085	2.611	—	0.133	2.5	2.490
Number of houses damaged	3,070,000	51,145	62,249	578,000	—	—	—	307,464	345,000	1,073,847	1,400,000
Number of cattle lost	—	20,139	—	67,104	6,090	6,547	—	37,250	82	263,589	14,200
Number of villages affected	28,260	—	4,026	—	7,900	1,370	—	5,200	1,686	7,507	31,960

Sources: Estimated based on Disaster Risk Management Plan, Sindh Province. Provincial Disaster Management Authority, November 2008.
Note: — = not available.

water supply in changing climatic conditions. In addition, it will significantly mitigate the waterlogging and salinity problems, thus reducing productivity losses.

Probabilistic analysis reveals an option value of alternative irrigation technologies and suggests a road map for a gradual technological substitution that would
minimize risk of exposure to droughts and floods, given available resources. Such
alternatives could be estimated in the next stage of the analysis when more data
become available.

Benefits and Costs of Interventions to Reduce Losses of Natural Resources in Sindh Province

The previous sections discussed the severity of natural resource degradation in
Sindh. The category of natural resource degradation with the highest economic
cost is agricultural losses resulting from salinity and waterlogging, followed by
losses from natural disasters. In addition, loss of productive land resulting from
seawater intrusion, loss of mangroves, and loss of fisheries also have significant
economic, social, and environmental implications. This section summarizes
the findings of the CBA conducted on selected interventions aiming to reduce
natural resource degradation. In particular, this included analysis of the following
stylized interventions: (a) emergency management; (b) capacity building in water
resource management of hydrological resources; (c) rehabilitation of existing
water-supply systems, including irrigation and small-scale drainage; (d) agricultural
extension; (e) reforestation; and (f) sustainable fisheries management. These
interventions are described with further detail below.

Stylized interventions considered in this chapter in their present form mitigate only a small fraction of the cost of natural resources degradation in Sindh.
However, most of them could be scaled up and replicated, depending on available financial resources. Capacity-building components presented for each intervention may create a positive scale effect that should be taken into account in
the next steps.

The goal of the CBA is to prioritize interventions based on benefit-cost ratios
(BCR), which indicates the monetary value of the benefits realized by implementing a project, compared with the amount it costs to execute the project.
The CBA in this study reveals substantial uncertainties associated with the
implementation of each intervention. While the expected net present value of
each of the interventions was analyzed for this chapter, a real options methodology was also applied to evaluate irreversible decisions with uncertain future
results, as discussed below. For each of the analyzed interventions, specific
assumptions had to be considered to assess combined uncertainties of benefits
and costs, and Monte Carlo simulations were performed. The concept of "stylized
interventions" is used in this section as a reminder that further analysis of the
selected interventions should be completed according to internationally accepted
rules and procedures for prefeasibility and feasibility studies.

As previously discussed, there are important interlinkages between different
categories of natural-resource degradation in Sindh. Thus, there are overlaps

between interventions; consequently, total benefits are likely to be smaller than the arithmetic sum of benefits from each individual intervention, if all interventions are implemented. In addition, interventions' results are not certain. Therefore, an uncertainty factor is introduced in the analysis and this factor becomes important in assessing the efficiency of the selected interventions. Overlapping distributions of BCR of different interventions in Sindh are presented in figure 4.5. In contrast to a conventional CBA that reports the mean (central) estimate only, this approach takes into account other important characteristics of the distribution of benefits and costs. Standard deviations (SD), along with the shape of the probability distribution function (PDF), are important factors to take into account. A relatively low BCR is not a sufficient reason to reject an intervention, if this intervention exhibits high probabilities of resulting in benefits that exceed the costs.

Emergency Management

This intervention aims to improve the response to emergencies in Sindh, mostly flood related. The intervention revises existing strategies, plans, and procedures related to emergency response, and using existing technologies, it provides sensitivity maps for critical areas of living as well as possible flood and other emergency scenarios for risk prone areas. As one of mitigations measures, the project establishes an emergency fund to finance mitigation measures and effective response strategies. Finally, an extensive capacity-building program targeting government officials and local community leaders would be developed to cover areas such as planning, mitigating and responding to emergencies.

On the basis of the aforementioned components, this study estimated that the intervention could save about 1,000 lives. Using a discount rate of 3 percent and an annual appreciation of VSL at 2 percent, the PV of the benefits from lives saved is estimated at PRs 7.9 billion. This is a conservative estimate of benefits,

Figure 4.5 **Distribution of Benefit-Cost Ratio for Emergency Management Intervention in Sindh Province**

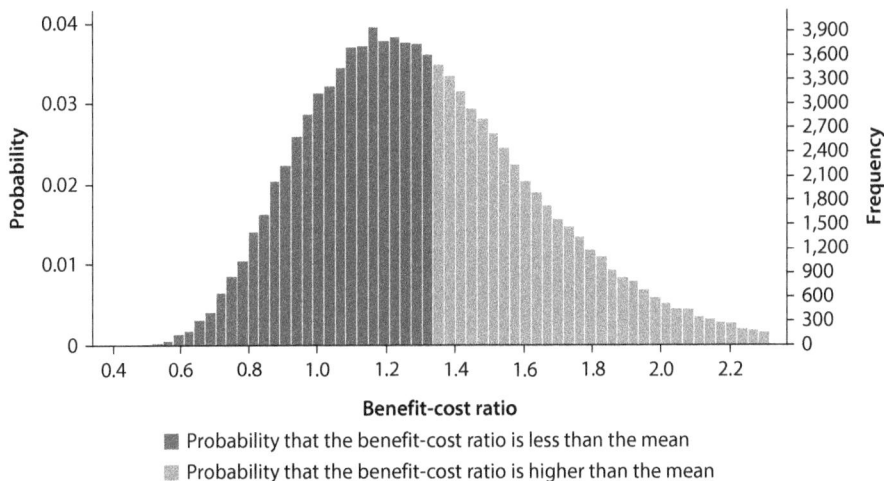

Probability that the benefit-cost ratio is less than the mean
Probability that the benefit-cost ratio is higher than the mean

since it does not consider the reduction in numbers of injured and affected people. The intervention's capitalized start-up and annual costs are estimated at PRs 5.9 billion. Thus, the BCR for the Emergency Management intervention is 1.3. Given that data on benefits and costs of the intervention are highly uncertain, the study conducted a sensitivity analysis (figure 4.5).

Capacity Building in Management of Hydrological Resources

The intervention's goal is to improve capacity for managing hydrological resources in Sindh, including its legal, institutional, and structural aspects, such as capacity building of the water management through training, strategic planning, institutional innovations, and modeling. Major activities under this intervention would include (a) preparation of a revised hydrological model of the Indus River in Sindh province; (b) capacity building (training and equipment) within water-management authorities at district and local levels; (c) preparation and adoption of the province-level strategy and district-level sectoral programs to implement new water-management practices (water-saving plans); (d) creation of new institutional settings (legal, organizational, and so forth); and (e) realization of components of a water-saving strategy related to the water-resource management (monitoring, planning, and so forth).

Capacity building creates an opportunity to deploy resources for interventions that address loss of productivity of soils resulting from salinity and waterlogging. In particular, the analysis estimates the benefits that would accrue in terms of reduction in yield losses for four major crops: rice, wheat, sugar cane, and cotton. The pricing of the intervention would be conducted during the first stage of project preparation and feasibility study. To assess the efficiency of the start-up costs, the study applied an option valuation methodology. Figure 4.6 presents the PDF of the interventions.

More research is needed to understand the true actual benefits and costs of this intervention. Investment in the initial research significantly narrows uncertainties

Figure 4.6 Probability Distribution Function of Benefits from Capacity Building in Management of Hydrological Resources in Sindh Province

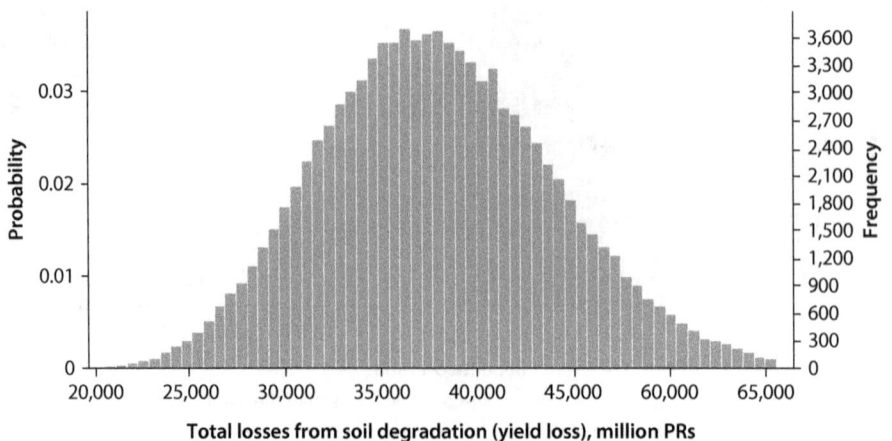

Total losses from soil degradation (yield loss), million PRs

and creates a possibility to deploy a full-scale intervention or abandon it. The benefits of this research stage are equal to an option value to deploy this intervention. This option value (an option to deploy a full-scale project) is 1.85 times higher than the cost of the required research.

Agricultural Extension Services for Climate Change Adaptation and Water Conservation

This intervention would bolster the capacity of the agricultural extension services (AES) to support practices for climate change adaptation, including changes in crops pattern, and use of improved irrigation practices, and water-saving technologies. The major activities of this intervention would include (a) institutional reorganization (if necessary) and capacity building of AES in Sindh (training, equipment, and human resources [HR]); (b) support of extension services educational facilities, including extension farms renovation, support of academia, equipping AES, and other services; and (c) support of introduction of new crop varieties through improvement of marketing chains, and provision of inputs and other sources.

The analysis estimated potential productivity for paddy production, assuming an increase of paddy yield from the average on Tatta and Badin districts to the potential yield found in the literature. The price of paddy is assumed at PRs 40,000 per ton; the assumed project success rate is between 40 percent and 90 percent. Financial cost of capital was estimated with hurdle rate[6] 30 percent, taken into account the cost of private capital and institutional barriers for project implementation. The expected benefit-cost ratio is about 1, reflecting high risk and institutional barriers for project implementation. However, if the intervention were scaled up, the BCR may increase 30 percent. Because data on benefits and costs of the intervention are highly uncertain, we applied sensitivity analysis to assess the effect of different parameters on the BCR (figure 4.7)

Figure 4.7 Benefit-Cost Ratio for the Agricultural Extension Intervention in Sindh Province

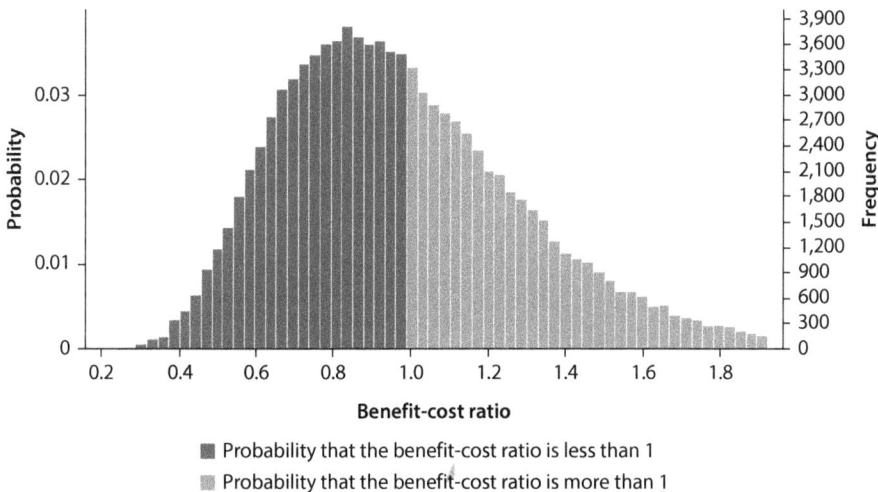

Probability that the benefit-cost ratio is less than 1
Probability that the benefit-cost ratio is more than 1

Rehabilitation of Existing Irrigation Water Supply Systems and Drainage

Implementation of this intervention would improve the efficiency and effectiveness of irrigation water distribution in Sindh. The intervention's activities would include (a) deepening and broadening the institutional reforms that are already underway in Sindh; (b) improving the irrigation system in a systematic way, covering key hydraulic infrastructure, main and branch canals, and distributaries and minors; and (c) enhancing long-term sustainability of the irrigation system through participatory irrigation management and developing institutions for improving operation and maintenance of the system and cost recovery. The intervention would result in rehabilitation of more than 1.8 million hectares or more than 30 percent of the irrigated area in Sindh, thus contributing to growth in agricultural production, employment and income.

Even a conservative estimate suggests that the intervention's BCR would be above 1, with confidence of more than 99 percent. The potential increase of the price of agricultural production would increase the benefits of this intervention. Thus, the BCR is higher than 1.5 with a 20 percent probability. This intervention has a lower risk than the other interventions assessed in this chapter. Figure 4.8 shows the sensitivity analysis of the intervention's BCR.

Reforestation Program

The intervention includes strengthening the capacity to transfer knowledge on reforestation practices. It would also include recruiting specialists who can provide extension services to farmers, as well as establishing tree nurseries and improving regulations, such as requirements for compulsory forestation programs in major canals and other key areas.

Major benefits from reforestation include habitat protection and carbon sequestration. However, high pollution from drainage canals and high probability of flooding, droughts, and erosion result in a high risk of plantation failure.

Figure 4.8 Benefit-Cost Ratio for the Water Sector Rehabilitation Intervention in Sindh Province

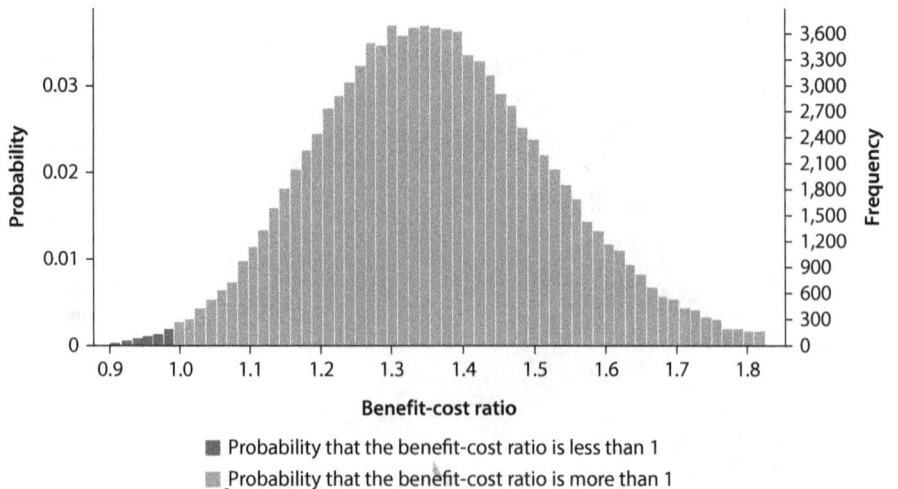

■ Probability that the benefit-cost ratio is less than 1
▨ Probability that the benefit-cost ratio is more than 1

Figure 4.9 Distribution of the Benefit-Cost Ratio for the Reforestation Intervention in Sindh Province

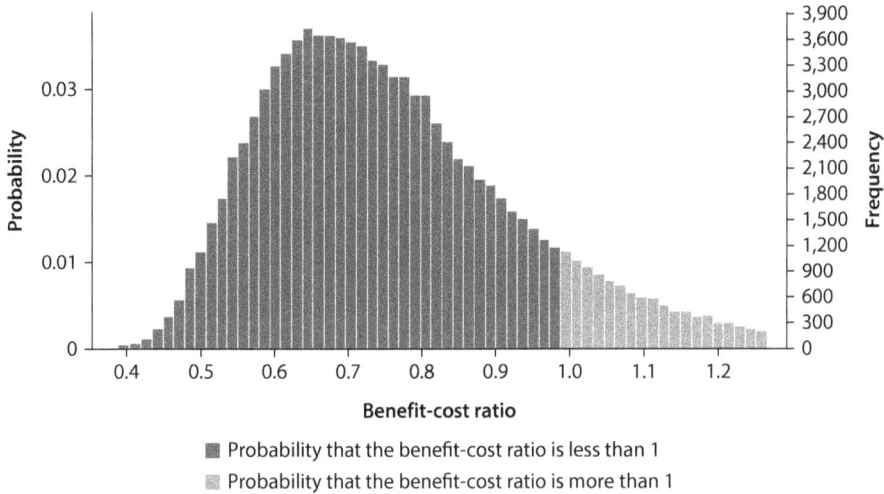

■ Probability that the benefit-cost ratio is less than 1
▨ Probability that the benefit-cost ratio is more than 1

Therefore, the analysis applied the hurdle rate to estimate benefits. The expected value of additional carbon sequestration, valued at social cost of carbon at US$20/ton, is relatively low. Figure 4.9 shows the results of the sensitivity analysis for the intervention's BCR.

The project BCR is less than 1. Benefits could be increased if additional interventions to protect new plantations from erosion and to clean up sewage waters were implemented. Cleaning up of sewage water would increase benefits from fishing while other interventions like sedimentation husbandry would decrease exposure of new plantations to extreme weather events.

Sustainable Fishery Management

This intervention would aim to establish sustainable fishery practices in Sindh's coastal areas. Its main activities would include (a) capacity building of the fisheries department (training, enforcement, management, and so forth); (b) identification, preparation, and implementation of management plans for critical habitat and fishery grounds; (c) introduction of sustainable fishery management practices in selected communities (districts); and (d) supporting regional initiatives in sustainable fish stock management within Pakistan's territory in the Arabian Sea.

Sustainable fishery management would increase fish catch by up to 20,000 tons per year. Project implementation would require a one-time cost of PRs 0.87 billion and an annual cost of PRs 0.13 billion. It was assumed that the targeted fish catch level would be achieved in 10 years. A major source of uncertainty for this intervention is the price of fish, which may significantly increase in the future. It could also decline slightly as a result of productivity increases.

A conventional CBA yields a negative expected net present value for this project. Nevertheless, the intervention would become economically feasible if the fish price increases. The initial capital investment creates a real option to

Figure 4.10 Benefit-Cost Ratio for the Sustainable Fishery Project in Sindh Province

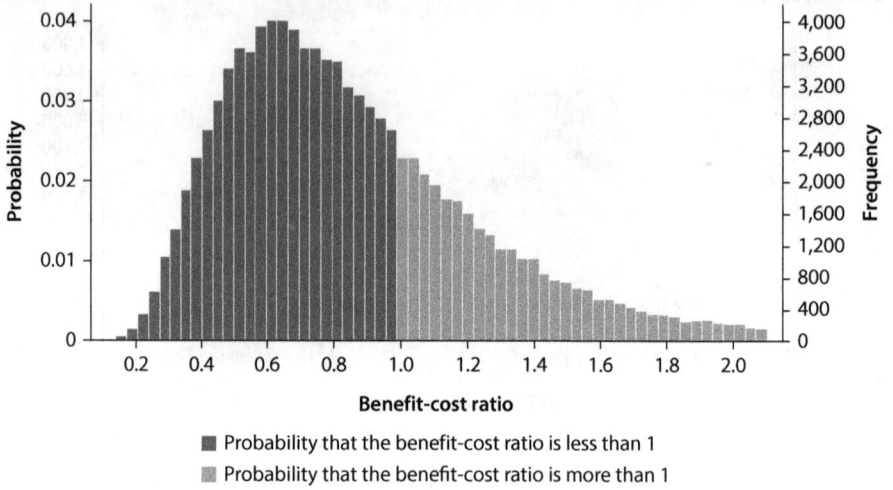

■ Probability that the benefit-cost ratio is less than 1
▨ Probability that the benefit-cost ratio is more than 1

Table 4.5 Benefit-Cost Ratios of the Selected Interventions in Sindh Province

Selected interventions	Mean benefit-cost ratio	SD	Benefit-cost ratio (80% CI)
Rehabilitation of existing water-supply systems including irrigation and small scale drainage	1.4	0.2	1.2–1.6
Emergency management	1.3	0.35	0.9–1.8
Agricultural extension	1	0.3	0.6–1.4
Sustainable fishery management	0.9	0.4	0.4–1.4
Reforestation program	0.8	0.2	0.6–1

Note: CI = confidence interval; SD = standard deviation.

increase productivity of the fishery sector, if the price of fish sufficiently increases to cover fishing costs and the project's operating costs. Even at PRs 16 per kilogram of fish, initial capital investment creates an option value equal to 1.043 billion PRs, reflecting the value of flexibility to start and scale up a sustainable fishery project, if the price of fish sufficiently increases. With respect to an option value, the benefit-cost ratio—calculated for the initial cost only—is about 1.2 (figure 4.10).

Recommendations

Out of the six interventions that could be undertaken to reduce natural resource degradation in Sindh, two exhibit a mean BCR above 1.3: emergency management and water-supply systems rehabilitation (see table 4.5 and figures 4.11 and 4.12). However, the variability range of the benefits is higher for the first intervention. Rehabilitation of water-supply systems has not only the highest BCR, but also the lowest risk of failure, with a 99 percent confidence that its benefits will exceed its costs.

Emergency management has a high expected BCR, but also exhibits the highest volatility, which is attributed to the random character of extreme weather

Figure 4.11 Benefit-Cost Ratio Probability Distribution for the Selected Interventions to Reduce the Cost of Natural Resource Degradation, Sindh Province

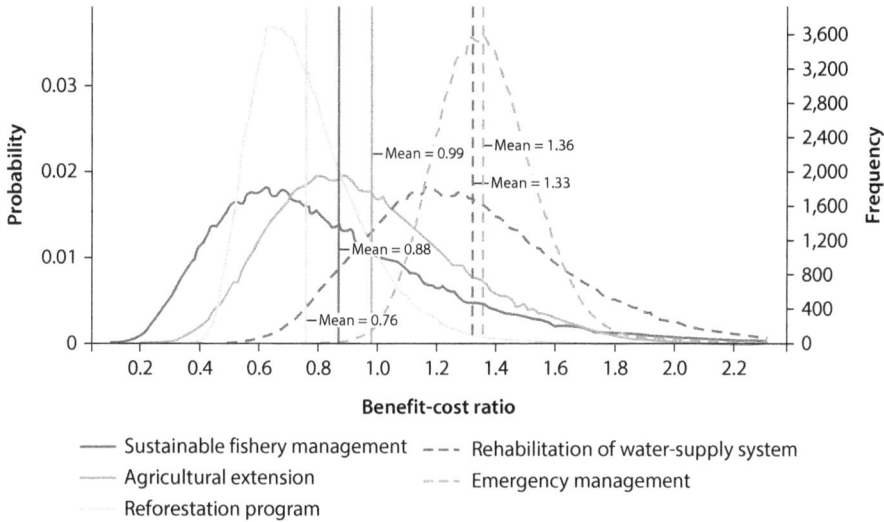

Figure 4.12 Mean Benefit-Cost Ratios for the Selected Stylized Interventions

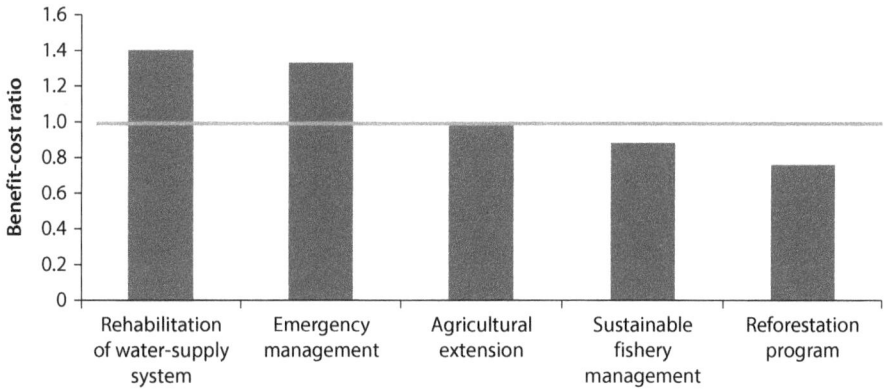

event occurrence in Sindh. This intervention could be characterized as extreme weather events risk management. Its implementation is justified based on a positive expected net present value, and on an option value to save more lives in case extreme weather events end up occurring more frequently than expected. Moreover, water-supply systems rehabilitation and emergency management have important cross-linkages: people affected by emergencies, particularly in the forms of flooding, are more vulnerable to diseases and deteriorating health. If the water-supply systems used for human consumption during emergencies are of poor quality, then human health is likely to deteriorate even further.

Agricultural extension has a BCR close to 1. However, removal of institutional barriers and reduction of financial risks along with an increase of success rate achieved by scaling up the project could increase the BCR by about 30 percent.

This intervention has important implications for human development and liveli-hoods in Sindh, as the province is the second largest contributor to agriculture production in the country.[7]

The last two interventions have lower BCRs. A reforestation program could be improved by including protective measures for new mangrove plantations, like sedimentation husbandry. In addition, it should be coupled with an inter-vention focused on cleanup of sewage that would reduce water pollution in the Indus River delta. Sustainable fishery management has an embedded option value because it provides flexibility to respond adequately to increases in fish prices. Taking into account this option value, the BCR of this intervention would increase to 1.2.

Regarding capacity building in management of hydrological resources in Sindh, more research is needed to understand its true actual benefits and costs. Investment in the initial research significantly narrows uncertainties and creates a possibility to deploy a full-scale intervention or abandon it. The benefits of this research stage are equal to an option value to deploy this intervention. This option value (an option to deploy a full-scale project) is 1.85 times higher than the cost of the required research.

On the basis of the benefit-cost analysis presented in this section, this chapter recommends implementing the agricultural extension and water-supply systems rehabilitation interventions with the highest priority. This is because, on top of relatively high BCRs, an increase in agricultural productiv-ity is vitally important for food security in Sindh. Large-scale drainage projects that were implemented in Sindh recently should take into account risks for ecosystems, especially in the coastal areas. Lack of data prevented conducting a CBA of such projects in this study. Although the expected agricultural ben-efits of these projects are high, their BCR could be negatively affected if they are associated with significant ecosystem damages. Emergency management is also one of the most efficient interventions to contain the cost of natural resources degradation in Sindh by saving lives that are at risk during extreme weather events. Other projects require further analysis. Because of synergy and overlapping results, an umbrella project for coastal area development in Sindh could be considered.

All the interventions assessed here are scalable and can therefore be imple-mented incrementally. In the context of significant uncertainty, a gradual imple-mentation creates opportunities for learning that helps to reduce uncertainties and dynamically adjust strategies of implementation that minimize the risk of sunk costs. In contrast to large-scale projects, scalable projects have an embedded value of flexibility that, if taken into account, further increases their BCR. This consideration is especially important for mangrove protection, which may exhibit significantly higher benefits resulting from reduction of pollution after Sindh's sewer systems are rehabilitated.

Analysis of stylized interventions demonstrates that small-scale projects gen-erate high BCRs. A number of other interventions may reduce the cost of natural resources degradation in Sindh. These interventions include, but are not limited to, the following:

- Radical changes in water-use practices, including increasing water productivity and quality management, while simultaneously substituting new economic activities for water-intensive agriculture
- Introduction of drought-resistant crop varieties
- Introduction of land-leveling technologies
- Promotion of alternative businesses for the local population, including support of local inland fisheries with hatcheries and shrimp ponds, as well as initial fish processing
- Improvement of fishery regulation
- For water resources quality improvements and marine water and wetlands protection, it is important to rehabilitate wastewater-treatment systems in Karachi, Hyderabad, and other big cities in the Indus River basin
- As an emergency option for water-supply systems, it is advisable to consider marine water desalinization plants for big cities
- Development of mechanisms for flood protection of critical economic infrastructure, and annual allocation of funds for maintaining existing flood-protection facilities and for introducing new approaches to Indus River flood protection.

These interventions should be supported by institutional strengthening, reform of regulatory systems, and economic instruments. Gradual elimination of water subsidies with simultaneous introduction of financing mechanisms to deploy new water efficient agricultural technologies should be at the core of a new regulatory system.

Sea-Level Rise in the Indus Watershed

The government of Sindh is particularly concerned about its vulnerability to climate change and the associated sea-level rise. To understand this risk better, this study assessed the situation of Sindh's coastal areas and the potential short-, medium-, and long-term effects of climate change.

Pakistan is highly dependent on the Indus River for its surface-water needs, making the country highly vulnerable to water pollution and basin degradation, both of which have important implications for human health and socioeconomic development. The Indus Delta is currently suffering major environmental problems caused by complex processes, but which appear to center on the significant reduction in fluvial inputs of water and sediment from the Indus River. The recent history of dam construction in the Indus catchment has reduced flows by an order of magnitude over the past century. Some authors see the concomitant loss of sediment input to the delta as resulting in lower accretion rates that are not able to keep pace with predicted future sea-level rise (for example, Inam,

Tabrez, and Rabbani [2008]). Although this is a problem shared by many of the world's delta regions, the impact appears to have been more acute in the Indus than elsewhere. Erosion of the delta coastal frontage appears to be another response to sediment starvation marked by progressive landward advance of sand cheniers. The response of the former mangrove vegetation cover has been equally serious, with massive reduction in mangrove extent and species (Saifullah 1997). The detailed impact on human use of the delta is unclear, but it is evident that the area is one of extreme poverty, caused, in part, by the region's physical and ecological degradation.

The analysis completed as part of this study finds that the Indus Delta is in the process of transitioning from a sediment-rich model to a sediment-poor model. Historical data indicate that the deltas of the Indus and the Ganges-Brahmaputra developed over the Quaternary and Holocene periods resulting from massive fluvial discharge and associated sediment loads, derived from the Himalayas, which offset the rise in sea level following glaciation. Although sea levels rose by more than 100 meters (m) after the last glacial period, the sediment-rich Indus delta continued to accrete seaward by as much as 100 m per year along parts of its coastal margins (Giosan and others 2006).

Sediment-poor deltas behave differently. They are characteristic of mid-latitude estuaries where fluvial sediment loads are low. As Holocene sea levels rose after glaciations, these estuaries regressed landward by a process referred to as "roll-over" (Townend and Pethick 2002). This involves erosion of the coastal fringes of the estuarine delta and landward transfer of the sediment along its estuarine channels to the inner margins where it becomes deposited. The delta rolls landward by recycling its existing sediment.

The current transition of the Indus Delta from the sediment-rich model to the sediment-poor model is a response to the massive reduction in fluvial inputs from upstream, following construction of the numerous barrages and dams along the course of the river. The geomorphological impact of the fall in sediment input has been to reduce the rate of accretion to below the annual eustatic sea-level rise so that the delta surfaces are, in effect, suffering a rise in relative sea level. In addition, sediment reduction has increased erosion of the coastal margins and a transfer of sediment landwards along the tidal creeks. Giosan and others (2006) show that this erosion is highest in the middle section of the delta (between Dabbo and Warri Creeks). They also show that, in contrast, there has been a slight advance of the extreme margins of the delta front, north of Khai Creek and south of Warri Creek. According to the best available information, the morphological response of the delta to this reduction in inputs will be exacerbated by the predicted rise in sea level as a result of global warming. The implications of such a transition and the complications resulting from sea-level rise are critical for the population of the delta, who are extremely vulnerable to changes in delta morphology.

The present transitional status of the delta suggests that it can develop in one of two ways. On the one hand, if sediment supply is restored, the delta could move back to a sediment-rich model—or at least to a condition in which sufficient sediment is available to maintain the existing delta morphology. Alternatively, if sediment supply is not restored or decreases even further, the delta will continue to "roll-over," that is, erode at its seaward margins and transfer sediment to its landward margins—in this case the landward margin is the slope between the low delta and high delta surface—so that existing sediment is recycled. This latter model implies that the existing delta area will be progressively reduced since landward migration is impeded by the high delta surface.

The maintenance of the existing delta morphology appears, a priori, to demand a major increase in the sediment supply now impounded by the barrage system on the Indus. However, first-order approximations suggest that, even under the present barrage regime, there is sufficient sediment discharge from the Indus River to keep pace with even the most extreme sea-level rise predictions by 2100 (approximately $1,800 \times 10^6$ cubic meters [m^3] per year is currently available for accretion on the delta sub-aerial surface). Although it is emphasized that this is a tentative preliminary sediment budget, it does appear that given the sediment supply as it was in the decade 1993–2003, there will be sufficient sediment to maintain the delta surface elevation relative to rising sea levels.

The alternative model developed under this study assumes that the sediment supply from the Indus River decreases to zero. This would lead to a sediment-poor recycling model as outlined earlier. Coastal erosion rates according to Giosan and óthers (2006) average between 10 m and 50 m per year along the central 100 km of the delta front. Assuming an average erosion rate of 30 m per year and a silt/clay content of 80 percent, this would yield an annual noncohesive sediment load of approximately 3×106 m^3. Some of this load will be carried into the delta along the tidal creeks and redeposited in the low delta zone. A first-order calculation suggests that this low delta surface zone has an area of 200,000 hectares so that deposition of the entire noncohesive sediment load from the coastal erosion would result in vertical accretion of approximately 1 millimeter (mm) per year—sufficient to keep pace with existing rates of eustatic sea-level rise. This would support the sediment-poor delta model with rollover, allowing the delta to migrate landward under a rising sea level without additional sediment inputs. However, it would not be sufficient to allow the entire tidal delta to maintain its surface elevation even under the existing 1 mm per year rate of sea-level rise. Thus, this model would result in progressive reduction in the area of the tidal delta. If coastal erosion rates increase in line with rising sea levels, it is possible that the entire coastal margin would be eroded by 2100.

These sediment budgets suggest that if sediment inputs remain as they were in 1993–2003 the delta would keep pace with sea-level rise—even under the most extreme predictions. This appears to be contradicted by the existing rates of coastal erosion, which indicate that the delta is already experiencing a sediment-poor rollover. The explanation of this apparent contradiction must be that the sediment supply from the Indus is no longer carried to the delta as a result of the loss of distributary channels. At present, only a single main channel flows from the Indus River, via the Khubar Creek, into the sea. The remaining delta surface does not receive sediment from the fluvial source. This deficit can only be made good if distributaries are re-established; this would mean increasing the fresh water supply from the Indus.

A major conclusion of this study on the sediment budget is that, although sufficient sediment appears available to maintain the Indus Delta under sea-level rise, the low water discharge from the Indus River and lack of distributaries for this flow restrict sediment supply to most of the tidal delta.

If the analytical work's hypothesis that the Indus Delta is in transition from a sediment-rich to a sediment-poor system is supported by further investigation and data, then it is suggested that management of the delta should concentrate on re-establishing minimum fresh water flows from the barrages and re-opening distributaries across the tidal delta, rather than attempting the more difficult task of re-establishing sediment supply across the barrages.

Since the inhabited areas of the Indus Delta are on the relatively high-level surface, predicted sea-level rise as a result of global warming is not likely to have a major direct impact on the population living there. The recent sea-level oscillation, during which the sea level dropped by 10 centimeters during the period 1960–90 and then rose again by the same amount, will have caused concern among both local people and coastal managers in view of the widespread publicity about global warming. However, this oscillation must be seen as a short-term fluctuation only. Increased fluvial flooding may result from sea-level rise propagating landward and impeding flood flows, but direct flooding by the sea is unlikely even under the most extreme sea-level rise predictions. The major impact of the predicted sea-level rise will be in the tidal delta, where loss of mangrove and fisheries will have a devastating impact on existing communities. These impacts are already occurring and will only be exacerbated by sea-level rise as a result of climate change. The major problem facing the Indus Delta is not global warming, but the impounding of the Indus River.

Prediction of Floods and Droughts in Pakistan

Over the past several years, Pakistan has been struck by several major hydro-meteorological hazards, including the catastrophic floods of 2010, the 2011 floods in Sindh, several land-falling tropical cyclones (TCs), and the recent droughts of 1998–2002 and 2009. Given the significant negative effects of natural disasters—particularly floods and droughts—on the development of Pakistan, and particularly of Sindh, this section discusses the results of an assessment on prospects for mitigating the adverse impacts of such hazards through improved extended-range forecasts of rainfall, stream flow, and TCs. Recent efforts have demonstrated that slow-rise floods and TC landfalls are predictable 10 days in advance (Hopson and Webster 2010; Webster and others 2010),[8] allowing sufficient lead time for planning to minimize the impacts of flooding. For example, precipitation and stream flow forecasts out to 10 days allow informed water resource management (for example, dam draw-down for irrigation and hydropower) that may mitigate flood impact.

A basic premise of this analysis is that no matter how good a disaster risk reduction (DRR) warning is for hydro-meteorological hazards, it requires timely and accurate forecasts for the warning system to be used effectively.

Geographic and Climatological Characteristics

Pakistan lies at the extreme western reaches of the southwest monsoon system, which causes substantial variability from year-to-year, oscillating between excessive and deficient rainfall (map 4.1). Excessive rainfall may lead to floods while deficient rainfall may result in drought. Pakistan's climate is principally monsoonal with maximum rainfall occurring in the summer months of June to September (figure 4.13), with more intense rainfall happening over the Bay of Bengal and

Map 4.1 Geographical Distribution of Rainfall in South Asia

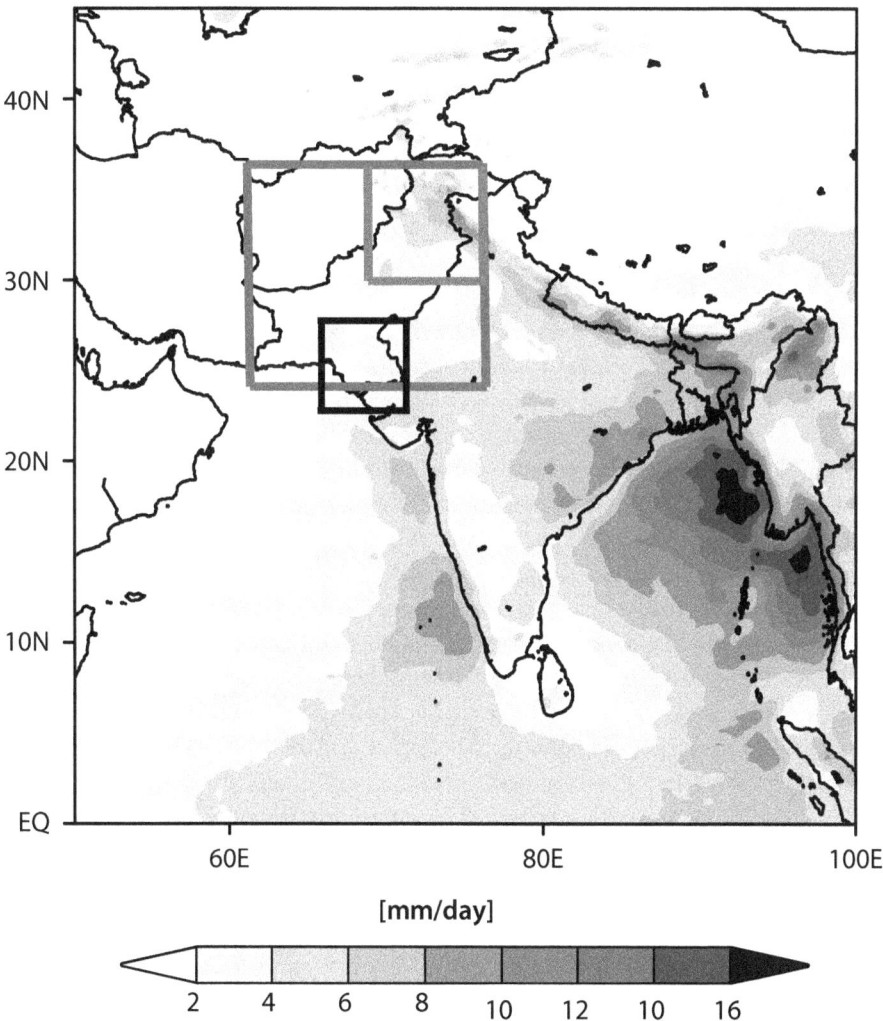

[mm/day]

2   4   6   8   10   12   10   16

Source: Webster 2011.

Figure 4.13 Climatological Distribution of Rainfall Averaged in Pakistan

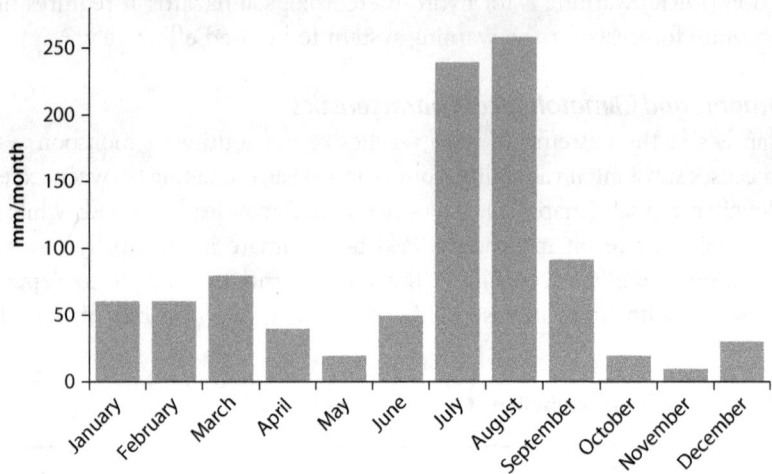

Source: Webster 2011.

decreasing westwards across the Ganges valley to Pakistan (figure 4.13). A smaller amount of rainfall occurs during winter, associated with extra tropical systems propagating into the region from the west. About 68 percent of the geographical area of Pakistan has an annual rainfall of 250 mm, whereas about 24 percent obtains an annual rainfall of 250–500 mm. Only 8 percent of Pakistan's area (in the Punjab and northern foothills) has annual rainfall exceeding 500 mm (map 4.1).

In this chapter, we consider slow-rise floods, flash floods, drought, and land-falling TCs that generate storm surges and excess rainfall. Slow-rise floods result from prolonged and intense monsoonal rain occur during the June–August/early September period. Pakistan is located to the north of the warm tropical Indian Ocean, which spawns TCs that occasionally affect the west coast of India or Pakistan (map 4.2). Most cyclones occur in the Bay of Bengal, five times more frequently than in the Arabian Sea. In addition, intense heating of the land surface, especially elevated land prior to the commencement of the monsoon rains, can lead to violent convective storms and torrential rainfall, often causing devastating localized flash floods. Flash floods occur in April–June, occasionally September–October, and sometimes in summer when the monsoon is inactive or in a "break phase" (figure 4.14).

Flash floods, slow-rise floods, and TCs occur fairly frequently in Pakistan. The landfall of a major TC along Pakistan occurs once every year or two. Flash floods occur most years ahead of the monsoon rains or during the break phase of the established monsoon. Slow rise floods occur in different parts of Pakistan every year with major inundations occurring every 3–5 years. The statistics of each hazard will be discussed in more detail later in this chapter together with a number of detailed case studies.

Map 4.2 Tropical Cyclone Tracks, 1980–2005

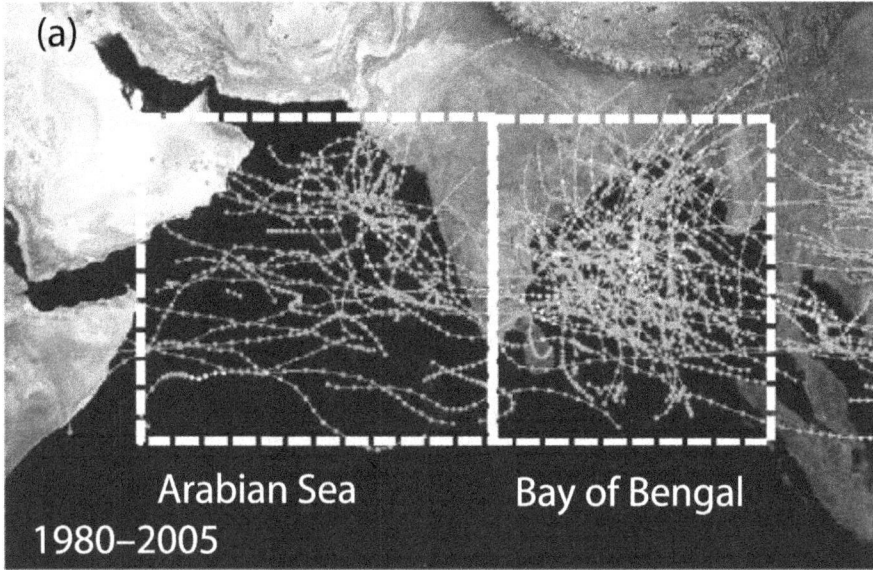

Source: Webster 2011.

Figure 4.14 Flood Type, by Month, in Pakistan, 1990–2010

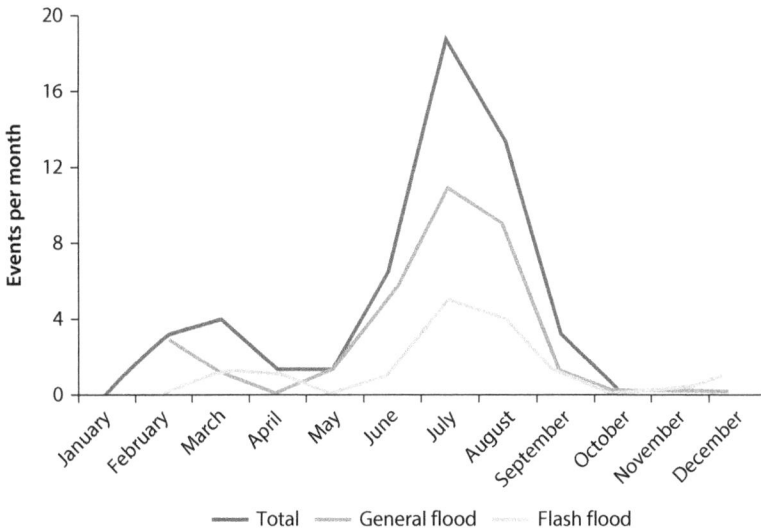

Source: Webster 2011, based on data from the Centre for Research on the Epidemiology of Disasters (CRED):
http://www.cred.be/disaster-types/natural-disasters.

The other hydro-meteorological hazard is drought. The reliable availability of fresh water for domestic, agricultural, and commercial usage is one of the major problems facing Pakistan. Long-lived droughts in Pakistan (for example, those in 1998–2002 and 2009) caused substantial hardship for the agrarian populace across broad areas of the country, while shorter-term droughts can cause hardship particularly in regions of rain-fed agriculture.

Climatology of Hydro-Meteorological Hazards in Pakistan
Drought

There are three major types of droughts, each differing in form and impact, and all relevant in the context of Pakistan in general, and Sindh in particular (Ahmad and others 2004; Chaudhry and others 2001):

1. A meteorological drought involves a reduction in region rainfall over a specific period (day, month, season, and year) defined formally as some percentage of the long-term climatological average. Such droughts are often associated with extremes of temperature that lead to an increase of evapotranspiration and consequent serious loss of soil moisture. A meteorological drought is especially devastating for regions that depend principally on precipitation for agriculture. Such rain-fed (barani) agricultural practices are used in areas where irrigation is unavailable or unaffordable.
2. A hydrological drought is defined by a reduction in water resources (for example, stream flow, reservoir levels, groundwater, and subsurface aquifer levels) within a region. A hydrological drought may result from a meteorological drought elsewhere. For example, a hydrological drought may exist in the southern Indus Valley as a result of reduced winter snowfall in the Himalayas or poor monsoon rainfall during the summer. River flow, so reduced, may limit water for irrigation.
3. An agricultural drought is the compound consequence of hydrological and meteorological droughts. About 30 percent of the total area of Pakistan in cultivated, out of which more than 75 percent is irrigated and the rest is rain-fed. The irrigated land may avoid a regional meteorological drought if there is no hydrological drought and water is supplied from regions receiving rainfall that is more abundant. The barani areas, lying in arid or semi-arid lands, are dependent almost entirely on local rainfall and thus are most vulnerable to any meteorological drought and relatively independent of hydrological drought. In these areas, underground water is mostly brackish and sweet water resources lie at greater and inaccessible depths.[9]

One of the major problems for the barani areas, and distinct from the irrigated regions, is that when rainfall occurs it is often intense and short-lived. It is estimated that more than 50 percent of the annual rainfall is lost through runoff. Not only is the water not used, but it also increases the hazard of erosion. Thus, the food crop and livestock production could be increased if the rain-fed water could be stored for later use in cultivation of crops.

Figure 4.15 Number of Floods, by Type and Administrative Province of Pakistan, 1990–2010

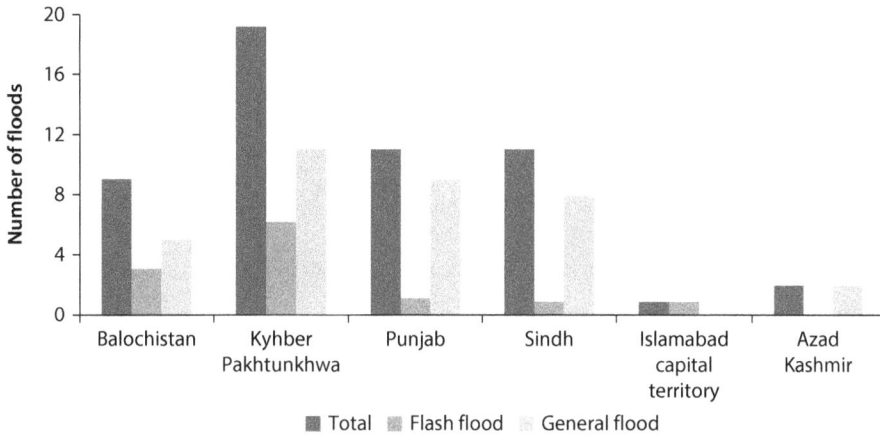

Source: Webster 2011, based on data from the Centre for Research on the Epidemiology of Disasters (CRED): http://www.cred
.be/disaster-types/natural-disasters.

Tropical Cyclones

Six percent of all TCs forming in the planet (5–6 per year) occur in the North
Indian Ocean (NIO), and 3–4 of these form in the Bay of Bengal. TCs are relatively rare in the Arabian Sea, but they do occur and occasionally affect Pakistan's
coast; in 2007 tropical Cyclone Gonu reached Category 5 on the Saffir-Simpson
scale.[10] The greatest impact of land-falling TCs comes from wind-induced storm
surges. These are especially catastrophic in near-coastal delta regions, such as the
southern sector of the Ganges-Brahmaputra delta in Bangladesh, the Irawaddy
delta in Myanmar, and the Indus delta in Pakistan.

Floods

Flash floods arise from precipitation associated with severe convection, typically during the pre-monsoon season or during a break period during summer,
and tend to be short-lived. Slow-rise floods tend to occur during excessive
rainfall periods during the summer monsoon and can have extended longevity,
often spreading slowly across large sectors of the country. Figure 4.15 shows the
number of floods as a function of province, showing that flooding is widespread
across the country.

Losses from Hydro-Meteorological Hazards in Pakistan

Over the past century, Pakistan has been subject to many severe natural disasters
causing significant death, injury, and property damage. Prevalent amongst these
are both slow- and fast-rise (flash) floods. Tables 4.6 and 4.7 show the significant
impact of floods amongst Pakistani natural disasters, in terms of both property
damage and number of people affected. Table 4.6 indicates the number of people
injured, displaced, and otherwise affected by natural disasters in Pakistan over the
past century. Eight of the 10 natural disasters in which more people were

Table 4.6 Top 10 Natural Disasters in Pakistan, by Number of People Affected

Disaster type	Year	Number affected
Flood	2010	20,359,496
Flood	2011	8,900,000
Flood	1995	7,000,450
Flood	1992	6,655,450
Flood	1992	6,184,418
Flood	2011	5,800,000
Flood	1976	5,566,000
Earthquake	2005	5,128,309
Flood	1973	4,800,000
Flood	1978	2,246,000
Drought	1999	2,200,000

Source: Webster 2011, based on data from the Centre for Research on the Epidemiology of Disasters (CRED): http://www.cred.be/disaster-types/natural-disasters.

Table 4.7 Top 10 Natural Disasters in Pakistan, by Losses

Disaster type	Year	Losses (US$ '000)
Flood	2010	9,500,000
Earthquake	2005	5,200,000
Storm	2007	1,620,000
Flood	1992	1,000,000
Flood	1973	661,500
Flood	1976	505,000
Flood	2007	327,118
Drought	1999	247,000
Flood	2001	246,000
Flood	2008	103,000

Source: Webster 2011, based on data from the Centre for Research on the Epidemiology of Disasters (CRED): http://www.cred.be/disaster-types/natural-disasters.

negatively affected were floods, including the top six events. Tables 4.6 and 4.7 also show that flood events occur much more frequently than other type of natural disaster.

Flood events comprise seven of 10 of the most costly natural disasters in Pakistan over the past century. Table 4.7 depicts the 10 natural disasters that have incurred the highest economic impacts Pakistan, including property and livestock damage, among others. This illustrates that not only do floods occur more frequently than other types of events—they also incur significant economic impacts. Indeed, the argument could be made that floods, collectively, have caused more economic damage than any other type of natural disaster event.

Recent Floods and Tropical Cyclones in Pakistan
Tropical Cyclones
A number of TCs have made landfall in Pakistan during the past 15 years. For example, a "very severe" or Category 3 TC (ARB 01) made landfall near the

Indian-Pakistan border in early June 1998. More than 10,000 fatalities occurred. On May 16, 1999, a very severe TC made landfall near Karachi. The total number killed exceeded 6,400 and there was significant damage and loss. Tropical Cyclone Yemnin made landfall on June 21, 2007, with a mortality of 730. In each of these three cases, damage was in the billions of dollars. In late May, 2011, Tropical Cyclone Phet developed in the mid-Arabian Sea and, eventually a category 4 system, moved eastward along the Pakistan coast making landfall near Thatta, Pakistan. The loss of life was relatively low.

In 2007, Tropical Cyclone Gonu became the first recorded category 5 cyclone in the Arabian Sea. The storm made landfall in Oman, killing 100 people with damage estimated at US$4.4 billion. If this storm had made landfall in Sindh, the impact might have been catastrophic.

The Pakistan Floods of 2010 and 2011

During the late boreal spring of 2010, the tropical Pacific Ocean entered a La Niña phase, which is conducive for above-average rainfall in the South Asian monsoon region. During July 2010, a disturbance propagated northward into the Bay of Bengal. This disturbance forced an active monsoon over the northern part of the Indian subcontinent, with rainfall extending across the Gangetic Plains between the Bay of Bengal in the east, to northern Pakistan in the west. Embedded in this active period were 5–6 distinct deluges that caused the devastating floods. In late July, some Pakistan stations recorded rainfall amounts exceeding 300 mm over a four-day period.[11] During the following days and weeks, flooding extended through the entire Indus Valley, eventually reaching the Arabian Sea and leaving behind a wake of devastation and destruction. In the end, the death toll was close to 2,000, and more than 20 million people were affected. An estimated 20,000 cattle were drowned. Power stations and transmission towers were destroyed along with other major infrastructure such as barrages, bridges, and roads. Irrigation systems were ruined and planting of subsequent crops delayed or abandoned with agricultural costs exceeding US$500 million. Overall, estimates of damage exceed US$40 billion.[12] In general, it was the poor that suffered the most and many will face the prospect of intergenerational poverty because of the perpetual flooding (Webster and Jian 2011).[13]

Map 4.3 shows the extent of the 2010 flooding. The flooding was a Pan-Pakistan event (panel a) with flooding occurring along the extent to the Indus River and tributaries. Map 4.4 shows the areal distribution of accumulated rainfall determined from satellite for the mid-July to early August.

In 2011, a period of torrential rainfall inundated the Sindh province (map 4.3, panel b). Although not as extensive as the 2010 floods, the damage was considerable. Four major precipitation pulses of rainfall (map 4.5, panel a) occurring within a month. The first occurred in early August, and three further pulses followed in late August and early September. Panels b and c of maps 4.5 show the accumulated rainfall for two periods: August 8–11, 2011, and August 30–September 3, 2011. Nearly 500 people lost their lives, with 8.9 million affected by the floods and 7 million acres of land were damaged.

Map 4.3 Extent of the Pan-Pakistan Flood, 2010, and the Sindh Province Flood, 2011

a. Extent of pan-Pakistan flooding, 2010   b. Extent of Sindh Province flooding, 2011

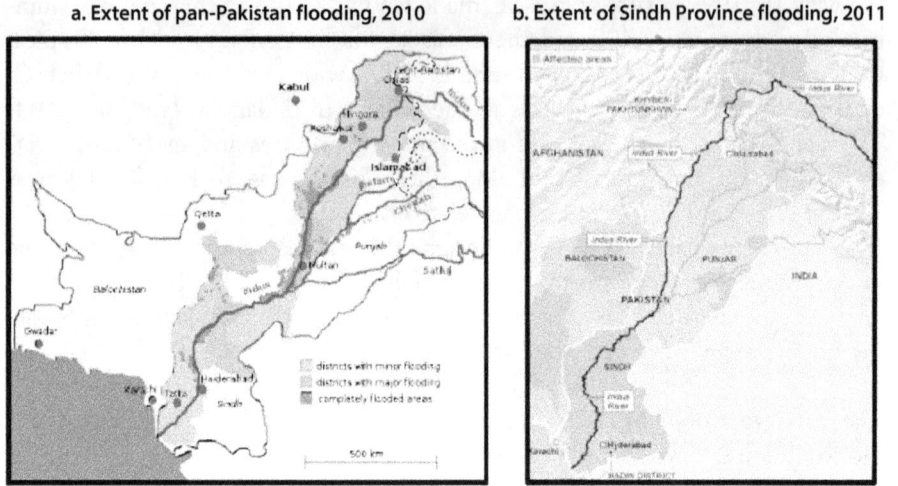

Sources: (a) http://geog.ucsb.edu/img/news/2011/707px-Indus_flooding_2010_en.svg.png; (b) http://www.digitalhen.co.uk/news/world-south-asia-14931833.
Note: Blue areas indicate the extended flooding.

Map 4.4 Accumulated Rainfall in Pakistan, July and August 2010

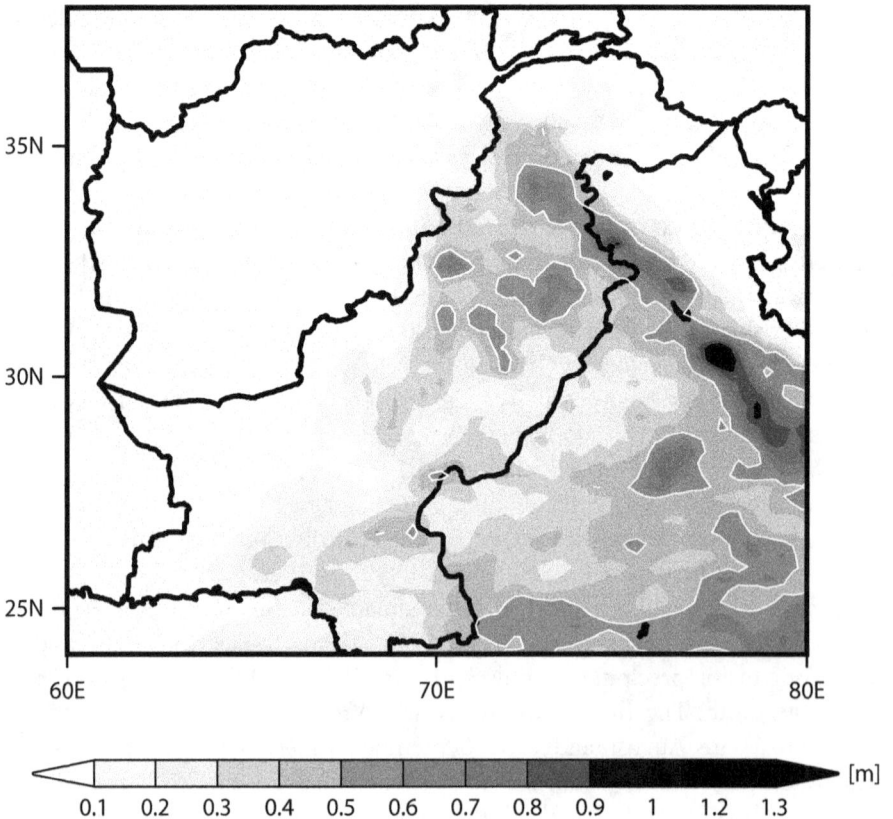

Source: Webster, Toma, and Kim 2011.

Map 4.5 Time Series of Rainfall Rate Comparing Actual Rainfall with Climate in Pakistan, 2011

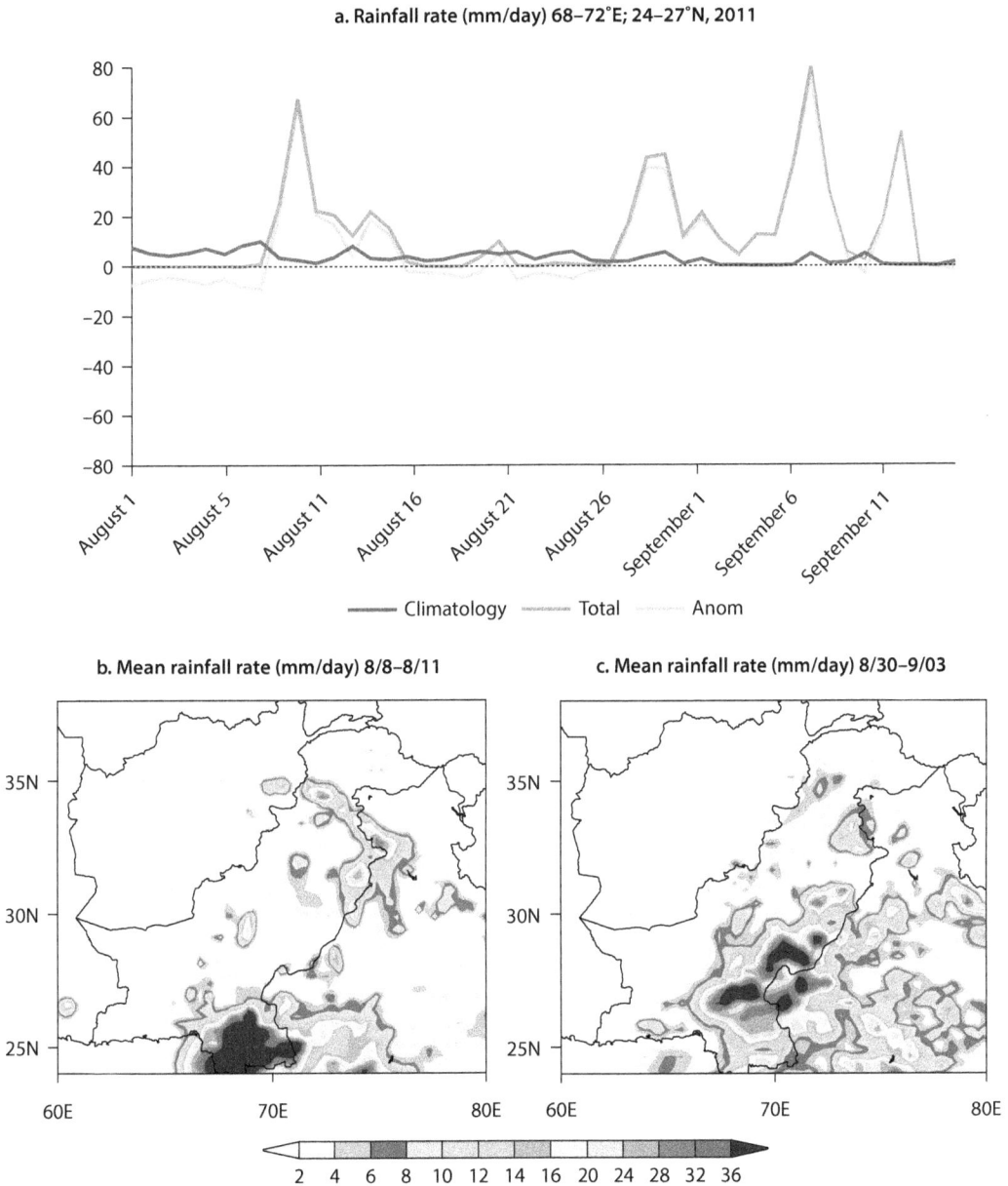

a. Rainfall rate (mm/day) 68–72°E; 24–27°N, 2011

Climatology ——— Total ——— Anom

b. Mean rainfall rate (mm/day) 8/8–8/11

c. Mean rainfall rate (mm/day) 8/30–9/03

2 4 6 8 10 12 14 16 20 24 28 32 36

Source: Webster 2011.
Note: Four pulses can be seen. Rainfall rates were computed using National Oceanic and Atmospheric Administration (NOAA) CPC Morphing Technique (CMORPH) Precipitation Product for the 2003–10 period (Joyce and others 2004).

Since 1900, there have been 67 reported flooding events in Pakistan, with a clustering of 52 events of varying severity in the past 30–40 years.[14] Some of these events (for example, 1950, 1973, 1976, 1977, 1992, 2001, 2007, and 2008) were also accompanied by large loss of life and property. The recent increase in number of floods is consistent with the increase in intensity of the global monsoon (Wang and others 2012). Alternatively, the increased number of floods could have resulted from changes in water management strategies, and increases of damage caused by a rapidly growing population.

Prediction of Hydro-Meteorological Hazards in Pakistan

Prediction of weather hazards days to weeks in advance has the potential to minimize some of the adverse impacts of these events.

Tropical Cyclone Prediction

In a recent study, Belanger and others (2012) examined the predictability of several key forecasting parameters using the European Centre for Medium Range Weather Forecasts (ECMWF) Variable Ensemble Prediction System (VarEPS) for TCs in the NIO, including TC genesis, pre-genesis, and post-genesis track, as well as intensity projections and regional outlooks of TC activity for the Arabian Sea and the Bay of Bengal. On the basis of the evaluation period of 2007–10, the VarEPS TC genesis forecasts demonstrate low false alarm rates and moderate to high probabilities of detection for lead times of one to seven days. The study concludes that the time horizon for successful prediction of genesis and subsequent tracks of the system is of the order 7–10 days. The system of prediction for Arabian Sea TCs is identical to that designed for the Bay of Bengal allowing a convenient adaptation.

The current TC system revolves around the World Meteorological Organization (WMO) designation of six regional specialized meteorological centers (RSMCs)[15] across the global tropics to facilitate the forecasting of TCs. The Indian Meteorological Department (IMD) is the RSMC responsible for the NIO.[16] In its RSMC capacity, the IMD provides the official forecasts and warnings for TCs. However, the IMD-RSMC only provides three-day forecasts of tropical cyclone tracks following observed cyclogenesis, resulting in far less lead time and skill relative to the forecasting system described in the previous paragraph. A three-day deterministic forecast is inadequate, especially in the less-developed world where more time is necessary for evacuation.

Slow-Rise Flood Prediction—the 2010 and 2011 Floods

How predictable was the rainfall that produced the flooding? Map 4.6, panel a, shows the total average precipitation for July 28–29, based on the CMORPH satellite observational dataset and the ECMWF forecast ensemble mean initialized four days before the event.

The forecast rainfall compares well with the observed rainfall, although ECMWF slightly underestimates the rainfall intensity in the northern part of the region. The ECMWF forecast showed average precipitation larger than 40 mm/day in some areas, which is more than three times larger than the U.S. National Oceanic and Atmospheric Administration's Climate Prediction Center Morphing Technique (CMORPH) climatological average for the region. Figure 4.16 shows the temporal evolution of the ECMWF forecast commencing on July 24, 2010, through August 9, 2010, for the Khyber Pakhtunkhwa province.

Map 4.6 Comparison between the Satellite-Observed Rainfall, July 28–29, 2010, and the ECMWF Forecast Made Four Days Earlier in Pakistan

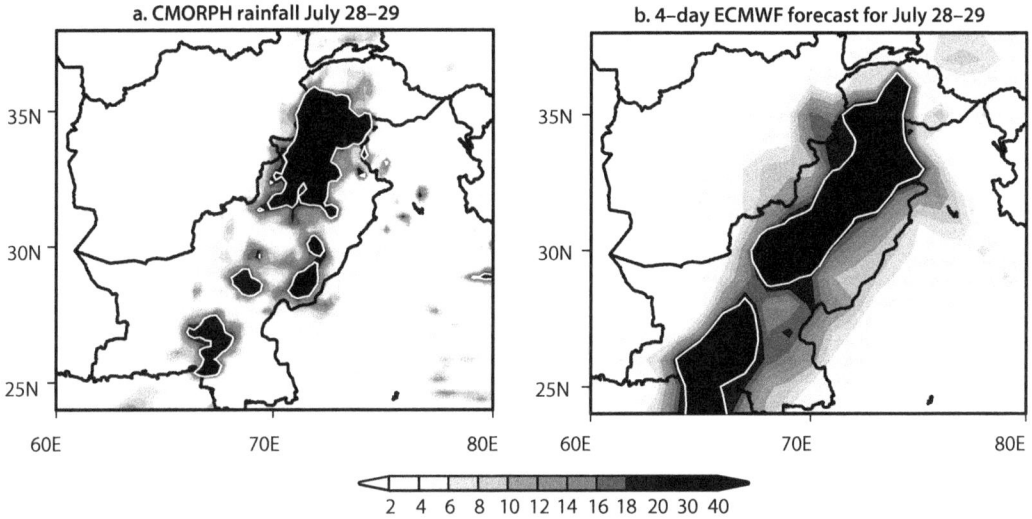

a. CMORPH rainfall July 28–29

b. 4–day ECMWF forecast for July 28–29

2 4 6 8 10 12 14 16 18 20 30 40

Source: Webster, Toma, and Kim 2011.
Note: CMORPH = Climate Prediction Center Morphing Technique; ECMWF = European Centre for Medium Range Weather Forecasts.

Figure 4.16 Forecasts of Rainfall Using the ECMWF System in Pakistan, July–August 2010

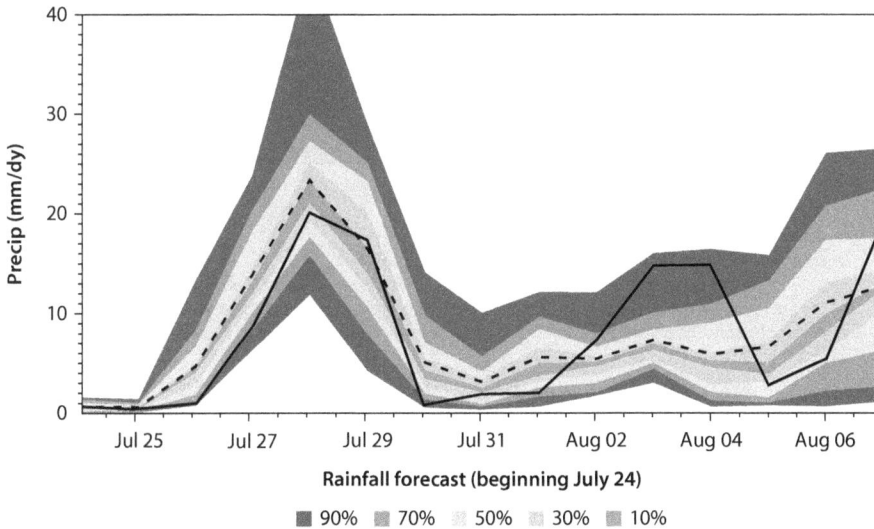

Rainfall forecast (beginning July 24)

■ 90%   ■ 70%   ■ 50%   ■ 30%   ■ 10%

Source: Webster, Toma, and Kim 2011.
Note: The blue line is the observed rainfall rate. The forecast was initialized on July 24, 2010. ECMWF = European Centre for Medium Range Weather Forecasts.

Figure 4.17 Forecast Lead-Time Diagram for Floods in Pakistan and Sindh Province

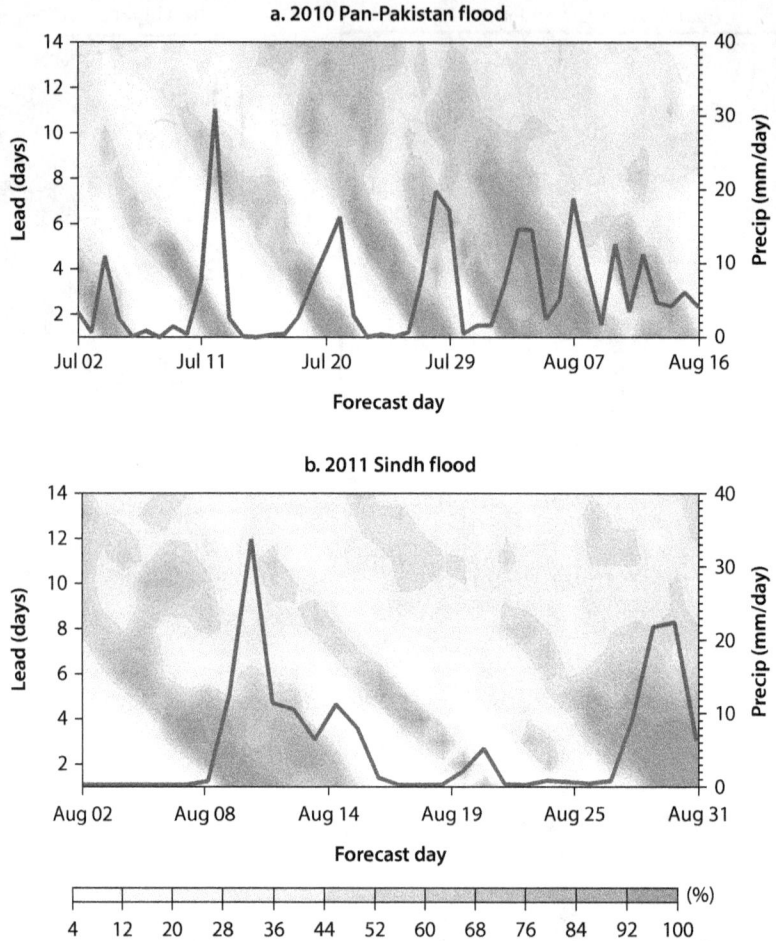

Source: Webster, Toma, and Kim 2011.

Note: The diagram shows the probability that the ECMWF forecast for the red region exceeds the observed CMORPH July-August Climatology Plus 1 Standard Deviation. The line represents the observed CMORPH rainfall [mm/day] averaged for the same region and the same time period (units on the left axis). CMORPH = Climate Prediction Center Morphing Technique; ECMWF = European Centre for Medium Range Weather Forecasts.

Figure 4.16 shows the probability distribution of precipitation based on the 51 ensemble members, with the ensemble mean plotted as the black dotted line and the CMORPH observed rainfall represented by the blue line. Good predictive skill of the July 28–29 major rainfall pulse is found up to eight days in advance.

A similar analysis was done for the rainfall associated with the August 2011 Sindh floods. Figure 4.17 shows the prediction of the August 2011 rainfall. Similar to the forecasts horizons found for the 2010 floods, strong predictability of 7–10 days was found ahead of each rainfall pulse. The aforementioned results demonstrate the ability of the ECMWF model to forecast major rainfall events at time scales longer than a week.

Prediction of Pakistan Stream Flow during the 2010 Flood

Floods are dynamic systems, both temporally and spatially. For example, a flood event that begins in the headwaters of the Indus in Pakistan's north may not have any immediate or significant regional impacts. Yet, as the floodwaters move downstream, the volume increases as stream flow from tributaries is added to the system. At a certain point downstream, this cumulative loading may result in a catastrophic flood. A catastrophic flood must be anticipated for the complete Indus Valley and across the boundaries of the provinces of Pakistan.

The flood forecasting system is based upon a sophisticated hydrological stream flow mode[17] forced by statistically rendered ECMWF ensemble forecasts. The model is full routing and allows for dams and barrages, irrigation withdrawal, different soil and vegetation types, and a full topography. The base river system of Pakistan is resolved at 0.125° (8 km) resolution (map 4.7, panel a). The main routes of the Indus and other major tributaries are resolved in some detail. The need for a model to take into account damming and irrigation drawdown can be seen from map 4.7, panel b, which shows the complexity of damming throughout Pakistan. The following characteristics are deemed necessary for the new Pakistan hydrological stream-flow model:

- The system must cover all rivers within Pakistan, because flooding is progressive from upstream and may flood a region receiving little precipitation.
- The system must also account for those rivers that lie across national boundaries such as in China and India (map 4.7a).
- The system must be probabilistic, providing estimates at all points across Pakistan of the probability of stream flow at a particular level and duration at

Map 4.7 Base Topography and River Routes of the Indus Basin and Major Dams and Barrages on the Indus and Tributaries

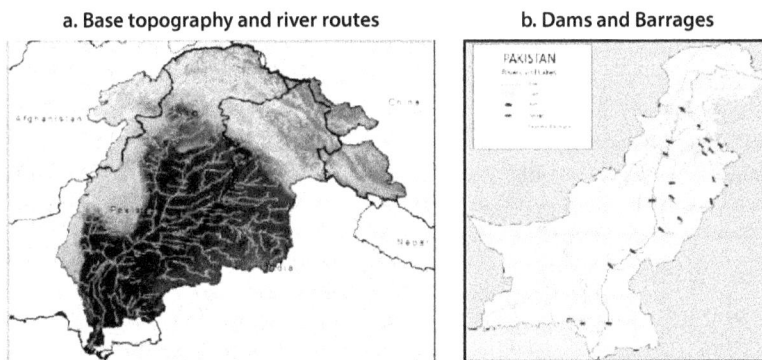

a. Base topography and river routes   b. Dams and Barrages

Source: Webster 2011.
Note: Panel a shows Shuttle Radar Topographic Mission (SRTM) elevations within the basin indicated as a color ramp from dark blue (low) to dark red (high). The derived stream a network is plotted in light blue, and the location of Tarbela Dam in Pakistan is noted by a red circle. Panel b shows major rivers and lakes of Pakistan (see http://en.wikipedia.org/wiki/List_of_rivers_of_Pakistan). Political boundaries are in red. The Tarbela Dam is shown as the red dot. The mountains in the north have elevations >5,000 m. The Indus delta (blue) is extremely flat and near sea level.

all points across Pakistan. Such a finding will allow user communities to determine the "risk" of flooding or low flow.

• The system must produce daily forecasts out to 10 days for all points in
  Pakistan, allowing anticipatory actions prior to warning or floods.
• The model should produce useable information for irrigation and water
  resource managers.

Unfortunately, stream flow data from Pakistan are largely unavailable with only
the inflow into the Tarbela Dam (red spot—see map 4.7a) available for 2011.
However, this data allowed a very basic calibration of the hydrological model.
Maps 4.7a and 4.7b show time series of forecasts of flow into the Tarbela Dam at
different lead times. Figure 4.18a shows each of the 51 ensemble members for
4-day, 7-day, and 10-day forecasts. Figure 4.18b shows the transformation into
probabilities determined from the spread of the ensembles in figure 4.18a. There
is a 95 percent probability of the stream flow at any forecast time being within
the green area, thereby indicating a very high probability that the stream flow will
be bounded by the limits of the green area. There is a 50 percent confidence that
the stream flow will lie within the red area at the indicated date. Furthermore,
there is a 25 percent probability of the flow above the red area. Assuming that
stream-flow flood values are known at a particular location, the probability of
exceedance can be determined and the forecast used in decision making.

Despite the lack of available data, the forecast of the stream flow during July
2010 at Tarbela Dam is very encouraging. With access to stream-flow data from
a much longer period, forecasts by the new hydrological stream-flow model for
Pakistan should improve substantially.

Flash Flood Prediction

Flash floods result from high precipitation rates persisting over a few hours that
occur in a region conducive to hydrological concentration (Doswell 1997).
Surface hydrological characteristics play a large role in the flash flood problem;
a given amount of rainfall in a given time may or may not result in a flash flood,
depending on factors as antecedent precipitation, soil permeability, terrain gradi-
ents, and so on. Therefore, flash flood forecasting involves both a hydrological
and a meteorological forecast.

Virtually all flash flood-producing rainfall is from convective storms; however,
not all convective storms produce flash floods; a major limiting factor is the duration of the relatively intense convective rainfalls. Most convective events do not
persist in any given catchment long enough to produce flooding, so the duration
of rainfall is the key issue. "Quasi-stationary convective events" are conducive to
flash flooding, such as the Leh flash flood of 2010 in northwest India (Rassmussen
and Houze 2012).

A number of difficult questions present challenges to the prediction of flash
floods:

• Is the meteorological situation conducive to the production of explosive convection and accompanying torrential rainfall?

Figure 4.18 Experimental Forecasts of Stream Flow into the Tarbela Dam in Northern Pakistan, 4-, 7-, and 10-Day Forecasts, 2010

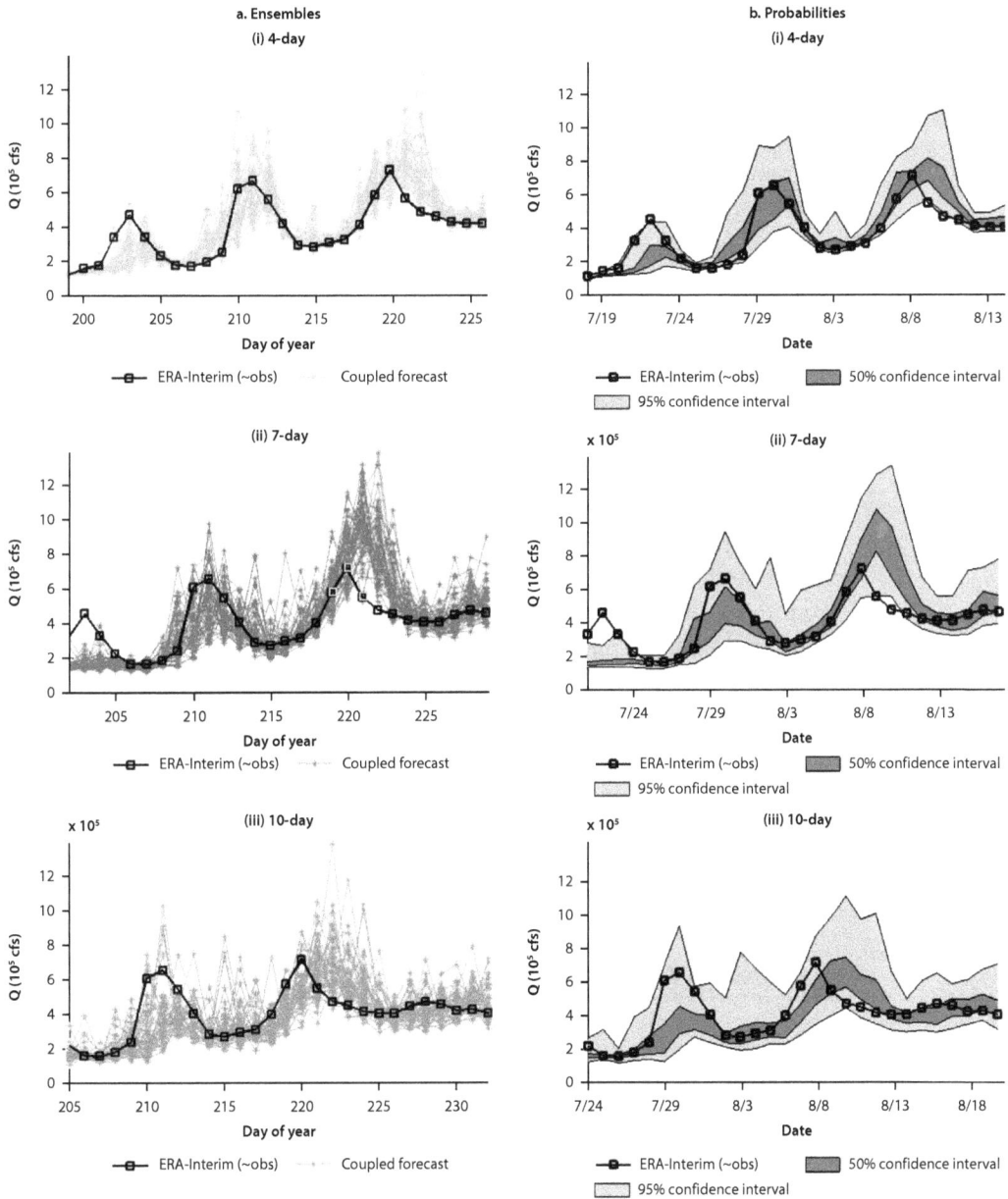

Source: Webster 2011.

Note: For the vertical axis, Q = flow rate; cfs = cubic feet per second. Lead-time plots representing accumulation of 15-day stream flow hindcasts in July–August 2010. Reconstructed stream flow in 2010 using ERA-Interim forcings is plotted as a black line. Panel a: Ensembles are plotted as colored lines to demonstrate the spread of stream flow hindcasts. Panel b: Probabilities are shown as confidence interval envelopes. Starting date of the forecasts is Julian day 195 2010 (July 14). Forecasts are shown are shown in two formats: panel a—the 50-member ensemble with each line representing a forecast, and panel b—the probabilities derived from the spread of the ensembles.

- Is the terrain over which the convection will occur such that the flow of water will be concentrated?
- Will the convection regenerate over such an area for a long enough period for there to be sufficient accumulation of precipitation for a flash flood to occur?

There are two forms of solutions to the prediction of flash floods: quantitative numerical and empirical statistical methods. Twice each day, the ECMWF operational model generates a global "control" run at a 12.5-km resolution. The ensemble runs an additional 50 models at a 25-km resolution. At these resolutions, topography is resolvable, but not necessarily at the required degree of resolution. Thus, a two-stage approach is suggested:

- Determine, using the control and the ensemble forecasts, a general sense of the degree of convective activity during the coming 1–10 days. If there is a general indication of the possibility of deep convection then:
- Run a very high-resolution mesoscale model over the area where there is a general expectation of severe convection using the ECMWF ensembles as boundary conditions. The model would be run many times in order to determine the probability of convection in a particular region. A candidate model would be the Weather Research Forecasting Model (WRF).[18] The outcome from this exercise would be the generation of probabilities of severe convection and flash floods in a particular region.

Model-based prediction of flash floods must be integrated with a detailed analysis of radar and satellite data (Houze 2012; Romatschke and Houze 2011).

Prediction of Droughts

The proposed drought prediction system calls for a three-tier overlapping prediction system: 1–15 days, 16–32 days, and 1–7 months. Table 4.8 assesses the skill for drought prediction for each of these spatial and temporal scales.

Table 4.8 Predictability of Hazards in Pakistan

Hazard type	Frequency	Predictive skill		
		1–7 months	15–30 days	1–10 days
Earthquakes	Decadal	None	None	None
Regional flood (for example, Sindh 2011)	Biannual	Low	Moderate	High
Pan-Pakistan flood (for example, 2010)	2–5 years	Low	Moderate	High
Flash floods	Multiple/year	Low	Moderate	Moderate
Tropical cyclone	1–2 years	Moderate	Moderate	High
Droughts (short duration: 20 days)	Annual	Low	Moderate	High
Droughts (long: months/years)	Decadal	Low	Moderate	High

Source: Webster 2011.
Notes:
No forecasting ability of earthquakes on any time scale exists at this time. Identification of high flood risk, but not regionally specific. Regionally specific at 10 days. Identification of nationwide flooding at 10 days. Identification of a period of higher risk. Identification of region at the 1–3 day horizon. Indication of cyclogenesis risk. Specific region of landfall. Indication of entering into break phase of the monsoon and hence "mini-drought." Indications that the drought will be prolonged or continuing.

Seasonal outlook (1–7 months). Coupled ocean-atmosphere climate models provide ensemble-based seasonal forecasts out through seven months. While the skill is often marginal beyond two months (see table 4.8), these outlooks can provide decision makers with "broad-brush" assessments of the coming seasonal climate and the ability to make strategic decisions. As prediction of seasonal rainfall improves, a major beneficiary would be the barani (rain-fed) agricultural sector, which could hedge against drought through the choice of drought-resistant crops.

Intra-seasonal outlook (15–30 days). Variability that exists on 20–60 day periods dominates the precipitation in Asia's monsoon regions. Such variability separates the monsoon into "active" or rainy periods and "break" or dry (mini-drought) periods. A forecast of an impending dry period can be crucial for agriculture. Empirical forecasting schemes do exist but modeling groups such as ECMWF are showing increased predictive skill in intra-seasonal variability of rainfall. Such forecasts would be especially important to water resource managers to allow for adequate storage. For the barani regions, reduction of intra-seasonal variability would allow optimization the timing of planting, harvesting, applications of fertilizer/pesticides, and water harvesting.

Weather forecasts (1–10 days). Forecasts of the absence or the abundance of rainfall in a particular region have been shown to possess substantial skill on timescales out to two weeks. Short-term forecasts allow user communities to make a wide-range of tactical decisions.

An assessment of the predictive skill of Pakistan hazards. Table 4.8 provides an assessment of the predictability of hydrometeorological hazards in Pakistan. Flash floods are currently poorly predicted. At best, it may be possible to determine risk of a period when flash flooding is probable but this may not be regionally specific except perhaps at rather short forecast horizons. TCs, floods, and droughts are more predictable at intermediate time scales. Depending on the phase of the Madden-Julian Oscillation,[19] forecasts are currently made with moderate skill out to 30 days in the Atlantic Ocean (Belanger, Curry, and Webster 2010). Forecasts of slow rise floods have been demonstrated to be highly skillful at the 1–10 day time scales. There is also a growing anticipation that seasonal predictions of rainfall will increase in their skill using improving couple ocean-atmosphere climate models, of use to both drought and flood forecasting.

Disaster Preparation and Response

To strengthen community resilience in the face of floods, TCs, and other natural disaster, countries in South Asia have begun to implement, to various degrees, DRR strategies. This section describes DRR and risk communication systems in general, with an emphasis on the importance of community level structures. It then describes the DRR and risk communication systems in place in Pakistan, with a special focus on flood response.

General Overview of DRR and Risk Communication Systems
Effective disaster management requires a vertically integrated structure that encompasses coordinated responsibilities and functions for various government institution types and levels (federal, state/district, and local) and recognizes that communities play a critical role in an effective DRR system. Because communities themselves are both the immediate entities affected by a natural disaster, and the first responders on the scene, contemporary disaster management approaches recognize "that community action for disaster risk management is a crucial element in promoting a 'culture of prevention' and creating safer communities."[20]

The UN World Food Programme notes: "[A] dollar invested today in DRR saves four or more dollars in the future cost of relief and rehabilitation."[21] Similarly, disaster management policies have transformed from reactive disaster response efforts to efforts that emphasize disaster planning, as well as response activities. Therefore, contemporary disaster risk response planning should involve both (a) top-down [governmental] planning activities, and (b) community-level planning structures and approaches.

The Asian Disaster Preparedness Center (ADPC)[22] has indicated that the following elements must be present in an integrated disaster-management structure:

- Institutionalization of the community-based disaster risk management in the policy, planning, and implementation of the government ministries and departments and donors in target countries
- Implementation of innovative programs to explore new dimensions in the community-level preparation and response practice
- Development of frameworks and tools to support the work of decision makers and practitioners
- Development of databases and publications to map the community-level preparation and response practices in various regions
- Development of new training tools to enhance the capacity of practitioners[23]

With specific regard to weather hazards, effective disaster planning and risk communication must include useful predictions of the weather hazard at time horizons that enable effective planning and communication to occur. Forecast information regarding TCs and floods, formation, tracks, and landfall—disseminated through the disaster management system, and down to and through communities—is a central element to effective and successful community resilience to weather hazards. In other words, a disaster management system and risk communication structure are necessary, but not sufficient, elements of effective risk response to weather hazards.

A flood event forecasting system integrated with a disaster management and risk communication scheme should include the following elements:

- The ability to provide probabilistic information as to when and where a flood event will occur and the location and magnitude of the flood crest

- Communication of the forecast information with communities using a pre-arranged system, and in terms that the recipients of the information can understand and use
- Integration of the forecast information with disaster management preparedness systems that are already in place to determine the appropriate types and levels of response that should be applied by communities, government institutions, and other stakeholders

This integrated approach will provide hazard information to communities in advance of a flood event whereby communities can reduce the possibility of injury, loss of life, and damage to property and livestock.

Current Pakistan Disaster Management

Pakistan's primary agency for DRR is the National Disaster Management Authority (NDMA). The NDMA was established after the 2005 earthquakes with the intention of establishing plans and facilitating government coordination in order to prepare and improve the response to natural disasters. While an important framework has been put in place, the magnitude of some recent disasters has exposed weaknesses in the implementation of NDMA policies. In addition, it is unclear whether the NDMA has integrated weather forecasting tools into its disaster preparation framework.

The NDMA was created through the policy and legal framework of the National Disaster Management Framework (NDMF).[24] The NDMF established a framework whereby Pakistan would be able to handle both anthropogenic and natural disasters better, on any scale. The framework is designed to address, implement, or create vulnerability assessments, multi hazard early warning systems, institutional arrangements for risk reduction and response, the promotion of disaster preparedness planning, community and local-level risk-reduction programs, training education and awareness, efforts and policies to mainstream DRR into development, and the development of emergency response systems and capacity-development policies for post-disaster recovery. The NDMA is the body that implements these action areas and develops and implements DRR planning policies at the federal, provincial, and district levels.

Following Pakistan's major earthquakes in 2005, assessments were made of the country's ability to prepare and respond to natural disasters. Among the lessons learned were focused approaches, the organization of lean structures, and a flexible organization. Furthermore, there must be a capacity to deal with all types of disasters. The NDMF and NDMA grew out of the recognition of these particular needs.

A central element of the NDMA's work is "mainstreaming"—that is, integrating DRR into federal, provincial, and district policies through a number of NDMA activities. These activities include preparing disaster response management plans for relevant ministries; developing the technical and physical capacities of respective ministries; assessing disaster risks associated with ministry assets and infrastructure; integrating vulnerability reduction measures in the implementation of

ministry programs; developing capacities for post-disaster assessments; and orga-
nizing emergency response, recovery, and rehabilitation.

From a structural and implementation perspective, the NDMA has had
limited success. While the agency fills a very important gap in planning for and
responding to natural disasters, it has been hindered from being able to implement some of its approaches and policies. The 2010 flooding of the Indus River
exposed severe cracks in Pakistan's DRR planning and response, under the
auspices of the NDMA. First, issues in successfully developing DRR policies and
responses at the local and district levels became apparent. Second, while the
NDMA had been established to work across government agencies, a disaster as
widespread as the 2010 Indus River floods indicated that the institutional capacity to respond to such a disaster (let alone prepare for it) was not sufficient. In
fact, a 2010 report from the International Policy and Leadership Institute found
that "NDMA failed to assert its role as the key government institution responsible for disaster management."[25]

Pakistan's efforts to establish a disaster preparation and response agency at
the national level are an important step forward. These efforts are intended
to facilitate policy planning and coordinates between national, provincial, and
district levels. However, significant problems continue to hinder NDMA's
response effectiveness:

The NDMF has a balance of DRR and disaster response approaches. However,
it is unclear the degree to which the NDMA has integrated forecasting capabilities (for floods, TCs, and localized storms) into its new DRR framework.
Providing long-lead forecasts and providing this information to local-level leaders
and institutions so that it can be integrated effectively into planning schemes is
critically important. Not providing this information in a timely manner can ren-
der much disaster planning ineffective and greatly exacerbate fatalities, property
loss, and the displacement of individuals.

Analyses indicate that the coordination envisioned through the NDMF has
not been realized. While DRR policies and planning efforts are underway at the
national level, this has not necessarily taken place, in kind, across the provincial
and district levels. These disaster response gaps were made overly evident during
the cataclysmic flooding of the Indus River in 2010.

Analyses also hold that Pakistan has a deficit of disaster response human
resources. The International Policy and Leadership Institute found that Pakistan's
national humanitarian relief, information management, and geographical information systems experts were in short supply. Pakistan and international development agencies must make it a priority to reinforce Pakistan's human capital in
areas that are central to disaster preparation and response—including analysts
that can engage in hydrologic and tropical cyclone forecasting, warning systems,
and information dissemination.

Emerging Issues: Potential Impacts of Climate Change

A critical element necessary for planning for the future in Pakistan is a comprehensive view of the climate as it evolves over the next hundred years. It is

possible that hydro-meteorological hazards in Pakistan will increase in intensity and frequency during the next century. Webster and Jian (2011) have suggested that there will be an increase in the stream flow in the Brahmaputra, Ganges, and Yangtze Rivers during the next century, with a shorter return time of severe floods. While the Indus River originates in the Tibetan Plateau in common with the Ganges and the Brahmaputra, the source of the summer stream-flow in the Indus is different. The basins of the Ganges and the Brahmaputra depend on copious monsoon rainfall to maintain their stream flow through summer, whereas the Indus, lying to the west of the main monsoon precipitation region, depends more on the ice and snow melt of the Himalaya and Tibetan plateau. While monsoon rains have been projected by the Intergovernmental Panel on Climate Change (IPCC) to become somewhat more intense during the next century, less is known about what may occur at the borders of the monsoon regions, including Pakistan.

In assessing the per capita freshwater availability in the coming century for the regions fed by the Ganges and Brahmaputra Rivers, projected population increase dominates a small increase in stream flow for a projected reduction in per capita water availability. Pakistan faces future challenges in terms of per capita freshwater availability, owing to rapidly increasing population and large uncertainty of the future Indus stream flow.

It is necessary to place climate change in context relative to the occurrence of hazards in the present climate. In Pakistan, regional flooding occurs nearly every year and Pakistan-wide floods every decade or so. Thus, the populace will experience a hazard a number of times each generation. However, given the severity of the impacts from currently hydrological hazards, it is prudent to attend to the reduction of their impacts in the near term. Societies or communities that learn to deal with current hazards will be best able to manage the impacts of future hazards.

Recommendations

Hydro-meteorological hazards recurrently affect Pakistan. Recent catastrophic events include the floods of 2010, the 2011 floods in Sindh, several land-falling TCs, and the recent droughts of 1998–2002 and 2009. Given the significant negative effects of natural disasters—particularly floods and droughts—on the development of Pakistan, and particularly of Sindh, the governments of Pakistan and Sindh should consider developing early warning system based on improved extended-range forecasts of rainfall, stream flow, and TCs. Recent efforts have demonstrated that slow-rise floods and tropical cyclone landfalls are predictable 10 days in advance (Hopson and Webster 2010; Webster and others 2010),[26] allowing sufficient lead time for planning to minimize the impacts of flooding.

The most critical recommendation from this analysis is to develop a comprehensive flood forecasting system that provides 10-day probability of impending regional floods. Given the cumulative nature of flooding through a delta, the system would have to include all of Pakistan and the cross-boundary tributaries to the north and east. In this regard, efforts should focus on the continued development of the new probabilistic hydrological forecast models and calibrating them using multiple years of Pakistani river data. Required data include a long (multi-year) history of stream flow measurements, dam levels and outflow, and flood levels throughout the basin. The model should be able to provide governmental agencies daily forecasts of the probability of flooding out to 10 days. In addition, the development of secondary basin models that extend across international boundaries could produce important benefits in terms of mitigating the negative effects of floods and could help reduce the costs of developing and operating the models.

In terms of developing the Pakistan Tropical Cyclone Forecast System, this study recommends (a) increasing the lead time of tropical cyclone forecasts and extending from the current three days deterministic forecast to 10–15 days; and (b) including a storm-surge component, which will require data on coastal bathymetry and tidal estimates.

Regarding the development of a Flash Flood Forecasting Capability, it is necessary to develop a detailed climatology of mesoscale convective clusters and their associated impacts. The tools (very high-resolution numerical weather models) and the necessary data (satellite and Doppler radar) may be available to produce short-term probabilistic forecasts of these convective events.

To establish a drought forecasting system, the study recommends developing a three-tier drought forecast system, based upon rainfall predictions. These would include (a) probabilistic forecasts of rainfall across Pakistan (1–15 days) on a 25-km scale to support agriculture and water resource management; (b) probabilistic extended dry periods across Pakistan (15–30 days), using the extended monthly forecasts adjusted statistically to forecast intra-seasonal variability of the South Asian monsoon, identifying periods of extended low rainfall; and (c) probabilistic drought across Pakistan (1–7 months) for regional forecasts.

To improve and test an integrated regional DRR and Risk Communication Strategy, the study recommends that the production of forecasts be complemented by an effort to disseminate them to user communities who should be trained in their utility. Such a strategy was adopted successfully for Bangladesh in 2007 and 2008 (Webster and others 2010). Different user groups will have differing needs. For example, water resource managers will have a keen interest in stream flow forecasts. Agriculturists in rain-fed areas would be more interested in rainfall/drought forecasts. The first step is to identify user groups in Pakistan and their needs. In addition, a communication and education plan should be adopted when the forecast products have reached maturity.

Conclusions

The annual cost of natural resource losses and natural disasters is calculated to be equivalent to 4–6 percent of Sindh's estimated GDP. Agricultural crop losses resulting from salinity and waterlogging contribute about 46 percent of the total annual cost, natural disasters about 33 percent, and the rest is the result of

Table 4.9 Summary of Natural Resource Degradation and Disaster Risk Management Interventions in Pakistan and Sindh Province

Timeframe	Category	Intervention
Short term	Natural resources degradation	Rehabilitation of existing water-supply systems, including irrigation and small scale drainage Emergency management
	Disaster risk management	Develop a three-tier drought forecast system be developed based on probabilistic modeling Develop an effective and efficient warning system that reaches all segments of the population in a timely manner

different categories of natural resource depletion. A CBA was conducted on six potential interventions that could be implemented to mitigate these costs: (a) emergency management; (b) capacity building in water resource management of hydrological resources; (c) rehabilitation of existing water-supply systems, including irrigation and small-scale drainage; (d) agricultural extension; (e) reforestation; and (f) sustainable fisheries management. Given the substantial uncertainties associated with the implementation of each intervention, the analysis also included a real options methodology to evaluate irreversible decisions with uncertain future results. On the basis of the analysis, this chapter recommends implementing the agricultural extension and water-supply systems rehabilitation interventions with the highest priority.

Over the past several years, Pakistan has been struck by several major hydro-meteorological hazards, including the catastrophic floods of 2010, the 2011 floods in Sindh, several land-falling TCs, and the recent droughts of 1998–2002 and 2009. The impacts of these hazards have been devastating. Given the significant negative effects of natural disasters—particularly floods and droughts—on the development of Pakistan, and particularly of Sindh, this section discusses the results of an assessment on prospects for mitigating the adverse impacts of such hazards through improved extended-range forecasts of rainfall, stream flow, and TCs. The study found that coupling a prediction system to a hazard warning system could result in the successful evacuation of regions that face storm-surge peril.

The interventions recommended based on the analyses discussed in this chapter are presented in table 4.9.

Notes

1. See appendix C for a more in-depth discussion of natural resource degradation priorities in Sindh and the benefit-cost analysis of interventions to mitigate them. Appendix D provides a more in-depth analysis of hydrometeorological hazards in Sindh.

2. 1 MAF (million acre feet) is equal to approximately 1.23 billion cubic meters.

3. Established during field trials with agronomic recommendations under the current agricultural practices as reported in Kahlown and Skogerboe (1998).

4. Inland fishery is the focus of Baig and Iftikhar (2006) that is the secondary data source for the estimates in this book. Marine fishery was considered as the source of "trash" fish species only in Baig and Iftikhar (2006).

5. Direct cost refers to the monetary value of the completely or partially destroyed assets, such as social, physical, and economic infrastructure immediately following a disaster; indirect costs are income losses and comprise both the change of flow of goods and services and other economic flows, such as increased expenses, curtailed production, and diminished revenue, which arise from the direct damage to production capacity and social and economic infrastructure (ADB and World Bank 2010).

6. The minimum annual percentage earned by an investment that will induce individuals or companies to put money into a particular security or project.

7. http://www.sindhagri.gov.pk/pdf%20reports/investment%20opp.pdf.

8. Also, see the Climate Forecasts Applications Network: http://cfanclimate.com.

9. http://www.pakistaneconomist.com/issue2000/issue17/i&e1.htm.

10. The Saffir-Simpson scale is a graded hurricane intensity scale. Different regions of the planet use alternative scales. However, a category 5 hurricane corresponds to the strongest of all tropical cyclones with maximum winds >250 km/hour.

11. http://www.pakmet.com.pk/FFD/index_files/rainfalljuly10.htm.

12. http://www.pakistanfloods.pk/; http://en.wikipedia.org/wiki/2010_Pakistan_floods.

13. Houze and others (2011), and Webster, Toma, and Kim (2011) discuss the meteorological and climatological causes of the torrential rain in 2010.

14. International Disaster Data Base, http://www.emdat.be.

15. See http://www.wmo.int/pages/prog/www/tcp/Advisories-RSMCs.html.

16. See http://www.imd.gov.in.

17. Based on Gao and others (2010), http://www.hydro.washington.edu/Lettenmaier /Models/VIC/Overview/ModelOverview.shtml.

18. http://www.wrf-model.org/index.php.

19. The Madden-Julian Oscillation is the dominant component of the intraseasonal (30–90 days) variability in the tropical atmosphere.

20. http://www.adpc.net/v2007/Programs/CBDRM/.

21. http://www.wfp.org/disaster-risk-reduction.

22. http://www.adpc.net/2011/?

23. http://www.adpc.net/v2007/Programs/CBDRM/.

24. Document available at: www.pakdipecho.org/docs/ndmf-1006.doc.

25. http://www.ygl-indo-pak.org/files/Pakistan%20Floods%20Malik.pdf.

26. Also, see the Climate Forecasts Applications Network: http://cfanclimate.com.

Bibliography

ADB (Asian Development Bank) and World Bank. 2010. *Pakistan Floods 2010: Preliminary Damage and Needs Assessment.* Washington, DC: World Bank.

Ahmad, S., Z. Hussain, A. S. Qureshi, R. Majeed, and M. Saleem. 2004. "Drought Mitigation in Pakistan: Current Status and Options for Future Strategies." Working Paper 85, International Water Management Institute, Colombo, Sri Lanka.

ANZDEC. 2005. *Pakistan: Sindh. The Asian Development Bank Coastal and Inland Community Development Project.* ADB (Asian Development Bank), Washington, DC. Project Number: PAK 37188. http://www.sida.org.pk.

Arby, M., and M. Rasheed. 2010. "Estimating Gross Provincial Accounts of Sindh." *Pakistan Business Review*, October.

Baig, S., and U. Iftikhar. 2006. "Are the Mangroves for the Future? Empirical Evidence of the Value of Miani Hor Mangrove Ecosystem as the Basis for Investments." Pakistan: International Union for Conservation of Nature (IUCN).

Belanger, J., J. A. Curry, and P. J. Webster. 2010. "Predictability of North Atlantic Tropical Cyclones on Intraseasonal Time Scales." *Monthly Weather Review* 138: 4362–74.

Belanger, J. I., P. J. Webster, J. A. Curry, and M. T. Jelinek. 2012. "Extended Predictions of North Indian Ocean Tropical Cyclones." *Weather and Forecasting* 27: 757–69.

Briscoe, J., and U. Qamar. 2005. *Pakistan: Water Economy Running Dry*. World Bank and Oxford University Press.

Chaudhry, Q. Z., M. M. Sheikh, A. Bari, and A. Hayat. 2001. "History's Worst Drought Conditions Prevailed over Pakistan." Pakistan: PAKMET. http://www.pakmet.com.pk/journal/historyworstdrought2001report.htm.

Doswell, C. D. III. 1997. "Flash Flood Forecasting: Techniques and Limitations." Presentation Given at the III Jornades de Meteorologia Eduard Fontsere, Sponsored by the Catalan Meteorological Society, Barcelona, Spain, November 15–16.

Eccleston, C. H. 2008. *NEPA and Environmental Planning: Tools, Techniques, and Approaches for Practitioners*. Boca Raton: CRC Press.

FAO (Food and Agriculture Organization of the United Nations). 2005. *Global Forest Assessment Report. Pakistan Country Report*. Rome, Italy: FAO.

Gao, H., Q. Tang, X. Shi, C. Zhu, T. J. Bohn, F. Su, J. Sheffield, M. Pan, D. P. Lettenmaier, and E. F. Wood. 2010. "Water Budget Record from Variable Infiltration Capacity (VIC) Model Algorithm." *Theoretical Basis Document for Terrestrial Water Cycle Data Records* (in review).

Giosan, L., S. Constantinescu, P. D. Clift, A. R. Tabrez, M. Danish, and A. Inam. 2006. "Recent Morphodynamics of the Indus Delta Shelf and Coast." *Continental Shelf Research* 26 (14): 1668–84.

Hopson, T. M., and P. J. Webster. 2010. "A 1–10 Day Ensemble Forecasting Scheme for the Major River Basins of Bangladesh: Forecasting Severe Floods of 2003–2007." *Journal of Hydrometeorology* 11: 618–41.

Houze, R. A., Jr. 2012. "Orographic Effects on Precipitating Clouds." *Review of Geophysics* 50, RG1001.

Houze, R. A., Jr., K. L. Rasmussen, S. Medina, S. R. Brodzik, and U. Romatschke. 2011. "Anomalous Atmospheric Events Leading to the Summer 2010 Floods in Pakistan." *Bulletin of the American Meteorological Society* 92: 291–98.

Inam, A., A. R. Tabrez, and M. M. Rabbani. 2008. "The State of the Environment of the Pakistan Coast." In *Asia-Pacific Coasts and their Management: States of Environment (Coastal Systems and Continental Margins)*, Vol. 11, edited by N. Mimura, 301–11. Springer.

IUCN Pakistan. 2005. "Mangroves of Pakistan. Status and Management." International Union for Conservation of Nature. http://iucn.org/.

Joyce, R. J., J. E. Janowiak, P. A. Arkin, and P. Xie. 2004. "CMORPH: A Method that Produces Global Precipitation Estimates from Passive Micro-wave and Infrared

Data at High Spatial and Temporal Resolution." *Journal of Hydrometeorology* 5: 487–503.

Kahlown, M., and G. Skogerboe. 1998. *Waterlogging Salinity and Crop Yield Relationship*. MREP Report 233, IIMI Report R-73. Fordwah Eastern Sadiqia (South) Irrigation and Drainage Project. The Marine Resource Education Program (MREP); Intelligent Image Management Inc. (IIMI).

Rassmussen, K. L., and R. A. Houze, Jr. 2012. "A Flash-flooding Storm at the Steep Edge of High Terrain: Disaster in the Himalayas." *Bulletin of the American Meteorological Society* 93 (11): 1713–24.

Romatschke, U., and R. A. Houze, Jr. 2011. "Characteristics of Precipitating Convective Systems in the South Asian Monsoon." *Journal of Hydrometeorology* 12: 13–26.

Saifullah, S. M. 1997. "Management of the Indus Delta Mangroves." *Coastal Systems and Continental Margins* 3: 333–46.

Townend, I. H., and J. Pethick. 2002. "Estuarine Flooding and Managed Retreat." *Philosophical Transactions of the Royal Society* A360 (1796): 1477–95.

Wang, B., J. Liu, H. J. Kim, P. J. Webster, and S. Y. Yim. 2012. "Recent Change of the Global Monsoon Precipitation (1979–2008)." *Climate Dynamics* 39: 1123–66.

Webster, P. J. 2011. *Prediction of Floods and Droughts in Pakistan*. Unpublished Consultant Report Commissioned by the World Bank, Washington, DC.

Webster, P. J., and J. Jian. 2011. "Probability, Uncertainty and Prediction: A Pathway towards the Alleviation of Poverty in the Developing World." *Philosophical Transactions of the Royal Society* 369 (1959): 1–30.

Webster, P. J., J. Jian, T. M. Hopson, C. D. Hoyos, P. Agudelo, H.-R. Chang, J. A. Curry, R. L. Grossman, T. N. Palmer, and A. R. Subbiah. 2010. "Extended-Range Probabilistic Forecasts of Ganges and Brahmaputra Floods in Bangladesh." *Bulletin of the American Meteorological Society* 91 (11): 1493–514.

Webster P. J., V. E. Toma, and H. M Kim. 2011. "Were the 2010 Pakistan Floods Predictable?" *Geophysical Research Letters* 38 (4): L04806.

World Bank. 2006. *Pakistan Strategic Country Environmental Assessment*. Report 36946-PK, Washington, DC.

CHAPTER 5

Institutional Analysis of Sindh Province's Environmental Sector

Abstract

Pakistan's system for environmental planning and management has evolved over time. The recent 18th Amendment to the Constitution has highlighted the need on part of Sindh to have its environmental planning and management system in place at the earliest. At present, environmental planning and development responsibility lies with the Environment Section at the Planning and Development Division, which makes important planning decisions in the province with respect to any new development plans, and supports the preparation and approval of policies at the provincial level. At the provincial level, environmental priority setting is not institutionalized and there is no formal mechanism in place to incorporate them into multi-year planning schemes, as is the case of the Medium Term Development Framework. Resource allocation in Sindh is based on annual disbursements according to departmental requests, but there is a lack of clearly defined criteria governing the process. There has been a haphazard trend in terms of resource allocation and funds releases to the environment priorities. Environmental management authorities have limited capacity in terms of management, technical, and financial aspects. Interinstitutional coordination among government of Sindh (GoS) departments needs to be enhanced for effective policy implementation and achieving desired results and developing synergies. Environmental management practices in Sindh have not yet incorporated the concept of results-based management, nor have they adopted formal mechanisms that promote organizational learning. Institutional mechanisms, particularly resources, to adequately manage and incorporate public participation into decision making are not yet incorporated in Sindh's institutional framework.

Introduction

The bulk of environmental degradation issues are best addressed through regulation, which requires strong institutional capacity of environmental institutions. Until recently, the federal Ministry of Environment was responsible for environmental priority setting and policy formulation in Pakistan, while the federal Pakistan Environmental Protection Agency (Pak-EPA) was the lead environmental enforcement agency. However, the passage of the 18th Amendment to the Constitution of Pakistan in 2010 resulted in the dissolution of the former ministry, a downscaling of the Pak-EPA's legal attributes, and the devolution of most environmental management responsibilities to the provinces. Then, in 2012, the GoP established the Ministry of Climate Change, which became the Climate Change Division in mid-2013.

A number of factors limit the development of institutional capacity of environmental institutions. For example, interviews and surveys conducted under World Bank support revealed that individuals from the private sector, professional organizations, business chambers, and some public officials perceive environmental goals to be at odds with economic growth. This perception limits the possibility for increasing the budgetary resources for the Sindh EPA, adopting reforms to strengthen it, or enhancing intersectoral coordination mechanisms. Other line agencies have virtually no incentives to endorse an initiative that would reduce their resources and power, or one that would require that these be used to address environmental problems, since these are currently not perceived as a priority for the province.

This chapter focuses on the findings of the institutional analysis of Sindh's environmental sector and consists of four sections. The next section details the institutional framework for the environment sector presently in place at Sindh. This section discusses the regulatory structure, organizational structure of environmental agencies, and details those organizations where environment is a crosscutting theme. The third section presents detailed analysis of the environmental management framework of Sindh. The analysis covers policies, programs, and priorities; capacity and coordination; implementation and learning; and participants in regulatory process. The fourth section provides conclusions and specific recommendations to address the institutional environmental framework, along with the rationale for selecting the proposed alternatives.

Institutional Framework for Environmental Regulation

The institutional framework for environmental regulation in Pakistan has undergone significant changes and revisions since initial efforts to establish a framework for environmental management occurred in 1975 when, as a follow-up to the 1972 UN Conference on the Human Environment in Stockholm, Pakistan created the Federal Ministry of Environment. The Pakistan Environmental Protection Ordinance (PEPO) was adopted in 1983. In 1992, Pakistan developed the National Conservation Strategy, and the first version of the National

Environmental Quality Standards (NEQS) was promulgated in 1993. The NEQS were originally issued under the PEPO. Consultations with major stakeholders were initiated in April 1996, and a revision of the NEQS for ambient air was approved by the Pakistan Environmental Protection Council (PEPC) in December 1999; the new version became effective in August 2000.

The Pakistan Environmental Protection Act (PEPA) of 1997 established a comprehensive framework for environmental management that includes a number of major environmental management entities and their specific responsibilities for environmental protection. These entities include the PEPC; the Pak-EPA; provincial environmental protection agencies in Punjab, Sindh, Khyber Pakhtunkhwa, and Baluchistan; and environmental tribunals (ETs) and magistrates created under PEPA, 1997, which have the power to hear environment-related cases and impose sanctions (for example, monetary fines and prison sentences) for noncompliance with environmental requirements.

Until recently, the umbrella responsibility for environmental priority setting and policy formulation in Pakistan rested with the federal Ministry of Environment, and the umbrella responsibility for regulatory enforcement with the federal Environmental Protection Agency (Pak-EPA). However, the passage of the 18th Amendment to the Constitution of Pakistan in 2010 resulted in the dissolution of the ministry and a downscaling of the Pak-EPA's scope of work. The Ministry of Environment was absorbed by the Ministry of National Disaster Response, which became the Ministry of Climate Change in 2012. However, in mid-2013, the ministry became the Climate Change Division. Recently, the GoS was the first provincial government to approve its Sanitation Strategy (a first-ever regulatory framework step after the 18th amendment to take care of sanitation management in provinces). Table 5.1 presents the overall chronology of events linked to environmental protection in Pakistan.

Analysis of Environmental Management Framework

Policies, Programs, and Priorities

The system for environmental planning and environmental management has improved in Pakistan since the creation of the PEPO in 1983. However, several shortcomings persist in the system's design and functioning for effectively managing and addressing environmental problems. The PEPA, 1997, established the PEPC, which had among its core functions (under section 4 (e) of PEPA) to "*co-ordinate integration of the principles and concerns of sustainable development into national development plans and policies.*" However, PEPC has not performed this function well because it has remained almost nonfunctional since its creation. Not only has PEPC failed to meet at least twice yearly as required under section 3 of PEPA 1997, but it also failed to meet at all between 2004 and 2010. As the apex environmental institution in Pakistan, PEPC's weak performance has hampered the effective functioning of environmental management organizations.

Table 5.1 Key Elements of the Environmental Management Framework for Pakistan and Sindh Province, 1983–2011

Actor regulation	Year	Main features/requirements
Pakistan Environmental Protection Ordinance	1983	Established the requirement to prepare an Environmental Impact Assessment for development projects.
National Environmental Quality Standards (NEQS)	1993	Issued standards applicable to industrial and municipal liquid effluents and industrial gaseous emissions.
Pakistan Environmental Protection Act (PEPA)	1997	Replaced the Pakistan Environmental Protection Ordinance of 1983. Established Pakistan Environmental Protection Council (PEPC), the apex body for environmental protection and the Pakistan Environmental Protection Agency (Pak-EPA). Provided a formal mandate for the Pak-EPA to propose NEQS and enforce approved standards. Enabled the government to levy pollution charges and establish Provincial Sustainable Development Funds. Authorized creation of Provincial EPAs as well as Environmental Tribunals.
Revised NEQS	1999	Relaxed NEQS, which were considered more stringent than those of other countries in the region, and adjusted them based on Pakistan's conditions and practices in South Asia.
Local government ordinance	2001	The responsibility for water supply and sanitation was nominally devolved to Tehsil municipal administrations, the second-lowest tier of local government in Pakistan, comparable to counties or subdistricts. However, the decentralization could not been implemented in all areas.
National Environment Policy	2005	Established goals and high priority objectives in several areas, including water supply, waste management, air pollution, and noise, among others.
National Sanitation Policy	2006	Promoted the grassroots concept of Community-led Total Sanitation in communities with less than 1,000 inhabitants. In larger communities, the National Sanitation Policy promoted a "component sharing model," under which sewage and wastewater-treatment facilities were provided by the communities in the case that local government developed disposal was not available. The objective was the safe disposal of excreta using latrines, the creation of an "open defecation free environment," safe disposal of liquid and solid waste, and the promotion of health and hygiene practices.
18th Amendment to Constitution	2010	Devolution of the Ministry of Environment, Ministry of Local Government, and Ministry of Health's responsibilities to provincial governments and downscaling of Pak-EPA's responsibilities.
Sindh Sanitation Strategy	2011	Guides the Province of Sindh's sector strategies and development framework for achieving the sector *vision* and *mission statement*. The Strategy has looked into promoting viable synergies and linkages among the actors in the sector development, including municipal government agencies, the private sector, NGOs, and others that can lead to setting up of a sector driven by outcome-based evaluation and investment.

The recent 18th Amendment to the Constitution has highlighted the need on part of the GoS to have its environmental planning and management system in place at the earliest possible time. Before the 18th Amendment, many of the issues related to development planning were managed at the federal level. However, since environment is now a devolved subject, the province has to develop an institutional and organizational framework that is adequate for its constitutional responsibilities.

Mostly, decision making in Sindh EPA is made at the highest level, which is at Director Cadre who provide policy/strategy suggestions to the Director General, who in turns passes it to the Environment Department for vetting and approval from the competent authority. At the time when this book was prepared, two of the very important positions of Director (Monitoring) and Director (Environmental Impact Assessment) were vacant, and additional responsibility was given to the Director (Technical).

Priority-Setting Process

Environmental priority setting is yet to be institutionalized in Sindh, because there are no formal mechanisms in place to identify priorities using analytical work and incorporate them in multi-year planning processes, as is the case of the Medium Term Development Framework. This situation is highlighted in the analysis of allocation and release funds of development schemes conducted as part of this study. The analysis reveals that a huge amount of money is allocated at the start of each development year, but only a meager amount is released (figure 5.1). The pattern is not consistent in terms of allocation and releases. Despite failures to utilize the available funds, a huge amount is again allocated at the start of each new year.

There are several characteristics of Sindh's planning and decision-making mechanisms that contribute to the observed disconnect in priority setting. First, there is a lack of analytical work and availability of data to support the governmental decision-making process. This is further aggravated by the lack of representation of certain sectors and stakeholders in the instances where decisions are made, resulting in a particularly apparent absence of the voices and concerns of the most vulnerable groups. Another missing key element is a formal mechanism for the allocation of financial and human resources according to key environmental priorities linked to poverty alleviation and social priorities.

Figure 5.1 Environmental Sector Annual Development Plan Allocation in Sindh Province, 2007–12

Million PRs

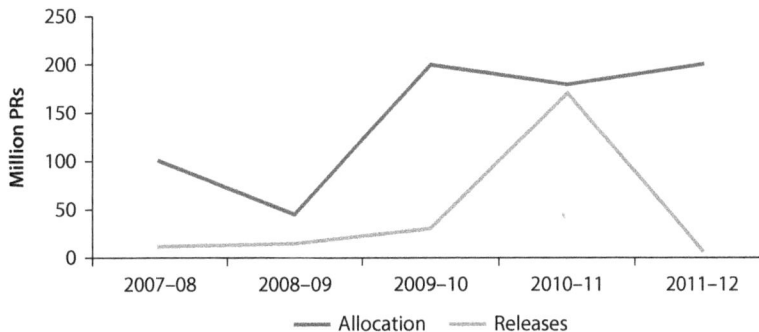

Source: Data provided by the Planning & Development Department, GoS.

Sustainability and Poverty Alleviation • http://dx.doi.org/10.1596/978-1-4648-0452-6

Regulatory Gaps

The recent final approval of the devolution of the attributions contained in the 18th Amendment Act of 2010 has greatly enhanced the jurisdiction and authority of the provincial and local governments in areas such as environment and natural resource management, while the powers of the federal government have been significantly curtailed. The devolution of environmental management responsibilities to the provinces has proceeded in an inconsistent and ad hoc manner. For example, in Punjab the government has already devolved environmental management responsibilities; however, the devolution has not taken place in Sindh, at least at the regulatory framework level.

Uncontrolled decentralization can be very ineffective, as local interests are in a better position to degrade and deplete the resources faster and more efficiently. Coordination is also critical for successful decentralization. Decentralization efforts may fail tremendously without a reasonable level of supervision and monitoring by central governments, as well as a without a good level of coordination between agencies. Even when local capacity is strong, the transfer of responsibilities may make the coordination of national policies difficult, particularly in federative systems (World Bank 2011).

Federal ministries such as Environment undertook regulatory functions before the 18th Amendment. In the post-18th Amendment context, there is uncertainty as to how the country will continue to regulate areas that are traditionally a responsibility of the national government, such as those pertaining to climate change, trans-boundary pollution, and so forth. Failing to regulate on these areas, or doing it in an inconsistent manner across provinces, would enhance the risks to the economy and society. These risks can be illustrated in the case of Sindh by the natural disasters that affected the province recently and that could become more severe in the future because of climate change. Responses to these phenomena require a national-level coordination framework containing provisions for activities ranging from the development of weather forecasts, to management of water flows in the Indus Delta. Both of these are examples of activities that would be more efficiently managed at the national level. In addition, the GoS has yet to develop the capacity to manage the responsibilities devolved by the 18th Amendment. The Planning and Development Department and concerned environmental management authorities have been burdened with additional responsibilities to have a regulatory framework in place at the earliest. For example, Planning and Development Department now needs to have a legal framework in place at provincial level. Although the environmental regulatory framework is still governed under PEPA 1997, the devolution now requires that each province have its own legal framework.

While decentralization of environmental management responsibilities offers a number of benefits, including the capacity to respond more effectively to local priorities, there are also significant tradeoffs and risks. For example, unequal definition and enforcement of environmental standards, as well as differences in the capacity of environmental agencies, could lead to more severe environmental degradation in different parts of the country. A 2011 World Bank study reported that even countries that use decentralized environmental management approaches maintain responsibilities impossible to delegate to regional entities (World Bank 2011). Some of the responsibilities are maintained centrally for reasons of efficiency but others are kept as central responsibilities because failure to do so has been determined to be potentially harmful to the environment and the population. Specifically, the responsibilities that tend to be maintained by the central government, regardless of the level of decentralization, deal with (a) enacting environmental standards and policies; (b) national and international trans-boundary issues, including international agreements; (c) coordination between local governments; and (d) research into environmental issues, such as climate change adaptation and mitigation (Environment Law Institute 2010). The challenge facing Sindh is to address these concerns effectively in its regulatory framework.

Capacity and Coordination

Resource Allocation

Resource allocation in Sindh is based on annual disbursements according to departmental requests. An analysis of resource allocation for various departments (where environment is a crosscutting theme) reveals that those departments have more priority than the environment as a whole. Analyses of 2011–12 Annual Development Plan (ADP) allocations reveal that a major share of the ADP budget is provisioned for Special Projects, Special Packages, and a Special Initiative Unit (figure 5.2).

Annual allocation in terms of staff and their nondevelopment budget for Sindh EPA has increased over time. Between 2010–11 and 2011–12, allocation in terms of budget increased from PRs 47,579,900 to PRs 53,692,700, whereas the number of total staff also increased from 138 to 168. This reveals that authorities have been updating their resources on a need basis, which is reflected in staffing of technical positions that are vital for effective management of technical issues.

Management Capacity

Sindh EPA has demonstrated its capacity to play an important role in helping improve the environmental performance of industries. It provided strong support for the implementation of Combined Effluent Treatment Plants (CETPs) for Korangi tanneries in Karachi, and issued warnings to those tanneries that were not paying their share of operations and maintenance costs for CETPs. In response to the efforts of the Sindh EPA, most of the tanneries at Korangi are paying monthly charges and arrears for the operation of CETPs. In the past 15 years, almost all the multinational industries have installed treatment plants under the enforcement campaigns of the Sindh EPA.

However, Sindh EPA's staff members are geographically concentrated in Karachi (Head Office), and in regional offices located in Hyderabad, and (table 5.2). Analysis of the total positions available/occupied reveals that a huge proportion of the total staff is based at Karachi and is only responsible for operations based in the Head Office and Karachi. Another crucial issue is number of vacant positions in the Sindh EPA.

Sustainability and Poverty Alleviation • http://dx.doi.org/10.1596/978-1-4648-0452-6

To carry out its responsibilities, Sindh EPA has been strengthening its organizational structures (for example by increasing sanctioned positions), has established its own environmental laboratories, and has set up district offices (Hyderabad and Sukkur). However, the agency is inadequately staffed with experts to monitor and enforce ambient air, water, and soil quality standards;

Figure 5.2 Annual Development Plan Allocations in Sindh Province, 2011–12
Million PRs

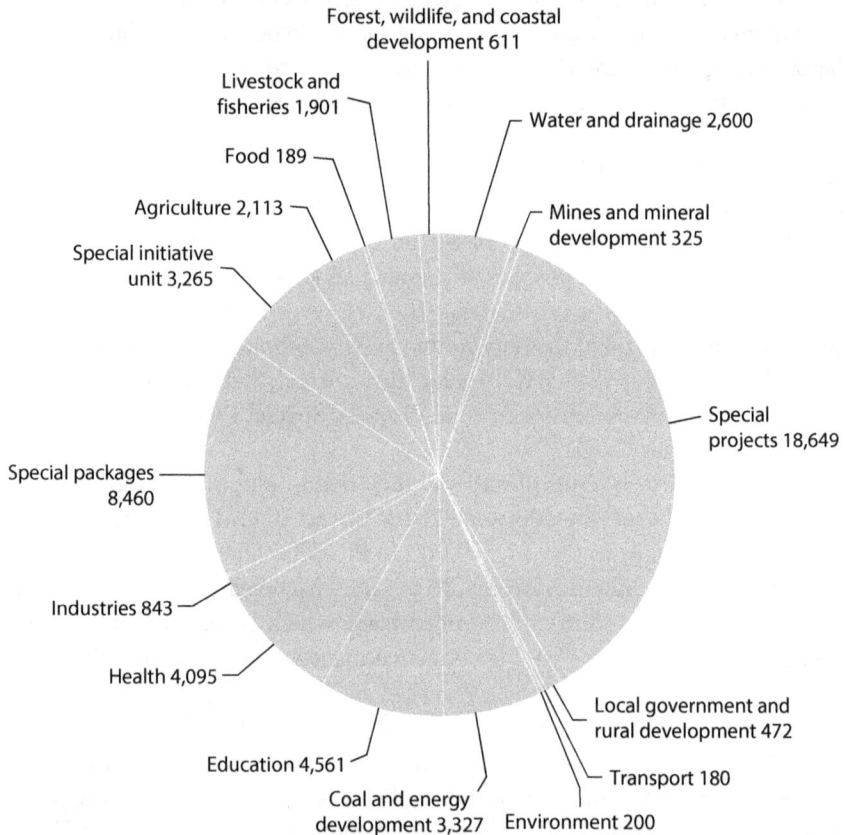

Forest, wildlife, and coastal development 611
Livestock and fisheries 1,901
Water and drainage 2,600
Food 189
Agriculture 2,113
Mines and mineral development 325
Special initiative unit 3,265
Special projects 18,649
Special packages 8,460
Industries 843
Health 4,095
Local government and rural development 472
Transport 180
Education 4,561
Coal and energy development 3,327
Environment 200

Source: Data provided by the Planning & Development Department, GoS.

Table 5.2 Location and Occupation of Environmental Protection Agency Staff Positions in Sindh Province

Office location	Positions
Karachi	119
Hyderabad	14
Sukkur	12
Total occupied	145
Total sanctioned	168
Positions vacant	23

Source: Data provided by the Sindh EPA, GoS.

protect valuable natural resources; review Environmental Impact Assessments (EIAs) of major and complex projects and monitor their implementation; and carry out meaningful public consultations with affected communities.

Because of these factors, the enforcement of mandatory regulations is lax, and stricter penalties that are sometimes available in the laws are almost never imposed because of, among other reasons, the lack of technical capacity to provide sound evidence of infractions, and the fear of political retribution. As examples, Sindh EPA generally has weak capacity to inspect and monitor projects during the EIA and Initial Environmental Examinations (IEE) processes.[1] Because of the lack of site inspection, the agency relies heavily on the IEE/EIA reports, many of which are of poor quality, to make their approval decisions. The concern here is that many projects have the tendency to be approved based on environmental assessments that are inadequate in that they do not account for the actual realities of the environment and ecological setting, as well as the potential impacts of projects (Luken 2009).

As a result of these capacity issues, the consequences for the province/country include (a) poor ambient quality; (b) continuing destruction of valuable natural resources; (c) disproportionate burden of disease on the poor and disadvantaged communities; (d) ineffective review process of EIAs, with long delays in the issuance of environmental permits, adding unnecessary costs to projects; and (e) an excessive judicialization of the environmental permitting process (Khan 2010; Miglino 2011).

Interinstitutional Coordination

Within the GoS, interinstitutional coordination responsibility lies with Environment Section of the Planning and Development Division. At present, the Environment Section is staffed by only one official who is responsible for all work related to environmental planning in the province. The Monitoring and Evaluation section of the Planning and Development Division is formally mandated to carry out the overall coordination among various departments. However, interinstitutional coordination is very weak among departments, and lack of a coordination mechanism was acknowledged by officials interviewed for this study. In particular, water and sanitation and solid waste management schemes are launched in the province, such as the Sindh Cities Improvement Program; but provincial environmental organizations in the province set-up were not engaged.

Despite all the directives contained in the regulations stressing the importance of coordination among concerned agencies, according to environmental agency officials, at present no formal mechanisms exist for agencies involved in environmental management to participate in a consultative process with other government agencies for setting priorities, development of long-term action plans, and assessment of performance/impacts of specific initiatives. Intersectoral coordination for the oversight of crosscutting issues is also nonexistent (Miglino 2011).

Implementation and Learning
Enforcement and Compliance

Enforcement of NEQS is low because of the impracticality of the discharge-based NEQS. In Karachi, most of the industries are located in industrial estates and these do not have land for the construction of wastewater-treatment plants. To have better compliance within industries for NEQS, Sindh EPA provided strong support for the implementation of CETPs for Korangi tanneries in Karachi. Sindh EPA issued notices and Environmental Protection Orders (EPOs) to tanneries that were not paying operations and maintenance costs of the treatment plant. In response to these notices, most of the tanneries are at present paying monthly charges and arrears for the operation of the Common Effluent Treatment Plant. Many such notices and EPOs were also issued to other industries and Sindh EPA staff have made field visits to persuade industries to comply NEQS. Recently, Sindh EPA has inspected many sugar mills, and issued notices. In response, many sugar mills have started the implementation of cleaner production measures and wastewater-treatment plants. As part of its efforts to persuade public entities, Sindh EPA also issued notices to the Karachi Port Trust on public complaints against coal dust pollution.

Organizational Learning

Environmental management practices in Sindh have not yet incorporated the concept of results-based management, nor have they adopted formal mechanisms that promote organizational learning. Transparency with respect to results-based performance is important, but so is transparency with respect to the effectiveness of environmental expenditures to address environmental priorities and administrative practices. Administrative performance indicators allow organizations to set measurable goals, periodically evaluate their achievements, and engage in processes of reforming and improving their practices (World Bank 2007). Over the past decades, the absence of such mechanisms in Sindh may have prevented environmental agencies from adapting their priorities and actions in order to provide a response to changing environmental needs.

A significant weakness in the environmental management framework in Sindh is the absence of systematic processes of learning from experiences that can help guide actions in the present and the future. Sindh's environmental system lacks a consistent evaluation system. Baselines are not created at the beginning of interventions and government institutions do not systematically conduct performance and impact evaluations. Without evaluation, the learning process is weak and institutional adjustment and adaptation does not build on experience.

Environmental Tribunals

Section 20 of PEPA, 1997, authorizes the federal government to establish as many ETs as it considers necessary and specify the territorial limits or class of cases under which each of them shall exercise jurisdiction. In accordance with the Act, the tribunals are staffed by Environmental Magistrates appointed by the federal and provincial governments among senior civil judges. The ETs and magistrates have the power to hear environment-related cases and impose sanctions for noncompliance with environmental requirements. Firms charged with noncompliance face the following *possible* penalties: imprisonment (a maximum of two years), monetary fines, closure of the firm, or confiscation of factory machinery, equipment, and other assets. EPAs, with the approval of the courts, may also continue to penalize the offending firm with each subsequent violation. Penalties are rare, however, as most firms formally charged with noncompliance to PEPA eventually implement required environmental measures. In the early 2000s, there were only a few cases of mild penalties being levied against offenders.

Currently there is a one ET in Sindh at Karachi. The tribunal is headed by a chairperson and two members: one member is a technical expert and the other is a legal expert. At present, the Environmental Protection Tribunal, Karachi, is not fully functional, primarily because some key posts are vacant.[2] The ET is the key fact-finding authority in cases and issues related to environmental pollution as per PEPA, 1997. Private individuals can also use ETs to seek relief for their grievances against the alleged polluters (World Bank 2012). To date, the ET has disposed of 28 of the filed 42 cases and issued various orders where relief was given to the grieved party.

By establishing a constitutional right to a clean environment and demonstrating a willingness to address matters of environmental policy, the courts have empowered citizens with legal standing, enabling them to enforce environmental laws through administrative and judicial proceedings. While this right has been established by the courts, there are no citizen suit provisions in the enabling environmental statutes. Existing and future laws would be needed in order to explicitly provide for citizen enforcement. Public interest advocacy can be a powerful force for improvements in environmental management, one that could be supported through environmental law associations and the establishment of environmental law clinics at universities.

Participants in Regulatory Process
Public Participation

In the past decade, efforts were undertaken to include public/industry participation in environmental management spaces. These efforts range from participation in the design of environmental regulations to the involvement of a diversity of actors in the implementation of environmental programs. For example, the Self-Monitoring and Reporting Program (SMART) was introduced by Pak-EPA in 2001. Under this initiative, all the industrial units were invited to submit the SMART reports as per the requirements of industry categories in which their unit was placed. Pak-EPA, in collaboration with Sindh EPA and leading NGOs of the country, did extensive outreach and dissemination activities to popularize the SMART program for industries (as large numbers of industrial units are based in Sindh, the focus/expectations for SMART were higher in the province). However, even after intensive outreach and trust-building exercises, the Pak-EPA and Sindh EPA could not secure the trust of industrial units (Khan 2010).

Institutional mechanisms, particularly resources, to adequately manage and incorporate public participation mechanisms into decision making are not provisioned in the Sindh set-up yet. Sindh EPA and various government departments/agencies at the provincial level have conducted dialogues involving diverse stakeholders to stir up environmental participation debate. These dialogues have provided important opportunities for voicing concerns of different environmental stakeholders. However, the numerous spaces for institutionalized public participation in Sindh have not provided a systematic forum to address environmental issues. Environmental issues do not consistently constitute a crosscutting element of the agendas of existing participatory mechanisms in place.

Accountability Mechanism

The absence of clear responsibilities and capacities among agencies with a mandate for environmental management dilutes public accountability. Likewise, the lack of apparent channels for citizens to voice their concerns and complaints, regarding the fulfillment of their rights, hampers accountability on environmental issues between the state and citizens (World Bank 2007).

At present, no such formal accountability mechanisms are in place for aspects of matters relating to environmental management in Sindh. Sindh EPA also does not have such provisions in its scope of work. Amidst the ongoing environmental governance challenges the province is facing, there is an immediate need for accountability mechanisms to promote good environmental governance in the province.

Mechanisms to disseminate information in a manner that is easily interpretable can allow communities to play a role as informal regulators, but also promotes accountability on the part of those being regulated. An example is the pioneering public disclosure scheme in Indonesia (PROPER) that encouraged small firms to improve their performance with respect to environmental pollution (World Bank 2005). Interestingly, in a second phase of the same program, the government has moved to make such a disclosure plan compulsory, rather than voluntary (World Bank 2007). Arguably, a compulsory plan forces greater social accountability than a voluntary program.

Environmental Awareness

The success of environmental policy is highly associated with public awareness. Individuals can be meaningfully involved in the environmental management process. Public environmental awareness and education can be increased by promoting public interest and environmental education, particularly among targeted groups, about relevant laws and regulations and about people's rights, interests, duties, and responsibilities, as well as about the social, environmental, and economic consequences of noncompliance.

Sindh EPA has a specific section dealing with public awareness, which has carried out some public awareness campaigns and has involved various civil society organizations—namely, the International Union for Conservation of Nature (ICUN) and the World Wildlife Fund, youths (in particular schools), and media for promoting responsible action in the community. Sindh EPA has not carried out effectiveness measurement of such awareness campaigns. Initiatives like these can be more effective if awareness activities are focused for encouraging public involvement in monitoring environmental performance of key polluters.

Conclusions and Recommendations

The analysis of the organizational structure of the environmental sector in Sindh points to the need to undertake several reforms in order to improve its performance. There is a clear need to build capacity of the relevant agencies to deliver and be responsive to environmental needs, and provide them with the incentives and mechanisms to coordinate with other agencies within and outside the sector.

Although Sindh has made some progress in its environmental management framework, many challenges remain. The following institutional challenges have been identified as the most important: (a) setting environmental priorities, (b) aligning environmental expenditure with priorities and improving the financial sustainability of environmental agencies, (c) strengthening interinstitution coordination, (d) fostering decentralization, (e) promoting enforcement and accountability, and (f) ensuring participation and social accountability.

Table 5.3 summarizes the recommendations that could be adopted to address the key issues emanating from the institutional analysis.

Table 5.3 Recommendations for Institutional Strengthening in Sindh Province

Timeframe[a]	Category	Policy recommendation	Responsible organization
Short term	Setting environmental priorities	Establish a small group in Sindh EPA for analytical work and environmental policy design	Planning and Development Department Sindh EPA
		Design and implement a policy (through laws and regulations) to set environmental priorities at the provincial, district, and local levels, based on learning mechanisms to periodically review and learn from the experiences of implementation of environmental policies	
Medium term		Install and implement systems to monitor and evaluate environmental management and the extent to which the objectives of environmental priorities are efficiently met	
		Periodically evaluate progress on the implementation of policies to tackle environmental priorities with the support of the accumulation of data, results, and experiences achieved through interinstitutional coordination and learning	
Short term	Aligning environmental expenditure with priorities and improving the financial sustainability of environmental agencies	Establish the leadership and institutional arrangements and capacities to set priorities in environmental policy design and implementation	Planning and Development Department Sindh EPA
Medium term		Align environmental expenditure with priorities and improve the financial sustainability of environmental agencies	
		Enhance capacity of environmental agencies on technical, financial, and managerial issues	
Medium term	Strengthening interinstitutional coordination	Set coordination incentives and quantifiable goals	Planning and Development Department Sindh EPA Line Departments with a mandate over areas associated with the province's environmental priorities
		Strengthen institutional learning and build the necessary feedback loops to mainstream improvements and change	
Medium term	Fostering decentralization	Carefully analyze for decentralization of Sindh EPA and define a decentralization scheme for environmental functions	Planning and Development Department Sindh EPA
		Improve interinstitutional coordination and planning, and build capacity to adequately harness decentralization of key environmental competencies	Line Departments with a mandate over areas associated with the province's environmental priorities District and municipal governments
Short term	Promoting enforcement and accountability	Strengthen an enforcement mechanism that consists of identifying a simple set of standards to measure the fulfillment of basic environmental rights	Planning and Development Department Sindh EPA
		Establish an accountability mechanism	Civil society organizations to be coordinated
Short term	Ensuring participation and social accountability	Establish a public disclosure mechanism	Planning and Development Department Sindh EPA
Medium term		Support the technical and financial capacity of accountability agencies to oversight environmental performance and creating an enabling environment for public participation and social accountability	Civil society organizations to be coordinated

Note: a. Short term: 1–3 years; Medium term: 3–7 years; Long term: 7 years and longer.

Notes

1. The IEE-EIA Regulations, 2000, provide details on the preparation, submission, and review of IEE/EIAs. EIAs are conducted for proposed projects that are expected to have serious environmental impacts, whereas projects with lesser environmental impacts require an IEE. Detailed sector-specific guidelines are prepared for industrial estates. Section 18 of IEE/EIA Regulations, 2000 state that "for the purpose of verification of any matter relating to the review or to the conditions of approval of an IEE or EIA prior to, during or after commencement of construction or operation of a project, dually authorized staff of the Federal Agency shall be entitled to enter and inspect the project site, factory building and plant and equipment installed therein."

2. Information is based on http://www.molaw.gov.pk/gop/index.php?q=aHR0cDov LzE5Mi4xNjguNzAuMTM2L21vbGF3Lw%3D%3D.

Bibliography

Environment Law Institute. 2010. *India 2030: Vision for an Environmentally Sustainable Future. Best Practices Analysis of Environmental Protection Authorities in Federal States.* Study commissioned by the World Bank. Washington, DC: World Bank. http://www .eli.org/pdf/india2030.pdf.

Khan, A. U. 2010. "Industrial Environmental Management in Pakistan." Study commissioned by the World Bank, Washington, DC.

Luken, R. A. 2009. "Equivocating on the Polluter-Pays Principle: The Consequences for Pakistan." *Journal of Environmental Management* 90 (11): 3479–84.

Miglino, L. 2011. "SEPSA: Environmental Management Component". Unpublished consultant report commissioned by the World Bank, Washington, DC.

World Bank. 2005. *Integrating Environmental Considerations in Policy Formulation Lessons from Policy-Based SEA Experience.* Environment Department Report 32783. Washington, DC: World Bank.

———. 2007. *Republic of Peru Environmental Sustainability: Country Environmental Analysis.* Report 40190-PE. Washington, DC: World Bank.

———. 2011. *Policy Options for Air Quality Management in Pakistan.* Report submitted to the Government of Pakistan. Washington, DC: World Bank.

———. 2012. *The Greening of Pakistan's Industrial Sector: A Necessary Condition for Meeting Pakistan's Economic Development Goals.* Unpublished consultant report, World Bank, Washington, DC.

CHAPTER 6

Policy Options to Strengthen Sindh Province's Environmental Management Framework

Abstract

Environmental health and natural resources degradation result in the deaths of nearly 40,000 people and cost Sindh between 11 and 19 percent of its GDP annually. Currently, the primary environmental policy instruments that are in place for mitigating these environmental risks are the Environmental Impact Assessment (EIA) procedures and the National Environmental Quality Standards (NEQS). These regulations are enforced in Sindh by the Pakistan Environmental Protection Agency (Pak-EPA) and the Sindh Environmental Protection Agency (Sindh EPA). Gaps in environmental policies, weak enforcement, and deficient technical capacity have characterized Sindh's environmental policy framework. Diverse instruments for environmental policy could be designed and implemented to address Pakistan's environmental priorities. These include (a) direct regulation by government (that is, so-called "command-and-control" measures); (b) economic and market-based instruments; and (c) others, including public disclosure, legal actions, and formal negotiation. This chapter examines each of the major types of environmental degradation in Sindh and proposes specific policies that could be used to address each priority environmental problem. The result would be a comprehensive set of environmental regulations that would have fewer gaps and bad incentives.

Introduction

The discussion below uses the analyses in previous chapters as a basis for identifying policy options that the government of Sindh (GoS) can utilize to significantly improve the environmental management framework. As a caveat, this book recognizes that the limited capacity of the provincial EPA combined with the time it will take to devolve environmental regulations to the provincial level means that regulatory enforcement is not likely to improve environmental outcomes in the short term. What follows is a combination of policies that could be implemented in the short term and medium term and could be used to best address environmental issues as the technical and regulatory capacity of the GoS improves over time.

Diverse instruments for environmental policy could be designed and implemented to address Pakistan's environmental priorities. These include (a) direct regulation by government (that is, so-called "command-and-control" measures); (b) economic and market-based instruments; and (c) others, including public disclosure, legal actions, and formal negotiation. This chapter examines each of the major types of environmental degradation in Sindh and proposes specific policies that could be used to address each priority environmental problem. The result would be a thicket of environmental regulations that would have fewer gaps and bad incentives.

This chapter contains five sections. We first describe Pakistan and Sindh's environmental policy framework. We then analyze this regulatory framework. Then, we examine each of the major types of environmental risk in Sindh and outline policy options that could be used to specifically target each priority environmental problem. In the last section, we summarize the analysis and recommendations of the analysis presented in this chapter.

Pakistan's Environmental Policy Framework

To address the aforementioned issues identified in previous chapters of this book, Pakistan has—over the course of three decades—slowly grown an environmental policy framework that largely relies on two instruments: (a) the EIA for new investment projects; and (b) emission and effluent discharge standards for point sources. In the early 2000s, Pakistan designed a water pollution fees scheme that has not been implemented yet. In recent years, Pakistan has experimented with environmental tribunals (ETs).

Environmental Impact Assessment

The EIA system is the most visible tool used to address environmental concerns in sectoral investments, and air quality and water pollution. According to Riffat and Khan (2006), the EIA process in Pakistan was adopted because of the influence of donor agencies such as the World Bank, Asian Development Bank, and different nongovernmental organizations (NGOs).[1] The Pakistan Environmental Protection Act (PEPA) of 1997 established the current use of EIA. In Sindh, public and private sector construction projects that exceed a certain project cost (depending on the type of project), must undertake an EIA. This EIA must (a) identify the possible negative environmental impacts of the project; (b) develop mitigations for these impacts; and (c) disclose impacts in public hearings. The resulting EIA documents are then presented to the appropriate environmental agency (either the Pak-EPA or the Sindh EPA) for review and project approval. In theory, the environmental agency has the power to withhold approval of the project if it believes that proponents have not identified all negative impacts or designed adequate mitigations for those impacts (GoP 1997).

National Environmental Quality Standards

The National Environmental Quality Standards (NEQS) were originally issued under the 1983 Environmental Protection Ordinance. In 1992, Pakistan developed the National Conservation Strategy, and the first version of the NEQS was promulgated in 1993. These standards established concentration requirements for municipal and industrial effluents, industrial gaseous emissions, and motor vehicle emissions; they also placed limits on noise pollution. Consultations with major stakeholders were initiated in April 1996, and a revised version of the NEQS for ambient air was approved in December 1999; the new version became effective in August 2000. Enforcement of the NEQS is the responsibility of the Pak-EPA and the provincial EPAs, including the Sindh EPA (World Bank 2012).

Pollution Charge System

Pollution charges provide an opportunity to implement the Polluter Pays Principle (PPP). In 2000, the Pak-EPA, in consultation with industry, industry associations, NGOs, and public-sector stakeholders, agreed on Pollution Charges for Industrial Sources. The 2001 rules included detailed formulas for reporting and paying pollution charges. They also defined parameters applicable to pollution charges and included clauses for escalation. After providing notification of comprehensive rules, Pakistan's environmental authorities did not implement the 2001 Pollution Charge Rules (Khan 2010).

Environmental Tribunals

Section 20 of the PEPA authorizes the federal government to establish as many ETs as it considers necessary and specify the territorial limits or class of cases under which each of them shall exercise jurisdiction. According to the PEPA, the ETs are staffed by Environmental Magistrates appointed by the federal and provincial governments among senior civil judges. The ETs are empowered to sentence repeat offenders to up to two years imprisonment and to order the permanent closure of a factory. By January 2011, two ETs were based in Karachi and Lahore. The tribunals in Karachi and Lahore have jurisdiction over other provinces and areas (World Bank 2012).

In cases where citizens or NGOs have sought environmentally related redress from courts, the cases have frequently taken many years to reach a decision, and then the decision has often been ignored. For example, in *Syed Mansoor Ali Shah vs. Government of Punjab* the Lahore High Court appointed the Lahore Clean Air Commission to develop and submit a report on feasible and specific solutions and measures for monitoring, controlling, and improving vehicular air pollution in the City of Lahore. However, the court ran into roadblocks and little was done to implement the measures arising from this case (World Bank 2006).

In theory, the aforementioned policy framework should provide a solid foundation for management of priority environmental problems. While the EIA procedures are meant to manage possible new sources of environmental damage, the NEQS are meant to regulate existing sources of damage. In theory, the NEQS provide firm guidelines on acceptable emission and effluent levels. If polluters exceed these limits, Pakistan and Sindh have empowered their environmental regulatory agencies to force polluters to comply with the law with measures. If regulators fail, the court system is also empowered to step in and force compliance with the law.

Sindh Province: Environmental Policy Issues and Opportunities

Gaps in environmental policies, weak enforcement, and deficient technical capacity have characterized Sindh's environmental policy framework. Environmental regulations only apply to, or are only enforced for, a limited subset of activities, and some of the most polluting activities are systematically neglected by environmental regulation. Government regulators lack resources to enforce the regulatory framework. Because of this, enforcement is selective. Compliance with regulations is extremely low. As a result, Sindh's policy framework is not effective at reducing environmental degradation in the province.

EIA Review

Pakistan's EIA regulations contain screening rules that determine which types of projects must undergo the EIA process. In practice, some projects are never screened by regulators. For government projects, the provincial planning and development department is the authority responsible for screening. However, the department's primary responsibility is to engage in strategic coordination of development schemes and it is usually pressured to expedite projects (Nadeem and Hameed 2008). Thus, EIA requirements are frequently ignored. Another cause of inadequate screening is that developers frequently fail to review the schedule of upcoming projects that require an EIA.

Even when an EIA is conducted, the assessment can be overly narrow in scope. Areas of concern to affected populations and government departments are often not reflected in the Terms of Reference for the EIA (and as a result, are not covered in final documents) (Nadeem and Hameed 2008). Analysis of cumulative impacts[2] and sustainability considerations is weak in EIAs (Nadeem and Hameed 2010). In Karachi for example, the cumulative, synergic, and long-term impacts of major urban projects are almost never considered in the city planning process. Case studies of EIAs done for four industrial projects found that either no evaluation of alternatives was carried out, or a generic statement—without supporting analysis—was included, which stated that the alternative was selected based on maximum production efficiency and safety criteria.[3]

Project proponents also face issues with the technical staff that they hire to conduct EIAs. Consultants have been known to submit reports without visiting affected sites to collect information (World Bank 2006). Generally speaking, proponents want consultants to conduct cheap, quick EIAs. Their intention is to highlight the project's benefits and justify the proposal in order to obtain environmental clearance (World Bank 2006).

EPAs often lack the technical capacity to assess the quality of EIA documents, and particularly to assess them in the context of broader sustainability considerations. As a result of a lack of clear criteria for evaluating EIAs, the clearance process is highly discretionary. Experts rarely review EIAs, even if they deal with issues that are not well understood by EPA personnel.[4] Although the EPA occasionally distributes EIA reports for comments, this is not done systematically and comments are rarely received (Aslam 2006). Often, the comments are requested from government departments or sectoral agencies concerned with the project, which are asked to respond prior to formal public hearing. Sindh has no independent EIA review body (Nadeem and Hameed 2008).

In Pakistan, the law requires that public notice be published in a newspaper 30 days before the hearing. In addition, the EIA documents must be made available to members of the public at a location where they can read them at will. However, illiteracy and lack of technical knowledge significantly constrain public participation (Nadeem 2010). While environmental reports generally state that stakeholders have been consulted, in a number of cases no meaningful public consultation has been pursued.

After granting the EIA approval, the competent authorities do not visit the project unless a complaint is filed that forces them to take action. In many cases, the EPA field staff does not routinely check the project's compliance with EIA approval conditions. In addition, the authenticity of the data contained in the yearly monitoring report is never checked. Furthermore, in many cases the proponent does not send the annual monitoring reports to the relevant authority unless there is some kind of ongoing investigation.

The aforementioned discussions shed light on the deficiencies of the EIA process about planning, review, and supervision. The EIA system needs to be strengthened. However, it is also not capable of bearing the weight that has been placed on it. EIA was intended to be an instrument that forced project proponents to think about environmental considerations and to provide a method for incorporating those considerations into their decision making. It was not intended to be a replacement for environmental regulators' responsibility to manage priority environmental problems. In the end, a better solution would be to create an environmental management system in which EIA is not the only conduit through which the productive sectors are required to deal with environmental considerations. Currently, any environmental consideration that is not present in the EIA is unlikely to be addressed ever. However, a system of diverse regulations and policy instruments would create fewer bad incentives and would be more likely to address Sindh's priority environmental problems.

Enforcement of Environmental Regulations

In terms of enforcing the NEQS, environmental agencies are unable to monitor pollutant discharge, and regulatory actions are only undertaken in response to public complaints. As such, regulatory enforcement is selective and shallow. Provincial agencies have undertaken very few enforcement actions. A survey of 57 tanneries and textile processing firms showed that two-thirds knew nothing about the NEQs. Even out of those firms that did have some awareness of the regulatory requirements, only three were in compliance. The majority of Pakistan's industrial firms are not only out of compliance with the national regulations, but they also are unaware that these regulations exist (World Bank 2012).

The provincial authorities, like the Sindh EPA, which are charged with the implementation of the existing legal and regulatory framework, have ambitious mandates, but in general, they face obstacles in their work because they have insufficient staff, small budgets, little administrative autonomy, and high staff turnover rates. The agencies have rarely been adequately staffed with experts to monitor and enforce ambient air, water, and soil quality standards, and protect valuable natural resources. As a result, the enforcement of mandatory regulations is lax, and stricter penalties that are sometimes available in the laws are almost never imposed because of, among other reasons, the lack of technical capacity to provide sound evidence of infractions and the fear of political retribution. Furthermore, use of the provincial EPA's limited resources is not typically based on priority setting supported by sound analytical work, including analysis of cost-effectiveness (Luken 2009; World Bank 2012).

Section 7 of the PEPA gives the responsible authority "full right of entry and inspection of the site, factory or premises at any time prior to, during or after the commencement of the operations relating to the project." However, this power is only selectively exercised, and, thus, actual compliance is low. EPA's ability to carry out their functions, particularly effective monitoring and enforcement, is constrained by problems in retaining staff and making effective use of professional skills and expertise (World Bank 2006).

Provinces are mired in administrative, funding, and staffing difficulties that prevent them from enforcing the NEQS. For example, provincial authorities have yet to issue discharge licenses because they are still waiting for guidance from the Pak-EPA. Provincial EPAs are also still waiting for guidance on how to apply stiffer enforcement actions—civil and criminal sanctions. Furthermore, there is no comprehensive monitoring system for environmental quality, so EPAs have difficulties identifying where the environmental standards are being exceeded (Luken 2009). In the absence of these tools, they lack levers with which to ensure compliance.

Policy Options to Address Sindh Province's Priority Environmental Problems

There are a variety of mechanisms for controlling environmental health and natural resources degradation. These include (a) direct regulation by government (that is, so-called "command-and-control" measures); (b) economic and market-based instruments; and (c) others, including public disclosure, legal actions, and formal negotiation. These mechanisms are discussed in more detail in the following paragraphs, which indicate which type of mechanism would be most adequate to address Sindh's priority environmental problems.

Outdoor and Household Air Pollution

In Sindh, outdoor and household air pollution results from market and policy failures. EIA is not a tool that lends itself to application for controlling air pollution since it is unsuitable for redressing market and policy failures. Experience in other countries indicates that economic instruments and command and control regulations are far more efficient and effective than EIA in controlling air pollution.

An economic instrument—tax differentiation—could be used to reduce vehicle-related emissions by encouraging motorists to switch from high- to low-sulfur diesel, and by encouraging clean car sales. Among the policy options to control outdoor air pollution, the GoS could consider differentiated taxes and fees on vehicles according to cylinder capacity, age, fuel efficiency, and other environmentally relevant characteristics. A strong system of enforcement and monitoring investments are key to enhancing the effectiveness of tax differentiation systems.

Command and control measures include ambient standards, emission standards, and technology- and performance-based standards. In Pakistan, the environmental regulatory framework includes requirements for ambient and emission standards. Since particulate matter with a diameter of less than 2.5 microns ($PM_{2.5}$) is a priority air pollutant, the government might consider issuing ambient and emission standards for this pollutant. For example, findings from scientific research suggest setting ambient air primary standards for $PM_{2.5}$ at 14.0 micrograms per cubic meter ($\mu g/m^3$) (annual average) and 35 $\mu g/m^3$ (24-hour average). Recommendations for technological standards include reducing the sulfur content in diesel to 500 parts per million (ppm) in the short term, and to 50 ppm in the medium term. Other technological standards might include requiring retrofit particle control technology for diesel vehicles, the use of catalytic converters, and banning the import of used cars.

To control household air pollution, the government might consider the use of a fuel-pricing policy aimed at fostering the use of substitutes for fuel wood. Another economic instrument to control household air pollution includes the implementation of subsidies for improved stoves targeted to poor families and people most affected by the adverse health impact of exposure to such pollution.

Inadequate Water Supply, Sanitation, and Hygiene

Reducing the incidence of waterborne diseases, for example, could be achieved through measures such as (a) reducing regulatory barriers to construction of water-supply and sanitation projects; (b) increasing subsidies for education campaigns for hand washing and household disinfection of water; (c) setting and enforcing strict standards for drinking water quality, particularly regarding substances having adverse health impacts, such as most-probable number of fecal coliform; and (d) setting standards for water usages that could impair human health, such as irrigation and recreation. For example, in Sindh, the government might consider prohibiting irrigation of vegetables with wastewater containing more than a most probable number of 2,000 fecal coliforms per 100 milliliters (mL).

Sustainability and Poverty Alleviation • http://dx.doi.org/10.1596/978-1-4648-0452-6

Public disclosure of water quality parameters has been very effective in fostering continuous improvements in drinking water quality. Reporting requirements include, for example, the Drinking Water Consumer Confidence Reports required by the U.S. EPA since 1999. Under this program, all suppliers of drinking water in the country are required to provide households with information on the quality of their drinking water, including specified information regarding water sources and actual and potential contamination. In Sindh, the government might consider implementing similar regulations requiring water utilities to disclose publicly parameters related to environmental health on monthly consumer water bills, such as pathogenic quality and data on morbidity and mortality associated with waterborne diseases by area served.

Natural Disasters

There are more relevant and effective measures for minimizing vulnerability to natural disasters than EIA. These include design and implementation of regulations relating to land-use plans, and identification of areas prone to risk of floods and other natural disasters. The government could implement policies on land-use planning for risk reduction that identify spatial uses for different human activities—housing, infrastructure, and productive activities like agriculture. The approach to zoning should emphasize disaster prevention and mitigation; and take into account critical constraints, risks, and limitations arising from both human activity and the environment.

In developed countries, the most frequent market-based instrument used to reduce vulnerability to natural disasters is disaster insurance. Unfortunately, disaster insurance is seldom used in developing countries for a variety of reasons, including the high probability of extreme weather events, the difficulty of spreading risk in small economies (relative to the magnitude of risk), the adverse selection problem, and thin markets for insuring risk (Freeman and others 2003). However, a number of potential risk-transfer mechanisms could be considered for Sindh: catastrophe insurance or bonds, access to an international insurance fund (such as that proposed by the United National Framework Convention on Climate Change), private-public partnerships (such as the Turkish Catastrophe Insurance Pool), and parametric earthquake insurance. These and similar initiatives should be considered further.

Deforestation and Loss of Biodiversity

In Pakistan, the markets for evaluating many environmental services simply do not exist. Very high transaction costs, for example, prevent the development of markets for valuing the ecological functions provided by the upper portions of watersheds. Polluters and loggers have few incentives to avoid downstream impacts associated with their wastewater discharges or harvesting practices since these social costs rarely translate into private ones. Another example of a market failure is the situation where private property rights are ill defined or unprotected. This provides the opportunity for overexploitation of natural resources and biodiversity as it is difficult to assess and distribute the costs and benefits of mitigating environmental degradation or abating pollution to individual polluters and parties affected by pollution or environmental degradation. To overcome these market failures, the government of Pakistan could consider implementing market-based instruments such as payments for environmental services.

Water Pollution

Despite persistent water pollution associated with municipal wastewater discharges and agricultural nonpoint sources, the attention of environmental agencies has been restricted to a few industrial activities. Effluent standards are the instruments in place for water pollution control. Typically, parameters for which limits have been established and regulated include primary pollutants such as biochemical oxygen demand (BOD), chemical oxygen demand (COD), total suspended solids, PH, temperature, odor, color, and taste. These limits are primarily of aesthetic and ecological significance, although they do also have some bearing on water use for recreational purposes or water use for productive purposes such as in agriculture and industry. Efforts to regulate water pollution might give emphasis to toxic and hazardous pollutants such as those that have potential adverse health impacts such as lead, copper, arsenic, cyanide, and chromium; or those that could destroy the livelihoods associated with natural resources such as the fisheries and mangroves in the delta of the Indus River.

Solid Waste Disposal

Inadequate waste disposal is also an environmental problem where EIA can prove ineffective without clear command and control regulations. There also is a blatant lack of environmental regulations for the disposal of solid wastes and for the management of hazardous wastes. Poor coverage of waste management services and lack of landfills, which has contributed to the proliferation of unsafe disposal methods and sites, are important factors contributing to the existing state of waste management in the country. Undoubtedly there is a need for detailed regulations that clearly address technical criteria—including, among others, siting of landfills, treatment of leachates, gas collection and management, management of surface or storm runoff in the event of flash flood—and that provide technical specifications for the design, construction, and operation of landfills. Clear regulations and instruments are also needed to address (a) technical specifications for design, construction, and operation of landfills; and (b) incentives for compliance, and sanctions for noncompliance, by waste generators and government officials responsible for waste management. Without such regulations, it would be unrealistic to expect EIAs prepared by project proponents prior to project implementation to suffice for waste management.

Hazardous Waste Disposal

One of the challenges to adequate management and disposal of hazardous wastes in Pakistan, and particularly in Sindh, is lack of adequate infrastructure to manage hazardous wastes. Policy failure is one of the main causes of hazardous waste pollution in Sindh. Explicit subsidies favor overuse of hazardous waste precursors.

For example, agrochemical subsidies contribute to the overuse of chemical inputs in agricultural production, leading to contamination of water, soil, and produce. If the cost of abating pollution exceeds the value of agricultural output, this provides a disincentive for polluters to invest in operation and maintenance of pollution abatement devices. To eliminate some of these disincentives, Sindh could, for example, tax chromium sulfate, which is a highly toxic input to the leather tanning process. The underlying notion is that a tax on a chromium sulfate would result in higher prices to tanneries, and would provide them with incentives to reuse and recycle chromium (World Bank 2012). OECD countries have imposed hundreds of environment-related taxes on inputs such as pesticides. Again, without first addressing the policy deficiencies that stimulate environmental degradation, it is not possible to achieve far-reaching improvements in environmental quality outcomes. In effect, Sindh needs specific regulations and instruments that address, among other aspects, appropriate pricing of inputs precursors of pollution and environmental degradation, and appropriate pricing of natural resources such as water.

Among the topics to develop in the hazardous waste regulations, the GoS might consider focused and unambiguous regulations that (a) provide sufficient detail to ensure adequate management and treatment of hazardous wastes; (b) allocate clear roles and functions to environmental authorities; (c) ensure segregation of hazardous from nonhazardous wastes; and (d) define liabilities associated with compliance with hazardous waste management and treatment. Clearly, each type of waste (hazardous and nonhazardous) should be dealt with by a separate piece of regulation. Furthermore, in order to ensure compliance, regulations should promote accountability by attributing specific responsibilities for specific, identifiable waste management functions—such as waste collection and disposal—to specific positions in the municipal governments, and using sanctions in the event of noncompliance by the officers that occupy such positions. Clearly, in Pakistan, hazardous waste management is well beyond the realm of EIA.

Water Resources Management

In the water sector, policy failure is evident in water subsidies that encourage inefficient water distribution and overconsumption of water among those with first access, while depriving the "tail-enders." In Pakistan, because of the low cost of water, together with low water tariff collection rates, water is wasted and used inefficiently. Government interventions that subsidize operation and maintenance costs of irrigation districts contribute to environmental problems such as soil salinization (World Bank 2005). The current regulatory framework does not provide incentives for ongoing operations to reduce waste of water; nor does the framework promote improved agriculture and irrigation practices to control soil salinity. In effect, in addition to EIA, Pakistan needs specific regulations and instruments that address, among other aspects, appropriate pricing of water, efficient allocation of water rights, and improved collection of water tariffs.

Sectoral Environmental Management

Since EIA is foremost a tool for environmental planning and not for environmental regulation or environmental management, alternative environmental policy instruments should be considered to address consequences of policy failure in infrastructure construction and maintenance that are evident in weak environmental planning and management. A case in point is the construction of transport, water resources and energy infrastructure. For example, for new roads and highways projects, in addition to a restructured EIA regulatory framework, Pakistan requires (a) precise, unambiguous command and control regulations in the form of technical specifications for construction, operation, and maintenance of roads and highways; (b) regulations for land-use zoning; (c) regulations for disposal of waste and dirt during road construction; and (d) pollution-control regulations for construction camps, and all potential urban and regional development activities induced by highway construction.

Conclusions

Pakistan's primary tool for environmental management is EIA, which is a planning tool that the proponents of large projects are supposed to use to foresee possible negative impacts and incorporate mitigations for these impacts into their project design. Pakistan also has a set of emissions and effluent standards—the NEQS—that industrial firms are supposed to comply with. Both of these instruments are enforced by the federal Pak-EPA and the Sindh EPA.

At present, in Pakistan, EIA is perhaps the only point of contact between the environment and productive sectors. However, its effectiveness is reduced because government agencies lack a uniform perspective on EIA's purpose. In developed countries, EIA is foremost a tool for environmental planning and not for environmental regulation or environmental management. However, in Pakistan, there is an ambiguity, especially amongst government authorities, as to whether EIA's purpose is to achieve environmental planning or environmental management. As a management tool, the EIA system requires proponents to create obstacles for themselves—in the form of projected negative impacts and planned mitigations—that they are understandably loathe to do. The result of a high-quality EIA would be increased costs, increased public awareness of negative impacts, and increased responsibilities of environmental management. Thus, proponents are incentivized to conduct low-quality EIAs. In practice, EIA in Pakistan suffers from low quality, lack of public participation, and poor oversight. EIAs also ignore potential cumulative and long-term impacts. Once approved, projects are rarely inspected for compliance with their own EIAs.

Given the current technical capacity, administrative status, and funding of provincial EPAs, the NEQS cannot be enforced. The EPAs currently lack the ability to civilly or criminally sanction firms that violate emissions or effluents standards. Thus, enforcement actions are taken forward on an ad hoc basis, usually in response to public complaint.

To effectively address Sindh's environmental priorities, a full range of environmental instruments could complement EIA regulations. These include (a) direct regulation by government (that is, so-called "command-and-control" measures); (b) economic and market-based instruments; and (c) others, including public disclosure, legal actions, and formal negotiation. This chapter examined each of the major types of environmental degradation in Sindh and proposed specific policies that could be used to address each priority environmental problem. The result would be a comprehensive set of environmental regulations that would have fewer gaps and bad incentives. Table 6.1 presents potential options specifically targeted to address the varied forms of environmental health and natural resources degradation that cause substantial economic and social damage in the province.

Table 6.1 Matrix of Policy Options for Sindh Province

Policy option	Type
Outdoor air pollution	
Differentiated schedule of taxes and fees on vehicles, according to cylinder capacity, age, fuel efficiency, and other environmentally relevant aspects	Economic
Issuance of ambient and emission standards for $PM_{2.5}$	Command
Reducing sulfur content in diesel to 500 ppm (short term) and 50 ppm (medium term)	Command
Requiring retrofit particle control technology for diesel vehicles	Command
Requiring the use of catalytic converters in vehicles	Command
Banning import of used cars	Command
Institution of a fuel pricing policy that is aimed at fostering the use of substitutes to fuel wood	Economic
Subsidies for improved stoves that are targeted to poor and most vulnerable families	Economic
Inadequate water supply, sanitation, and hygiene	
Reducing regulatory barriers to construction of water-supply and sanitation projects	Economic
Increasing subsidies for education campaigns for hand washing and disinfection of water	Economic
Setting and enforcing strict standards for drinking water quality, with a particular emphasis on substances that have the most adverse health impacts	Command
Setting standards for water usages that could impair human health, such as irrigation and recreation	Command
Requiring suppliers of drinking water to provide households with information on the quality of their drinking water	Public Disclosure
Natural disasters	
Design and implementation of land-use regulations	Command
Identification of areas that are prone to risk of floods and other natural disasters	Command
Exploration of risk-transfer mechanisms to insure against economic losses from natural disasters	Economic
Water pollution	
Refocus regulatory efforts on pollutants with most potential for adverse health or economic impacts	Command

table continues next page

Table 6.1 Matrix of Policy Options for Sindh Province *(continued)*

Policy option	Type
Solid waste management	
Creation of detailed regulations that (a) address technical specifications for the design, construction, and operation of landfills; and (b) outline incentives for compliance, and sanctions for noncompliance, by waste generators and government officials responsible for waste management	Command
Hazardous waste management	
End or redesign subsidies that encourage the overuse of hazardous waste precursors	Economic
Development of regulation that (a) provides sufficient technical detail to ensure adequate management and treatment of wastes; (b) allocates clear roles and functions to environmental authorities; (c) segregates hazardous from nonhazardous wastes; and (d) defines the liabilities associated with compliance with hazardous waste management and treatment	Command
Water resources management	
Reducing water subsidies that encourage inefficient water distribution and overconsumption of water by those with first access	Economic
Development of precise and unambiguous technical specifications for the construction, operation, and maintenance of roads and highways	Command
Development of regulations for disposal of dirt and waste from movement during road construction	Command
Development of regulations for pollution control in all camps and potential urban and regional development activities induced by highway construction	Command

Notes

1. The international history of EIA dates back to the establishment of the National Environmental Policy Act (NEPA) by the United States in 1969. The United States was the first country to develop EIA reports based on NEPA. Federal agencies were required to prepare an environmental impact statement for any project that would "significantly affect" the quality of human environment, by assessing environmental consequences in development projects, analyzing alternatives, and ordering a public disclosure of the report to affected groups. NEPA opened U.S. federal decision making to the public to ensure that environmental values are considered in pursuit of other societal goals (Eccleston 2008). Thus, the Act requires agencies to consider environmental impacts in the early stages of planning and decision making. NEPA's vision was to force all agencies of the federal government to integrate environmental concerns into their planning and decision making. In the United States, EIA is built upon an open plan in which the views of other agencies, NGOs, and the public are solicited at every stage of the process. There is no prescribed list of impacts that must be included in EISs beyond the specification that direct, indirect, connected, similar, and cumulative actions must be considered. In the United States, public consultation is an integral part of an EIA process that is characterized by contentious public hearings and active involvement by activist NGOs and community organizations. When these groups do not receive adequate consideration by project proponents, they often pursue injunctions against the project in court. Thus, in the United States, there is a tendency to include impacts of questionable significance, rather to exclude them, partly because of the fear of legal challenge.

2. In EIA practice in the United States, "cumulative impact" refers to the effect on the environment that results from the incremental impact of the action when added to other past, present, and reasonably foreseeable future actions, regardless of which agency (federal or nonfederal) or person undertakes such other actions (Burris and Canter 1997).

3. Information provided from answers of Mr. Syed Nadeem Arif, Director, Environmental Management Consultants (EMC), during an interview with Luis Miglino, April 12, 2010, in Karachi.

4. According to Mr. Mughal (the Sindh EPA's Director General), the most important shortcomings in the agency are (a) shortage of qualified staff—they have only 4–5 professionals to take care of all EIA requirements in the whole Sindh province; and (b) insufficient budget to properly address all the agency's mandates. These limitations, plus the low quality of most EIAs that are submitted to the agency, are the reason why the system is not working as well as is expected by major stakeholders (project sponsors, civil society, sectorial agencies, and so forth). He is trying to overcome the problem by using panel experts that are created on an ad hoc basis to review large and/or complex projects. He has no money to pay panel members, and it is becoming harder to find people willing to work on a pro bono basis. (This interview was held by Mr. Miglino to Mr. Mughal on April 13, 2010, 4:00 PM, in Karachi.)

Bibliography

Aslam, F. 2006. "Environmental Impact Assessment in Pakistan: Overview, Implementation and Effectiveness". KTH Architecture and the Built Environment, Trita-LWR master's thesis, ISSN 1651-064X. LWR-EX-EX-06-24.

Burris, R. K., and L. W. Canter. 1997. "Cumulative Impacts Are Not Properly Addressed in Environmental Assessments." *Environmental Impact Assessment Review* 17 (1): 5–18.

Eccleston, C. H. 2008. *NEPA and Environmental Planning: Tools, Techniques, and Approaches for Practitioners.* CRC Press.

Freeman, P. K., L. A. Martin, J. Linnerooth-Bayer, R. Mechler, G. Pflug, and K. Warner. 2003. *Disaster Risk Management: National Systems for the Comprehensive Management of Disaster Risk and Financial Strategies for Natural Disaster Reconstruction.* Washington, DC: Inter-American Development Bank.

GoP (Government of Pakistan). 1997. "Pakistan Environmental Protection Act." GoP, Islamabad.

Khan, A. U. 2010. "Industrial Environmental Management in Pakistan." Study commissioned by the World Bank, Washington, DC.

Luken, R. A. 2009. "Equivocating on the Polluter-Pays Principle: The Consequences for Pakistan." *Journal of Environmental Management* 90 (11): 3479–84.

Nadeem, O. 2010. "Public Participation in Environmental Impact Assessment of Development Projects in Punjab, Pakistan." Department of City and Regional Planning, University of Engineering and Technology, Lahore, Pakistan.

Nadeem, O., and R. Hameed. 2008. "Evaluation of Environmental Impact Assessment System in Pakistan." Department of City and Regional Planning, University of Engineering and Technology, Lahore, Pakistan.

————. 2010. "Exploring the Potential and Constraints to Implementing the International Best Practice Principles of EIA Follow-up: The Case of Pakistan." *Journal of American Science* 6 (12): 108–21.

Riffat, R., and D. Khan. 2006. "A Review and Evaluation of the Environmental Impact Assessment Process in Pakistan." *Journal of Applied Sciences in Environmental Sanitation* 1: 17–29.

World Bank. 2005. "Integrating Environmental Considerations in Policy Formulation Lessons from Policy-Based SEA Experience." Environment Department Report 32783. World Bank, Washington, DC.

————. 2006. *Pakistan Strategic Country Environmental Assessment.* Report 36946-PK. Washington, DC: World Bank.

————. 2012. "The Greening of Pakistan's Industrial Sector: A Necessary Condition for Meeting Pakistan's Economic Development Goals". Unpublished consultant report. World Bank, Washington, DC.

CHAPTER 7

Conclusions and Outlook

Abstract

The World Bank's support has contributed to building sustainable capacity by providing a methodology that enables the government of Sindh (GoS) to identify and rank environmental problems based on sound analytical work and consider the effects of different categories of environmental degradation. This methodology also helps the GoS to analyze the effectiveness and efficiency of alternative interventions for addressing priority environmental problems. Finally, World Bank assistance has helped the GoS establish a social learning mechanism to identify the shortcomings of proposed interventions and continuously improve them, as well as consider the involvement of different stakeholder groups.

The analytical work presented in this book constitutes the first formal assessment of the severity of environmental degradation in Sindh. It also provides a badly needed framework and the province's first roadmap for carrying out investments, policy reforms, and institutional strengthening activities that would result in better environmental conditions. The methodologies and approach adopted by the analytical work can be replicated in the future to evaluate progress in reducing environmental conditions, identifying policy and intervention improvements, and determining the most efficient use of scarce resources. The Sindh EPA and the Planning and Development Department are now aware of the large potential gains to be realized from adopting reforms, promoting investments, and building institutional capacity to respond to the province's environmental problems.

Introduction

This book has reviewed the analytical work developed as part of the technical assistance provided by the World Bank to the GoS. The main objectives of the assistance were to (a) create a mechanism for ranking the province's environmental problems; (b) assess the efficiency and cost-effectiveness of alternative interventions to address priority environmental problems; and (c) identify the policy reforms, technical assistance, and investments that are needed to strengthen environmental sustainability in Sindh. This chapter summarizes the book's findings and the perspectives for environmental management in Sindh. The first section focuses on Sindh's priority environmental problems. The next section summarizes the results of the analysis on alternative interventions to address such priority problems. The subsequent section centers on the policy options for strengthening environmental sustainability in Sindh. The last section concludes with the outlook for environmental management in Sindh.

Sindh Province's Priority Environmental Problems

Even under conservative assumptions, the cost of environmental health problems, natural resource degradation, and natural disasters in the Sindh province is equivalent to 11–19 percent of the province's gross domestic product (GDP) for 2009 (with a midpoint estimate of 15 percent of GDP).[1] The most important environmental problems in Sindh are associated with environmental health, which have an annual cost that is equivalent to about 10 percent of Sindh's GDP. Among environmental health problems, the most costly are those related to inadequate water supply, sanitation, and hygiene. Outdoor air pollution and household air pollution are also pressing challenges. The problems associated with degradation of natural resources and losses from floods and other natural disasters have an annual cost that represents 5.1 percent of Sindh's GDP (table 7.1; figure 7.1).

Household air pollution from the use of solid fuels—wood, biomass, and charcoal—for cooking causes substantial adverse health effects, particularly

Table 7.1 Annual Cost of Environmental Degradation in Sindh Province, 2009
Percentage of Sindh's GDP

	Low	Midpoint	High
Environmental health			
Water, sanitation, and hygiene	2.88	3.32	3.77
Lead exposure	1.56	2.54	3.52
Outdoor air pollution	0.81	1.42	2.03
Road traffic accidents	0.68	1.15	1.62
Household air pollution	0.69	0.92	1.15
Road traffic noise	0.40	0.67	0.99
Subtotal	*7.0*	*10.0*	*13.1*
Natural resources			
Agricultural losses resulting from salinity and waterlogging	1.60	2.40	3.10
Losses from natural disaster	1.70	1.70	1.70
Loss of mangroves	0.30	0.70	1.00
Loss of productive land from seawater intrusion	0.30	0.40	0.40
Loss of fisheries	0.10	0.10	0.10
Subtotal	*4.0*	*5.3*	*6.3*
Total	11.0	15.3	19.4

Figure 7.1 Annual Cost of Environmental Degradation and Natural Disasters in Sindh Province, Midpoint Estimate, 2009

Percentage of Sindh's GDP

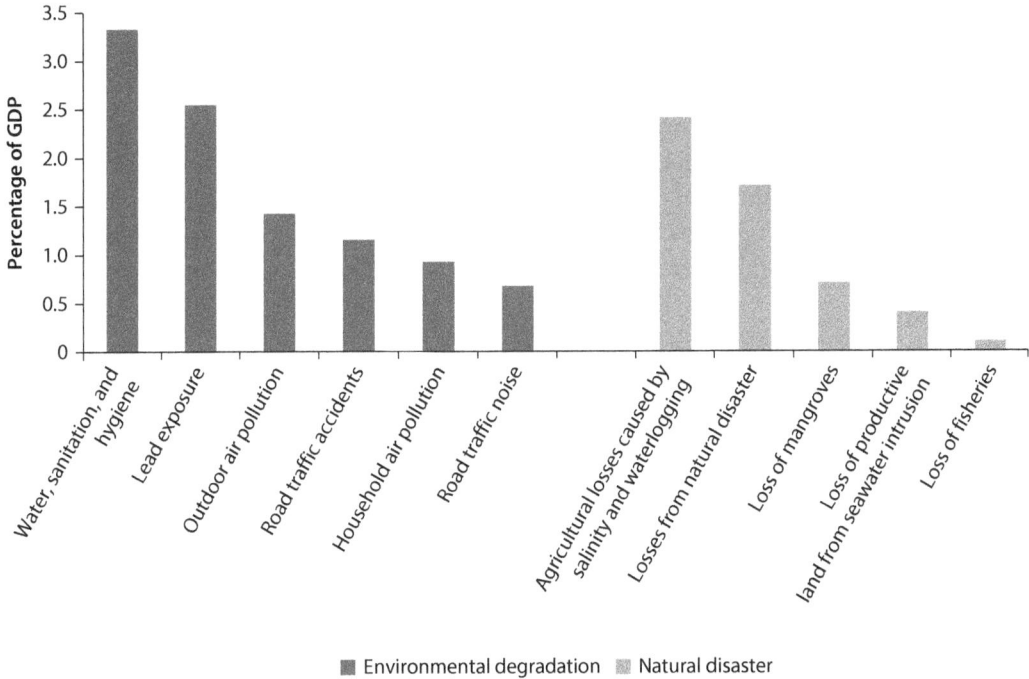

among adult women and young children, because these groups tend to spend the most time in household environments. Use of wood/biomass fuels in the house-hold environment causes air pollution levels that are often several times higher than outdoor air pollution levels in urban areas in Sindh.

Significant institutional challenges hinder the efforts of the GoS to success-fully address environmental health and resource degradation issues. After the 18th Amendment to the Constitution in 2010, the former Ministry of Environment was dissolved. A new Ministry of Climate Change was given a mandate for transboundary pollution issues, climate change, and development of national level policies on environment. However, the ministry became the Climate Change Division in mid-2013.

Provincial governments were given the power to legislate on environmental matters within the broad framework on environment developed by the Climate Change Division. In response to this power, the province of Sindh adopted the Pakistan Environmental Protection Act of 1997, without any substantial amend-ments. This suggests that the province has yet to develop adequate capacity to effectively use the legislative powers that emanated from the Amendment in a way that responds more clearly to provincial priorities. In addition, gaps in envi-ronmental policies, weak enforcement, and inadequate technical capacity have given Sindh an environmental management framework that is not optimally suited to reducing severe environmental degradation in the province.

Alternative Interventions to Address Priority Environmental Problems

Environmental degradation in Sindh is severe, but there are a number of possible interventions to mitigate its effects. An analysis of the benefits and costs of alternative actions sheds light on the most effective interventions for mitigating Sindh's priority environmental problems.

Improving Drinking Water, Sanitation, and Hygiene

It is estimated that each rupee spent on water-supply interventions will yield a benefit of between PRs 3.5 and 5.8 (that is, its benefit-cost ratio or BCR). The indication is that each of these interventions provides a very high rate of return (figure 7.2). The largest benefits arising from all the water-supply interventions are health improvements, followed by the increased water quantity expected from improving Karachi's piped water supply and providing an improved water supply to households in rural areas. Time-savings benefits are also substantial for households that currently do not have a water supply on their premises. The three water-related interventions with the highest BCR are improving the Karachi piped water supply, reopening temporarily closed schemes, and providing rural households with an on-premise water supply.

Improving Outdoor Air Quality

Aggressively implementing well-targeted interventions could improve ambient air quality, measured as particulate matter (PM) with a diameter of less than 2.5 microns ($PM_{2.5}$), in Karachi by 40–50 percent over the next 10–15 years. Interventions include (a) reducing sulfur in diesel and fuel oil, (b) retrofitting in-use diesel vehicles with PM emission control technology, and (c) controlling PM emissions from motorcycles. Fuel oil in Pakistan generally has a sulfur content that averages around 3 percent, though some fuel oil with 1 percent sulfur is being imported. PM emission rates from combustion of fuel oil are greatly influenced by sulfur content. Reducing sulfur from 3 percent to 1 percent in Sindh's urban areas is estimated, by this book, to have health benefits of US$35–47 per ton of fuel oil. The cost of low-sulfur fuel oil in international markets fluctuates and has recently been

Figure 7.2 Benefit-Cost Ratios of Water-Supply Interventions in Sindh Province

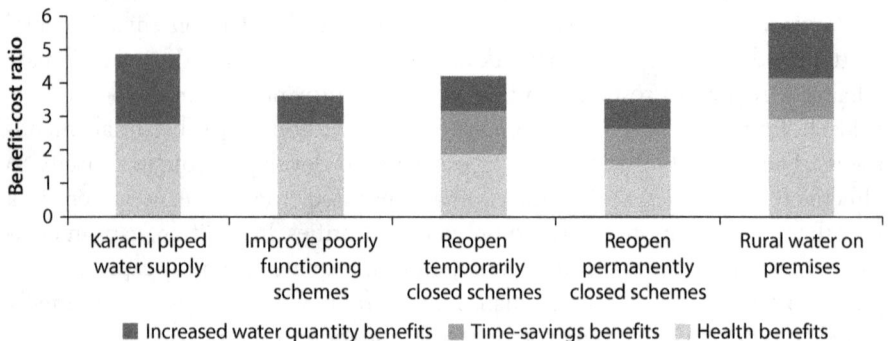

Increased water quantity benefits ■ Time-savings benefits ■ Health benefits

around US$50 per ton. Because of this low BCR, use of low-sulfur fuel oil should only be targeted at users within Karachi, where high population density means that health benefits will be the highest, and thus, the intervention's benefits are likely to exceed its costs. There are additional health benefits of low-sulfur fuel oil that are not assessed in this book. An example is reduced sulfur dioxide emissions, which would result in decreased formation of secondary particulates. Reducing the sulfur content of diesel is a more certain beneficial intervention. The estimated BCR for cleaner diesel is in the range of 1.5–2.4 for large buses and trucks (figure 7.3).

More stringent PM emission standards and control options can be implemented for diesel vehicles once low-sulfur diesel is available. Euro standards can be mandated on new diesel vehicles (and secondhand imports) and PM control technologies can effectively be installed on in-use diesel vehicles, such as diesel oxidation catalysts and diesel particulate filters.

Controlling Household Air Pollution

Replacing unimproved wood/biomass stoves with improved wood/biomass stoves or with LPG stoves (or, alternatively, CNG stoves) would result in benefits that are several times higher than the associated costs (figure 7.4).

Figure 7.3 Benefit-Cost Ratios of Low-Sulfur Fuels in Karachi

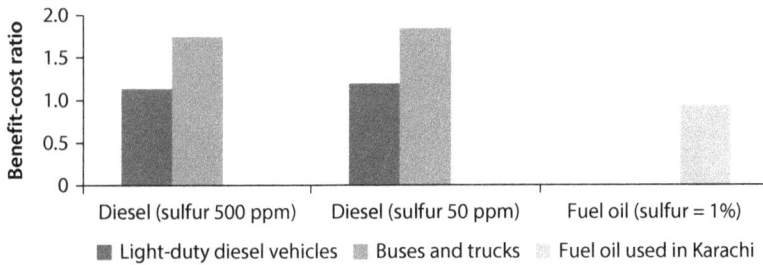

Note: Midpoint estimate of incremental cost of low-sulfur fuels.

Figure 7.4 Benefit-Cost Ratios for Use of Improved Wood/Biomass Stoves among Rural Households in Sindh Province

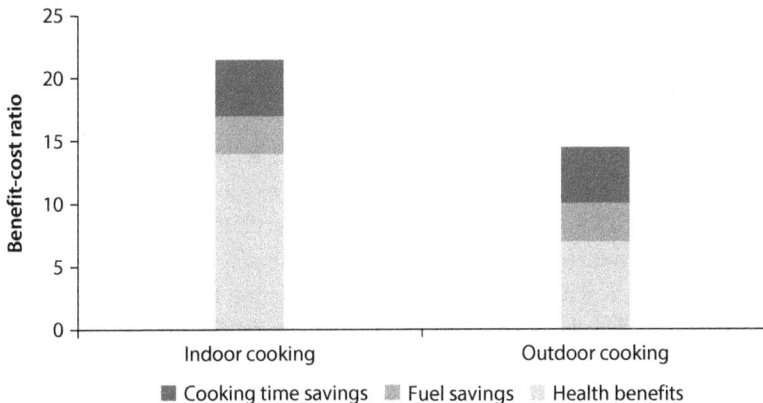

Figure 7.5 Benefit-Cost Ratio Probability Distribution for the Selected Interventions to Reduce the Cost of Natural Resource Degradation in Sindh Province

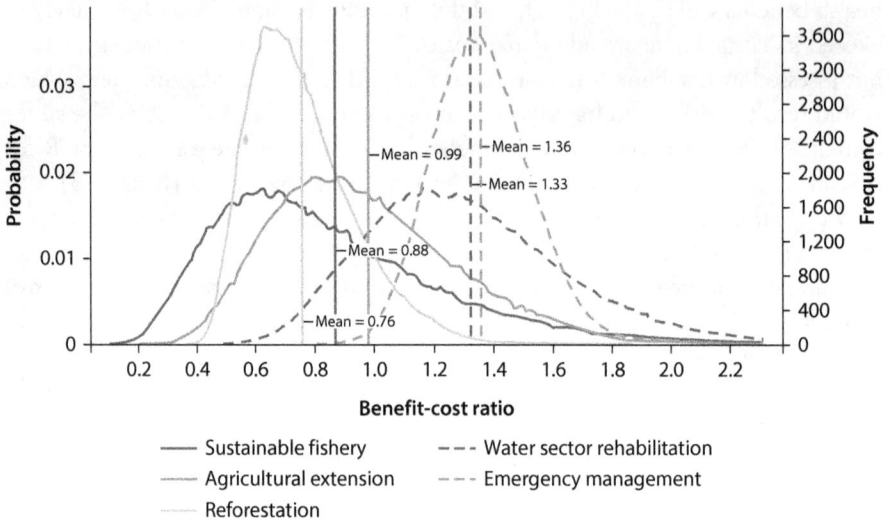

Figure 7.6 Mean Benefit-Cost Ratios for Selected Stylized Interventions to Reduce Natural Resource Degradation in Sindh Province

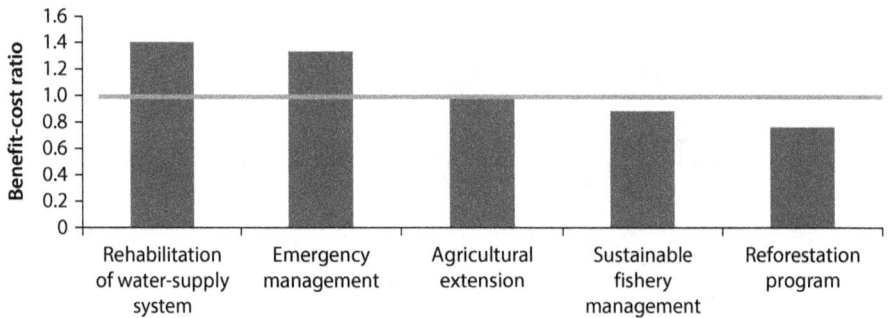

For reducing natural resources degradation from climate change, two interventions exhibit a mean BCR above 1.3: emergency management and rehabilitation of water-supply systems (figures 7.5 and 7.6). Rehabilitation of water-supply systems has the highest BCR, as well as the lowest risk of failure, with 99 percent confidence that the BCR is greater than one.

Emergency management has a high expected BCR, but also exhibits the highest volatility. This volatility is attributed to the random character of extreme weather events in Sindh. This intervention could be characterized as risk management for extreme weather events. Its implementation is justified based on a positive expected net present value and on an option value to save more lives in case of relatively high frequency of extreme weather events (right tail of benefits distribution). Moreover, water-supply systems rehabilitation and emergency management have important cross-linkages. Persons affected by emergencies, particularly flooding, are more vulnerable to diseases and deteriorating health. If emergency-affected persons do not have access to a good water-supply system, their health is likely to deteriorate further.

The most critical emergency management intervention is the development of a comprehensive flood forecasting system that provides the 10–day probability of impending regional floods. Given the cumulative nature of flooding through a delta, the system would have to include all of Pakistan, as well as the cross-boundary tributaries to the north and east. Forecasts can be complemented by an effort to disseminate the forecasts to user communities and train these communities in their utility. Because little attention has been given to the forecasting of severe convective clusters and the flash floods they produce, development of a detailed climatology of mesoscale convective clusters and their associated impacts should be encouraged. The use of Doppler radar in Pakistan, if possible, would be of great use in analyzing which conditions are conducive to convective cluster formation. Satellite imagery with pattern recognition will enhance the accuracy of extreme weather forecasts.

Policy Options for Strengthening Environmental Sustainability in Sindh Province

Supporting Environmental Institutions

The recently established CCD, the Sindh Environmental Protection Agency (EPA), and other units at the provincial level should be given the support they need to undertake their relatively new roles pursuant to the 18th Amendment. Technical capacity building must be a continual process to eliminate the lack of relevant expertise in operating environmental institutions, particularly at the provincial level. The capacity of the Sindh EPA should therefore be expanded by increasing the number of staff as well as their levels of professional education and experience. Funding will also be needed to augment the Sindh EPA's capacity to conduct environmental monitoring and enforce compliance with environmental regulations.

Setting Priorities

Currently, there are no formal mechanisms in place in Sindh to identify priorities using analytical work and incorporate them into multi-year planning processes. Also missing are mechanisms to incorporate the concerns of groups most severely affected by environmental degradation into Sindh's planning processes, as well as clear criteria to efficiently allocate scarce financial and human resources for environmental management in the province. The creation of a group within the Sindh EPA to conduct, in collaboration with the Planning and Development Department, the analytical work for priority identification would provide analytically sound foundations for setting environmental priorities across sectors and budget allocation in response to those priorities. The budgetary allocation for the environment should be informed by a priority-setting mechanism such as an analysis of the cost of environmental degradation.

Promoting Coordination

A necessary condition for improving coordination among environmental authorities and line departments is to establish a system for collecting credible data on the institutional performance of environmental agencies. These data are needed for planning coordinated activities and monitoring institutional performance. Disseminating and publicly disclosing such data those data can create strong incentives for compliance with coordinated plans and for improved institutional performance.

Strengthening the Demand Side of Accountability and Creating an Enabling Environment for Social Accountability

It is crucial that a more systematic effort be made to raise awareness of environmental issues. Possible avenues for raising awareness include publication of data in support of key environmental indicators (including health statistics or pollution loads) and greater use of public forums to discuss environmental issues. Sindh has a wide range of participatory channels, such as the vernacular electronic and print media, FM radio channels, Kawish (newspaper in Sindhi language), and the main national television channels, which could become conduits for social accountability.

Developing and Implementing Alternative Environmental Policy Instruments

A variety of policy options could be designed and implemented to overcome Sindh's environmental health issues and natural resources degradation. These policies could be tailored to target specific environmental challenges and include (a) direct regulation by government (that is, so-called "command-and-control" measures); (b) economic and market-based instruments; and (c) others, including public disclosure and legal actions.

Environmental impact analysis and National Environmental Quality Standards (NEQS) should provide an adequate foundation for management of priority environmental problems in Sindh. While the EIA procedures are meant to manage possible new sources of environmental damage, the NEQS are meant to regulate existing sources of damage. The NEQS were designed to provide firm guidelines on acceptable emission and effluent levels. If polluters exceed these limits, Pakistan and Sindh have empowered their environmental regulatory agencies to force polluters to comply with the law using civil and criminal measures. If regulators fail, the court system is also empowered to step in and force compliance with the law.

However, gaps in environmental policies, weak enforcement, and deficient technical capacity have rendered Sindh's environmental management framework ineffective to reduce environmental degradation in the province. Environmental regulations only apply to, or are only enforced for, a limited subset of activities, and some of the most polluting activities are systematically neglected by environmental regulation. Government regulators lack resources to enforce the regulatory framework. Because of this, enforcement is selective and compliance with regulations is extremely low.

Problems with EIA in Sindh include inadequate screening, overly narrow scope for EIAs that are conducted, the poor quality of EIA reports, inadequate capacity to evaluate EIA documents, insufficient public participation, and a general lack of monitoring of the project's compliance with the EIA's approval conditions. The EIA system needs to be strengthened, but it is also not capable of bearing the weight that has been placed on it. EIA was intended to be an instrument that forced project proponents to think about environmental considerations and to provide a method for incorporating those considerations into their decision making. It was not intended to be a replacement for environmental regulators' responsibility to manage priority environmental problems. In the end, a better solution would be to create an environmental management system in which EIA is not the only conduit through which the productive sectors are required to deal with environmental considerations.

In terms of enforcing the NEQS, environmental agencies are unable to monitor pollutant discharge, and regulatory actions are only undertaken in response to public complaints. As such, regulatory enforcement is selective and shallow. In addition, provinces are mired in administrative, funding, and staffing difficulties that prevent them from enforcing the NEQS. For example, provincial authorities have yet to issue discharge licenses because they are still waiting for guidance from the Pak-EPA.

To effectively address Sindh's environmental priorities, a full range of environmental instruments could complement EIA regulations. These include (a) direct regulation by government (that is, so-called "command-and-control" measures); (b) economic and market-based instruments; and (c) others, including public disclosure, legal actions, and formal negotiation. This book examined each of the major types of environmental degradation in Sindh and proposed specific policies that could be used to address each priority environmental problem. The result would be a comprehensive set of environmental regulations that would have fewer gaps and bad incentives.

Outlook

Sindh has paid extraordinarily high costs for the environmental degradation that has taken place. Findings from this analytical work indicate that roughly 40,000 people died in Sindh in 2009 from major environmental health hazards. Nearly half of these deaths were caused by inadequate household water, sanitation, and hygiene; nearly one-quarter were from outdoor air pollution in urban areas (including Karachi); and the remainder were caused by household air pollution, road traffic noise, and road traffic accidents. The striking figures presented herein provide ample support for the need to improve environmental outcomes. On the basis of the highest BCR and likely urgency of the problems identified, this book has identified both short- and medium-term recommendations to aid the GoS in developing and implementing strategies to tackle environmental health risks and environmental degradation issues.

The World Bank's support has contributed to building sustainable capacity by providing a methodology that enables the GoS to (a) identify and rank environmental problems based on sound analytical work and consider the effects of different categories of environmental degradation; (b) analyze the effectiveness and efficiency of alternative interventions to address priority environmental problems; and (c) establish a social learning mechanism to identify the shortcomings of proposed interventions and continuously improve them, as well as consider the involvement of different stakeholder groups.

Currently, there is no priority-setting mechanism in Sindh and the scarce available resources are not used to address the categories of environmental degradation that are causing the most significant effects. This study constitutes the first formal assessment of the severity of environmental degradation in the province. It also provides a badly needed framework and the province's first roadmap for carrying out investments, policy reforms, and institutional strengthening activities that would result in better environmental conditions. The methodologies and approach adopted by this analytical work can be replicated in the future to evaluate progress in reducing environmental conditions, identifying policy and intervention improvements, and determining the most efficient use of scarce resources.

This book has provided a comprehensive vision of the main environmental and natural resource degradation challenges faced by the Province of Sindh. The multi disciplinarity and methodological rigor that characterized the analytical work have helped initiate discussions with governmental agencies, NGOs, and other stakeholders on the need to address environmental problems as a priority in Sindh. The Sindh EPA and the Planning and Development Department are now aware of the large potential gains to be realized from adopting reforms, promoting investments, and building institutional capacity to respond to the province's environmental problems.

Note

1. The analysis of the costs of environmental degradation (COED) completed under this analytical work indicates the categories of environmental degradation that are causing the most significant costs. The government of Sindh and the World Bank agreed to use COED as the basis for identifying environmental priorities. The use of economic valuation to rank priorities is the state-of-the-art methodology adopted by the World Bank for this type of work (Ahmed and Sánchez-Triana 2008; OECD-DAC 2006; World Bank 2005, 2011). In addition to the COED, the World Bank conducted a household survey and had meetings with stakeholders in the high-level committee created by the government of Sindh to discuss the findings of the analytical work.

Bibliography

Ahmed, K., and E. Sánchez-Triana. 2008. *Strategic Environmental Assessment for Policies. An Instrument for Good Governance*. Washington, DC: World Bank.

OECD-DAC (Organisation for Economic Co-operation and Development—DAC Development Co-operation Directorate [DCD-DAC]). 2006. *Applying Strategic*

Environmental Assessment: Good Practice Guidance for Development Co-Operation. Paris: OECD Publishing.

World Bank. 2005. "Integrating Environmental Considerations in Policy Formulation Lessons from Policy-Based SEA Experience." Environment Department Report 32783. Washington, DC: World Bank.

———. 2011. *Policy Options for Air Quality Management in Pakistan*. Report submitted to the Government of Pakistan. Washington, DC: World Bank.

Environmental Health Priorities for Sindh Province

Abstract

Among the consequences of Sindh's environmental problems are increased mortality and morbidity, and the resulting costs to individuals, families, communities, and the province as a whole. This chapter appears after the book's Conclusions and Outlook chapter, because chapter 8 delves in depth into some of the technical considerations underlying calculation of the benefits and costs entailed in various categories of possible environmental health interventions. Chapter 8 discusses two methods for measuring the costs of increased mortality: the human capital value (HCV) and the value of statistical life (VSL) approach. The chapter also presents two other methods for calculating the costs of increased morbidity: the cost-of-illness (COI) approach includes medical treatment costs and the value of income and time lost to illness; the second approach equates cost of illness to individuals' willingness to pay (WTP) for avoiding an episode of illness. Growing numbers of cost-benefit analysis (CBA) studies in developing countries have investigated the potential benefits and costs of environmental-health interventions targeting water supply and sanitation, household drinking water point-of-use (POU) treatment, and hygiene improvements. This chapter analyzes those studies' methodologies (and their associated calculations and assumptions), results, and possible implications for Sindh. Major topic areas explored in this chapter include household water supply, sanitation, and hygiene; and outdoor and household air pollution. The chapter breaks down each of these topic areas into subtopics, and presents detailed cost-benefit analyses of various interventions for each subtopic.

Health Valuation Methods

The health effects estimated in this book impose a substantial cost to individuals, households, and society. Income and contributions to household activities are lost from premature mortality, illness, and neuropsychological impairments

Table 8.1 Economic Cost of a Premature Death Applied to Sindh Province
Million PRs

	HCV	VSL	Applied to
Children, birth to 4 years old	4.61	—	OAP, RTA, noise, WSH, HAP
Children, birth to 15 years old	5.71	—	RTA
Adults (10 years loss of life)	1.27	5.02	OAP, noise, WSH, HAP
Adults (30 years loss of life)	3.48	5.02	RTA

Note: HAP = household air pollution; HCV = human capital value; OAP = outdoor air pollution; RTA = road traffic accidents; VSL = value of statistical life; WSH = water, sanitation, and hygiene; — = not available.

(IQ losses). Illness also involves cost of medical treatment. Road accidents cause substantial material damage. These costs can be quantified in monetary terms by means of valuation techniques used in economics. Cost of premature mortality is commonly estimated by using the human capital value (HCV) or a value of statistical life (VSL). The HCV is the present value of lost future income from time of death. The VSL is based on individuals' willingness-to-pay (WTP) for a reduction in the risk of death. The HCV can also be applied to estimate the cost of IQ losses.

Two valuation techniques are also commonly used to estimate the cost of illness. The cost-of-illness (COI) approach includes cost of medical treatment and value of income and time lost to illness. The second approach equates cost of illness to individuals' WTP for avoiding an episode of illness. Studies in many countries have found that individuals' WTP to avoid an episode of an acute illness is generally much higher than the cost of treatment and value of income and time losses (Alberini and Krupnick 2000; Cropper and Oates 1992; Dickie and Gerking 2002; Wilson 2003). A conservative estimate would be that WTP is twice as high as COI.

In this study of Sindh province, the cost of health effects is presented as a range. The lower bound of the range reflects the use of HCV for child and adult mortality and COI for morbidity. The upper bound reflects the use of HCV for child mortality, VSL for adult mortality, and WTP for morbidity (table 8.1). The HCV for adults is substantially lower than the VSL, but nearly the same for children. In the absence of WTP studies in Sindh, WTP is assumed to be twice the COI. Estimates of COI are presented in the following subsections.

Household Water Supply, Sanitation, and Hygiene

An increasing number of cost-benefit analysis (CBA) studies from developing countries shed light on potential benefits and costs of various aspects of water supply and sanitation, household drinking water point-of-use (POU) treatment, and hygiene improvements. Recent CBAs include the following:

- A study of household water supply, sanitation, and POU water treatment in a range of conditions in developing countries by Whittington and others (2009)

- A global-regional study of household water supply, sanitation, and POU water treatment by Hutton, Haller, and Bartram (2007)
- A Middle East and North Africa regional study of household water supply, sanitation, POU water treatment, and hand washing by Larsen (2011a)
- A study of hand-washing promotion in Burkino Faso by Borghi and others (2002)
- Studies of household water supply, sanitation, POU water treatment, and hand-washing promotion in
  - Colombia by Larsen (2005);
  - Mexico by Larsen (2007b);
  - Nicaragua by World Bank (2010);
  - Peru by Larsen and Strukova (2006);
  - the Philippines by Larsen (2009);
  - Qena, the Arab Republic of Egypt, by ECON (2007);
  - Senegal by Larsen (2007a); and
  - the Sundarbans of India by Larsen (2011b).

CBAs of various household sanitation options in Cambodia, Indonesia, the Philippines, Vietnam, and the Yunnan province of China have also been completed by the Economics of Sanitation Initiative (ESI) of the Water and Sanitation Program (WSP).

There are also several recent cost-effectiveness analysis (CEA) studies of water, sanitation, and hygiene interventions. Clasen and others (2007b), and Clasen and Haller (2008) present a global-regional CEA of various household water treatment options at water source and POU. Haller, Hutton, and Bartram (2007) presents a global-regional CEA of improved water supply, sanitation, and household water treatment. Shrestha and others (2006) evaluates the health benefits of home-based chlorination and safe water storage in rural Uganda. Cairncross and Valdmanis (2006) presents a global CEA of household water supply, sanitation, and hygiene (WSH) promotion. Larsen (2003) presents a global-regional CEA of water, sanitation, and hygiene interventions. These studies provide estimates of the cost of averting a disability-adjusted life year (DALY), while Larsen (2003) estimates costs per death averted.[1]

Benefits of Interventions

A portion of the costs of inadequate household WSH estimated in chapter 2 of this book (see the "Inadequate Water Supply, Sanitation, and Hygiene" section) can be avoided by implementing the interventions discussed in chapter 3 of this book (see the "Improving Drinking Water Supply, Sanitation, and Hygiene" section). The avoided costs are then the monetized health benefits of the interventions. Monetized health benefits of a particular intervention (k) in population group (i) are given by the following set of equations:

$$B_i = \beta_k H_i / AF \qquad (8.1)$$

$$H = H_i + H_j \tag{8.2}$$

$$H_i / P_i = 1/(1 - \beta_k) * H_j / P_j \tag{8.3}$$

$$P = P_i + P_j \tag{8.4}$$

where B_i is the monetary value of health benefits of the intervention; β_k is the percentage reduction in estimated health effects of WSH from the intervention; H_i and H_j are the health effects of WSH in monetary terms (before interventions) in the intervention group and nonintervention group, respectively, with H as estimated in chapter 2 of this book; P_i and P_j are the intervention and nonintervention population; P is the population of Sindh; and AF is the attributable fraction of disease and mortality from WSH. As the health effects of WSH estimated in chapter 2 of this book are exclusively associated with diarrheal disease and mortality and health effects indirectly caused by diarrheal disease, $AF = 0.88$ per the global estimate by Pruss and others (2002) and Prüss-Üstün and others (2004).

Seven literature review and meta-analysis studies of the international evidence of the effectiveness of interventions in reducing diarrheal illness[2] were used to determine β_k (table 8.2). These studies indicate that the most effective interventions are improved hand washing with soap (32–48 percent) and household POU treatment of drinking water (29–60 percent), followed by improved

Table 8.2 Reduction in Diarrheal Disease from Water Supply, Sanitation, and Hygiene Interventions in Sindh Province[a]

Interventions	Intervention effectiveness (% reduction in diarrheal disease)	Applied in this study (β_k) (%)
Improved water supply	25% (Fewtrell and others 2005)	20–25
	21% (point-of-use) (Waddington and Snilstveit 2009)	
Water quality improvement (point-of-use treatment)	35% mainly chlorination and disinfection (Fewtrell and others 2005)	30
	29% chlorination (Arnold and Colford 2007)	
	40–60% chlorination or filtration (Clasen and others 2007a)[b]	
	44% mainly chlorination, filtration, or disinfection (Waddington and Snilstveit 2009)	
Improved sanitation	32% (Fewtrell and others 2005)	15–35
	36% (Cairncross and others 2010)	
	31% sewer, 35% toilet (Waddington and Snilstveit 2009)	
Hand washing with soap	44% (Fewtrell and others 2005)	40
	47% (Curtis and Cairncross 2003)	
	48% (Cairncross and others 2010)	
	32% LMIC, 39% HIC (Ejemot and others 2009)	
	37% (Waddington and Snilstveit 2009)	

a. Summary of review and meta-analysis studies. b. Studies reporting rate ratio or risk ratio. POUT = point-of-use treatment. LMIC = low- and middle-income countries. HIC = high-income countries.

sanitation (31–36 percent). Provision of improved water supply is found to be the least effective intervention (21–25 percent), but provision of piped water supply with high quality at household tap may approach the effectiveness of household POU treatment if quality of other sources of water is poor. However, Cairncross and others (2010) question the effectiveness of household POU treatment in terms of the quality of the studies that have assessed the effectiveness of POU treatment and propose that the reduction in diarrheal disease is only 17 percent. Clasen and others (2010) reviewed sanitation intervention studies and found there is sufficient evidence that improved sanitation effectively reduces diarrheal disease, but conclude that the evidence is not sufficient to estimate the magnitude of effectiveness.

On the basis of these review and meta-analysis studies, values for β_k applied in this assessment in Sindh are in the range of 15–40 percent (table 8.2). The following sections discuss these values further.

Household Water Supply

Five household water-supply interventions are assessed (table 8.3). These interventions likely represent only a subset of household water-supply interventions needed in Sindh to provide the population with plentiful and safe water for protection of health and for increasing the convenience of and opportunities for improving personal and domestic hygiene practices. Upgrading and/or rehabilitation of piped water-supply schemes require assessment of each individual scheme in terms of water source, water treatment, distribution network, and technical requirements for continuous water supply. The assessment here is therefore only indicative of benefits and costs of upgrading and/or rehabilitation of the schemes. It might also be that upgrading and/or rehabilitation of some or many of these schemes is unviable for technical or economic reasons. As for the rural population that relies on nonpiped water sources, a first priority is to

Table 8.3 Assessment of Benefits and Costs for Selected Household Water-Supply Interventions in Sindh Province

Interventions	Descriptions	Improvements and benefits
Karachi piped water supply	Rehabilitation and upgrading of water-supply distribution network and water treatment	Improved water quality; increased water quantity and reliability of supply
Upgrading/rehabilitation of piped water-supply schemes	Improve poorly functioning schemes	Improved water quality through water treatment and rehabilitation of water distribution networks; increased water quantity and reliability of supply
	Reopen temporarily closed schemes	Improved water quality through water treatment and rehabilitation of water distribution networks; increased water quantity and reliability of supply; and reduced time to water source for the population that relied on these schemes, but are now using water sources at a distance from their dwelling
	Reopen permanently closed schemes	
Rural water supply	Provide high quality water on premises	Reduced time to water source; increased water quantity and convenience; improved water quality

provide high-quality water to those households that currently rely on unsafe drinking water located at a distance of more than 30-minute round-trip from their dwelling. A second rural priority is to address water quality problems for households with unsafe water within a 30-minute round-trip or on premises.

Benefits of Interventions

Key benefit parameters of the water-supply interventions are presented in table 8.4. Water treatment and improvement in distribution networks can provide substantial improvements in water quality at household taps. An effectiveness of 25 percent in reducing diarrheal disease is attributed to improvement in piped water supply in Karachi, and improvement in poorly functioning piped water-supply schemes in other parts of Sindh as these schemes are currently plagued by water quality problems (PCRWR 2010). An effectiveness of 20 percent is applied to the other interventions as water quality problems of currently used water sources are found to be less severe than in the poorly functioning piped water-supply schemes. These rates of effectiveness are in the range found in the review and meta-analysis studies by Fewtrell and others (2005) and Waddington and Snilstveit (2009).

Some of the water-supply interventions will also provide time savings in the collection of household water. Time savings are the average time that households currently spend on a round-trip to their water source, as reported in the PDHS (2006–07) by NIPS/Macro (2008). There are no time savings from the interventions to improve piped water supply in Karachi and from improving poorly functioning piped water-supply schemes elsewhere in Sindh, as the

Table 8.4 Key Benefit Parameters of Water-Supply Interventions in Sindh Province

	Karachi piped water supply	Upgrading/rehabilitation of piped water-supply schemes			Rural water supply
	Rehabilitation and upgrading of water-supply network and water treatment	Improve poorly functioning schemes	Reopen temporarily closed schemes	Reopen permanently closed schemes	Provide water on premises
Intervention effectiveness (% reduction in diarrheal disease)	25	25	20	20	20
Incremental water supply (liters/person/day)	50	20	30	30	30
Water collection time savings (minutes/household/day)	0	0	18	18	19
Value of incremental water supply (PRs/m^3)	40	40	40	40	40
Value of time savings (% of average wage rate)	50	50	50	50	50
Average wage rate (PRs/hour)	88	62	62	62	36

location where households receive their water does not change. Households that previously used the now temporarily or permanently closed piped water supply schemes have to access water elsewhere and will benefit from time savings if these schemes are reopened. In addition, rural households currently without water on premises will benefit from time savings by receiving water on premises. These time-savings benefits are valued at 50 percent of wage rates in Sindh. The wage rate applied to Karachi is the urban wage rate. The wage rate applied to the upgrading/rehabilitation of piped water-supply schemes is the average of the urban and rural wage rate, as these households are predominantly in secondary cities and towns with lower average wage rates that the overall urban population. The wage rate applied to rural water supply is the average rural wage rate.

An additional nonhealth benefit of the water-supply interventions is increased quantity of water available to households. Households in developing countries with no access to plentiful water supply are often willing to pay several U.S. dollars per cubic meter of water from private vendors, reflecting the value these households place on water (Kjellen and McGranahan 2006). It is assumed here that the value to households of incremental water supply is PRs 40 per m^3 for an incremental volume of 20–50 liters per person per day.

Estimated total annual health and nonhealth benefits of the water-supply interventions are in the range of PRs 1,140–1,657 per person when health benefits are valued using the HCV for child and adult mortality and the COI approach for morbidity. The estimated benefits are in the range of PRs 1,402–1,867 when using HCV for child mortality, VSL for adult mortality, and WTP for avoiding morbidity (table 8.5).

Table 8.5 Benefits of Water-Supply Interventions in Sindh Province

	Karachi piped water supply	Upgrading/rehabilitation of piped water-supply schemes			Rural water supply
	Rehabilitation and upgrading of water-supply network and water treatment	Improve poorly functioning schemes	Reopen temporarily closed schemes	Reopen permanently closed schemes	Provide water on premises
Annual health benefits per person (PRs) ("low" valuation)	848	848	679	679	679
Annual health benefits per person (PRs) ("high" valuation)	1,110	1,110	888	888	888
Annual value of increased water quantity per person (PRs)	730	292	438	438	438
Annual value of time savings per person (PRs)	0	0	541	541	333
Total annual benefit per person (PRs) "low"	**1,578**	**1,140**	**1,657**	**1,657**	**1,450**
Total annual benefit per person (PRs) "high"	**1,840**	**1,402**	**1,867**	**1,867**	**1,659**

Note: "Low" reflects using HCV for child and adult mortality and COI for morbidity. "High" reflects using HCV for child mortality, VSL for adult mortality, and WTP for morbidity.

Health benefits constitute 41–79 percent of total benefits, and are highest for the upgrading/rehabilitation of poorly functioning piped water-supply schemes (74–79 percent) and lowest for the temporarily closed and permanently closed piped water-supply schemes (41–48 percent). Nonhealth benefits constitute 20–58 percent of total benefits, and are lowest for the upgrading/rehabilitation of poorly functioning piped water-supply schemes (21–26 percent) and highest for the temporarily closed and permanently closed piped water-supply schemes (52–59 percent). The benefits of time savings are similar to the benefits of increased water quantity for the interventions with time savings.

Costs of Interventions

Cost of water-supply interventions includes initial capital cost and incremental operations and maintenance (O&M) cost (table 8.6).

The piped water-supply system in Karachi is in dire need of rehabilitation and upgrading, just to meet current water demands. ADB 2005 presents potential water-supply projects in Karachi amounting to around US$120–130 million simply to address deficiencies in existing infrastructure. This includes rehabilitation and strengthening of existing water-supply network (US$80–85 million) and expansion of two water treatment plants (US$40–45 million).[3] This capital cost amounts to around PRs 2,100 per capita (2009 prices), assuming the improvements would benefit 6 million people or somewhat less than half of Karachi's population.

The Pakistan Institute of Development Economics (PIDE) presents a review and analysis of the costs of water-supply and sanitation projects in each province of Pakistan (PIDE 2002). A hand pump is the most common source of household water supply in small cities, towns, and rural areas in Sindh. The cost of a hand pump water supply in Sindh ranged from PRs 5,400 per household for an individual household scheme, to PRs 17,500 for a scheme shared by tens of

Table 8.6 Costs of Water-Supply Interventions in Sindh Province

	Karachi piped water supply	Upgrading/rehabilitation of piped water-supply schemes			Rural water supply
	Rehabilitation and upgrading of water-supply network and water treatment	Improve poorly functioning schemes	Reopen temporarily closed schemes	Reopen permanently closed schemes	Provide water on premises
Capital cost (PRs/person)	2,100	2,100	2,500	3,000	1,600
Annual incremental O&M cost (% of capital cost)	5	5	5	5	5
Annualized capital cost (PRs/person)	247	247	294	352	188
Annual incremental O&M cost (PRs/person)	105	105	125	150	80
Total annual cost per person (PRs)	**352**	**352**	**419**	**502**	**268**

households (2009 prices). A cost of PRs 10,000 per household (or PRs 1,600 per person) is applied in the CBA here to reflect a scheme that provides safe and plentiful water on household premises.

The cost per person of upgrading/rehabilitating piped water-supply schemes will vary depending on the condition of each scheme and the number of people served by each scheme. It is here assumed that on average the cost of improving poorly functioning schemes will be PRs 2,100 per person—the same as the cost of rehabilitation and upgrading of piped water supply in Karachi. The cost of upgrading/rehabilitating temporarily and permanently closed piped water-supply schemes will likely be higher—here assumed to be PRs 2,500 and PRs 3,000, respectively, per person.

Useful life of the water-supply interventions is assumed to be 20 years. Capital cost is discounted at an annual rate of 10 percent. Annual incremental O&M cost is assumed to be 5 percent of capital cost. O&M costs are thus 42 percent of annualized capital costs. Estimated total annual cost per person ranges from PRs 268 for rural water supply on premises to PRs 502 for reopening of permanently closed piped water-supply schemes.

Benefit-Cost Ratios

Benefit-cost ratios (BCRs) for the water-supply interventions are presented in table 8.7. "Low" reflects valuation of health benefits using HCV for child and adult mortality and COI for morbidity. "High" reflects valuation using HCV for child mortality, VSL for adult mortality, and WTP for avoiding morbidity.

Table 8.7 Benefit-Cost Ratios of Household Water-Supply Interventions in Sindh Province

	Karachi piped water supply	Upgrading/rehabilitation of piped water-supply schemes			Rural water supply
	Rehabilitation and upgrading of water-supply network and water treatment	Improve poorly functioning schemes	Reopen temporarily closed schemes	Reopen permanently closed schemes	Provide water on premises
"Low" health benefits					
Health benefits only	2.4	2.4	1.6	1.4	2.5
Health and time-savings benefits	2.4	2.4	2.9	2.4	3.8
Health, time savings, and increased water quantity	4.5	3.2	4.0	3.3	5.4
"High" health benefits					
Health benefits only	3.2	3.2	2.1	1.8	3.3
Health and time-savings benefits	3.2	3.2	3.4	2.8	4.6
Health, time savings, and increased water quantity	5.2	4.0	4.5	3.7	6.2

Note: "Low" reflects valuation of health effects using HCV for mortality and COI for morbidity. "High" reflects using HCV for child mortality, VSL for adult mortality, and WTP for morbidity.

BCRs for the interventions range from 3.3–3.7 for upgrading/rehabilitation of permanently closed piped water schemes to 5.4–6.2 for rural water supply on premises. The BCRs are all greater than one even when only health benefits are included.

At least six million people in Karachi would benefit from rehabilitation and upgrading of the piped water-supply system. About five million people would benefit from improving poorly functioning piped water-supply schemes elsewhere in Sindh. Approximately nine million people in rural areas do not have their water source on premises and would benefit from the rural water-supply intervention. About five million people relied on the now temporarily closed piped water-supply schemes, and 1.7 million on the now permanently closed schemes. These population figures suggest that at least 70 percent of the population in Sindh would benefit from these interventions.

Household Treatment of Drinking Water

About 15 percent of households in Sindh treat their drinking water at POU by an appropriate method. Several methods of household POU treatment of drinking water are available, including boiling of water, chlorination, filter devices, and solar disinfection. Most of the studies reviewed in the meta-analysis studies in table 3.2 assessed the effectiveness of chlorination, filtering and disinfection. Very few studies assessed boiling of water. The most common method of POU treatment in Sindh is, however, boiling of water and this is the most common method practiced worldwide (Rosa and Clasen 2010). However, boiled water is subject to a higher risk of recontamination from hands and utensils (as water is often stored for periods of time before consumed) than, for example, water subjected to chlorination. POU treated drinking water therefore requires hygienic storage and hygienic POU water withdrawal methods.

In a study in Karachi, Luby and others (2001) found a 99.8 percent reduction in coliforms in drinking water among households that received a plastic water storage vessel with a high-quality spout and regular supply of diluted hypochlorite solution for water treatment. Nearly 70 percent of the households used their vessel two years after distribution, while most of the other households' vessel was broken. Also in Karachi, Luby and others (1999) found that only 18–24 percent of household water samples were free of coliforms among households reporting to boil *or* filter their drinking water and 38 percent among households reporting to boil *and* filter their drinking water. Water samples from households with clean kitchens were more than four times more likely to be free of coliforms than samples from households with dirty kitchens.

Clasen and others (2008a) found in a study in rural Vietnam that stored samples of self-reported boiled drinking water contained 97 percent less thermotolerant coliforms (TTC) than the source water. About 37 percent of samples of stored boiled water were free of TTC and 38 percent fell within the low risk category of 1–10 TTC per 100 milliliters (mL) of water. Most households stored the boiled water in closed thermo-flasks. Mean TTC in samples from the thermo-flasks was 1.8 per 100 mL compared to around 8 per 100 mL in samples from plastic jugs and aluminum vessels. In a study in India, Clasen and others (2008b) found that samples of stored self-reported boiled drinking water contained 99 percent less fecal coliforms (FC) than the source water, and 60 percent of stored water samples were free of FC. These improvements in drinking water quality are, according to Clasen and others (2008b), similar to improvements found in studies of chlorination or filtering.

Benefits of Interventions

An effectiveness of 30 percent in reducing diarrheal disease is applied here in the benefit-cost assessment. This is at the low end of effectiveness found in the review and meta-analysis studies by Arnold and Colford (2007), Clasen and others (2007a), Fewtrell and others (2005), and Waddington and Snilstveit (2009) (see table 3.1), and substantially lower than the ≥55 percent reduction in diarrheal disease found by Luby and others (2006) in Karachi. The relatively low rate of effectiveness applied is motivated by the questioning of effectiveness by Cairncross and others (2010).

On the basis of an effectiveness of 30 percent, the health benefits of household drinking water treatment are on average PRs 6,514–7,404 per child younger than five years of age and PRs 160–385 per person five years or older (table 8.8). The reason for the much lower benefits for the population five years or older is the much lower incidence of diarrheal disease and mortality in this population group than among children younger than five years of age.

Costs of Interventions

Cost of household drinking water treatment has three components—namely direct cost of water treatment, time spent on water treatment, and cost of promotion programs to encourage households to treat their drinking water.

Boiling of drinking water is the treatment method most widely practiced in Sindh and is therefore the method assessed here. Assessment is undertaken for children younger than five years of age and older household members separately (table 8.9). It is assumed that 1 liter is boiled per person per day for the population five years or older and 0.5 liters for children younger than five years of age. The estimated cost of boiling is calculated at PRs 1.2 per liter of water. On an annual

Table 8.8 Benefits of Household Drinking Water Treatments in Sindh Province

	Children younger than five years of age	Population 5 years of age and older
"Low" valuation of health benefits	6,514	160
"High" valuation of health benefits	7,404	385

Note: "Low" reflects valuation of health effects using HCV for mortality and COI for morbidity. "High" reflects using HCV for child mortality, VSL for adult mortality, and WTP for morbidity.

Table 8.9 Annual Private Costs per Person Consuming Boiled Drinking Water in Sindh Province

Drinking water boiled for children <5 years (liters/child/day)	0.5
Drinking water boiled for population 5+ years (liters/person/day)	1.0
Time used for boiling drinking water (minutes/household/day)	10
Average household size	6.3
Value of time (% of average wage rate)	50
Average wage rate (PRs/hour)	58.7
Annual cost of boiling drinking water per child <5 years (PRs)	219
Annual cost of boiling drinking water per person 5+ years (PRs)	437
Annual cost of time used for boiling water per person (PRs)	283

basis, this is PRs 219 per year for children younger than five years, and PRs 437 per year for the population five years of age or older. This cost is estimated by assuming that households will boil water by using wood, as this is the predominant fuel used for cooking in Sindh. Stove efficiency is assumed to be 15 percent, reflecting efficiencies of unimproved wood/biomass stoves. Cost of fuel is PRs 5.6 per kilogram (kg), which was the retail price of fuel wood in Karachi in 2009 reported in FBS (2011). Water is assumed to be boiled for 10 minutes. This cost component is less than 10 percent of the cost of bringing water to a boil. If an improved wood/biomass stove is used for boiling, the cost of boiling would be around PRs 131 per child and PRs 262 per person five years or older.

The estimated cost of boiling water is substantially higher than the cost of alternative POU treatment methods in Pakistan (Aziz 2008). The BCRs presented here are thus conservative compared to ratios for alternative methods, assuming effectiveness in reducing diarrheal disease is about the same.

Time used for boiling of drinking water is assumed to be 10 minutes per household per day. This is substantially less time than it takes to bring the required amount of water per household to a boil and the time of boiling, but much of this time can simultaneously be spent on other household activities. Time is valued at 50 percent of the average wage rate. Thus, cost of time used for boiling is PRs 283 per person per year.

Costs of household drinking water treatment include a treatment promotion program. Program cost and assumptions about household response rates are the same as for hand washing (see section on hand washing). Three promotion program scenarios are assessed, with program response rates ranging from 10 to 20 percent (table 8.10).

Studies have evaluated the sustainability of POU treatment around the world. Waddington and Snilstveit (2009) found that studies conducted over longer periods tend to show smaller effectiveness of POU treatment in reducing diarrheal disease than studies of shorter duration, and evidence suggests compliance rates and therefore impact may fall markedly over time. Hunter (2009) reviewed a large number of POU treatment studies, and concluded that use of ceramic filters is especially effective and more sustainable over the long term, compared to other treatment methods assessed (biosand, chlorine, and combined

Table 8.10 POU Drinking Water Treatment Program Response Rates and Annualized Costs in Sindh Province

	Scenario 1	Scenario 2	Scenario 3
Program response rate (% of program targets with behavioral change)	10	15	20
Program cost per program target (US$)	0.40	1.20	5.00
Program cost per target person with behavioral change (US$)	4.00	8.00	25.00
Annualized program cost per person with behavioral change (PRs)			
1 year of POU drinking water treatment	314	628	1,961
2 years of POU drinking water treatment	181	362	1,130
3 years of POU drinking water treatment	126	252	789

Note: US$1 = PRs 78.44 in 2009. Discount rate is 10%.

coagulant-chlorine). Benefits and costs of POU treatment is therefore evaluated for practice sustained for a period ranging from one to three years. Annualized program cost is PRs 126–1,961 per person, depending on program response rate and duration of sustained POU treatment behavior.

Benefit-Cost Ratios

Table 8.11 presents the BCRs of household drinking water treatment (that is, boiling) for children younger than five years. Benefits of the program are reduced diarrheal illness and mortality. "Low" reflects valuation of health effects using the HCV for child and adult mortality and the COI approach for morbidity. "High" reflects valuation using HCV for child mortality, VSL for adult mortality, and WTP for morbidity. BCRs are presented for response rates to the promotion program; these rates range from 10 to 20 percent, with drinking water treatment sustained for 1–3 years.

All the BCRs are greater than 1 and increase with the length of time drinking water treatment is sustained and decline with higher program response rate due to the higher program cost per person to induce behavioral change.

A drinking water treatment promotion program targeting treatment for young children may also promote drinking water treatment in the population five years or older with or without additional program promotion cost. In the case of no additional program costs, the BCR is 0.2 when benefits are valued using the HCV for mortality and COI for morbidity, and 0.5 when benefits are valued using VSL for mortality and WTP for morbidity. These estimates are based on the same benefit and cost parameters as for children younger than five years old, except that the cost of water boiling is higher and program promotion cost is assumed to be zero for this population group.[4] In the event that additional cost of promotion is incurred, the BCRs would be lower than those presented above. However, if other treatment options at lower cost are used, as presented in Aziz (2008), the BCRs for the population five years or older may very well be greater than one.

Table 8.11 Benefit-Cost Ratios of Household Drinking Water Treatment for Health Protection of Children Younger than Five Years Old in Sindh Province

	Low			High		
Program response rate (%)	10	15	20	10	15	20
Water treatment is sustained for 1 year	8.0	5.8	2.6	9.1	6.6	3.0
Water treatment is sustained for 2 years	9.5	7.5	4.0	10.8	8.6	4.5
Water treatment is sustained for 3 years	10.4	8.6	5.0	11.8	9.8	5.7

Note: "Low" reflects valuation of health effects using HCV for mortality and COI for morbidity. "High" reflects using HCV for child mortality, VSL for adult mortality, and WTP for morbidity. Benefits and costs are discounted at an annual rate of 10%.

Table 8.12 Assessment of Benefits and Costs for Selected Sanitation Interventions in Sindh Province

Interventions	Descriptions	Improvements and benefits
Karachi sewerage improvements	Improvement of sewerage networks and sewage collection	Improved community-wide sanitation and hygiene conditions
Household sewerage connection	Connecting household toilets to sewerage network in small cities and towns	Reduced risk of cross-contamination of water supply
Sanitation upgrade	Upgrade to higher levels of sanitation (for example flush toilet with safe drainage)	Reduced risk of disease transmission
Household access to nonshared toilet facility	Improved toilet facility to households without access to toilet	Phase out open defecation in rural areas, small cities and towns
		Improved community-wide sanitation and hygiene conditions
		Reduced risk of contamination of water supply
		Reduced risk of disease transmission
	Improved toilet facility to households currently sharing a facility with other households	Access to private toilet facility Improved hygiene conditions

Household Sanitation

This section assesses five sanitation interventions (table 8.12). These interventions likely represent only a subset of sanitation interventions needed in Sindh to promote and ensure good hygienic household and community conditions, minimize risks of contamination of household water supply (wells, piped water networks), minimize risks of fecal-oral transmission for protection of health, and protect water and land resources and the broader environment. Wastewater treatment—necessary to achieve some of these objectives and coastal protection—is not assessed here because of data constraints.

The vast majority of households in Karachi have a flush toilet with connection to a sewerage network. However, the sewerage networks in many parts of Karachi suffer from poor connectivity and broken and undersized sections with much wastewater consequently discharged to the drainage system for storm water. The consequences of this situation are high risks of cross-contamination of the piped water distribution network and contamination of floodwater by raw sewage during the rainy season (ADB 2005). One of the five sanitation interventions assessed in the CBA here is therefore improvements of sewerage networks and sewage collection in Karachi.

In small cities and towns, more than 70 percent of households with a toilet facility have flush toilets. About 20–25 percent of these flush toilets drain to other places than a sewer, septic tank, or sanitary pit. One of the sanitation interventions is therefore connection of these households to a sewerage system.

A large majority of households with other toilets in small cities, towns, and rural area have toilets classified as unimproved. This includes more than half of households with flush toilets in rural areas, which drain to other places than to sewer, septic tank, or sanitary pit. Households with unimproved toilet facilities can benefit from an upgrading to an improved facility. As a flush toilet appears to be the toilet facility desired by most of the population, the upgrade assessed is installing a flush toilet with connection to at least a septic tank or sanitary pit (including connecting existing flush toilets to at least a septic tank or sanitary pit).

Similarly, for households without access to a toilet facility (that is, more than 50 percent of the rural population), or for households currently sharing a toilet facility (15 percent of the entire population), the intervention assessed is installing a nonshared flush toilet with connection to at least a septic tank or sanitary pit.

Benefits of Interventions

Key benefit parameters of the sanitation interventions are presented in table 8.13. An intervention effectiveness of 15–35 percent in reducing diarrheal disease is applied. The upper bound is within the range reported by Fewtrell and others (2005), Waddington and Snilstveit (2009), and Cairncross and others (2010).

Table 8.13 Key Benefit Parameters of Sanitation Interventions

	Karachi sewerage improvements	Household sewerage connection	Sanitation upgrade	Access to nonshared toilet facility	
	Improvement of sewerage networks and sewage collection	Connecting household toilets to sewerage network in small cities and towns	Upgrade to higher levels of sanitation	Improved toilet facility to households without access to toilet	Improved toilet facility to households currently sharing a toilet
Intervention effectiveness (% reduction in diarrheal disease)	20	20	30	35	15
Access time savings per person per day (minutes)	0	0	0	5	3
Value of time savings (% of average wage rate)	n.a.	n.a.	n.a.	50	50
Average wage rate (PRs/hour)	n.a.	n.a.	n.a.	36	54

Note: n.a. = not applicable.

Sustainability and Poverty Alleviation • http://dx.doi.org/10.1596/978-1-4648-0452-6

Providing an improved toilet to households currently without access to a toilet (open defecation) is assumed to have the highest effectiveness, followed by the sanitation upgrade intervention. The effectiveness of an improved, nonshared toilet facility for those currently sharing a toilet with other households is assumed to be 15 percent. This effectiveness is applied to two households for every household receiving the intervention, assuming that two households are currently sharing a toilet. An effectiveness of 20 percent is applied to the two *sewerage* improvements and connection interventions. This may be a conservative estimate but some of health benefits of avoiding water-supply contamination from sewage are already captured in the water-supply interventions.

Households benefiting from access to a nonshared toilet facility will benefit from some time savings—that is, five minutes saved per person per day for not having to rely on open defecation and three minutes per person per day for not having to use a facility shared by multiple households. These time savings benefits are valued at 50 percent of wage rates in Sindh for the population 15 years and older. A weighted average of urban and rural wage rates is applied to households currently sharing a toilet, and the rural wage rate is applied to households currently without access to toilet, because most of these households are rural (see the third section of chapter 2 of this book).

Estimated total annual health and nonhealth benefits of the sanitation interventions are in the range of PRs 679–1,508 per person when health benefits are valued using the HCV for child and adult mortality and the COI approach for morbidity. The estimated benefits are in the range of PRs 888–1,875 when using HCV for child mortality, VSL for adult mortality, and WTP for avoiding morbidity (table 8.14). Health benefits constitute 78–100 percent of total benefits.

Costs of Interventions

Cost of sanitation interventions includes initial capital cost and incremental O&M cost (table 8.15). ADB (2005) presents potential sanitation infrastructure projects in Karachi amounting to around US$110–120 million simply to address deficiencies in existing sewer and drainage infrastructure. This includes rehabilitation and strengthening of the existing sewer network (US$80–85 million), and rehabilitation of the existing network for storm water drainage and interconnections with the sewer network (US$30–35 million). This capital cost amounts to around PRs 1,900 per capita (2009 prices), assuming the improvements would benefit 6 million or somewhat less than half of Karachi's population.

PIDE (2002) presents a review and analysis of the costs of sanitation projects in each province of Pakistan. Cost of public sewer connection was in the range of PRs 8,400–15,000 per household in Sindh and Punjab (2009 prices). A midpoint cost of about PRs 12,000 per household or PRs 1,900 per person is applied in the CBA here for sewerage connection in small cities and towns.

A flush toilet is the most common household toilet facility in both urban and rural areas of Sindh. According to PIDE (2002), the cost of a flush toilet

Table 8.14 Benefits of Sanitation Interventions in Sindh Province

	Karachi sewerage improvements	Household sewerage connection	Sanitation upgrade	Access to nonshared toilet facility	
	Improvement of sewerage networks and sewage collection	Connecting household toilets to sewerage network in small cities and towns	Upgrade to higher levels of sanitation	Improved toilet facility to households without access to toilet	Improved toilet facility to households currently sharing a toilet
Annual health benefits per person (PRs) ("low" valuation)	679	679	1,018	1,188	1,018
Annual health benefits per person (PRs) ("high" valuation)	888	888	1,332	1,554	1,332
Annual value of time savings per person (PRs)	0	0	0	320	284
Total annual benefit per person (PRs) "low"	**679**	**679**	**1,018**	**1,508**	**1,302**
Total annual benefit per person (PRs) "high"	**888**	**888**	**1,332**	**1875**	**1,616**

Note: "Low" reflects using HCV for child and adult mortality and COI for morbidity. "High" reflects using HCV for child mortality, VSL for adult mortality, and WTP for morbidity.

Table 8.15 Costs of Sanitation Interventions

	Karachi sewerage improvements	Household sewerage connection	Sanitation upgrade	Access to nonshared toilet facility	
	Improvement of sewerage networks and sewage collection	Connecting household toilets to sewerage network in small cities and towns	Upgrade to higher levels of sanitation	Improved toilet facility to households without access to toilet	Improved toilet facility to households currently sharing a toilet
Capital cost (PRs/person)	1,900	1,900	1,600	1,600	1,600
Annual incremental O&M cost (% of capital cost)	5	5	5	5	5
Annualized capital cost (PRs/person)	223	223	210	210	210
Annual incremental O&M cost (PRs/person)	95	95	80	80	80
Total annual cost per person (PRs)	**318**	**318**	**290**	**290**	**290**

connected to a twin pit was around PRs 10,000 per household or PRs 1,600 per person (2009 prices). This cost is applied to the sanitation upgrade and the access to a nonshared toilet facility.

The useful life of the first two sewerage network improvements and connections interventions is assumed to be 20 years, and 15 years for the interventions involving installation of a flush toilet. Capital cost is discounted at an annual rate of 10 percent. The annual incremental O&M cost is assumed to be 5 percent of capital cost. O&M costs are thus 38–42 percent of annualized capital costs. Estimated total annual cost per person is in the range of PRs 290–318.

Benefit-Cost Ratios

BCRs for the sanitation interventions are presented in table 8.16. "Low" reflects valuation of health benefits using HCV for child and adult mortality and COI for morbidity. "High" reflects valuation using HCV for child mortality, VSL for adult mortality, and WTP for avoiding morbidity.

BCRs for the interventions range from 2.1–2.8 for the sewerage improvements and connection interventions to 5.2–6.5 for improved toilet facility to households currently without access to a toilet.

As much as half or more of the population in Karachi could benefit from the sewerage improvement intervention. About 1.2 million would benefit from connecting flush toilets to sewerage in small cities and towns. Approximately 6 million people mostly in rural areas would benefit from sanitation upgrade. About 10 million people in rural areas currently without access to a toilet facility would benefit from improved toilet facilities. More than 5 million people currently sharing a toilet facility with other households would benefit from a nonshared toilet facility.

Table 8.16 Benefit-Cost Ratios of Sanitation Interventions in Sindh Province

	Karachi sewerage improvements	Household sewerage connection	Sanitation upgrade	Access to nonshared toilet facility	
	Improvement of sewerage networks and sewage collection	Connecting household toilets to sewerage network in small cities and towns	Upgrade to higher levels of sanitation	Improved toilet facility to households without access to toilet	Improved toilet facility to households currently sharing a toilet
"Low" health benefits					
Health benefits only	2.1	2.1	3.5	4.1	3.5
Health and time-savings benefits	2.1	2.1	3.5	5.2	4.5
"High" health benefits					
Health benefits only	2.8	2.8	4.6	5.4	4.6
Health and time-savings benefits	2.8	2.8	4.6	6.5	5.6

Note: "Low" reflects valuation of health effects using HCV for mortality and COI for morbidity. "High" reflects using HCV for child mortality, VSL for adult mortality, and WTP for morbidity.

Hand Washing with Soap

Studies of the effectiveness of improved hand washing with soap have assessed reduction in incidence of diarrheal illness (or reduced prevalence during a specific time period) among young children resulting from improved hand-washing practices among mothers and caretakers, as well as among older children and adults resulting from their own hand washing. Hand washing by mothers and caretakers of young children involves hand washing with soap at critical times such as after going to the toilet, after cleaning a child, and before preparing meals and feeding a child. The meta-analyses of these studies by Curtis and Cairncross (2003) and Fewtrell and others (2005) suggest that the reduction in incidence of diarrheal illness is about the same for children younger than five years of age and the population five years of age or older. However, as baseline diarrheal disease incidence and mortality is much higher among young children than among older children and adults, a CBA is here undertaken separately for children younger than five years of age and the population five years of age or older.

Benefits of Interventions

An effectiveness of 40 percent in reducing diarrheal disease from improved hand washing with soap is applied. This is approximately the midpoint of effectiveness found in the review and meta-analysis studies by Fewtrell and others (2005), Curtis and Cairncross (2003), Ejemot and others (2009), and Waddington and Snilstveit (2009). However, the effectiveness applied is lower than the more than 50 percent reduction in diarrheal incidence from hand washing with soap found in Karachi by Luby and others (2004, 2006).

On the basis of an effectiveness of 40%, the health benefits of improved hand washing with soap are on average PRs 8,686–9,872 per child younger than five years of age and PRs 214–513 per person five years or older (table 8.17). The reason for the much lower benefits for the population five years or older is the much lower incidence of diarrheal disease and mortality in this population group than among children younger than five years of age.

Cost of Interventions

The cost of hand washing with soap has three components—namely, the cost of soap and water, the time spent on hand washing, and the cost of promotion programs to encourage households to wash their hands with soap.

Table 8.17 Benefits of Hand Washing with Soap in Sindh Province

	Children younger than five years of age	Population 5 years of age and older
"Low" valuation of health benefits	8,686	214
"High" valuation of health benefits	9,872	513

Note: "Low" reflects valuation of health effects using HCV for mortality and COI for morbidity. "High" reflects using HCV for child mortality, VSL for adult mortality, and WTP for morbidity.

Table 8.18 Annual Private Costs per Person of Improved Hand Washing in Sindh Province

Water use for improved hand washing (liters/person/day)	3
Soap consumption (soaps/person/month)	1.2
Cost per soap (PRs)	22
Time used for hand washing (minutes/person/day)	5
Value of time (% of average wage rate)	50
Average wage rate (PRs/hour)	58.7
Annual cost of water per person (PRs)	44
Annual cost of soap per person (PRs)	317
Annual cost of time used for hand washing per person (PRs)	893
Total annual private cost per person (PRs)	**1,253**

Table 8.18 presents the estimated annual costs of soap and water and time spent on hand washing. Water use for improved hand washing is assumed to be 3 liters per person per day, or 1.1 m³ per person per year. The cost of water supply to household premises is assumed to be PRs 40 per m³. Water collection time is not included because more than 80 percent of households in Pakistan have water on premises (NIPS/Macro 2008). Luby and others (2009) report soap purchases of about one bar of soap per person per month in a Karachi community that previously participated in a hand-washing promotion program. Soap distribution to households during the promotion program was about 1.4 bars of soap per person per month. Consumption of 1.2 bars of soap per person per month is applied here. The price of a bar of soap (Lifebuoy) was PRs 22 in 2009, as reported for Karachi in FBS (2011).

It is also assumed that improved hand washing takes five minutes per day. This time is valued at 50 percent of the average wage rate. Thus, total private cost of improved hand washing with soap is estimated at PRs 1,253 per person per year.

Promotion program cost per household depends critically on household response rate to the program. Three hand-washing programs that provide program costs and response rates are presented in table 8.19. Response rates—that is, improved hand washing behavior—range from 10 to 18 percent of targeted households. Program cost ranges from around US$0.40 to US$5 per targeted household, and thus from US$3.50 to US$28 per household with improved behavior. The CBA here therefore presents benefits and costs of promotion programs with response rates ranging from 10 to 20 percent (table 8.20).

Promotion program cost per household on an annualized basis also depends on the sustainability of improved hand-washing practices among those responding to the program. Luby and others (2009) found that households that participated in a hand washing with soap promotion program in Karachi demonstrated better hand-washing technique than nonparticipating households two years after the program, but showed no difference in soap purchases and diarrhea incidence. However, a study of communities in six countries in Asia and Africa found that improved hygiene behavior from intervention programs is sustained several years

Table 8.19 A Review of Costs and Effectiveness of Hand-Washing Promotion Programs in Selected Countries

	Guatemala	Thailand		Burkino Faso
Target area	National	Rural villages		One city
Targeted households	With children younger than 5 years old	All	All	With children younger than 3 years old
Number of targeted households	1,570,000	10,000	6,550	38,600
Duration of program implementation	1 year	3–4 months	3–4 months	3 years
Response rate (% of target population)	10	11	16	18
Program cost ('000 US$)	560	6	7.7	194
Program cost per target household (US$)	0.4	0.6	1.2	5.0
Program cost per target household with behavioral change (US$)	**3.6**	**5.4**	**7.4**	**28**

Sources: Derived from Borghi and others (2002), Pinfold and Horan (1996), and Saade, Bateman, and Bendahmane (2001).

Table 8.20 Hand-Washing Program Response Rates and Annualized Costs in Sindh Province

	Scenario 1	Scenario 2	Scenario 3
Program response rate (% of program targets with behavioral change)	10	15	20
Program cost per program target (US$)	0.40	1.20	5.00
Program cost per target person with behavioral change (US$)	4.00	8.00	25.00
Annualized program cost per person with behavioral change (PRs)			
1 year of improved hand washing	314	628	1,961
2 years of improved hand washing	181	362	1,130
3 years of improved hand washing	126	252	789

Note: US$1 = PRs 78.44 in year 2009. Discount rate is 10%.

after interventions (Shordt and Cairncross 2004). Therefore, benefits and costs of hand washing with soap are evaluated here for practice sustained for a period ranging from one to three years.

Three hand-washing promotion program scenarios are applied in the CBA here in terms of program costs, household response rates, and sustained duration of improved hand washing with soap (table 8.20). These scenarios are in line with the findings from the review of programs in table 8.19. Program cost per person (mother or caretaker of children younger than five years of age) with behavioral change ranges from US$4 to US$25. This translates to an annualized cost of PRs 126–1,961 per person with improved hand washing because of the promotion program, depending on program response rate and sustained duration of improved hand washing.

Benefit-Cost Ratios
BCRs of a promotion program for improved hand washing with soap among mothers and caretakers of young children are presented in table 8.21. Benefits of

Table 8.21 Benefit-Cost Ratios of Hand Washing with Soap for Health Protection of Children Younger than Five Years in Sindh Province

	Low			High		
Promotion program response rate (%)	10	15	20	10	15	20
Improved hand washing is sustained for 1 year	5.5	4.6	2.7	6.3	5.2	3.1
Improved hand washing is sustained for 2 years	6.1	5.4	3.6	6.9	6.1	4.1
Improved hand washing is sustained for 3 years	6.3	5.8	4.3	7.2	6.6	4.8

Note: "Low" reflects valuation of health effects using HCV for mortality and COI for morbidity. "High" reflects using HCV for child mortality, VSL for adult mortality, and WTP for morbidity. Benefits and costs are discounted at an annual rate of 10%.

the program are reduced diarrheal illness and mortality in children younger than five years of age.[5] "Low" reflects valuation of health effects using the HCV for child and adult mortality and the COI approach for morbidity. "High" reflects valuation using HCV for child mortality, VSL for adult mortality, and WTP for morbidity.

BCRs are presented for promotion program response rates ranging from 10 to 20 percent, with improved hand washing sustained for one to three years. All BCRs are greater than one and increase with the length of time improved hand washing is sustained, and decline with a higher program response rate because of the higher program cost per person to induce behavioral change.

A hand-washing promotion program targeting mothers and caretakers of young children may also promote improved hand-washing practices with soap among the population five years or older, with or without additional program promotion cost. In the case of no additional program costs, the BCR is 0.2 when benefits are valued using the HCV for mortality and COI for morbidity, and 0.4 when benefits are valued using VSL for mortality and WTP for morbidity. These estimates are based on the same benefit and cost parameters as for children younger than five years old, except that program promotion cost is assumed to be zero for this population group.[6] In the event that additional cost of promotion is incurred, the BCR would be lower than those presented. The reason for the low BCRs for the population five years or older is the much lower incidence of diarrheal disease and mortality in this population group than among children younger than five years old.

Outdoor Air Pollution

An increasing number of CBA studies from developing countries shed light on potential benefits and costs of various interventions to improve urban air quality. These studies include the following:

- For China, Blumberg and others (2006)
- For Bogotá, Colombia, Larsen (2005)
- For Mexico City, Stevens, Wilson, and Hammitt (2005)
- For Lima, Peru, ECON (2006)

- For Dakar, Senegal, Larsen (2007a)
- For the Philippines, Larsen (2009)
- For the Middle East and North Africa region, Larsen (2011a).

Larsen, Hutton, and Khanna (2009) reviewed most of these programs. The focus of these studies is on particulate matter (PM) as PM is considered the pollutant with the largest health effects in most urban areas. Interventions evaluated in these studies are control of emissions from motorized transport. There are also CBA studies in developing countries evaluating the control of emission from industry and power plants. Low-sulfur diesel and fuel oil.

This book estimates that the health benefits of using 500 parts per million (ppm) diesel in road transport amounts to at least US$2.3–3.5 per barrel of diesel for light diesel vehicles and large diesel buses and trucks used primarily within Karachi. Lowering the sulfur content further to 50 ppm would provide additional health benefits of US$3.0–4.6 per barrel. These estimates are based on PM emission reductions of 20 percent and 33 percent for diesel with 500-ppm and 50-ppm sulfur content, respectively.

The additional cost of providing 500-ppm and 50-ppm sulfur diesel depends on several factors related to cost of refinery upgrading and market conditions. A study of 145 refineries in 12 Asian countries estimated the cost of refinery upgrading to produce lower sulfur diesel. Bringing diesel sulfur content from mostly >5,000 ppm to 500 ppm would cost an additional US$1.3–2.4 per barrel. Bringing the sulfur content from 3,000 to 500 ppm would cost US$0.50–1.10 per barrel. In addition, bringing diesel sulfur content from 500 to 50 ppm would cost an additional US$2–3 per barrel (Enstrat 2003). In the wholesale petroleum product market in the United States in the past two years, the price difference between >500-ppm diesel and 15–500-ppm diesel was on average about US$2.7 per barrel and the difference between 15–500-ppm diesel and <15 ppm diesel was on average US$1.5 per barrel (EIA 2012). An incremental cost range of US$1.5–2.5 per barrel for lowering the sulfur content to 500 ppm and US$2–3 per barrel for lowering sulfur from 500 to 50 ppm is applied in the assessment in this book.

Based in the potential reductions of particulate matter emissions and the costs of reducing the sulfur content in diesel described above, estimated health benefits per dollar spent (that is, benefit-cost ratio) on cleaner diesel are in the range of about US$1–1.5 for light duty diesel vehicles and US$1.5–2.4 for large buses and trucks for both 500-ppm and 50-ppm diesel (figure 8.1).

The majority of diesel vehicles in the high-income countries of the European Union are fitted with EURO 3–5 PM emission-control technology. Most diesel vehicles in Pakistan do not comply with EURO 1 PM emission standards because of high sulfur content in diesel. Now that diesel with 500-ppm sulfur content will be the norm in Pakistan this year, new (and secondhand imported) diesel vehicles can comply with EURO 2 emission standards. This will reduce PM emissions quite substantially even compared with EURO 1 standards (figures A.2, A.3).

Figure 8.1 Benefit-Cost Ratios of 500-ppm and 50-ppm Sulfur Diesel in Karachi

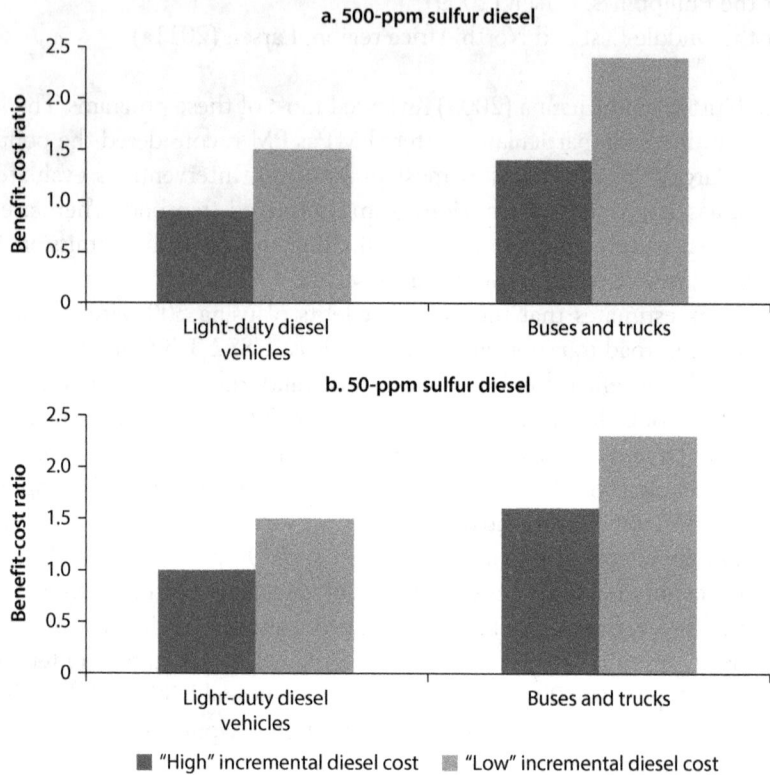

a. 500-ppm sulfur diesel

b. 50-ppm sulfur diesel

■ "High" incremental diesel cost   ■ "Low" incremental diesel cost

Reducing sulfur in diesel to 50 ppm would allow implementation of Euro 4 standards. PM emissions per km driven by Euro 1 compliant diesel passenger and light commercial vehicles (LCV) are 4.2–5.6 times higher than PM emissions from Euro 4 compliant vehicles (figure 8.2). For heavy-duty diesel vehicles, the situation is even worse. Euro 1 compliant vehicles emit 18–30 times more PM per kWh of engine power than Euro 4 compliant vehicles (figure 8.3).

Retrofitting of In-Use Diesel Vehicles

PM control technologies can effectively be installed on in-use diesel vehicles, such as diesel oxidation catalysts (DOC) and diesel particulate filters (DPF), once low-sulfur diesel is available. DOCs require a maximum of 500-ppm sulfur in diesel and DPFs require a maximum of 50-ppm to function effectively. Pakistan can therefore equip diesel vehicles with DOCs this year.

DOCs had been installed in more than 50 million diesel passenger vehicles and more than 1.5 million buses and trucks worldwide already five–six years ago (UNEP 2006). All new on-road diesel vehicles in the United States and Canada are equipped with a high-efficiency DPF. In addition, all new diesel cars and vans in the EU were equipped with DPF from 2009. Worldwide, more than 250,000 heavy-duty vehicles have been retrofitted with DPF (UNEP 2009). DOCs and

Figure 8.2 European Union Diesel Vehicle Emission Standards for PM
Grams per kilometer traveled

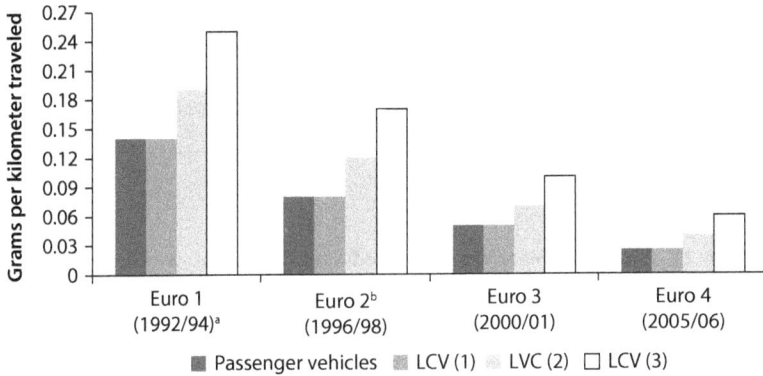

Source: Adapted from www.dieselnet.com.
a. The earlier year is for passenger vehicles. The later year is for light commercial vehicles (LCV) by weight class 1–3. b. Applicable for IDI engines. Slightly less stringent limits apply for DI engines.

Figure 8.3 European Union Heavy-Duty Diesel Engines Emission Standards for PM
Grams per kilowatt-hour

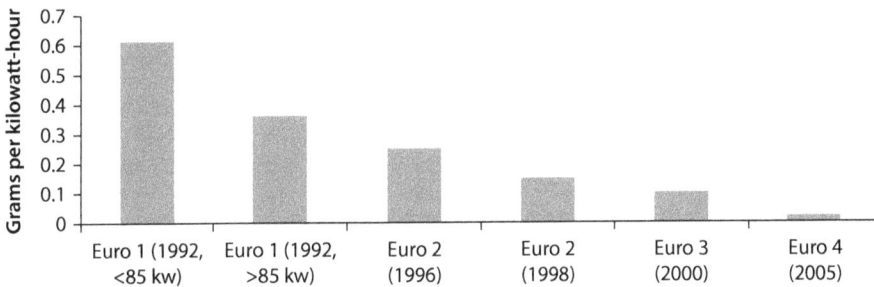

Source: Adapted from www.dieselnet.com

DPFs have also been used for retrofitting of buses and trucks in many countries and locations on a wider scale or in demonstration projects (table 8.22).

Retrofitting Euro 1 or pre-Euro 1 diesel vehicles with a DOC generally reduces PM emissions by 20–30 percent, although reductions of as much as 20–50 percent have been reported. A DPF reduces PM emissions by more than 80 percent (table 8.23). Potential candidates for a DOC, or a DPF once 50-ppm sulfur diesel becomes available, are high usage commercial diesel vehicles that are on the roads of Karachi today and primarily used within the city. Health benefits of retrofitting per vehicle per year are estimated in this book in the range of about US$95–568 for a DOC and US$216–1,295 for a DPF depending on type of vehicle and annual usage (table 8.24). These estimates are based on a PM emission reduction of 25 percent for DOCs and 85 percent for DPFs.

Table 8.22 Use of Diesel Oxidation Catalysts and Diesel Particulate Filters on Diesel Vehicles for Particulate Matter Emission Control in Selected Countries

Technology	Examples of implementation
DPF on new diesel vehicles	Canada, Europe, United States
DOC and DPF retrofitting of in-use vehicles	Chile; China; Europe; Hong Kong, SAR China; India; Japan; Mexico; Taiwan, China; Thailand; United States

Source: UNEP 2006.

Table 8.23 Particulate Matter Emission Reductions from Retrofitting of In-Use Diesel Vehicles in Karachi

	Vehicle PM emission reductions	Main sources of data
Diesel oxidation catalyst (DOC)	20–30% and 20–50%	MECA (2009)
Diesel particulate filter (DPF)	>85%	UNEP (2009)

Table 8.24 Estimated Health Benefits of Retrofitting Diesel Vehicles in Karachi with DOC and DPF in Sindh Province

	Diesel oxidation catalyst (DOC) Vehicle usage		Diesel particulate filter (DPF) Vehicle usage	
	35,000 km/ year	70,000 km/ year	35,000 km/ year	70,000 km/ year
Heavy-duty trucks	284	568	647	1,295
Large buses	208	417	475	949
Minibuses	133	265	302	604
Light-duty vans	95	189	216	432

A DOC costs US$1,000–2,000 and a DPF as much as US$6,000–10,000 (MECA 2009; UNEP 2009; USEPA 2012). The expected number of years that the vehicle will continue to be in use and years that the devices will be effective is therefore an important consideration. Estimated health benefits of a DOC only exceed its cost (that is, benefit-cost ratio >1 for retrofitting of very high usage vehicles (for example, 70,000 km/year) and a relatively long useful life of the DOC (for example, 10 years). If the DOC's useful life is only 5 years, then health benefits only exceed the cost of the DOC for heavy-duty trucks even when vehicles are used 70,000 km per year (figure 8.4).[7] Estimated health benefits of a DPF is currently lower than its cost for all classes of diesel vehicles, but should be reassessed once 50–ppm sulfur diesel is available in the future.

Conversion of Light-Duty Diesel Vehicles to CNG

Health benefits of compressed natural gas (CNG) conversion are estimated in this book in the range of about US$455–1,288 per vehicle per year depending on type of vehicle and annual usage (table 8.25).

Figure 8.4 Benefit-Cost Ratios of Retrofitting In-Use Diesel Vehicles with DOC in Sindh Province

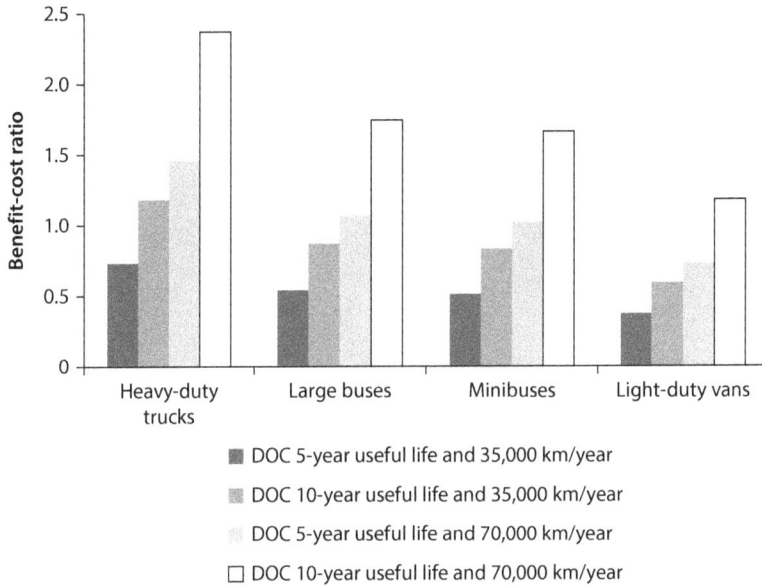

- DOC 5-year useful life and 35,000 km/year
- DOC 10-year useful life and 35,000 km/year
- DOC 5-year useful life and 70,000 km/year
- DOC 10-year useful life and 70,000 km/year

Table 8.25 Estimated Health Benefits of Conversion to CNG

	Vehicle usage	
	35,000 km/year	70,000 km/year
Minibuses	644	1,288
Light-duty vans	455	909

Conversion of such vehicles to CNG in Pakistan is reported to cost in the range of PRs 150,000–200,000 per vehicle, or US$1,900–2,550 at exchange rates in 2009 (*Daily Times* 2012). Applying a cost of PRs 200,000, estimated health benefits per dollar spent on conversion to CNG (that is, BCR) are in the range of US$1–3 for diesel minibuses and US$0.7–2.2 for light duty diesel vans depending on the length of expected remaining useful life of vehicles and their annual usage (figure 8.5).[8] The BCRs for vans are somewhat lower than for minibuses because of a difference in estimated PM emissions per kilometer of vehicle use.

Household Air Pollution

An increasing number of CBA studies from developing countries shed light on potential benefits and costs of controlling household air pollution (HAP) from cooking with solid fuels such as coal, charcoal, wood, and other biomass

Figure 8.5 Benefit-Cost Ratios of Converting In-Use Diesel-Fueled Minibuses and Vans to CNG

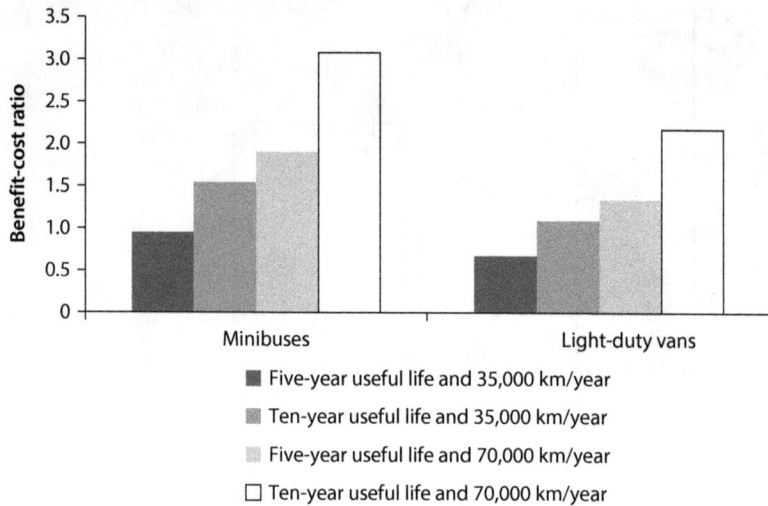

fuels (for example, agricultural residues, animal dung, and straw/shrubs/grass). Recent CBAs include the following:

- a global-regional study (Hutton and others 2006)
- a global-regional cost-effectiveness study (Mehta and Shahpar 2004) and studies of the following regions:
  - Colombia (Larsen 2005)
  - Nicaragua (World Bank 2010)
  - Peru (Larsen and Strukova 2006)
  - the Philippines (Larsen 2009)
  - the Sundarbans of India (Larsen 2011b)
  - Uganda (Habermehl 2007)

Habermehl presents a CBA for improved wood and charcoal stoves, and the other studies look at improved wood stoves as well as switching to cleaner fuels such as liquefied petroleum gas (LPG). These studies all find that the benefits of replacing unimproved wood stoves with improved wood stoves by far exceeds the cost of stoves and stove promotion programs. For replacing wood stoves with LPG stoves, the studies show however mixed results depending primarily on estimates of the value of wood/biomass savings. Larsen, Hutton, and Khanna (2009) review most of these studies.

Interventions
Benefits and costs that are quantified and those not quantified in this chapter are presented in table 8.26.

Table 8.26 Benefits and Costs of Assessed Interventions in Sindh Province

Interventions	Benefits quantified	Public costs quantified	Private costs quantified	Benefits and costs not quantified
Improved wood/ biomass stoves for cooking	Health improvements; reduced wood/ biomass consumption; reduced cooking time	Promotion program	Purchase of stove	Environmental benefits of reduced wood/ biomass consumption; household status benefits; reduced fatigue and physical ailments from fuel collection
LPG stoves for cooking	Health improvements; reduced wood/ biomass consumption; reduced cooking time	Promotion program	Purchase of stove and LPG	Environmental costs and benefits of fuel switching (for example, greenhouse gas emission implications); household status benefits; reduced fatigue and physical ailments from fuel collection

Benefits of Interventions

An improved wood or biomass cooking stove reduces immediate exposure to smoke. It has higher fuel efficiency and cleaner fuel burning than an unimproved stove, and may be attached to a chimney or hood to vent smoke from the indoor environment to the outside. Most previous CBA studies evaluate an improved stove that reduces the health effects of HAP from wood/biomass fuels by 30–70 percent relative to the use of an unimproved wood/biomass stove. An LPG stove eliminates the remaining health effects of wood/biomass fuel use.

Benefits are here assessed for an improved wood/biomass stove of such characteristics that it reduces the risk of health effects of HAP from solid fuels by 50 percent compared to the use of an unimproved wood/biomass stove. Switching from such an improved wood/biomass stove to LPG would eliminate the remaining health effects of HAP from solid fuels—that is, by another 50 percent relative to the health effects of using unimproved wood/biomass stoves. Switching directly from an unimproved wood/biomass stove to LPG would remove 100 percent of the health effects of HAP from solid fuels. Table 8.27 presents these intervention scenarios, with $(C) = (A) + (B)$.

Most CBA studies also evaluate nonhealth benefits of improved wood/ biomass stoves or LPG stoves. These benefits may include reduced wood/ biomass use and time savings from reduced cooking time associated with improved wood/biomass stoves or LPG stoves, and potential environmental benefits arising from reduced need for fuel wood.

An improved wood/biomass stove is assumed to reduce fuel consumption by 40 percent relative to consumption by an unimproved stove. This is a conservative assumption relative to many improved stoves available that may save as much as 50–60 percent of fuel consumption. Switching from an improved wood/biomass stove to LPG would result in another 60 percent wood/biomass fuel savings relative to an unimproved wood/biomass stove (table 8.27).

Studies have also found that cooking with an improved wood/biomass stove or LPG/natural gas stove saves cooking time relative to cooking with an unimproved stove. Siddiqui and others 2009 report that daily fuel burning time for cooking in a semirural community outside Karachi was 30 minutes less in

Table 8.27 Benefits of Interventions in Sindh Province

	Improved instead of unimproved wood/ biomass stove (a)	LPG instead of improved stove (b)	LPG instead of unimproved stove (c)
Effectiveness (% reduction in health effects)	50	50	100
Wood/biomass savings (%)	40	60	100
Time savings (reduced cooking time in minutes per day)	20	20	40

households using natural gas than in households using wood, and that time spent in the kitchen was 40 minutes less. It is here therefore assumed that an LPG stove would provide time savings of 40 minutes per household per day relative to an unimproved wood/biomass stove and 20 minutes per household per day relative to an improved wood/biomass stove. An improved wood/biomass stove would thus provide 20 minutes of time savings per day relative to an unimproved wood/biomass stove (table 8.27).

When estimating the potential health benefits of controlling HAP from household use of solid fuels, consideration must be given to cooking practices, smoke ventilation characteristics of dwellings, and type of stoves used by households. Cooking practices and smoke ventilation characteristics of dwellings (such as conditions of exposure to HAP) can be incorporated in a CBA by applying a ventilation factor as applied earlier in this book. Thus, each of the three aforementioned interventions is evaluated for two different household conditions, one in which households are cooking indoors (ventilation factor = 1.0) and one in which households are cooking outdoors (ventilation factor = 0.5). These ventilation factors (VFs) are applied to the risk of health effects from use of wood and other biomass fuels when estimating the health benefits of HAP control.

The health benefits of interventions in indoor and outdoor cooking environments ($i = 1,2$) are given by the following set of equations:

$$B_i = \beta H_i \text{ for } i = 1,2 \tag{8.5}$$

$$H = H_1 + H_2 \tag{8.6}$$

$$H_1/P_1 = VF_1{}^* H_2/P_2 \tag{8.7}$$

where B_i is the monetary value of health benefits of interventions; β is the percentage reduction in estimated health effects of HAP from interventions; H_i is the health effects of HAP in monetary terms (before interventions), with H as estimated earlier in this book; P_i is the population cooking outdoors or indoors with wood/biomass; and $VF_1 = 0.5$ is the ventilation factor.

The values of β are 0.5 for switching from unimproved to improved wood/biomass stoves, 1.0 for switching from unimproved wood/biomass stoves to LPG stoves, and 0.5 for switching from improved wood/biomass stoves to LPG stoves. Table 8.28 presents the estimated benefits.

According to the Household Integrated Economic Survey 2007–08 (FBS 2009), rural households in Sindh spent about PRs 285.5 on fuels per month. Most of this expenditure is on firewood. Adjusting for inflation, using firewood prices in Karachi reported in FBS (2011), an average rural household spent an estimated PRs 4,613 per year on fuels in 2009. Sindhu (2006) reports that households using wood/biomass in Pakistan used 82 percent of their total fuel consumption on cooking and 18% on heating and water boiling. As temperatures are generally higher in Sindh than in the rest of Pakistan during the winter months, a Sindh household spends a higher share of energy on cooking. It is here therefore assumed that a Sindh household spends 90 percent of their fuel consumption on cooking. Thus, an average rural household spent about PRs 4,150 on cooking fuels per year in 2009. This figure includes the market value of self-collected fuels for own consumption (FBS 2009). On the basis of estimated annual cooking fuel expenditure, the expected value of fuel savings from the interventions are in the range of PRs 1,660–4,150 per household per year in 2009 (table 8.28).

Time savings involving cooking are valued at 50 percent of the average wage rate. The rural wage rate is applied as most of the households using wood/biomass live in rural areas, and is estimated at PRs 40 per hour based on the estimated wage of PRs 58.7 in all-Sindh in 2009 (see appendix G). Therefore, the value of cooking-involved time savings from the interventions is approximately PRs 2,430–4,860 per household per year (table 8.28).

Table 8.28 Estimated Value of Health and Nonhealth Benefits of Interventions in Sindh Province, 2009

	Improved instead of unimproved wood/ biomass stove	LPG instead of improved stove	LPG instead of unimproved stove
Health benefits for households cooking outdoors—"Low"	2,827	2,827	5,655
Health benefits for households cooking outdoors—"High"	4,795	4,795	9,589
Health benefits for households cooking indoors—"Low"	5,655	5,655	11,309
Health benefits for households cooking indoors—"High"	9,589	9,589	19,178
Value of fuel savings	1,660	2,490	4,150
Value of cooking time savings	2,430	2,430	4,860

Note: "Low" reflects valuation of health benefits using HCV for mortality and COI for morbidity. "High" reflects using HCV for child mortality, VSL for adult mortality, and WTP for morbidity.

Costs of Interventions

Unit costs of improved wood/biomass and LPG stoves, assumption about the useful life of stoves, and estimated LPG consumption that is required to replace wood/biomass consumption are presented in table 8.29.

To inform households of the benefits of improved wood/biomass stoves and cleaner fuels, and encourage them to adopt these stoves and fuels, a promotion program can be designed and implemented. The cost of such a program should be reflected in the CBA. There is, however, little information on the program cost per household adopting improved stoves or cleaner fuels, but cost of hygiene promotion programs can serve as an indication. Table 8.30 provides estimates of program promotion cost per household based on Saade, Bateman, and Bendahmane (2001), Pinfold and Horan (1996), and Borghi and others (2002) in Guatemala, Thailand, and Burkino Faso. Program cost is annualized over three years, equivalent to the assumed useful life of the improved wood/biomass cooking stove. The midpoint cost estimate of PRs 252 per household is applied in the CBA.

Total annualized cost of interventions per household is presented in table 8.31. Stove cost amounts to about 54 percent and promotion program cost to about

Table 8.29 Unit Costs of Interventions in Sindh Province

			Source
Cost of improved wood/biomass stove	800	PRs per stove	Based on reported stove prices in Pakistan
Average useful life of an improved stove	3	Years	Assumption
Cost of LPG stove	4,800	PRs per stove	International prices
Average useful life of an LPG stove	10	Years	Assumption
LPG fuel consumption (required to replace wood/biomass consumption)	108	Kg/household/ year	Estimated assuming a 15% energy efficiency of unimproved wood/ biomass stoves and 55% efficiency of an LPG stove
LPG fuel cost	85	PRs per kg	Price in Pakistan in December 2009
Discount rate applied to annualize the cost of stoves	10%	Annual rate	Assumption

Table 8.30 Promotion Program Cost per Household

	Scenario 1	Scenario 2	Scenario 3
Program response rate (% of targeted households switching stove)	10	15	20
Program cost per program target (US$)	0.4	1.2	5
Program cost per household switching stove (US$)	4	8	25
Program cost per household switching stove (PRs)	314	628	1,961
Annualized program cost per household switching stove (PRs)	**126**	**252**	**789**

Note: US$1 = PRs 78.44 in year 2009. Program cost is annualized over three years. Discount rate is 10%. Program cost per household switching stove is equal to program cost per household targeted by the program, divided by the program response rate.

Table 8.31 Total Cost of Intervention in Sindh Province, 2009

	Improved instead of unimproved wood/ biomass stove	LPG instead of improved stove	LPG instead of unimproved stove
Annualized stove cost	292	710	710
Annualized promotion program cost	252	252	252
LPG fuel cost	n.a.	9,208	9,208
Total annual cost	**544**	**10,170**	**10,170**

Note: n.a. = not applicable.

Table 8.32 Benefit-Cost Ratios of Interventions to Control Household Air Pollution from Solid Cooking Fuels in Sindh Province

		Households cooking outdoors		Household cooking indoors	
		Low	High	Low	High
1	Improved wood/biomass stove (health only)	5.2	8.8	10.4	17.6
	Improved wood/biomass stove (health and fuel savings)	8.2	11.8	13.4	20.7
	Improved wood/biomass stove (health, fuel, and time savings)	12.7	16.3	17.9	25.1
2	LPG from unimproved stove (health only)	0.56	0.94	1.11	1.9
	LPG from unimproved stove (health and fuel savings)	0.96	1.4	1.5	2.3
	LPG from unimproved stove (health, fuel, and time savings)	1.4	1.8	2.0	2.8
3	LPG from improved stove (health only)	0.28	0.47	0.56	0.94
	LPG from improved stove (health and fuel savings)	0.52	0.72	0.80	1.2
	LPG from improved stove (health, fuel, and time savings)	0.76	0.96	1.04	1.4

Note: "Low" reflects valuation of health effects using HCV for mortality and COI for morbidity. "High" reflects using HCV for child mortality, VSL for adult mortality, and WTP for morbidity. Positive benefit-cost ratios are highlighted.

46 percent for the improved wood/biomass cooking stove intervention. For the LPG stove interventions, LPG fuel cost is about 90 percent of the total cost, while the cost of stove and promotion program only constitutes 10 percent.

Benefit-Cost Ratios

Benefit-cost ratios (BCRs) of the three interventions to control HAP from household use of solid cooking fuels are presented in table 8.32. "Low" reflects valuation of health effects using the HCV for child and adult mortality and the COI approach for morbidity. "High" reflects valuation using HCV for child mortality, VSL for adult mortality, and WTP for morbidity. BCRs are presented for outdoor and indoor cooking. Fuel saving benefits is the value of reduced wood/biomass fuel requirements for cooking when switching to an improved and more energy efficient wood/biomass stove or an LPG stove. Time saving benefits stem from reduced cooking time.

The BCRs for replacing unimproved wood/biomass stoves with improved wood/biomass stoves are greater than one (that is, benefits > costs) for households cooking outdoors or indoors. The BCRs are very robust. All BCRs are greater than one, even if only health benefits are included and the cost of an improved wood/biomass stove would be PRs 5,000 instead of PRs 800, or annualized program promotion cost would be PRs 2,500 instead of PRs 252 per household, or the useful life of the stove is only six months instead of three years.

The BCRs of switching to LPG stoves from unimproved wood/biomass stoves are greater than one in most cases and only less than one for outdoor cooking when only health benefits are included and these health benefits are valued using the "low" valuation approach. The BCRs of switching to LPG stoves from improved wood/biomass stoves are greater than one only for indoor cooking and when fuel and time savings are included.

All BCRs are highly insensitive to the discount rate applied. This is because the stove cost is a minor part of overall costs, with program-promotion costs being higher than the annualized cost of improved wood/biomass stoves and the cost of LPG being much higher than the annualized cost of LPG stoves.

Notes

1. There are also single-intervention studies. For example, Meddings and others (2004) presents a CEA of household sanitation (latrines) improvements in Kabul, Afghanistan.

2. Diarrheal mortality is assumed to decline in proportion to reduction in incidence of diarrheal illness.

3. Other components of the projects are metering of water service connections (US$30–35 million) and around US$165–170 for construction of two seawater desalinization plants to meet water demand requirements.

4. In this case, the BCR is independent of program response rate and period of sustained drinking water treatment, and is determined solely by health benefits and private cost of water treatment.

5. Mothers and caretakers are also likely to benefit from improved hand washing in terms of reduced diarrheal illness. These benefits are not included here and thus the benefit-cost ratios are likely to be conservative.

6. In this case, the BCR is independent of program response rate and period of sustained improved hand washing practice, and is determined solely by health benefits and private cost of hand washing.

7. A cost of a DOC of US$1,500 was applied for heavy-duty trucks and large buses, and a cost of US$1,000 for minibuses and light-duty vans. A discount rate of 10 percent was applied to annualize the cost of the DOC.

8. A discount rate of 10 percent was applied to annualize the cost of conversion to CNG.

Bibliography

ADB (Asian Development Bank). 2005. *Karachi Mega Cities Preparation Project*. Final report, Vol. 1, TA 4578-Pakistan, Manila, Philippines.

Alberini, A., and A. Krupnick. 2000. "Cost-of-Illness and Willingness-to-Pay Estimates of the Benefits of Improved Air Quality: Evidence from Taiwan." *Land Economics* 76: 37–53.

Arnold, B., and J. M. Colford. 2007. "Treating Water with Chlorine at Point-of-Use to Improve Water Quality and Reduce Child Diarrhea in Developing Countries: A Systematic Review and Meta-analysis." *American Journal of Tropical Medicine and Hygiene* 76 (2): 354–64.

Aziz, M. A. 2008. *Pakistan Safe Drinking Water and Hygiene Promotion Project*. Technical and Marketing Review of POU Technologies, USAID, Washington, DC.

Blumberg, K., K. He, Y. Zhou, H. Liu, and N. Yamaguchi. 2006. *Costs and Benefits of Reduced Sulfur in China*. The International Council on Clean Transportation. www .theicct.org.

Borghi, J., L. Guinness, J. Ouedraogo, and V. Curtis. 2002. "Is Hygiene Promotion Cost-effective? A Case Study in Burkino Faso." *Tropical Medicine and International Health* 7 (11): 960–69.

Cairncross, S., C. Hunt, S. Boisson, K. Bostoen, V. Curtis, I. C. Fung, and W. P. Schmidt. 2010. "Water, Sanitation and Hygiene for Preventing Diarrhoea." *International Journal of Epidemiology* 39: i193–i205.

Cairncross, S., and V. Valdmanis. 2006. "Water Supply, Sanitation, and Hygiene Promotion." In *Disease Control Priorities in Developing Countries*, edited by D. T. Jamison, J. G. Breman, A. R. Measham, G. Alleyne, M. Claeson, D. B. Evans, P. Jha, A. Mills, and P. Musgrove, 771–92. Oxford University Press and the World Bank.

Clasen, T., K. Bostoen, W. P. Schmidt, S. Boisson, I. C. Fung, M. W. Jenkins, B. Scott, S. Sugden, and S. Cairncross. 2010. "Interventions to Improve Disposal of Human Excreta for Preventing Diarrhoea (Review)." *The Cochrane Library* 6.

Clasen, T., and L. Haller. 2008. *Water Quality Interventions to Prevent Diarrhea: Cost and Cost-effectiveness*. Geneva: Public Health and the Environment, World Health Organization.

Clasen, T., L. Haller, D. Walker, J. Bartram, and S. Cairncross. 2007a. "Cost-effectiveness of Water Quality Interventions for Preventing Diarrhoeal Disease in Developing Countries." *Journal of Water and Health* 5 (4): 599–608.

Clasen, T., C. McLaughlin, N. Nayaar, S. Boisson, R. Gupta, D. Desai, and N. Shah. 2008a. "Microbiological Effectiveness and Cost of Disinfecting Water by Boiling in Semi-urban India." *American Journal of Tropical Medicine and Hygiene* 79 (3): 407–13.

Clasen, T., W.-P. Schmidt, T. Rabie, I. Roberts, and S. Cairncross. 2007b. "Interventions to Improve Water Quality for Preventing Diarrhoea: Systematic Review and Meta-analysis." *British Medical Journal* 334: 782–91.

Clasen, T., D. H. Thao, S. Boisson, and O. Shipin. 2008b. "Microbiological Effectiveness and Cost of Boiling to Disinfect Drinking Water in Rural Vietnam." *Environmental Science and Technology* 42 (12): 4255–60.

Cropper, M., and W. Oates. 1992. "Environmental Economics: A Survey." *Journal of Economic Literature* 30: 675–740.

Curtis, V., and S. Cairncross. 2003. "Effect of Washing Hands with Soap on Diarrhoea Risk in the Community: A Systematic Review." *The Lancet Infectious Diseases* 3: 275–81.

Daily Times. 2012. http://www.dailytimes.com.pk/default.asp?page=2012%5C01%5C16 %5Cstory_16-1-2012_pg7_26.

Dickie, M., and S. Gerking. 2002. "Willingness to Pay for Reduced Morbidity." Presented at Economic Valuation of Health for Environmental Policy: Assessing Alternative Approaches, Orlando FL, March 18–19.

ECON. 2006. "Urban Air Pollution Control in Peru." Prepared for the Peru Environmental Analysis, World Bank. ECON Analysis, Oslo.

———. 2007. "Mitigating the Cost of Environmental Impacts from Inadequate Water Supply and Sanitation and Hygiene in Rural Qena, Egypt." Commissioned by the World Bank. ECON Analysis, Oslo.

EIA (Energy Information Administration). 2012. *Petroleum Marketing Monthly, February 2012*. Washington, DC: Energy Information Administration, Department of Energy.

Ejemot, R. I., J. E. Ehiri, M. M. Meremikwu, and J. A. Critchley. 2009. "Hand Washing for Preventing Diarrhea (Review)." *The Cochrane Library* 3.

Enstrat International Ltd. 2003. *Cost of Diesel Fuel Desulphurisation for Different Refinery Structures Typical of the Asian Refinery Industry*. Final report prepared for the Asian Development Bank, Washington, DC.

FBS (Federal Bureau of Statistics). 2009. "Household Integrated Economic Survey 2007–08." Islamabad: Federal Bureau of Statistics.

———. 2011. *Pakistan Statistical Yearbook 2011*. Islamabad: Federal Bureau of Statistics.

Fewtrell, L., R. B. Kaufmann, D. Kay, W. Enanoria, L. Haller, and J. M. Colford. 2005. "Water, Sanitation and Hygiene Interventions to Reduce Diarrhea in Less Developed Countries: A Systematic Review and Meta-analysis." *The Lancet Infectious Diseases* 5: 42–52.

Habermehl, H. 2007. *Economic Evaluation of the Improved Household Cooking Stove Dissemination Programme in Uganda*. German GTZ.

Haller, L., G. Hutton, and J. Bartram. 2007. "Estimating the Costs and Health Benefits of Water and Sanitation Improvements at Global Level." *Journal of Water and Health* 5 (4): 467–80.

Hunter, P. R. 2009. "Household Water Treatment in Developing Countries: Comparing Different Intervention Types Using Meta-regression." *Environmental Science and Technology* 43 (23): 8991–97.

Hutton, G., L. Haller, and J. Bartram. 2007. "Global Cost-benefit Analysis of Water Supply and Sanitation Interventions." *Journal of Water and Health* 5 (4): 481–502.

Hutton, G., E. Rehfuess, F. Tediosi, and S. Weiss. 2006. *Global Cost-benefit Analysis of Household Energy and Health Interventions*. Department for the Protection of the Human Environment, World Health Organization, Geneva.

Kjellen, M., and G. McGranahan. 2006. "Informal Water Vendors and the Urban Poor." Human Settlements Discussion Paper Series, International Institute for Environment and Development, London.

Larsen, B. 2003. "Hygiene and Health in Developing Countries: Defining Priorities through Cost-Benefit Assessments". *International Journal of Environmental Health Research* 13: S37–46.

———. 2005. "Cost-benefit Analysis of Environmental Protection in Colombia." Prepared for the Ministry of Environment, Housing and Land Development. Background paper for the Colombia Country Environmental Analysis: Colombia Mitigating Environmental Degradation to Foster Growth and Reduce Inequality. Washington, DC: World Bank.

———. 2007a. "A Cost-benefit Analysis of Environmental Health Interventions in Urban Greater Dakar, Senegal." Commissioned by the World Bank, ECON/Roche, Canada.

———. 2007b. *Cost-benefit Analysis of Water Supply, Sanitation and Hygiene Interventions in Mexico*. Report prepared for the World Bank.

————. 2009. *Cost-benefit Analysis of Selected Environmental Health Interventions: International Evidence and Applications to the Philippines.* Report prepared for the Philippines CEA, World Bank.

————. 2011a. *Benefits and Costs of Select Environmental Health Interventions in the MENA Countries.* Report prepared for the World Bank/CMI.

————. 2011b. "Environmental Health in the Sundarbans of India: A Benefit-Cost Assessment of Select Interventions." Prepared for the Climate Change Adaptation, Biodiversity Conservation and Socio-Economic Development of the Sundarbans Area of West Bengal, World Bank Technical Assistance, World Bank, Washington, DC.

Larsen, B., G. Hutton, and N. Khanna. 2009. "Air Pollution." In *Global Crisis, Global Solutions: Costs and Benefits,* edited by B. Lomborg, 7–49. Cambridge University Press.

Larsen, B., and E. Strukova. 2006. "A Cost-benefit Analysis of Improved Water Supply, Sanitation and Hygiene and Indoor Air Pollution Control in Peru." Prepared for the Peru Country Environmental Analysis: Environmental Sustainability A Key to Poverty Reduction in Peru. Washington, DC: World Bank.

Luby, S. E., A. H. Syed, N. Atiullah, M. K. Faizan, and S. Fisher-Hoch. 1999. Limited Effectiveness of Home Drinking Water Purification Efforts in Karachi, Pakistan. *International Journal of Infectious Diseases* 4 (1): 3–7.

Luby, S., M. Agboatwalla, A. Bowen, E. Kenah, Y. Sharker, and R. M. Hoekstra. 2009. Difficulties in Maintaining Improved Handwashing Behavior, Karachi, Pakistan." *American Journal of Tropical Medicine and Hygiene* 81 (1): 140–45.

Luby, S., M. Agboatwalla, J. Painter, A. Altaf, W. L. Billheimer, and R. Hoekstra. 2004. "Effect of Intensive Hand-washing Promotion on Childhood Diarrhea in High-Risk Communities in Pakistan: A Randomised Controlled Trial." *Journal of the American Medical Association* 291 (21): 2547–54.

Luby, S., M. Agboatwalla, J. Painter, A. Altaf, W. Billhimer, B. Keswick, and R. M. Hoekstra. 2006. "Combining Drinking Water Treatment and Hand Washing for Diarrhoea Prevention, A Cluster Randomized Controlled Trial." *Tropical Medicine and International Health* 11 (4): 479–89.

Luby, S., M. Agboatwalla, A. Razz, and J. Sobel. 2001. "A Low-Cost Intervention for Cleaner Drinking Water in Karachi, Pakistan." *International Journal of Infectious Diseases* 5 (3): 144–50.

MECA (Manufacturers of Emission Controls Association). 2009. *Retrofitting Emissions Controls on Diesel-Powered Vehicles.* Report by the Manufacturers of Emission Controls Association. Washington, DC. www.meca.org.

Meddings, D., L. Ronald, S. Marion, J. Pinera, and A. Oppliger. 2004. "Cost Effectiveness of A Latrine Revision Programme in Kabul, Afghanistan." *Bulletin of the World Health Organization* 82 (4): 281–89.

Mehta, S., and C. Shahpar. 2004. "The Health Benefits of Interventions to Reduce Indoor Air Pollution from Solid Fuel Use: A Cost-Effectiveness Analysis." *Energy for Sustainable Development* 8 (3): 53–59.

NIPS (National Institute of Population Studies)/Macro. 2008. "Pakistan Demographic and Health Survey 2006–07." National Institute of Population Studies, Pakistan, and Macro International Inc., Islamabad.

PCRWR (Pakistan Council of Research in Water Resources). 2010. *Technical Assessment Survey Report of Water Supply Schemes in Sindh Province.* Prepared by M. A. Tahir, M. K. Marri, and F. ul Hassan. PCRWR. Ministry of Science and Technology, Pakistan.

PIDE (Pakistan Institute of Development and Economics). 2002. *Cost and Impact Analysis of Water Supply and Environmental Sanitation in Pakistan.* Islamabad: PIDE and UNICEF.

Pinfold, J., and N. Horan. 1996. "Measuring the Effect of a Hygiene Behaviour Intervention by Indicators of Behaviour and Diarrhoeal Disease." *Transactions of the Royal Society of Tropical Medicine and Hygiene* 90: 366–71.

Pruss, A., D. Kay, L. Fewtrell, and J. Bartram. 2002. "Estimating the Burden of Disease from Water, Sanitation and Hygiene at the Global Level." *Environmental Health Perspectives* 110 (5): 537–42.

Prüss-Üstün, A., D. Kay, L. Fewtrell, and J. Bartram. 2004. "Unsafe Water, Sanitation and Hygiene." In *Comparative Quantification of Health Risks: Global and Regional Burden of Disease Attributable to Selected Major Risk Factors*, edited by M. Ezzati. Geneva: World Health Organization.

Rosa, G., and T. Clasen. 2010. "Estimating the Scope of Household Water Treatment in Low- and Medium-Income Countries." *American Journal of Tropical Medicine and Hygiene* 82 (2): 289–300.

Saade, C., M. Bateman, and D. Bendahmane. 2001. *The Story of a Successful Public-Private Partnership in Central America: Hand Washing for Diarrheal Disease Prevention.* Published by BASICS II, EHP, UNICEF, USAID, and World Bank.

Shordt, K., and S. Cairncross. 2004. *Sustainability of Hygiene Behaviour and the Effectiveness of Change interventions: Findings and Implications for Water and Sanitation Programmes from a Multi-Country Research Study.* Amsterdam, the Netherlands: IRC International Water and Sanitation Centre.

Shrestha, R., E. Marseille, J. Kahn, J. R Lule, C. Pitter, J. M. Blandford, R. Bunnell, A. Coutinho, F. Kizito, R. Quick, and J. Mermin. 2006. "Cost-Effectiveness of Home Based Chlorination and Safe Water Storage in Reducing Diarrhea among HIV-Affected Households in Rural Uganda." *American Journal of Hygiene and Tropical Medicine* 74 (5): 884–90.

Siddiqui, A. R., K. Lee, D. Bennett, X. Yang, K. H. Brown, Z. A. Bhutta, and E. B. Gold. 2009. Indoor Carbon Monoxide and PM2.5 Concentrations by Cooking Fuels in Pakistan. *Indoor Air* 19: 75–82.

Sindhu, A. S. 2006. "Indoor Air Pollution: The Case of Pakistan. Rural Development Policy Institute (RDPI), Pakistan." Presentation at the South Asia Regional Workshop on Indoor Air Pollution, Health and Household Energy, Kathmandu, February 26–27.

Stevens, G., A. Wilson, and J. Hammitt. 2005. "A Benefit-cost Analysis of Retrofitting Diesel Vehicles with Particulate Filters in the Mexico City Metropolitan Area." *Risk Analysis* 25 (4): 883–99.

UNEP (United Nations Environment Programme). 2006. "Opening the Door to Cleaner Vehicles in Developing and Transition Countries: The Role of Lower Sulphur Fuels." UNEP Partnership for Clean Fuels and Vehicles. Nairobi, Kenya.

———. 2009. "Cleaning Up Urban Bus Fleets with Focus on Developing and Transition Countries." United Nations Environment Program. http://www.unep.org/transport /pcfv/PDF/Retrofit.pdf.

USEPA (United States Environmental Protection Agency). 2012. http://www.epa.gov /cleandiesel/technologies/retrofits.htm.

Waddington, H., and B. Snilstveit. 2009. "Effectiveness and Sustainability of Water, Sanitation, and Hygiene Interventions in Combating Diarrhoea." *Journal of Development Effectiveness* 1 (3): 295–335.

Whittington, D, W. M. Hanemann, C. Sadoff, and M. Jeuland. 2009. "Water and Sanitation." In *Global Crisis, Global Solutions: Costs and Benefits*, edited by B. Lomborg, 355–429. Cambridge University Press.

Wilson, C. 2003. "Empirical Evidence Showing the Relationships between Three Approaches for Pollution Control." *Environmental and Resource Economics* 24: 97–101.

World Bank. 2010. *Environmental Health in Nicaragua: Evaluating Costs and Setting Priorities*. Report 55453-NI. Washington, DC: World Bank.

Baseline Health and Child Nutritional Status

Data Sources

Reliable data on the health and nutrition status of the population in Sindh province are for the most part not readily available. Public health information systems rarely contain complete and reliable data on cause-specific adult and child mortality, child nutritional status, and incidence of infectious diseases. Such data are essential for estimating the health effects or disease burden from environmental health risk factors. This book therefore relies on household surveys in Pakistan and data reported by the World Health Organization (WHO) that combined provide indications of several dimensions of health and nutrition in Sindh needed for this study of environmental health. The main household surveys with relevant health statistics are the Pakistan Demographic and Health Survey 2006–07 (PDHS 2006–07 by NIPS/Macro 2008), the Pakistan Social and Living Standards Measurement Surveys (PSLM 2008–09, 2010–11, by GoP 2010, 2011), and the Pakistan Demographic Survey 2007 (PDS 2007 by GoP 2009). In addition, this study also relies on several surveys from Pakistan on child nutritional status, and estimates of cause-specific structure of child and adult mortality in Pakistan by WHO (2009b, 2010, 2011). The reference year for this study is 2009. Health and nutrition data have therefore been converted and estimated for this year.

Child Mortality and Morbidity

According to the PDS 2007, the under-five child-mortality rate in Sindh was around 90.4 per 1,000 live births in 2006. On the basis of rates of decline in under-five child-mortality rates in all-Pakistan from 2006 to 2009, the under-five child mortality in Sindh may have been approximately 83.7 per 1,000 live births in 2009. On the basis of a crude birthrate of 24.7 per 1,000 population in Sindh (GoP 2009) and a population of 35.7 million, an estimated 73,741 children younger than five years of age died in Sindh in 2009.[1]

WHO provides estimates of cause-specific child mortality in 2008 for all WHO member states (WHO 2010). According to these estimates, about 46 percent of mortality among children younger than five years old in Pakistan was from infectious and parasitic diseases, and 54 percent from other causes (figure A.1). For the purposes of this book, it is assumed that the structure of child mortality in Sindh is the same as estimated for all Pakistan. Deaths from malaria, at 0.1 percent of child mortality in Pakistan, are ignored, because malaria mortality is highly location specific.

The PDHS 2006–07 and PSLMs contain important information on prevalence of diarrhea and symptoms of respiratory infections in children younger than five years of age. The PDHS 2006–07 (see NIPS/Macro 2008) carried out during September–February (largely dry season) reports a two-week diarrheal prevalence rate of 23.6 percent in Sindh province. The PSLM 2008–09 and 2010–11 report a 30-day diarrheal prevalence rate of 12 percent in Sindh province. Annual incidence (I) of diarrhea per child per year is calculated as follows:

$$I = P^* 52/(w+d/7)$$ (A.1)

where P is the prevalence rate, w is the prevalence period measured in weeks (that is, two weeks or 30 days) and d is average duration of disease (diarrhea) measured

Figure A.1 Estimates of Cause-Specific Mortality among Children under Five Years of Age in Pakistan, 2008
Percent

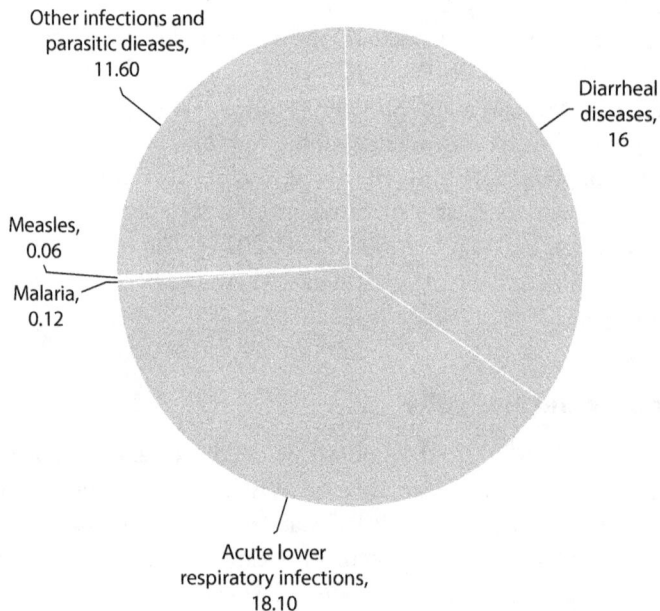

Other infections and parasitic dieases, 11.60

Diarrheal diseases, 16

Measles, 0.06

Malaria, 0.12

Acute lower respiratory infections, 18.10

Source: Produced from WHO estimates of mortality among children in Pakistan in 2008 (WHO 2010).

in days. This formula accounts for the fact that the prevalence captures some of the diarrheal cases that started before the prevalence period and will end after the prevalence period. Annual incidence is therefore adjusted by the "*d* / 7" factor in the denominator. Average duration of diarrhea is assumed to be four days. Therefore, the incidence of diarrhea is 4.8 cases per child per year according to the PDHS (2006–07) by NIPS/Mcro (2008), and 1.3 cases per child per year according to the PSLM (2008–09 and 2010–11) by GoP (2010 and 2011). Thus, the surveys indicate very different annual incidence rates that unlikely are caused by changes in conditions causing diarrheal disease. One factor of importance is the prevalence period used in the surveys. Many mothers may have difficulty precisely recalling whether or not their child had diarrhea in the past 30 days or even two weeks. For example, the PDHS 2006–07 also asks mothers if their child had diarrhea in the past 24 hours. About 9.6 percent of children had diarrhea in the past 24 hours in Sindh, suggesting an incidence of seven cases per child per year. Thus, it seems that some of the difference in prevalence rate of diarrhea may be due to difference in the recall period used in the survey, and that the longer is the recall period the lower and less accurate is the reported prevalence rate. In this study, the PDHS (2006–07) is given a weight of two-thirds and the PSLM surveys a weight of one-third in estimating annual incidence of diarrhea. Thus, the estimated incidence is 3.6 cases per child per year, and assumed to be the same in 2009.

The PDHS (2006–07) reports on cough; cough accompanied by short, rapid breathing; and cough accompanied by short, rapid breathing that is chest related in children younger than five years of age. The latter is a proxy for pneumonia or acute lower respiratory infection (ALRI) and is used in this book to estimate ALRI morbidity in children younger than five caused by household use of wood and other biomass fuels. Cough with short, rapid breathing reported as not being chest related is used in this book as an indicator of acute upper respiratory infection (AURI). Its prevalence rate is used to estimate AURI morbidity in children younger than five years old caused by household use of wood and biomass.

The two-week prevalence rate of ALRI among children in Sindh province was 17 percent, and the prevalence rate of cough with short, rapid breathing was more than 24 percent (the latter rate includes the cases of ALRI). Analysis of the all-Pakistan data does, however, indicate seasonal variations with prevalence rates peaking in December–January and reaching the lowest rates in September, with seasonal variations somewhat smaller in Sindh. The survey was administered during September–February, and thus likely does not reflect even lower prevalence rates during March–August. Adjusting for seasonality suggests a prevalence rate of ALRI of 13 percent and rate of cough with short, rapid breathing of 20 percent. Consequently, by subtracting the cases of ALRI, the prevalence of AURI is 7 percent.

These seasonally adjusted prevalence rates are converted to an annual incidence of 1.1 cases of ALRI and 1.2 cases of AURI per child per year (this does not include cough that is not accompanied by short, rapid breathing) using equation A.1, assuming an average duration of 30 days for ALRI and 7 days for AURI. It is here assumed that that the incidence rate was the same in year 2009.

Child Nutritional Status

Commonly used indicators of poor nutritional status in children are underweight, stunting, and wasting. Underweight is measured as weight-for-age relative to an international reference population.[2] Stunting is measured as height-for-age, and wasting is measured as weight-for-height. Underweight is an indicator of chronic or acute malnutrition or a combination of both. Stunting is an indicator of chronic malnutrition, and wasting an indicator of acute malnutrition. Underweight status among children younger than five years of age is most commonly used in assessing the risk of mortality and morbidity from poor nutritional status (Fishman and others 2004).

A child is defined as moderately underweight or stunted if his or her weight or height is in the range of –2 to –3 standard deviations (SD) below the weight or height of the median child in the international reference population, and severely underweight or stunted if the child's weight or height is below –3 SD from the weight or height of the median child in the reference population. The standard deviations are also called z-scores and noted as WAZ (weight-for-age z-score).

A WHO nutrition database is used here to provide some perspectives on the nutritional status among children younger than five years of age in Sindh.[3] The database draws on household surveys such as the Pakistan National Nutrition Survey (2001–02) by PIDE (2002), the Pakistan Multiple Indicator Cluster Survey 1995 (MICS) (UNICEF 1995), the National Health Survey of Pakistan (1990–94) by PMRC (1998), and the Pakistan Demographic and Health Survey (1990–91) by NIPS and IRD/Macro (1992). Prevalence rates of moderate and severe underweight among children younger than five in 2001 are higher in Pakistan, and in Sindh in particular, than in most developing countries (tables A.1, A.2). Prevalence rates seem to have declined more in Pakistan in general than in Sindh province from 1990 to 2001.

The prevalence rates of underweight in tables A.1 and A.2 are based on the WHO international reference population that was established a few years ago (WHO 2006). However, Fishman and others (2004) used the National Center for Health Statistics (NCHS) reference population when estimating mortality and morbidity from child underweight. Prevalence rates of moderate and severe underweight (≤ 2 SD) are higher with the NCHS international reference

Table A.1 Prevalence of Underweight in Children Younger than Five Years Old in Pakistan, 1990–2001

Percent

	1990–91	1990–94	1995	2001
Moderate and severe underweight	39.0	35.3	34.2	31.3
Severe underweight	17.5	14.6		12.7

Source: http://apps.who.int/nutrition/landscape/search.aspx.
Note: Prevalence rates are based on WHO (2006) international reference population.

Table A.2 Prevalence of Underweight in Children Younger than Five Years Old in Sindh Province, 1990–2001

Percent

	1990–91	*1990–94*	*2001*
Moderate and severe underweight	47.2	36.9	42.3
Severe underweight	22.9	15.2	18.7

Source: http://apps.who.int/nutrition/landscape/search.aspx.
Note: Prevalence rates are based on WHO (2006) international reference population.

Table A.3 Prevalence of Underweight in Children Younger than Five Years Old in Pakistan, 2001

Percent

	NCHS	*WHO*
Moderate and severe underweight	38	31
Severe underweight	13	13

Source: www.childinfo.org, based on recalculations by WHO of the Pakistan National Nutrition Survey (2001–02).

Table A.4 Assumed Prevalence Rates of Underweight in Children Younger than Five Years Old in Sindh Province, 2009

	Standard deviations	*Prevalence rates (%)*
Mild underweight	−1 to −2	30
Moderate underweight	−2 to −3	28
Severe underweight	<−3	14

Note: Based on the NCHS international reference population.

population than with the WHO child growth standards, while prevalence of severe underweight is about the same (table A.3).

Data from the Pakistan National Nutrition Survey 2010 needed to estimate the prevalence of child underweight in Sindh using the NCHS reference population were not available at the time this book was being prepared. Therefore, projections from 2001 to 2009 are necessary. If the rate of decline in child underweight prevalence was the same during 2001–2009 as during 1990–2001, prevalence of moderate and severe underweight in Pakistan might have been around 25 percent and severe underweight around 9 percent in 2009. In Sindh, the respective rates might have been 37 percent and 14 percent in 2009. Converting these prevalence rates from the WHO child growth standards suggests that prevalence of moderate and severe underweight in Sindh was 42 percent and severe underweight was 14 percent in 2009 using the NCHS reference population (table A.4).

In estimating mortality and morbidity from child underweight, Fishman and others (2004) also rely on the prevalence rate of mild underweight.

However, the prevalence of mild underweight is not reported in most survey reports on nutrition and would need to be calculated from the original survey data. These Pakistani data are however not readily available. By international comparison, the prevalence rate of mild underweight in Sindh might have been around 30 percent in 2009.

Adult Mortality and Morbidity

Data on cause-specific mortality and morbidity among adults are needed for estimating health effects of outdoor air pollution and road traffic noise in urban areas, and water, sanitation, and hygiene throughout Sindh. In addition, data on cause-specific mortality and morbidity among adult females are needed for estimating health effects of household air pollution.

Tables A.5–A.8 present the mortality data used for urban areas. Urban crude death rate is estimated from various Pakistani data sources while the structure of mortality is from WHO for Pakistan as a whole. It is assumed that the structure of adult mortality is the same in Sindh as in Pakistan overall and that the structure has not changed from 2004 to 2009.

Data from WHO (2009a), and gender- and age-specific mortality in the South-East Asian Region D (SEAR D) of WHO (2004), were used to estimate the structure of mortality among women 30 or more years of age in Pakistan (table A.7). Using these estimates and broader demographic data, cause-specific mortality among women 30 or more years of age in Sindh is estimated and presented in table A.8 for 2009. The demographic data for Sindh are a female crude

Table A.5 Baseline Mortality Data for Pakistan

Health indicator	Numerical value (%)	Source of data
Crude urban mortality rate (per 1,000 population)	6.0	Estimate for urban Sindh based on PDS 2007 (GoP 2009); PDHS 1990–91 (NIPS and IRD/Macro 1992) and 2006–07 (NIPS/Macro 2008)
Cardiopulmonary mortality (% of crude morality)	40	WHO 2008 data for Pakistan (WHO 2011)
Cardiopulmonary (CP) mortality among population 30+ years of age (% of all CP)	80	WHO 2008 data for Pakistan (WHO 2011) and adjusted to the urban population
Cardiopulmonary mortality among population 30+ years (% of crude mortality)	32	= 40% × 80%
Lung cancer (% of crude mortality)[a]	0.52	WHO 2008 data for Pakistan (WHO 2011)
Ischemic heart disease mortality (% of crude mortality)	13.3	WHO 2008 data for Pakistan (WHO 2011)
Cerebrovascular disease mortality (% of crude mortality)	6.9	WHO 2008 data for Pakistan (WHO 2011)

a. Practically all lung cancer mortality is among the population 30 or more years of age.

Table A.6 Structure of Mortality, by Age Group in Pakistan, 2004

Percent

	0–14 years	15–59 years	60+ years	All ages
Diarrhea	11.7	1.6	1.9	5.3
Acute lower respiratory infections (ALRI)	15.2	4.3	10.9	10.8
Ischemic heart disease	0.2	12.4	25.3	13.1
Cerebrovascular disease	0.1	3.8	14.4	6.7
Hypertensive heart disease	0.0	0.5	0.7	0.4
Rheumatic and inflammatory heart disease	0.5	2.1	1.8	1.4
Other cardiovascular disease	0.3	2.4	4.8	2.6
Chronic obstructive pulmonary disease (COPD)	0.0	4.7	7.4	4.1
Tuberculosis	0.7	12.8	3.6	4.9
Lung cancer	0.0	0.8	1.7	0.9
Other causes	71.3	54.5	27.4	49.9
Total	100.0	100.0	100.0	100.0

Source: Produced from WHO (2009a) data.

Table A.7 Structure of Mortality among Women in Pakistan, 2004

Percent

	Structure of mortality among women (all age groups)	Mortality among women 30+ years (% of all-age female mortality)
Ischemic heart disease	12.2	97.4
Cerebrovascular disease	7.0	99.0
Hypertensive heart disease	0.4	96.8
Rheumatic and inflammatory heart disease	1.5	77.1
Chronic obstructive pulmonary disease (COPD)	3.9	99.9
Lung cancer	0.4	98.9

Sources: WHO (2009a) and Global Burden of Disease data by WHO.

Table A.8 Estimated Annual Cases of Mortality in Sindh Province among Adult Women 30 Years of Age or Older in Sindh Province, 2009

	Annual numbers of deaths
Chronic obstructive pulmonary disease (COPD)	3,310
Ischemic heart disease	10,150
Cerebrovascular disease	5,918
Hypertensive heart disease	363
Rheumatic and inflammatory heart disease	1,014
Lung cancer	310

mortality rate of 5 per 1,000 population (GoP 2009) and a total female population of 17.0 million in 2009.[4] Again, it is assumed that the structure of adult
female mortality is the same in Sindh as in Pakistan overall and that the structure
has not changed from 2004 to 2009.

Morbidity in adults relevant for this study is the same diseases as for mortality.
Data on cardiovascular and lung cancer morbidity are, however, not available.
Thus only diarrhea and COPD morbidity is included in this study (diarrhea in
population five years or older is discussed in the main body of this book).

Data on COPD in Pakistan are scarce, but the National Health Survey of
Pakistan (1990–94) indicates that the prevalence rate of chronic bronchitis (CB)
among women was around 2,470 per 100,000 women. Because CB is a major
subset of COPD, this CB prevalence rate is applied to estimate health effects
of household air pollution in Sindh.[5] As reported in Nishtar (2007), the same
survey indicates that the CB prevalence in urban areas was 1,857 per 100,000
population (males and females), which rate is applied for estimating CB from
outdoor air pollution.

Notes

1. This birthrate is calculated from data in the PDS (2007) by GoP (2009). Sindh's 2009
   population was estimated based on its 2006 population (PDS 2007), and adjusted to
   2009 by the population growth reported in FBS (2011).

2. The recently published WHO (2006) international reference population (representing a diverse group of countries) is increasingly replacing the international reference
   population defined by the National Center for Health Statistics (NCHS), United
   States.

3. http://apps.who.int/nutrition/landscape/search.aspx.

4. The Sindh's total female population in 2006 was 16.0 million (GoP 2009). This
   figure is here adjusted to 2009 by an annual population growth rate of 2.15 percent
   (FBS 2011).

5. A more recent study of rural women and household air pollution in Peshawar indicates that the prevalence of CB might be even higher (Akhtar and others 2007).

Bibliography

Akhtar, T., Z. Ullah, M. H. Khan, and R. Nazli. 2007. "Chronic Bronchitis in Women Using
   Solid Biomass Fuel in Rural Peshawar, Pakistan." *Chest* 132: 1472–75.

FBS (Federal Bureau of Statistics). 2011. *Pakistan Statistical Yearbook 2011.* Federal
   Bureau of Statistics, Pakistan.

Fishman, M. S., L. E. Caulfield, M. De Onis, M. Blossner, A. A. Hyder, L. Mullany, and
   R. E. Black. 2004. "Childhood and Maternal Underweight." In *Comparative
   Quantification of Health Risks—Global and Regional Burden of Disease Attributable
   to Selected Major Risk Factors*, edited by M. Ezzati, A. D. Lopez, A. Rodgers, and
   C. J. L. Murray. Geneva: World Health Organization.

GoP (Government of Pakistan). 2009. "Pakistan Demographic Survey 2007." Statistics
   Division, Government of Pakistan.

————. 2010. "Pakistan Social and Living Standards Measurement Survey 2008–09." Statistics Division, Government of Pakistan.

————. 2011. "Pakistan Social and Living Standards Measurement Survey 2010–11." Statistics Division, Government of Pakistan.

NIPS (National Institute of Population Studies)/Macro. 2008. "Pakistan Demographic and Health Survey 2006–07." National Institute of Population Studies and Macro International Inc., Islamabad.

NIPS (National Institute of Population Studies), Demographic and Health Surveys IRD/ Macro International Inc. 1992. "Pakistan Demographic and Health Survey 1990–91." National Institute of Population Studies, Demographic and Health Surveys IRD and Macro International Inc., Islamabad.

Nishtar, S. 2007. *Health Indicators of Pakistan—Gateway Paper II*. Islamabad: Heartfile.

Pakistan Medical Research Council. 1998. *National Health Survey of Pakistan 1990–94*. Islamabad: Pakistan Medical Research Council.

PIDE. 2002. "Cost and Impact Analysis of Water Supply and Environmental Sanitation in Pakistan." Pakistan Institute of Development Economics and UNICEF, Islamabad, Pakistan.

UNICEF (United Nations International Children's Emergency Fund). 1995. *Multiple Indicator Cluster Survey*. New York: UNICEF.

WHO (World Health Organization). 2004. *Comparative Quantification of Health Risks: Global and Regional Burden of Disease Attributable to Selected Major Risk Factors*. Geneva: WHO.

————. 2006. *WHO Child Growth Standards: Length/Height-for-Age, Weight-for-Age, Weight-for-Length, Weight-for-Age: Methods and Development*. Geneva: WHO.

————. 2009a. "Estimated Deaths and DALYs Attributable to Selected Environmental Risk Factors." WHO Member States, 2004.

————. 2009b. "Estimated Deaths by Cause and WHO Member State, 2004." Department of Measurement and Health Information, WHO, Geneva. http://www.who.int /quantifying_ehimpacts/national/countryprofile/intro/en/index.html.

————. 2010. *World Health Statistics 2010*. Geneva: WHO.

————. 2011. "Estimated Total Deaths by Cause, Sex and WHO Member State, 2008." Department of Measurement and Health Information, WHO, Geneva.

Health Effects of Outdoor Particulate Matter Air Pollution

Health effects of exposure to outdoor particulate matter (PM) include both premature mortality and morbidity. Ostro (2004) reviewed studies of premature mortality and presents exposure-response functions in terms of relative risk (RR) of premature mortality from exposure to PM (table B.1). Exposure to PM is expressed in terms of annual average ambient concentrations (X). A lower threshold value (X_0) of PM is specified, below which health effects are assumed to be nonexistent or minimal. Estimation of acute lower respiratory infections (ALRI) mortality among children younger than five years of age is based a linear function of particulate matter with a diameter of less than 10 microns (PM_{10}) exposure, while cardiopulmonary (CP) and lung cancer (LC) mortality among the population 30 or more years of age is based on a log-linear function of particulate matter with a diameter of less than 2.5 microns ($PM_{2.5}$) exposure. The β-coefficient for ALRI is derived from five studies in Brazil, Mexico, and Thailand. The β-coefficient for CP and LC is derived from Pope and others (2002). Pope and others found elevated risk of CP and LC mortality from long-term exposure to $PM_{2.5}$ in a study of a large population of adults 30 or more years of age in the United States. CP mortality includes mortality from respiratory infections, cardiovascular disease, and chronic respiratory disease. The World Health Organization used this study by Pope and others when estimating global mortality from outdoor air pollution (WHO 2004, 2009).

Annual average $PM_{2.5}$ ambient concentrations are much higher in many cities in developing countries than observed in Pope and others (2002). Therefore, Ostro (2004) recommends a log-linear function for estimating CP and LC mortality, as presented in table B.1. Estimated annual average $PM_{2.5}$ ambient concentration levels in Karachi and other cities in Sindh are, however, as high as 55–88 micrograms per cubic meter ($\mu g/m^3$). The numerical value of the β-coefficient for the log-linear function presented in Ostro (2004) may therefore result in an overestimate of mortality from $PM_{2.5}$. Recent research suggests that the *marginal increase* in RR of mortality from $PM_{2.5}$ declines with increasing

Table B.1 Particulate Matter Exposure-Response Functions Applied to Cities in Sindh Province

Mortality	Population group	Functional form	β coefficient	Lower threshold value (X_0)
Acute lower respiratory infection	Children younger than 5 years of age	$RR = \exp(\beta(X - X_0))$	0.00166	$PM_{10} = 10 \ \mu g/m^3$
Cardiopulmonary	Adults 30+ years of age	$RR = [(X + 1)/(X_0 + 1)]^\beta$	0.13[a] (0.15515)	$PM_{2.5} = 7.5 \ \mu g/m^3$
Lung cancer	Adults 30+ years of age	$RR = [(X + 1)/(X_0 + 1)]^\beta$	0.23218	$PM_{2.5} = 7.5 \ \mu g/m^3$

Source: Ostro 2004.
Note: a. Estimated from Pope and others (2009).

concentrations of $PM_{2.5}$ (Pope and others 2009). Pope and others (2009) derives a shape of the $PM_{2.5}$ exposure-response function based on studies of mortality from active cigarette smoking, secondhand cigarette smoke (SHS), and outdoor $PM_{2.5}$ air pollution. $PM_{2.5}$ exposure in Karachi and other cities in Sindh falls somewhere between the exposure levels in the studies of outdoor air pollution and SHS on the one hand, and active cigarette smoking on the other hand. Applying these results to the estimated $PM_{2.5}$ concentration levels in cities in Sindh indicates that the β-coefficient for CP mortality is around 0.13 for $PM_{2.5}$ concentrations of 55–88 $\mu g/m^3$, instead of 0.15515 reported in Ostro (2004). Therefore, a coefficient of 0.13 is applied to the cities in Sindh to estimate CP mortality from $PM_{2.5}$. Using β = 0.15515 instead of β = 0.13 would result in a 16 percent higher estimate of CP mortality.

Pope and others (2009) do not report an exposure-response relationship for LC mortality. Therefore, the β-coefficient in Ostro (2004) is applied to the cities in Sindh. This may result in an overestimate of LC mortality from PM in these cities, but as estimated LC mortality from PM is only about 2 percent of total estimated mortality from PM, the effect of this overestimation on total estimated mortality from PM is small.

The attributable fraction of mortality due to $PM_{2.5}$ among the exposed population is as follows:

$$AF = (RR - 1)/RR \tag{B.1}$$

Estimated relative risks (RR) and attributable fractions (AF) of mortality caused by PM in cities in Sindh are presented in table B.2. The AF for the cities as a whole are adjusted for effects of multiple risk factors, that is, for impacts of water, sanitation, and hygiene on ALRI mortality among children and for road traffic noise on a subset of CP mortality among adults (appendix H).

The adjusted AF are multiplied by annual ALRI, CP, and LC mortality among the exposed population to arrive at estimated annual mortality due to annual average PM ambient concentrations. The following equation is applied:

$$M_i = P_i * C * \alpha_i * AF_i^A * 1{,}000 \tag{B.2}$$

where i refers to ALRI, CP, or LC mortality; M is estimated annual cases of mortality from PM exposure; P is population (millions) exposed to PM; C is crude

Table B.2 Relative Risks and Attributable Fraction of Mortality from PM$_{2.5}$ in Cities in Sindh Province, 2009

Mortality	ALRI		Cardiopulmonary		Lung cancer	
Population group	Children <5 years of age		Population 30+ years of age		Population 30+ years of age	
Pollutant	PM$_{10}$		PM$_{2.5}$		PM$_{2.5}$	
β-coefficient per 1 μg/m^3 of PM	0.00166		0.13		0.23218	
	RR	AF (%)	RR	AF (%)	RR	AF (%)
Karachi	1.33	25.0	1.36	26.3	1.73	42.0
Hyderabad	1.30	23.3	1.34	25.6	1.70	41.0
Sukkur	1.21	17.4	1.29	22.6	1.58	36.7
Larkana	1.21	17.2	1.29	22.5	1.58	36.6
Mirpur Kas	1.23	18.9	1.31	23.4	1.61	37.9
Nawabshah	1.21	17.1	1.29	22.4	1.57	36.5
Jacobabad	1.21	17.4	1.29	22.6	1.58	36.7
Shikarpur	1.19	16.0	1.28	21.8	1.55	35.5
Tando Adam	1.19	16.0	1.28	21.8	1.55	35.5
Khaipur	1.19	15.9	1.28	21.7	1.55	35.4
Dadu, Tando Allah Yar, and Khandh Kot	1.19	16.0	1.28	21.8	1.55	35.5
Total (unadjusted)	n.a.	23.7	n.a.	25.7	n.a.	41.1
Total (adjusted)	n.a.	20.4	n.a.	24.0	n.a.	41.1

Note: n.a. = not applicable.

mortality rate (or death rate among children younger than five years old) per 1,000 population; α is the share of ALRI, CP, or LC in total mortality; and AF^A is the adjusted attributable fraction. Appendix A presents the data applied in equation B.2.

Table B.3 presents the morbidity health end points affected by PM pollution included in this study of Sindh. Cases of chronic bronchitis (CB) are estimated as follows:

$$CB = \alpha * P * 10 * 0.01 * \beta(X-X_0)/(1+0.01) * \beta (X-X_0) \qquad (B.3)$$

where α is the prevalence rate of CB per 100,000 population; P is exposed population (millions); $\beta = 0.9$; X is annual average ambient concentration of PM$_{10}$; and $X_0 = 10$ is the lower threshold level of PM below which it is assumed that the impact on CB prevalence is nonexistent of minimal. Annual cases of the other health end points (H$_i$) are estimated as follows:

$$H_i = \beta_i * P_i *10 * (X-X_0) \qquad (B.4)$$

where P$_i$ is the relevant population age group (millions). Appendix A presents the baseline health and demographic indicators used to estimate morbidity from PM.

Table B.3 Morbidity Health End Points from Particulate Matter Exposure in Sindh Province

Health end point	Exposure response	β (per 1 $\mu g/m^3$ of PM_{10})
Chronic bronchitis	Change in prevalence of CB in adult population	0.90%
Hospital admissions	Cases per 100,000 population	1.2
Emergency room visits	Cases per 100,000 population	23.54
Restricted activity days	Cases per 100,000 adults	5,750
Lower respiratory illness in children	Cases per 100,000 children	169
Respiratory symptoms	Cases per 100,000 adults	18,300

Sources: Abbey and others 1995; Ostro 1994.

Bibliography

Abbey, D., M. Lebowitz, P. Mills, and F. Petersen. 1995. "Long-Term Ambient Concentrations of Particulates and Oxidants and Development of Chronic Disease in a Cohort of Nonsmoking California Residents." *Inhalation Toxicology* 7: 19–34.

Ostro, B. 1994. "Estimating the Health Effects of Air Pollution: A Method with an Application to Jakarta." Policy Research Working Paper Series 1301, World Bank. Washington DC.

———. 2004. *Outdoor Air Pollution: Assessing the Environmental Burden of Disease at National and Local Levels.* Environmental Burden of Disease, Series 5. Geneva: World Health Organization.

Pakistan Medical Research Council. 1998. *National Health Survey of Pakistan 1990–94.* Islamabad: Pakistan Medical Research Council.

Pope, C. A., III, R. T. Burnett, D. Krewski, and others. 2009. "Cardiovascular Mortality and Exposure to Airborne Fine Particulate Matter and Cigarette Smoke: Shape of the Exposure-Response Relationship." *Circulation* 120: 941–48.

Pope, C. A., III, R. T. Burnett, M. J. Thun, E. Calle, D. Krewski, K. Ito, and G. Thurston. 2002. "Lung Cancer, Cardiopulmonary Mortality, and Long-Term Exposure to Fine Particulate Air Pollution." *Journal of the American Medical Association* 287: 1132–41.

WHO (World Health Organization). 2004. *Comparative Quantification of Health Risks: Global and Regional Burden of Disease Attributable to Selected Major Risk Factors.* Geneva: WHO.

———. 2009. "Estimated Deaths by Cause and WHO Member State, 2004." Department of Measurement and Health Information, WHO, Geneva. http://www.who.int/quantifying_ehimpacts/national/countryprofile/intro/en/index.html.

APPENDIX C

Health Effects of Road Traffic Noise

WHO (2011) provides a methodology for estimating health effects of road traffic noise. Health end points included in this methodology are ischemic heart disease (IHD), noise-induced cognitive impairment (NICI) in children, sleep disturbance, tinnitus, and annoyance.[1] The report and methodology is a product of several years of work, including WHO (2007a, 2007b). While WHO (2011) does not include the effect of noise on cerebrovascular disease (stroke), a recent prospective cohort study of more than 160,000 people in Denmark assessed the relationship between road traffic noise and stroke. Effects of noise on cerebrovascular (CBV) disease are therefore included in this assessment of the population in Sindh.

Exposure-response functions for three of the health end points in WHO (2011) are presented in table C.1. The function for IHD is expressed as an odds ratio (OR). Sleep disturbance and annoyance is expressed as highly sleep disturbed (HSD) people and highly annoyed (HA) people, respectively, as a percentage of the exposed population. Table C.2 presents the percentage of children with NICI because of noise exposure. The incidence rate ratio (IRR) for stroke (CBV disease outcome) from noise exposure is presented in table C.3, based on Sørensen and others (2011). Sørensen and others found that a 10 dB(A) (decibel a-weighted) higher level of traffic noise was associated with 1.14 times higher risk of stroke in all age groups and 1.27 times higher risk among 64 or more year olds.

The exposure-response relationships for IHD and stroke (CBV) are applied to mortality only, given that reliable data on incidence of IHD and stroke morbidity are not readily available for Sindh. The attributable fraction (AF) of IHD and CBV mortality from noise exposure is estimated as follows:

$$AF = \left(\sum_{i=1}^{n} P_i RR_i - 1 \right) / \sum_{i=1}^{n} P_i RR_i \qquad \text{(C.1)}$$

where i refers to noise exposure levels in increments of 5 dB for IHD and 10 dB for CBV; P_i is the percentage of the population exposed to noise level, i; and RR_i is the relative risk of IHD or CBV mortality at noise exposure level, i. RR is approximated by the OR for IHD and the IRR for CBV.

Table C.1 Health Effects of Noise Exposure

Health end point	Exposure-response relationship	Noise-exposure range (dB(A))
Ischemic heart disease	$OR = 1.63 - 6.13 * 10^{-4} * L^2 + 7.36 * 10^{-6} * L^3$	$55 \leq L \leq 80$ (16-hour day)
Sleep disturbance	$HSD = 20.8 - 1.05 * L + 0.01486 * L^2$	$45 \leq L \leq 70$ (night)
Annoyance	$HA = 0.5118 * (L-42) - 1.436 * 10^{-2} * (L-42^2)$ $+ 9.868 * 10^{-4} * (L-42^3)$	$45 \leq L \leq 75$ (24 hours)

Source: WHO 2011.

Table C.2 Noise-Induced Cognitive Impairment in Children

Noise exposure range dB(A), 24 hours	Children developing NICI (%)
<55	0
55–65	20
65–75	50
>75	75

Source: WHO 2011.

Table C.3 Incidence Rate Ratio for Stroke (Cerebrovascular) from Noise Exposure

Noise-exposure range dB(A), 24 hours	All age groups	>64 years of age
<55	1.0000	1.0000
55–65	1.1400	1.2700
65–75	1.2996	1.6129
>75	1.4815	2.0484

Source: Based on Sørensen and others (2011).

The AF of the population with NICI (children), or that is HSD or HA as a result of noise exposure, is estimated as follows:

$$AF = \sum_{i=1}^{n} P_i D_i \tag{C.2}$$

where i and P_i are defined for noise exposure levels in increments of 5 dB (A) for HSD and HA and 10 dB(A) for NICI, and D_i is the percentage of the population with NICI, HSD, or HA at exposure level i. D_i for HSD and HA is calculated from the exposure-response functions in table C.1. Table C.2 presents D_i for NICI in children.

On the basis of the population distribution in relation to noise exposure level in chapter 2, the AF for each health end point is presented in table C.4. These results indicate that 12–19 percent of IHD mortality and 14–21 percent of CBV mortality in cities with a population >100,000 is due to traffic-noise exposure,[2] 27–44 percent of children have NICI, 9–14 percent of the population is HSD, and 14–22 percent of the population is HA as a result of noise in these cities.

Table C.4 Estimated Attributable Fraction of Mortality and Population Affected by Noise

Percent

	Karachi			Other cities with 100K+ population		
	Low	*Medium*	*High*	*Low*	*Medium*	*High*
IHD	14	17	19	12	14	17
CBV (all ages)	17	19	21	14	17	19
NICI (children)	33	38	44	27	33	38
HSD	11	12	14	9	11	12
HA	16	19	22	14	16	19

Note: IHD = ischemic heart disease; CBV = cerebrovascular; NICI = noise-induced cognitive impairment; HSD = highly sleep disturbed; HA = highly annoyed.

The AFs for mortality in table C.4 are not adjusted for effects of multiple risk factors, that is, outdoor air pollution. For the cities with more than 100,000 population as a whole, the unadjusted AF for IHD is in the range of 13.6–18.7 percent and the adjusted AF in the range of 12.4–16.7 percent with a medium of 14.6 percent. The unadjusted AF for CBV is in the range of 16.1–20.7 percent and the adjusted AF in the range of 14.5–18.3 percent with a medium of 16.5 percent (appendix H).

Notes

1. Tinnitus is defined as the sensation of sound in the absence of an external sound source. This health end point is not included in this assessment for Sindh province because of lack of data.

2. The estimate of CBV mortality is based on the IRR for all age groups. Using the IRR for the population 64+ years of age gives a 10–13 percent higher mortality estimate.

Bibliography

Sørensen, M., M. Hvidberg, Z. J. Andersen, R. B. Nordsborg, K. G. Lillelund, J. Jakobsen, A. Tjonneland, K. Overvad, and O. Raaschou-Nielsen. 2011. "Road Traffic Noise and Stroke: A Prospective Cohort Study." *European Heart Journal* 32: 737–44.

WHO (World Health Organization). 2007a. *Experts Consultation on Methods of Quantifying Burden of Disease Related to Environmental Noise.* Copenhagen: WHO Regional Office for Europe.

———. 2007b. *Quantifying Burden of Disease from Environmental Noise: Second Technical Meeting Report.* Copenhagen: WHO Regional Office for Europe.

———. 2011. *Burden of Disease from Environmental Noise: Quantification of Healthy Life Years Lost in Europe.* Copenhagen: WHO Regional Office for Europe.

Mortality from Inadequate Water, Sanitation, and Hygiene

Inadequate water, sanitation, and hygiene (WSH) are directly and indirectly affecting population health in Pakistan. Directly, poor WSH causes diarrheal infections and other health effects, which in turn lead to mortality, especially in young children. Indirectly, poor WSH contributes to poor nutritional status in young children through the effect of diarrheal infections.[1] Poor nutritional status in turn increases the risk of child mortality from disease (Fishman and others 2004). Child underweight is the nutritional indicator most commonly used in assessing the risk of mortality from poor nutritional status (Fishman and others 2004).

Estimating the indirect health effects of diarrhea from WSH is undertaken in two stages. First, the fraction of under-five child mortality attributable to child underweight is estimated, following the methodology in Fishman and others (2004). Second, a fraction of under-five child mortality from underweight is attributed to diarrheal infections from WSH in early childhood, using the approach in Fewtrell and others (2007).

An alternative approach to estimating the fraction of mortality attributable to diarrheal infections from WSH is the methodology developed in Larsen (2007) and World Bank (2008). This, however, requires estimation of counterfactual prevalence rates of child underweight (prevalence of underweight in the absence of diarrheal infections) from original survey data of child nutritional status. As the original survey data in Pakistan are not readily available for this study, and the last survey in Pakistan is as old as 2001–02, the approach in Fewtrell and others (2007) is used here. The approach in Fewtrell and others gives a somewhat lower estimate of indirect mortality from WSH than the Larsen and World Bank methodology.

Estimates of increased risk of cause-specific mortality in children younger than five years of age with mild, moderate, and severe underweight is presented in table D.1, based on Fishman and others (2004).

Table D.1 Relative Risk of Mortality from Severe, Moderate, and Mild Underweight in Children Younger than Five Years Old

	Severe	Moderate	Mild	None
Acute lower respiratory infections	8.1	4.0	2.0	1.0
Diarrhea	12.5	5.4	2.3	1.0
Measles	5.2	3.0	1.7	1.0
Malaria	9.5	4.5	2.1	1.0
Other causes of mortality[a]	8.7	4.2	2.1	1.0

Source: Fishman and others 2004.
Note: Relative risks are in relation to nutritional status according to the NCHS international reference population.
a. Only other infectious diseases (except HIV) are included here (see Fewtrell and others 2007).

These relative risk ratios are applied to prevalence rates of child underweight (see appendix A) to estimate attributable fractions (AF$_j$) of mortality by cause, j, from child underweight as follows:

$$AF_j = \frac{\sum_{i=1}^{n} P_i (RR_{ji} - 1)}{\sum_{i=1}^{n} P_i (RR_{ji} - 1) + 1} \tag{D.1}$$

where RR$_{ji}$ is the relative risk of mortality from cause, j, for children in each of the underweight categories, i, in table B.1, and P$_i$ is the prevalence rate of underweight.

Annual cases of mortality from child underweight (by cause, j, in table D.1) are estimated as follows:

$$M_j = C * U5MR * AF_j \beta_j \tag{D.2}$$

where C is annual live childbirths (thousands), U5MR is the under-five child mortality rate (per 1,000 live births), and β_j is the fraction of under-five mortality by cause j (cause-specific mortality in 2008 is taken from WHO [2010]).

Annual under-five child mortality from water, sanitation, and hygiene (W) is then estimated as follows:

$$W = \sum_{j=1}^{j=m} \gamma_j M_j \tag{D.3}$$

where γ_j is the fraction of child underweight mortality (M$_j$) attributed to WSH through diarrheal infections in early childhood. WHO (Fewtrell and others 2007) uses $\gamma_j = 0.5$ for ALRI, measles, malaria, and "other infectious diseases," which is applied here. For diarrhea, 88 percent of cases globally are attributed to WSH (Pruss and others 2002; Prüss-Üstün and others 2004). The additional indirect effect through child underweight on diarrheal mortality is therefore minimal and ignored here.

Table D.2 Estimated Annual Mortality in Children Younger than Five Years Old from Poor Water, Sanitation, and Hygiene, 2009

	Annual mortality among children younger than five years old	Attributable fraction from WSH (%)	Annual mortality from WSH
Diarrheal diseases	11,771	88	10,359
Acute lower respiratory infections	13,358	29	3,868
Measles	44	29	13
Malaria	NE	NE	NE
Other infectious and parasitic diseases	8,541	35	2,979
Other causes	39,942	0	0
Total	73,656	23	17,218

Note: NE = not estimated.

Using equations D.1–D.3 provides estimates of under-five child mortality from WSH as presented in table D.2. The attributable fraction (AF) for ALRI has been adjusted for multiple risk factors in relation to household air pollution in rural areas and outdoor air pollution in urban areas. The unadjusted AF is 34 percent (appendix H). Overall, 23 percent of child mortality is attributed to WSH of which 60 percent are directly from diarrheal disease and 40 percent is through the effect of diarrheal disease on child underweight and consequent infectious disease mortality.[2]

Notes

1. Repeated infections, and especially diarrheal infections, have been found to significantly impair weight gains in young children. Studies documenting and quantifying this effect have been conducted in communities with a wide range of infection loads in a diverse group of countries such as Bangladesh (Bairagi and others 1987; Becker, Black, and Brown 1991; Black, Brown, and Becker 1984); the Gambia (Rowland, Cole, and Whitehead 1977; Rowland, Rowland, and Cole 1988); Guatemala (Martorell and others 1975); Guinea-Bissau (Molbak and others 1997); Indonesia (Kolsteren and others 1997); Mexico (Condon-Paoloni and others 1977); Peru (Checkley and others 1997); the Philippines (Adair and others 1993); Sudan (Zumrawi, Dimond, and Waterflow 1987); and Tanzania (Villamor and others 2004). World Bank (2008) provides a review of these studies.

2. These estimates are based on the under-five mortality rate discussed in appendix A.

Bibliography

Adair, L., B. M. Popkin, J. VanDerslice, J. Akin, D. Guilkey, R. Black, J. Briscoe, and W. Flieger. 1993. "Growth Dynamics during the First Two Years of Life: A Prospective Study in the Philippines." *European Journal of Clinical Nutrition* 47 (1): 42–51.

Bairagi, R., M. K. Chowdhury, Y. J. Kim, G. T. Curlin, and R. H. Gray. 1987. "The Association between Malnutrition and Diarrhoea in Rural Bangladesh." *International Journal of Epidemiology* 16 (3): 477–81.

Becker, S., R. E. Black, and K. H. Brown. 1991. "Relative Effects of Diarrhea, Fever and Dietary Energy Intake on Weight Gain in Rural Bangladeshi Children." *American Journal of Clinical Nutrition* 53: 1499–503.

Black, R. E., K. H. Brown, and S. Becker. 1984. "Effects of Diarrhea Associated with Specific Enteropathogens on the Growth of Children in Rural Bangladesh." *Pediatrics* 73: 799–805.

Checkley, W., R. H. Gilman, L. D. Epstein, M. Suarez, J. F. Diaz, L. Cabrera, R. E. Black, and C. R. Sterling. 1997. "Asymptomatic and Symptomatic Cryptosporidiosis: Their Acute Effect on Weight Gain in Peruvian Children." *American Journal of Epidemiology* 145: 156–63.

Condon-Paoloni, D., J. Cravioto, F. E. Johnston, E. R. De Licardie, and T. O. Scholl. 1977. "Morbidity and Growth of Infants and Young Children in a Rural Mexican Village." *American Journal of Public Health* 67: 651–56.

Fishman, M. S., L. E. Caulfield, M. De Onis, M. Blossner, A. A. Hyder, L. Mullany, and R. E. Black. 2004. "Childhood and Maternal Underweight." In *Comparative Quantification of Health Risks—Global and Regional Burden of Disease Attributable to Selected Major Risk Factors*, edited by M. Ezzati, A. D. Lopez, A. Rodgers, and C. J. L. Murray. Geneva: World Health Organization.

Fewtrell, L., A. Prüss-Üstün, R. Bos, F. Gore, and J. Bartram. 2007. *Water, Sanitation and Hygiene: Quantifying the Health Impact at National and Local Levels in Countries with Incomplete Water Supply and Sanitation Coverage*. Environmental Burden of Disease Series 15. Geneva: World Health Organization.

Kolsteren, P. W., J. A. Kusin, and S. Kardjati. 1997. "Morbidity and Growth Performance of Infants in Madura, Indonesia." *Annals Tropical Pediatrics* 17 (3): 201–08.

Larsen, B. 2007. *Cost of Environmental Health Risk in Children Under Five Years of Age: Accounting for Malnutrition in Ghana and Pakistan*. Report prepared for the World Bank Environment Department, World Bank, Washington, DC.

Martorell, R., J. P. Habicht, C. Yarbrough, A. Loehtig, R. E. Klein, and K. A. Western. 1975. "Acute Morbidity and Physical Growth in Rural Guatemalan Children." *Pediatrics* 129: 1296–301.

Molbak, K., M. Andersen, P. Aaby, N. Hojlyng, M. Jakobsen, M. Sodemann, and A. P. da Silva. 1997. "Cryptosporidium Infection in Infancy as a Cause of Malnutrition: A Community Study from Guinea-Bissau, West Africa." *American Journal of Clinical Nutrition* 65 (1): 149–52.

Pruss, A., D. Kay, L. Fewtrell, and J. Bartram. 2002. "Estimating the Burden of Disease from Water, Sanitation and Hygiene at the Global Level." *Environmental Health Perspectives* 110 (5): 537–42.

Prüss-Üstün, A., D. Kay, L. Fewtrell, and J. Bartram. 2004. "Unsafe Water, Sanitation and Hygiene." In *Comparative Quantification of Health Risks: Global and Regional Burden of Disease Attributable to Selected Major Risk Factors*, edited by M. Ezzati. Geneva: WHO.

Rowland, M. G., T. J. Cole, and R. G. Whitehead. 1977. "A Quantitative Study into the Role of Infection in Determining Nutritional Status in Gambian Village Children." *British Journal of Nutrition* 37: 441–50.

Rowland, M. G., S. G. Rowland, and T. J. Cole. 1988. "Impact of Infection on the Growth of Children from 0 to 2 Years in an Urban West African Community." *American Journal of Clinical Nutrition* 47: 134–38.

Villamor, E., M. R. Fataki, J. R. Bosch, R. L. Mbise, and W. W. Fawzi. 2004. "Human Immunodeficiency Virus Infection, Diarrheal Disease and Sociodemographic Predictors of Child Growth." *Acta Paediatrica* 93 (3): 372–79.

World Bank. 2008. *Environmental Health and Child Survival: Epidemiology, Economics, Experiences*. Washington, DC: World Bank.

WHO (World Health Organization). 2010. *World Health Statistics 2010*. Geneva: WHO.

Zumrawi, F. Y., H. Dimond, and J. C. Waterflow. 1987. "Effects of Infection on Growth in Sudanese Children." *Human Nutrition and Clinical Nutrition* 41: 453–61.

APPENDIX E

Health Effects of Household Use of Solid Fuels

Combustion of solid fuels for cooking is a major source of household air pollution (HAP) in developing countries. Combustion of these fuels is associated with an increased risk of several health outcomes. The evidence from studies around the world is summarized in meta-analyses by Desai, Mehta, and Smith (2004) and Smith, Mehta, and Feuz (2004) (table E.1). Risks of health outcomes from use of solid fuels reported from these meta-analyses are generally for fuel wood and other biomass fuels relative to the risks from use of liquid fuels (for example, liquefied petroleum gas [LPG]).[1] Many studies have also found an increased risk of lung cancer from the use of coal.

Three recent meta-analyses shed further light on acute respiratory infections (ARI), chronic obstructive pulmonary disease (COPD), and chronic bronchitis (table E.2). Dherani and others (2008) find a somewhat lower relative risk of ALRI in children younger than five years of age than Desai and others and Smith and others. However, Po, FitzGerald, and Carlsten (2011) find a substantially higher relative risk of ARI in children of various ages from studies that did not necessarily distinguish between upper and lower respiratory infections. For COPD, Kurmi and others (2010), and Po, FitzGerald, and Carlsten (2011), both find a lower relative risk than Desai and others, and Smith and others. These recent meta-analyses also report relative risks of chronic bronchitis (a subset of COPD).

Studies of health effects of outdoor ambient particulate matter (PM) have found that exposure to PM increases the risk of cardiovascular mortality (Pope and others 2002). No such study is available for HAP from use of solid fuels because of the data intensity of such studies. However, a recent study in Guatemala found that cooking with wood using an improved chimney stove is associated with a 3.7 mm Hg lower systolic blood pressure among adult women compared to systolic blood pressure among women cooking with wood on open fire (McCracken and others 2007). This reduction in systolic blood pressure is from a partial removal of particulate matter with a diameter of less than 2.5 microns ($PM_{2.5}$) exposure from the use of solid fuels.[2] Switching from use of

Table E.1 Health Outcomes and Relative Risks from Household Use of Solid Fuels

Evidence	Health outcome	Population group (years)	Relative risk ratios (RR)
Strong	Acute lower respiratory infection	Children <5	2.3
	Chronic obstructive pulmonary disease	Women ≥30	3.2
	Lung cancer (from exposure to coal smoke)	Women ≥30	1.9
Moderate–I	Chronic obstructive pulmonary disease	Men ≥30	1.8
	Lung cancer (from exposure to coal smoke)	Men ≥30	1.5
Moderate–II	Lung cancer (from exposure to biomass smoke)	Women ≥30	1.5
	Tuberculosis	All ≥15	1.5

Sources: Desai, Mehta, and Smith 2004; Smith, Mehta, and Feuz 2004.

Table E.2 Health Outcomes and Relative Risks from Recent Meta-Analyses

		Relative risk ratios		
Health outcome	Population group	Dherani and others (2008)	Kurmi and others (2010)	Po, FitzGerald, and Carlsten (2011)
Acute respiratory infection	Children	1.8[a]	—	3.5[b]
Chronic obstructive pulmonary disease	Adult women	—	2.8[c]	2.4
Chronic bronchitis	Adult women	—	2.3[c]	2.5

Note: — = not available.
a. Acute lower respiratory infection in children younger than 5 years of age.
b. Acute upper and lower respiratory infection in children of various ages.
c. Some of the studies included in the meta-analysis were of adults in general.

wood on an open fire to use of nonsolid fuels such as LPG can be expected to result in a larger reduction in systolic blood pressure. The reduction may be approximately 6 mm Hg. Elevated systolic blood pressure is associated with an increased risk of cardiovascular disease (Lawes and others 2004). Relative risks of cardiovascular mortality from an increase of 6 mm Hg in systolic blood pressure are presented in table E.3 (see appendix F). As a reference, Wilkinson and others (2009) use a relative risk of 1.2 for ischemic heart disease mortality in adult women based on a study of the shape of the PM exposure-response relationship by Pope and others (2009).

The aforementioned international studies provide a basis for establishing the relative risks of health effects from the use of wood and other biomass for cooking in Sindh province. Table E.4 presents the relative risks applied in this study Sindh. These relative risks are applied to children younger than five years old and adult women in households using these fuels, as these are the household members that are most exposed to air pollution from cooking. Tuberculosis in women is not included, as the evidence base is only moderate (Desai, Mehta, and Smith 2004).

Table E.3 Relative Risk of Cardiovascular Disease in Women 30 Years of Age or Older, from the Use of Solid Fuels without an Improved Stove

Health outcome	Relative risk ratio
Ischemic heart disease	1.2
Cerebrovascular disease	1.3
Hypertensive heart disease	1.5
Other cardiovascular disease	1.1

Sources: Based on Lawes and others (2004) and McCracken and others (2007).

Table E.4 Relative Risks of Health Effects from Cooking with Wood and Biomass Applied to Sindh Province

Health outcome	Relative risk ratio
Children <5 years	
Acute lower respiratory infection	2.0
Acute upper respiratory infection	2.0
Women ≥30 years	
Chronic obstructive pulmonary disease	2.8
Chronic bronchitis	2.4
Ischemic heart disease	1.2
Cerebrovascular disease	1.3
Hypertensive heart disease	1.5
Other cardiovascular disease	1.1
Lung cancer	1.5

Note: Risk ratios are relative to cooking with liquid fuels (gas, biogas, and kerosene).

The relative risk of ALRI in children applied to Sindh is somewhat higher than reported by Dherani and others but lower than the risk reported for ARI in general by Po and others. The relative risk of AURI in children applied here is well below that reported by Po and others. Thus, it likely results in a conservative estimate of AURI effects from solid fuel use. The relative risk for COPD is an average of the risks reported in the meta-analyses reviewed, and is applied to mortality. For morbidity, the relative risk of CB is applied because data on CB prevalence in Pakistan is more readily available than on COPD prevalence.

Notes

1. Other biomass fuels used for cooking are mostly straw/shrubs/grass, agricultural crop residues, and animal dung.

2. Although the improved chimney stove removes the smoke from the kitchen, household PM exposure reduction is smaller than the exposure reduction in the kitchen because smoke reenters dwellings and people are exposed to the smoke outside dwellings. For example, the Guatemala study found a 90 percent reduction in $PM_{2.5}$ concentrations in the kitchen from the improved chimney stove, but only a 20 percent reduction in the bedroom.

Bibliography

Desai, M. A., S. Mehta, and K. Smith. 2004. "Indoor Smoke from Solid Fuels: Assessing the Environmental Burden of Disease at National and Local Levels." Environmental Burden of Disease Series 4, World Health Organization, Geneva.

Dherani, M., D. Pope, M. Mascarenhas, K. Smith, M. Weber, and N. Bruce. 2008. "Indoor Air Pollution from Unprocessed Solid Fuel Use and Pneumonia Risk in Children Aged under Five Years: A Systematic Review and Meta-Analysis." *Bulletin of the World Health Organization* 86: 390–98.

Kurmi, O. P., S. Semple, P. Simkhada, W. C. Smith, and J. G. Ayres. 2010. "COPD and Chronic Bronchitis Risk of Indoor Air Pollution from Solid Fuel: A Systematic Review and Meta-Analysis." *Thorax* 65: 221–28.

Lawes, C. M. M., S. Vander Hoorn, M. R. Law, P. Elliott, S. MacMahon, and A. Rodgers. 2004. "High Blood Pressure." In *Comparative Quantification of Health Risks: Global and Regional Burden of Disease Attributable to Selected Major Risk Factors*, edited by M. Ezzati, A. D. Lopez, A. Rodgers, and C. J. L. Murray. Geneva: World Health Organization.

McCracken, J. P., K. R. Smith, A. Díaz, M. A. Mittleman, and J. Schwartz. 2007. "Chimney Stove Intervention to Reduce Long-Term Wood Smoke Exposure Lowers Blood Pressure among Guatemalan Women." *Environmental Health Perspectives* 115 (7): 996–1001.

Po, J. Y. T., J. M. FitzGerald, and C. Carlsten. 2011. "Respiratory Disease Associated with Solid Biomass Fuel Exposure in Rural Women and Children: Systematic Review and Meta-Analysis." *Thorax* 66: 232–39.

Pope, C. A., III, R. T. Burnett, M. J. Thun, E. Calle, D. Krewski, K. Ito, and G. Thurston. 2002. "Lung Cancer, Cardiopulmonary Mortality, and Long-Term Exposure to Fine Particulate Air Pollution." *Journal of the American Medical Association* 287: 1132–41.

Pope, C. A., III, R. T. Burnett, D. Krewski, M. Jerrett, Y. Shi, E. E. Calle, and M. J. Thun. 2009. "Cardiovascular Mortality and Exposure to Airborne Fine Particulate Matter and Cigarette Smoke: Shape of the Exposure-Response Relationship." *Circulation* 120: 941–48.

Smith, K., S. Mehta, and M. Feuz. 2004. "Indoor Air Pollution from Household Use of Solid Fuels." In *Comparative Quantification of Health Risks: Global and Regional Burden of Disease Attributable to Selected Major Risk Factors*, edited by M. Ezzati, A. D. Lopez, A. Rodgers, and C. J. L. Murray. Geneva: World Health Organization.

Wilkinson, P., K. R. Smith, M. Davis, H. Adair, B. G. Armstrong, M. Barrett, N. Bruce, A. Haines, I. Hamilton, T. Oreszczyn, I. Ridley, C. Tonne, and Z. Chalabi. 2009. "Public Health Benefits of Strategies to Reduce Greenhouse-Gas Emissions: Household Energy." *The Lancet* 374 (9705): 1917–29. doi:10.1016/S0140-6736(0961713-X.

Cardiovascular Mortality from Household Air Pollution

The first randomized intervention trial to measure the health benefit of household air pollution control was conducted in Guatemala in 2002–04. An intervention group received and cooked with a well-maintained improved wood stove with chimney and the control group cooked with wood on open fires. Particulate matter with a diameter of less than 2.5 microns ($PM_{2.5}$) exposure and blood pressure was measured over the study period in women 38 years of age or older. $PM_{2.5}$ exposure was 264 micrograms per cubic meter ($\mu g/m^3$) in the control group cooking with wood on open fires and 102 $\mu g/m^3$ in the intervention group cooking with improved chimney stoves. The improved stove intervention was associated with a 3.7 mm Hg lower systolic blood pressure (McCracken and others 2007).[1] This reduction in systolic blood pressure is from a partial removal of $PM_{2.5}$ exposure from the use of solid fuels.[2] Switching from use of wood on an open fire to use of nonsolid fuels such as LPG can be expected to result in a larger reduction in systolic blood pressure. The reduction may be approximately 6 mm Hg. Lawes and others (2004) presents relative risks of cardiovascular disease from a 10 mm Hg decrease in systolic blood pressure by age group (table F.1).

The relative risk of cardiovascular disease in women by age group from use of solid fuels without an improved stove (versus the use of nonsolid fuels) can be estimated as follows:

$$RR_{ij} = \exp(\beta_{ij} * \Delta \text{ mm Hg}) \qquad (F.1)$$

where

$$\beta_{ij} = \ln (1/RR_{ij}^{10}/10) \qquad (F.2)$$

with RR_{ij}^{10} being the relative risks in table F.1 for disease "i" and age group "j" and Δ mm Hg = 6. The relative risk of disease "i" for the population aged 30 or more years (that is, RR_i) can then be calculated from RR_{ij} and the disease

Table F.1 Relative Risk Ratios of Cardiovascular Disease from a 10 mm Hg Decrease in Systolic Blood Pressure

Disease type	Age group (years)				
	30–44	45–59	60–69	70–79	80+
Ischemic heart disease	0.52	0.60	0.75	0.80	0.94
Cerebrovascular disease	0.42	0.50	0.64	0.73	0.83
Hypertensive heart disease	0.16	0.40	0.57	0.65	0.63
Other cardiovascular disease	0.66	0.76	0.83	0.90	0.92

Source: Lawes and others 2004.

Table F.2 Relative Risk Ratios of Cardiovascular Disease, in Women 30 Years of Age or Older, from the Use of Solid Fuels without an Improved Stove

Disease type	Relative risk ratio
Ischemic heart disease	1.19
Cerebrovascular disease	1.26
Hypertensive heart disease	1.51
Other cardiovascular disease	1.12

incidence by age group. Table F.2 presents RR_i from the use of solid fuels without an improved stove. As a reference, Wilkinson and others (2009) use a relative risk of 1.2 for ischemic heart disease mortality in adult women based on a study of the shape of the PM exposure-response relationship by Pope and others (2009).

Notes

1. The diastolic blood pressure was 3.0 mm Hg lower.
2. Although the improved chimney stove removes the smoke from the kitchen, household PM exposure reductions are smaller than the exposure reduction in the kitchen because smoke re-enters dwellings and people are exposed to the smoke outside dwellings. For example, the Guatemala study found a 90 percent reduction in $PM_{2.5}$ concentrations in the kitchen from the improved chimney stove, but only a 20 percent reduction in the bedroom.

Bibliography

Lawes, C. M. M., S. Vander Hoorn, M. R. Law, P. Elliott, S. MacMahon, and A. Rodgers. 2004. "High Blood Pressure." In *Comparative Quantification of Health Risks: Global and Regional Burden of Disease Attributable to Selected Major Risk Factors*, edited by M. Ezzati, A. D. Lopez, A. Rodgers, and C. J. L. Murray. Geneva: World Health Organization.

McCracken, J. P. K. R. Smith, A. Díaz, M. A. Mittleman, and J. Schwartz. 2007. "Chimney Stove Intervention to Reduce Long-Term Wood Smoke Exposure Lowers Blood Pressure among Guatemalan Women." *Environmental Health Perspectives* 115 (7): 996–1001.

Pope, C. A., III, R. T. Burnett, D. Krewski, M. Jerrett, Y. Shi, E. E. Calle, and M. J. Thun. 2009. "Cardiovascular Mortality and Exposure to Airborne Fine Particulate Matter and Cigarette Smoke: Shape of the Exposure-Response Relationship." *Circulation* 120: 941–48.

Wilkinson, P., K. R. Smith, M. Davis, H. Adair, B. G. Armstrong, M. Barrett, N. Bruce, A. Haines, I. Hamilton, T. Oreszczyn, I. Ridley, C. Tonne, and Z. Chalabi. 2009. "Public Health Benefits of Strategies to Reduce Greenhouse-Gas Emissions: Household Energy." *The Lancet* 374 (9705): 1917–29.

APPENDIX G

Valuation of Mortality

Approaches for Valuation of Mortality

Economists commonly use two distinct methods of valuation of mortality to estimate the social cost of premature death—that is, the human capital approach (HCA) and the value of statistical life (VSL). The first method was dominant in the past, but the VSL approach has increasingly replaced it in the past couple of decades. This book applies the HCA as a lower bound and VSL as a higher bound in estimating the cost of adult mortality. For child mortality, the HCA is applied.

Human Capital Approach

The HCA is based on the economic contribution of an individual to society over the individual's lifetime. Death involves an economic loss that is approximated by the loss of all future income of the individual. Future income is discounted to reflect its value at the time of death. The discount rate commonly applied is the rate of time preference. Thus the social cost of mortality, according to the HCA, is the discounted future income of an individual at the time of death. If the risk of death, or mortality risk, is evenly distributed across income groups, average expected future income is applied to calculate the social cost of death. Mathematically, the present value of future income, or human capital value (HCV), is expressed as follows:

$$HCV_0 = PV_0(I) = \sum_{i=k}^{i=n} I_0(1+g)^i / (1+r)^i \qquad (G.1)$$

where PV_0 (I) is present value of income (I) in year 0 (year of death), g is annual growth in real income, and r is the discount rate (rate of time preference). As equation G.1 shows, the equation allows for income to start from year k, and ending in year n. In the case of children, $i \in \{15,\ldots,65\}$, assuming the lifetime income on average starts at age 15 and ends at retirement at age 65. This book applies an annual growth of real income of 2 percent and a discount rate of 3 percent.

An important issue is often raised regarding the HCA. This centers on the application of this valuation approach to individuals who do not participate in the economy—that is, to individuals not having an income, such as the elderly, family members taking care of the home, and children. One may think of an extension of the HCA that recognizes the value of nonpaid household work at the same rate as the average income earner, or at a rate equal to the cost of hiring a household helper. In this case, the HCA can be applied to the death of nonincome earners and children (whether or not children will become income earners or take care of the home during their adult life). In the case of the elderly, the HCA would assign zero economic value to old individuals who have either retired from the workforce or do not make significant contributions to household work. This obviously is a serious shortcoming of the HCA approach. Therefore, the HCV for adults is calculated here based on the number of years lost to premature death, that is, on average 10 years of life because of outdoor air pollution and 30 years because of road traffic accidents.

An estimate of average annual income is needed to estimate the HCV. The following equation is one option to estimate annual income:

$$I_0 = gdp_0 * I_L/L_0 \tag{G.2}$$

where gdp_0 is GDP per capita in the year of death, I_L is the labor income share of GDP, and L_0 is the labor participation rate (percentage of total population). Sindh's GDP per capita is estimated at PRs 100,336 (US\$1,279) in 2009 (see table G.2 below). The labor income share is assumed to be 50 percent of GDP. Labor participation is 33 percent of the total population (FBS 2010). Therefore, annual average income is estimated at approximately PRs 152,000 per working person.

Alternatively, annual income can be estimated from the HIES 2007–08 (FBS 2009). The reported monthly household income in Sindh reported by this survey was PRs 14,819. Adjusting this figure by the nominal increase in GDP per capita to 2009 reported in FBS (2011) indicates that monthly household income in Sindh in 2009 might have been about PRs 19,825. Dividing this figure by the average number of employed household members of 2.04 (FBS 2009) and multiplying by 12 months per year, indicates that annual average income was PRs 116,620 per person working. This income figure is nearly 25 percent lower than the figure estimated by equation G.2. An average of the two income figures—that is, PRs 134,345—is applied here to estimate the HCV. The HCV, or cost of premature mortality according to the HCA, is presented for children (average age of 1 year, 2.5 years, and 10 years at time of death) and adults in table G.1.

Value of Statistical Life

While the HCA involves economic valuation of the death of an individual, VSL is based on valuation of mortality risk. Everyone in society is constantly facing a certain risk of dying. Examples of such risks are occupational fatality risk, risk of traffic accident fatality, and environmental mortality risks. Individuals adjust their

Table G.1 Cost of Mortality (per Death) Using Human Capital Approach

Population group	Human capital value (PRs)
Adults (30 years loss of life)	3,477,093
Adults (10 years loss of life)	1,273,763
Children at 10 years of age	5,711,559
Children at 2.5 years of age	4,824,922
Children at 1 year of age	4,614,495

behavior and decisions in relation to such risks. For example, individuals demand a higher wage (a wage premium) for a job that involves a higher than average occupational risk of fatal accident, individuals may purchase safety equipment to reduce the risk of death, individuals and families may be willing to pay a premium or higher rent for properties (land and buildings) in a cleaner and less polluted neighborhood or city—or some combination of the preceding circumstances.

Through the observation of individuals' choices and willingness to pay for reducing mortality risk (or minimum amounts that individuals require to accept a higher mortality risk), it is possible to estimate the value to society of reducing mortality risk, or, equivalently, measure the social cost of a particular mortality risk. For example, it may be observed that a certain health hazard has a mortality risk of 1/10,000. This means that one individual dies from this hazard for every 10,000 individuals. If each individual on average is willing to pay PRs 200 for eliminating this mortality risk, then every 10,000 individuals are collectively willing to pay PRs 2 million. This amount is the VSL. Mathematically it can be expressed as follows:

$$VSL = WTP_{Ave} * 1/R \tag{G.3}$$

where WTP_{Ave} is the average willingness-to-pay per individual for a mortality risk reduction of magnitude R. In the example above, R = 1/10,000 (or R = 0.0001) and WTP_{Ave} = PRs 200. Thus, if 10 individuals die from the health risk illustrated above, the cost to society is 10* VSL = 10* PRs 2 million = PRs 20 million.

The main approaches to estimating VSL are through revealed preferences and stated preferences of people's WTP for a reduction in mortality risk or their willingness to accept (WTA) an increase in mortality risk. Most of the studies of revealed preferences are hedonic wage studies, which estimate labor market wage differentials associated with differences in occupational mortality risk. Most of the stated preference studies rely on contingent valuation methods (CVM), which in various forms ask individuals about their WTP for mortality risk reduction.

Studies of WTP for a reduction in risk of mortality have been carried out in numerous countries, but there are no such studies from Pakistan. A commonly used approach to estimate VSL in Pakistan is therefore to use a benefit transfer (BT) based on meta-analyses of WTP studies from other countries.

Several meta-analyses have been conducted in the past decade, including Mrozek and Taylor (2002), Viscusi and Aldy (2002), Kochi, Hubbell, and Kramer (2006), and Navrud and Lindhjem (2010). Meta-analyses assess characteristics that determine VSL, such as household income, size of risk reduction, other individual and household characteristics, and often characteristics of the methodologies used in the original WTP studies.

Most of the meta-analyses of VSL are based entirely or predominantly on hedonic wage studies. The meta-analysis by Navrud and Lindhjem (2010), prepared for the OECD, is however exclusively based on stated preference studies, arguably of greater relevance for valuation of mortality risk from environmental factors than hedonic wage studies. These stated preference studies are from a database of more than 1,000 VSL estimates from multiple studies in more than 30 countries, including in developing countries with a range of GDP per capita that at the lower end is similar to that of Pakistan (www.oecd.org/env/policies /VSL). Navrud and Lindhjem provide an empirically estimated BT function from these stated preference studies that can be readily applied to estimate VSL in Pakistan and Sindh province:

$$VSL = e^{(0.0433 + 1.022 \ln(gdp) - 0.445 \ln(r))} \tag{G.4}$$

where *VSL* is expressed in purchasing power parity (PPP) adjusted dollars, *gdp* is GDP per capita in PPP adjusted dollars, and *r* is the change in risk of mortality.[1] The VSL is then converted to Rupees by multiplying by the PPP rate of 29.37 PRs/dollar in 2009, which is the ratio "GDP in rupees/PPP adjusted GDP in dollars" in 2009 from World Bank (2011).

Table G.2 presents estimates of GDP per capita in Pakistan and Sindh. Pakistan per capita figures in rupees are calculated from GDP at market prices (average of the years 2008–09 and 2009–10 reported in FBS [2011]). These figures are converted to U.S. dollars and PPP adjusted dollars using the exchange rate and PPP rate from World Bank (2011). Sindh's GDP is reported to have been 27 percent of Pakistan's GDP in 2007. Sindh's population was 22.3 percent of Pakistan's population in 2007 (GoP 2009). Thus, GDP per capita in Sindh was 21 percent higher than that of Pakistan. Applying this differential to 2009 provides the figures for Sindh in table G.2.

Applying the BT function (equation G.4) also involves specifying change in mortality risk (r). The mortality risk from environmental factors depends on the environmental factor at hand. Most stated preference studies of VSL use a mortality risk in the range of 1/10,000–5/10,000 per year. Applying this range of mortality risk and the estimated PPP adjusted GDP per capita in Sindh in 2009

Table G.2 GDP Per Capita, Pakistan and Sindh Province, 2009

	PRs	US$	PPP dollars
Pakistan	82,981	1,058	2,825
Sindh province	100,336	1,279	3,416

Table G.3 Estimated Value of Statistical Life, 2009

Change in annual mortality risk (r)	VSL (PPP adjusted dollars)	VSL (Million PRs)
r = 0.0001 (1/10,000)	257,076	7.55
r = 0.00025 (2.5/10,000)	170,993	5.02
r = 0.0005 (5/10,000)	125,609	3.69

provides estimates of VSL in Sindh in 2009, as presented in table G.3. This study applies the VSL of PRs 5.02 million, reflecting a mortality risk of 2.5/10,000 per year.[2]

Notes

1. This BT function implies that the income elasticity is 1.022, meaning that VSL varies across countries in proportion to their PPP-adjusted GDP per capita level.

2. In perspective, the estimated VSL for the high-income OECD countries in 2009 using equation G.4 and a mortality risk of 2.5/10,000 is about US$2.2 million, reflecting a GDP per capita of US$39,000.

Bibliography

FBS (Federal Bureau of Statistics). 2009. *Household Integrated Economic Survey 2007–08.* Pakistan: Federal Bureau of Statistics.

———. 2010. *Labor Force Survey 2008–09.* Pakistan: Federal Bureau of Statistics.

———. 2011. *Pakistan Statistical Yearbook 2011.* Pakistan: Federal Bureau of Statistics.

GoP (Government of Pakistan). 2009. *Pakistan Demographic Survey 2007.* Statistics Division, Government of Pakistan.

Kochi, I., B. Hubbell, and R. Kramer. 2006. "An Empirical Bayes Approach to Combining and Comparing Estimates of the Value of a Statistical Life for Environmental Policy Analysis." *Environmental and Resource Economics* 34 (3): 385–406.

Mrozek, J., and L. Taylor. 2002. "What Determines the Value of Life? A Meta-Analysis." *Journal of Policy Analysis and Management* 21 (2): 253–70.

Navrud, S., and H. Lindhjem. 2010. "Meta-Analysis of Stated Preference VSL Studies: Further Model Sensitivity and Benefit Transfer Issues." Prepared for the Environment Directorate, OECD.

Viscusi, W. K., and J. E. Aldy. 2002. "The Value of a Statistical Life: A Critical Review of Market Estimates throughout the World." Discussion Paper 392, Harvard Law School, Cambridge, MA.

World Bank. 2011. *World Development Indicators.* Washington, DC: World Bank.

APPENDIX H

Adjusting Mortality Estimates for Multiple Risk Factors

Several of the environmental risk factors assessed in this book cause an increase in the same disease-specific mortality in a particular age group of the population. In urban areas, this is the case for outdoor air pollution (OAP) and noise, and for outdoor air pollution and water, sanitation, and hygiene (WSH). In rural areas, this is the case for household air pollution (HAP) and WSH (table H.1). WSH cause diarrheal disease that in turn contributes to child underweight with consequent increase in risk of infectious disease mortality, for example, acute lower respiratory infections (ALRI) as discussed in appendix D.

When more than one of the environmental risk factors assessed in this book causes the same disease-specific mortality in urban or rural areas, then total disease-specific mortality from these risk factors is overestimated if simply added up by risk factor. To avoid this double-counting the joint attributable fraction (AF^T) formula for n risk factors can, under certain conditions, be applied to estimate total mortality from the specific disease (i):

$$AF_i^T = 1 - \Pi_{k=1}^{n}(1 - AF_i^k) \tag{H.1}$$

However, this formula does not provide the "adjusted" AF_i for each risk factor so that:

$$AF_i^T = \sum_{k=1}^{n} (\text{"adjusted" } AF_i^k) \tag{H.2}$$

As an approximation, the adjusted attributable fraction for each individual risk factor is calculated here as follows:

$$\text{"adjusted" } AF_i^k = AF_i^k * AF_i^T / \sum_{k=1}^{n} AF_i^k \tag{H.3}$$

where the adjusted attributable fractions satisfy equation H.2. As seen in table H.2, the joint AFs are 4–10 percentage points lower than the sum of the individual unadjusted AFs, and the individual adjusted AFs are 1.6–5.4

Table H.1 Disease-Specific Mortality Caused by Environmental Risk Factors

Disease-specific mortality	Geographic domain	Environmental risk factors
ALRI mortality in children	Urban	Outdoor air pollution (OAP) and water, sanitation, and hygiene (WSH)
	Rural	Household air pollution (HAP) and water, sanitation, and hygiene (WSH)
Cardiopulmonary disease mortality in adults	Urban	Outdoor air pollution (OAP) and noise (N)[a]
	Rural	Household air pollution (HAP) only[b]

Note: a. Ischemic heart disease and cerebrovascular disease mortality.
b. Use of solid fuels (the household air pollution factor assessed in this book) is predominantly a rural issue in Sindh.

Table H.2 Estimated Adjusted Attributable Fractions from Multiple Risk Factors

Disease-specific mortality	Geographic domain	Environmental risk factors	Unadjusted AF (%)	Joint AF (%)	Adjusted AF (%)
ALRI mortality in children	Urban	OAP	23.69	49.71	20.38
		WSH	34.10		29.33
	Rural	HAP	29.14	53.30	24.56
		WSH	34.10		28.74
Ischemic heart disease mortality	Urban	OAP	25.67	37.70	23.12
		Noise	16.19		14.58
Cerebrovascular disease mortality	Urban	OAP	25.67	39.38	22.91
		Noise	18.45		16.47

Note: The unadjusted AFs are from the individual sections of this book.

percentage points lower than the individual unadjusted AFs. As ischemic heart disease and cerebrovascular disease mortality is only a subset of cardiopulmonary disease mortality, the adjusted attributable fraction for cardiopulmonary mortality caused by OAP only declines from 25.67 percent to 24.02 percent.

The individual sections of this book apply the adjusted AFs to estimate mortality from each environmental risk factor. It should be noted, however, that the joint AF formula as applied here hinges on two key assumptions (Gakidou and others 2007). First, exposures to the risk factors are uncorrelated. Data are not available to confirm that this assumption holds. However, there is no evidence suggesting that drinking water quality, sanitation, and hygiene conditions in urban areas are correlated with PM ambient air quality. In addition, while road traffic noise and air pollution from road traffic is likely correlated, road traffic pollution constitutes only a fraction of total PM pollution in, for example, Karachi (Mansha and others 2011). In rural areas, about 90 percent of households are using solid fuels for cooking (the HAP factor assessed in this book), while poor drinking water quality and sanitation varies greatly across rural areas. Thus, any correlation is weak at the most. The second assumption is that the hazardous effects of one risk factor are not mediated through any of the other risk factors.

Bibliography

Gakidou, E., S. Oza, C. V. Fuertes, A. Y. Li, D. K. Lee, A. Sousa, M. C. Hogan, S. Vander Hoorn, and M. Ezzati. 2007. "Improving Child Survival through Environmental and Nutritional Interventions." *Journal of the American Medical Association* 298 (16): 1876–87.

Mansha, M., B. Ghauri, S. Rahman, and A. Amman. 2011. "Characterization and Source Apportionment of Ambient Air Particulate Matter (PM2.5) in Karachi." *Science of the Total Environment* 425: 176–83.

Particulate Matter Emissions in Karachi

Sources of PM Emissions

Many sectors and human behaviors contribute to PM outdoor air pollution in Karachi, including road vehicles; industry and power generation; fuels used by the domestic, commercial, and public sectors; burning of solid waste; the construction sector; resuspended PM as a result of poor cleaning of streets; natural dust from areas outside the city; salt particles from the sea; and burning of agricultural crop residue.

About 2 million motorized vehicles travel the roads of Karachi. More than 6,000 registered industrial units operate in the city (Amjad 2010), and the city contributes an estimated 30 percent of national industrial production and an even larger share of national manufacturing value added (Hasan 2007; http://www.urckarachi.org). As much as 10,000–12,000 tons of solid waste is generated daily, of which a substantial amount is burned within the city (CDGK 2007; Dawn 2011).

The government has and is taking actions to curtail outdoor air pollution. Growth in petroleum product consumption over the past 20 years has been reduced with increased use of cleaner natural gas. Pakistan now has more than 2.5 million vehicles fueled by compressed natural gas (CNG) and is the country with the most such vehicles in the world (MoF 2011). Euro 2 diesel with 500 parts per million (ppm) sulfur is being fully implemented this year. Low-sulfur fuel oil (S = 1 percent) is being imported in some quantities, in contrast to the fuel oil with an average sulfur content of about 3 percent supplied by the domestic refineries. Full-size CNG buses have been introduced in Karachi. Plans have been developed to convert rickshaws with two-stroke gasoline engines to four-stroke CNG. The banning of two-stroke motorcycles has been discussed. A ban on the burning of solid waste in the city has been put in place, although strict enforcement yet has to take effect. Some actions have also been taken to deal with numerous industrial polluters.

Energy Consumption

Primary commercial energy consumption in Pakistan was nearly 50 million tons of oil equivalents (TOE) in 2009, of which 46 percent was natural gas, 39 percent was oil products, 8 percent was coal, and 6–7 percent was hydro and nuclear (table I.1). Power production and transport were the largest consumers of oil products. Industry was the predominant consumer of coal (mainly brick kilns and cement industry). Power, industry, and the residential sectors were the largest consumers of natural gas, but with 10 percent of natural gas consumed by the transport sector.

Coal consumption doubled from 2001 to 2010, and natural gas and oil product consumption increased by 66 percent and 8 percent, respectively, over the same period. Gas consumption increased the most in the industrial sector (by about 5 million TOE), and by about 2 million TOE in each of the residential, power, and transport sectors. Oil product consumption declined in the residential (−80 percent and industrial (−49 percent) sectors, and increased marginally in the transport (+9 percent) and power (+36 percent) sectors (MoF 2011).

Around one-third of Pakistan's primary fossil fuel consumption was consumed in Sindh in 2008–09. Sindh's shares of natural gas and coal consumption were 40 percent and 36 percent, respectively (table I.2). Electricity generation and

Table I.1 Primary Commercial Energy Consumption in Pakistan, 2009
thousand TOE

	Coal/peat	Oil	Natural gas	Hydro	Nuclear	Total	Sectoral shares (%)
Power	71	8,623	6,751	2,416	754	18,615	38
Industry	4,051	979	7,997	n.a.	n.a.	13,027	26
Transport	0	8,878	2,201	n.a.	n.a.	11,079	22
Residential	0	593	4,877	n.a.	n.a.	5,470	11
Commercial/public	0	352	821	n.a.	n.a.	1,173	2
Agriculture	0	61	0	n.a.	n.a.	61	0
Total	4,122	19,486	22,647	2,416	754	49,425	100
Fuel shares (%)	8.3	39.4	45.8	4.9	1.5	100.0	n.a.

Source: International Energy Agency (2010). http://www.iea.org/stats/balancetable.asp?COUNTRY_CODE=PK.
Note: n.a. = not applicable.

Table I.2 Fossil Fuel Primary Energy Consumption, 2008–09
thousand TOE

	Sindh	Pakistan	Sindh (% of Pakistan)
Oil	3,785.1	18,226.8	21
Natural gas[a]	9,755.8	24,137.9	40
LPG	96.4	570.0	17
Coal	1,689.4	4,732.8	36
Total	15,326.7	47,667.5	32

Source: Produced from data in HDIP (2009).
Note: a. Excluding feedstock for the fertilizer industry.

industry in Sindh consumed 34 percent and 37 percent, respectively, of fossil fuels used by these sectors in Pakistan (figure I.1).

Primary fossil fuel consumption in Karachi is here estimated at around 2.7 million metric tons of petroleum products, 1.4 million metric tons of coal, and about 6.2 million metric tons TOE of natural gas (table I.3).[1] The estimates are based on primary energy consumption in Sindh, the population of Karachi, and data on industry and the power and road transport sectors. Industry, power, and road transport are the largest consumers of fossil fuel energy in Karachi. The power sector is the largest consumer of fuel oil, the transport sector of diesel, and industry and power of natural gas. Coal is almost exclusively consumed by the industrial sector.

Most of the fuel oil has a high sulfur content averaging around 3 percent. Diesel has also had high sulfur content, but has from this year been reduced to 500 ppm (0.05 percent). High sulfur content creates higher PM emissions from combustion and contributes to secondary particulates (sulfates). Coal is primarily consumed by the cement industry, and PM emissions depend on process and PM emission-control technology.

Although only around 3 percent of households in Karachi use wood/biomass for cooking (NIPS/Macro 2008), total wood/biomass consumption is around 96,000 tons per year if households on average use about 1.5 tons per year. This results in a substantial amount as PM emissions because emissions per ton of wood/biomass are much higher than per ton of petroleum products and natural gas.

Figure I.1 Fossil Fuel Primary Energy Consumption in Sindh Province, 2008–09

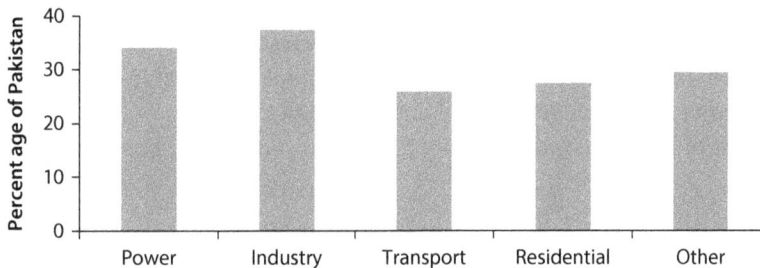

Source: Produced from data in HDIP (2009).

Table I.3 Estimated Primary Fossil Fuel Consumption in Karachi, 2008–09

'000 tonnes (metric tons)

	Fuel oil	Diesel	Gasoline	Natural gas ('000 TOE)	Coal
Domestic	11	n.a.	n.a.	1,077	n.a.
Industry	122	122	n.a.	2,693	1,400
Road transport	n.a.	1,433	311	406	n.a.
Power	546	n.a.	n.a.	1,862	n.a.
Public and commercial	57	57	n.a.	152	n.a.
Total	736	1,612	311	6,190	1,400

Note: n.a. = not applicable.

Road Vehicles

There were 2.1 million registered motor vehicles in Sindh province in 2010, up from 1.4 million in 2001 (figure I.2). Nearly half of these vehicles were motorcycles, one-third were passenger cars (motor cars, jeeps, station wagons), and nearly 10 percent were agricultural tractors (most of the "other" category) in 2010. Registered vehicle growth in Sindh was 52 percent from 2001 to 2010. The fastest growth was among three-wheelers (77 percent), motorcycles (63 percent), and taxis (53 percent), and the slowest growth was among buses/minibuses (27 percent).

Sindh had 27 percent of all registered motor vehicles in Pakistan in 2010. Relative to its population share of about 22 percent of Pakistan's population, Sindh has disproportionately many passenger cars, taxis and three-wheelers, but much less buses/minibuses. Registered buses/minibuses per 100,000 population were one-third lower in Sindh than in the rest of Pakistan in 2010 (FBS 2011).

The number of registered motor vehicles may represent an underestimate of the actual number of vehicles. The *Economic Survey of Pakistan 2010–11* reports a 25 percent higher number of motor vehicles in Pakistan than the number of registered vehicles in 2010 (MoF 2011). The difference is mainly due to a larger number of passenger cars and motorcycles. If the difference is similar in Sindh province, then total number of motor vehicles in Sindh was 2.6 million instead of 2.1 million in 2010.

The actual number of motor vehicles in Karachi is uncertain and is likely higher than the number of registered vehicles. Here, it is estimated at around 2 million vehicles, based on registered vehicles and a larger number of passenger cars and motorcycles, as indicated by the *Economic Survey of Pakistan 2010–11* (table I.4). A majority of passenger cars, as many as 90 percent of taxis, 40–45 percent of minibuses, and some rickshaws now use CNG. More than 40 percent of buses are over 15 years of age, but some CNG buses have recently

Figure I.2 Registered Motor Vehicles in Sindh Province ('000), 2001–10

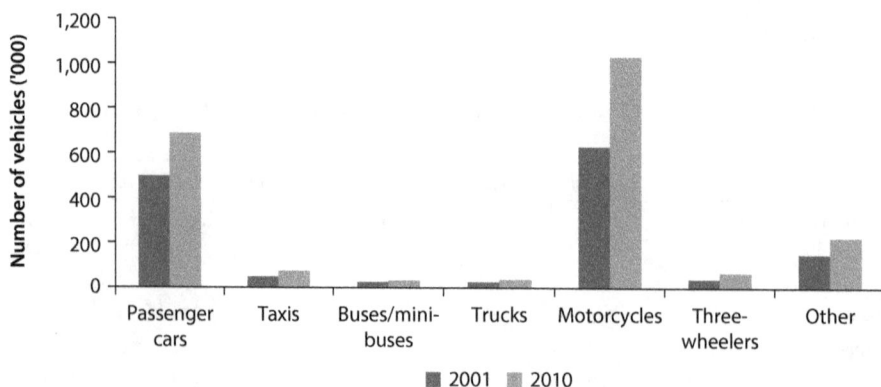

Source: Produced from FBS (2011).

Table I.4 Estimated Vehicles in Karachi, 2010

Passenger cars	844,000
Taxis	61,000
Buses/minibuses	22,000
Trucks	28,000
Vans and pickups	96,000
Motorcycles	905,000
Rickshaws	55,000
Total motor vehicles	2,011,000

Figure I.3 Transport Sector Fuel Mix in South and East Asia (% of Total Transport Fuel), 2009

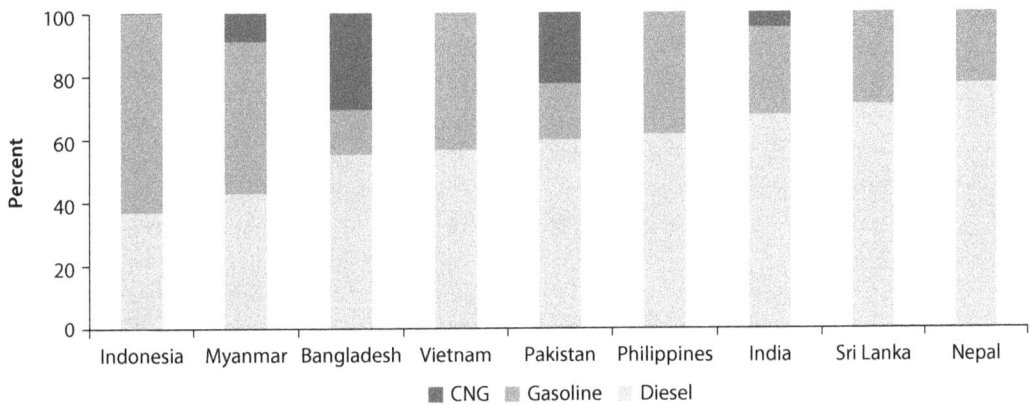

Source: International Energy Agency. http://www.iea.org/Textbase/stats/.

been introduced. A vast majority of motorcycles have two-stroke engines, most of which are highly polluting.

The diesel share of road transport fuels in Pakistan is around 60 percent, and ranges from 37 percent to 78 percent in other larger developing countries in South and East Asia with a GDP per capita (PPP) of less than US$ 5,000 (figure I.3) The diesel share in Pakistan is comparable to the shares in large high-income countries such as Germany and the United Kingdom (56–57 percent), Italy (67 percent), and France (78 percent), but higher than in Japan (35 percent) and the United States (27 percent). However, PM emissions per diesel vehicle in Pakistan are many times higher than in these high-income countries because of stringent emission controls in the high-income countries.

Industry and Power Generation

Industry and the power sector consist of numerous large, medium, and small stationary sources of PM emissions. Many industrial plants are located in industrial areas of Karachi, including SITE, Landhi, Korangi, Malir and Bin Qasim, Textile City, Northern Bypass Industrial Zone, and North Karachi (Amjad 2010;

CDGK 2007; Sajjad and others 2010). Large industrial and power plants that often can be major sources of PM emissions include two refineries in Korangi; one fertilizer plant, one integrated steel mill, and one cement plant in Bin Qasim; and eight fossil fuel-fired power plants in Bin Qasim, Korangi, and SITE.

There are seven oil refineries in Pakistan. Their combined crude oil processing capacity was about 13 million tons per year in 2008–09 (HDIP 2009). Two of the refineries are located in Korangi (National Refinery and Pakistan Refinery) and one is located in Baluchistan about 45 kilometers (km) from Karachi (Bosicor Refinery). The two refineries in Korangi processed more than 4 million tons of crude oil in 2008–09 (HDIP 2009). The refinery in Baluchistan processed more than 0.9 million tons of crude and is in the process of constructing an adjacent refinery with a capacity of 120,000 barrels per day, or about a 45 percent increase in Pakistan's total capacity. One refinery in Punjab is already producing low-sulfur diesel (500 ppm) to comply with Euro II standard, and other refineries are in the process of upgrading their facilities.

There are about 10 fertilizer plants in Pakistan of which the largest, Fauji Fertilizer Bin Qasim Ltd., is located in Bin Qasim in Karachi. The plant produces around 1.1–1.2 million tons of fertilizer per year (FFBL 2011).

Steel production in Pakistan is about 4 million tons per year from one large integrated steel mill (Pak Steel Mills), 168 reporting smelters, and 300 reporting re rolling mills (MIP 2012). According to MAC (2006), the steel sector is larger than this, with 450 foundries, 82 scrap smelters, and more than 60 steel pipe mills, and an additional number of re-rolling mills. Pak Steel Mills produces about 1 million tons of steel per year and is located in Bin Qasim about 40 km east (southeast) of Karachi. Numerous other foundries, mills, and smelters are located in other areas of the city.

The All Pakistan Cement Manufacturer Association (APCMA) provides a list of 24 cement companies with at least 30 cement plants in Pakistan. The production capacity of these plants was around 44 million tons of cement per year in 2010, up from 16 million tons in 2000. Total production was 31–34 million tons of cement per year during the period 2009–11. At least eight cement plants are located in Sindh province. Seven of these plants are located more than 50 km from Karachi. The eighth plant, Pakistan Slag Cement, has a production capacity of about 0.25 million tons per year (800 tons per day) and is located in Zulfiqarabad (Bin Qasim) in Karachi.

Karachi is served by electricity from power plants in Karachi and the national grid. The Karachi Electricity Supply Company (KESC) is responsible for electricity distribution from its own power plants and purchases from other power plants in Karachi and the national grid. KESC purchases nearly half of the electricity it distributes from other power companies. Total installed capacity of power plants in Karachi was over 2,500 MW in 2010 (table I.5). These plants consumed 1.86 million TOE of natural gas and 0.53 million TOE of fuel oil in 2008–09 (HDIP 2009). About 50 percent of fuel oil consumption was at the Bin Qasim Power Station, 20 percent at the power station of Gul Ahmed Energy, and nearly 30 percent at the station of Tapal Energy.

Table I.5 Power Stations in Karachi, 2010

KESC power plants	Location	Installed capacity (MW)
Bin Qasim Power Station	Port Qasim Industrial Area	1,260
Korangi Thermal Power Station	Korangi Creek	250
Combined Cycle Power Station	Korangi Creek	220
GEJB- 1	SITE, Karachi	100
GEJB- 2	Korangi Industrial Area	125
	Subtotal	**1,955**
Other power plants in Karachi		
Gul Ahmad Energy Ltd.	Korangi	136
Tapal Energy Ltd.	Karachi	126
Engro Energy Ltd.	Karachi (operational in 2010)	217
Karachi Nuclear Power Plant	Karachi	137
	Subtotal	**616**

Sources: HDIP 2009 and KESC 2011.

KESC has plans to convert two of the six units of the Bin Qasim Power Station to coal, because the cost of coal per unit of energy content was less than half the cost of fuel oil. A 560 MW Bin Qasim gas-fired power plant (II) is near completion and is expected to be operational in 2012 (KESC 2011).

A study of the brick-making sector estimated that there were around 3,000 brick kilns in Pakistan in 1990, of which 624 were located in Sindh province (TurkPak 1991). This figure has now increased to 8,000–15,000 in the country (Awan 2010) and one source reports that there are now 1,500 brick kilns in Sindh (Express Tribune 2011). Brick making is largely a rural industry and is spread throughout the provinces of Pakistan (Awan 2010). Therefore, brick kilns are not likely to be a major source of outdoor air pollution in Karachi, but represent a major source of PM pollution in areas they are located and for the large number of workers employed in the sector.

The aforementioned industrial plants represent only a fraction of industrial plants in Karachi. Numerous plants are located throughout the city and cause pollution from combustion of fuels and their production processes.

Solid Waste

Approximately 9,000 tons of waste was generated each day in Karachi per estimate in 2005 (CDGK 2007). By 2011, this had increased to 12,000 tons per day, according to one estimate (Dawn 2011). An estimated 50–60 percent of waste is collected and transferred to landfills where open burning is common. The remaining is recycled, burnt, or illegally dumped. About 55 percent of waste is organic, 5 percent is garden waste, 18 percent is inert, 15 percent is recyclable or reusable, and 7 percent is suitable for incineration (CDGK 2007). Large quantities of waste are dumped on the banks of Lyari and Malir River (Korangi) and other unofficial disposal sites in the city. Burning of some of the waste is common at these sites.

Sustainability and Poverty Alleviation • http://dx.doi.org/10.1596/978-1-4648-0452-6

Much collected waste never reaches designated landfills, but is diverted to unofficial sites where some of the waste is recycled. Ali and Hasan (2001) identified at least 20 such sites in Karachi, several of which are in Korangi. Some of the waste is also delivered to pottery makers where it is used as fuel. Burning of waste is common at many sites, including the landfills were waste is burnt to retrieve metals. Burning of solid waste is now illegal in Karachi but effective enforcement is yet to be properly implemented.

Source Contribution to PM Ambient Air Quality

Determining the contribution of various sources of emissions to ambient PM air concentrations in Karachi requires detailed emission inventories, emission-dispersion estimates, and source apportionment studies. The contribution of a ton of PM emissions to ambient concentrations in the city, and how many people that are affected by these emissions, largely depends on the location of the emission source and vertical height of emission release (stack height).

During the months of March to October, with winds from the southwest and west-southwest, emissions from the southern sections of the city are likely polluting large parts of Karachi. However, winds during these months likely carry at least some of the emissions from Bin Qasim and Malir away from areas in Karachi with high populations. This is also to some extent likely to be the case with emissions from at least some sections of Korangi and Landhi. These towns do, however, have a combined population of more than 3 million (CDGK 2007), a large share of which is affected by emissions originating in these towns throughout the year.

During the months of November to February, with very light winds from the east-northeast and north-northeast and very little rain, emissions from the northern and northeastern sections of the city (including Bin Qasim, Landhi, and Malir) are likely to have much larger effect on several sections of the city than during March to October.

In light of these factors, PM emissions from various sectors are here assigned a weight that represents how much of a ton of emissions from a sector is contributing to ambient PM concentrations and population exposure in Karachi—that is, how much of a ton is ending up in the urban air shed of Karachi. PM emissions from road vehicles within the city, oil and gas consumption by the domestic/public/commercial sectors, and household use of wood/biomass are assigned a weight of 100 percent as these emission sources are widely distributed throughout the city; thus practically all emissions end up in the urban air shed. On the low end, PM emissions from brick kilns are assigned a weight of 20 percent, since most kilns are located on the outskirts of the city. Thus, a large fraction of emissions drifts away from the city most of the year because of wind conditions in Karachi. The weights assigned to PM emissions from the refineries, power plants, and the cement plant are in the range of 40–50 percent as they are mainly located in Bin Qasim and Korangi. PM emissions from ferrous metal sources are assigned a somewhat higher weight of 60 percent. One large ferrous metal source is the integrated steel mill in Bin Qasim, but numerous scrap smelters, foundries, and smaller mills are located in various locations of the city. PM emissions from oil and gas combustion by industry and from other industrial processes are assigned a weight of 75 percent, since these emission sources are more scattered around the city than the aforementioned large sources. PM emissions from solid waste burning are assigned a weight of 70 percent as burning is more dispersed throughout the city than the large industrial sources but likely somewhat less than other industrial plants.

Annual tons of particulate matter with a diameter of less than 10 microns (PM_{10}) and particulate matter with a diameter of less than 2.5 microns ($PM_{2.5}$) emissions ending up in the urban air shed of Karachi from the sources discussed above are estimated as follows:

$$PM_{10}^S = \sum_{i=1}^{n} w_i PM_{10}^i \qquad (I.1)$$

$$PM_{2.5}^S = \sum_{i=1}^{n} s_i w_i PM_{2.5}^i \qquad (I.2)$$

where w_i are the source-specific weights discussed above and s_i are the source-specific $PM_{2.5}$ fractions of PM_{10} (see appendix J for estimates of $PM^{(i)}$). Annual tons of secondary particulates (PM^P) and PM from area wide sources (PM^A) are estimated as follows:

$$PM_{2.5}^P = pPM_{2.5}^T \text{ and } PM_{10}^P = PM_{2.5}^P / s_p \qquad (I.3)$$

$$PM_{10}^A = (PM_{2.5}^S + PM_{2.5}^P - s_T(PM_{10}^S + PM_{10}^P))/(s_T - s_A) \qquad (I.4)$$

$$PM_{2.5}^A = s_A PM_{10}^A \qquad (I.5)$$

where $s_p = 0.95$, $s_A = 0.2$, and $s_T = 0.48$ are the $PM_{2.5}$ fraction of PM_{10} for secondary particulates, area wide PM, and PM ambient air concentrations in Karachi, respectively. The parameter, $p = 12.4$ percent, is from a recent $PM_{2.5}$ apportionment study in Karachi by Mansha and others (2011). The value of s_T is derived from Alam and others (2011) and is the same value applied to estimate PM_{10} concentrations from the data on $PM_{2.5}$ concentrations in Karachi. Equations I.3 and I.4 are solved iteratively to arrive at an estimate of annual tons of secondary particulates and PM from area wide sources, and total annual tons of PM ending up in the urban air shed of Karachi.[2]

Annual identifiable source-specific PM emissions are estimated at 20,000–28,000 tons of PM_{10}, of which 16,000–22,000 tons are $PM_{2.5}$. About 70–80 percent of these emissions are estimated to end up in the urban air shed of Karachi (see equations I.1 and I.2), with the remaining emissions drifting away from the city. With the additions of secondary particulates and PM from area wide sources, total annual PM_{10} that causes the PM ambient concentrations in Karachi is estimated at 43,000–51,000 tons of which 21,000–25,000 tons are $PM_{2.5}$ (table I.6). The secondary particulates (sulfates and nitrates) are formed in the atmosphere from sulfur dioxide and nitrogen oxide emissions originating from fuel combustion and industrial processes. The area wide sources of PM include natural dust carried by the wind from outside the city, resuspended road dust, construction dust, agricultural residue burning, and salt particles from the sea.

The estimates suggest that more than 50 percent of PM_{10} in Karachi is from areawide sources, but these sources are less than one-quarter of $PM_{2.5}$ (table I.7). The difference stems from the fact that most of PM from area wide sources is larger particulates. As for $PM_{2.5}$, the main identifiable sources are road vehicles, industry, secondary particulates, and burning of solid waste. About two-thirds of PM from industry appears to be from iron and steel industries, and metal smelters. A share of PM from area wide sources can potentially also be controlled through improved street cleaning, containment of construction dust, and restrictions on agricultural residue burning.

Annual emissions of PM_{10} in Karachi from road vehicles are estimated at more than 6,100 tons in 2009 (table I.8). Two-stroke motorcycles and rickshaws contribute about one-third of these emissions, diesel-fueled minibuses and small diesel trucks (vans and pickups) another third, and heavy-duty trucks

Table I.6 Estimated Particulate Matter Emissions in Karachi, 2009

	Urban air shed PM_{10}		Urban air shed $PM_{2.5}$	
	Low	High	Low	High
Source-specific emissions	15.2	19.4	13.1	15.8
Secondary particulates (sulfates, nitrates)	2.7	3.2	2.6	3.0
PM from area wide sources[a]	25.1	28.5	5.0	5.7
Total	43.0	51.1	20.7	24.6

Note: a. Includes natural dust, sea particles, construction dust, resuspended road dust, and agricultural residue burning.

Table I.7 Estimated Source Contribution to Ambient Particulate Matter Concentrations in Karachi, 2009

Percent

	PM_{10}	$PM_{2.5}$
Road vehicles	12–14	24–28
Industry	13–15	19–20
Solid waste burning	4–7	8–14
Domestic (wood/biomass)	2.3–2.7	4–5
Domestic/public/commercial (oil, gas consumption)	0.9–1.0	1.5–1.7
Power plants	0.5–0.6	0.8–0.9
Secondary particulates (sulfates, nitrates)	6–7	12–13
PM from area wide sources[a]	56–58	23–24
Total	100	100

Note: a. Includes natural dust, sea particles, construction dust, resuspended road dust, and agricultural residue burning.

Table I.8 Estimated Annual PM$_{10}$ Emissions from Road Vehicles in Karachi, 2009

	Number of vehicles	PM (tons/year)	PM (% of total)
Rickshaws (two-stroke)	50,000	700	11
Motorbikes (two-stroke)	905,000	1,425	23
Small trucks (diesel) (vans and pickups)	96,000	1,296	21
Minibuses (diesel)	11,500	644	11
Buses, large (diesel)	3,000	185	3
Heavy-duty trucks (diesel)	28,000	1,680	27
Other vehicles	917,500	203	3
Total	2,011,000	6,133	100

over one-fourth. Large buses contribute 3 percent, and all other vehicles about 3 percent. These emission estimates are very rough orders of magnitude and depends on the accuracy of the number of vehicles and applied emission factors (see appendix K).

A recent PM chemical analysis and apportionment study in Karachi by Mansha and others (2011) finds that about 16 percent of ambient PM$_{2.5}$ is from soil and road dust; nearly 19 percent is road vehicle emissions; 13 percent is principally from ferrous metal sources (including the iron and steel industry, and metal smelters); 40 percent is from fuel burning by industry, road vehicles, and power plants; and 12 percent is secondary particulates (sulfates, nitrates). The study did not report contributions from burning of solid waste and domestic use of wood/biomass as separate categories; however, these contributions may be reflected in fuel burning by industry, road vehicles, and power plants.

Notes

1. The estimates do not include aviation and maritime fuel consumption.
2. The same approach was used for Senegal (Larsen 2007), Peru (ECON 2006), and Colombia (Larsen 2005).

Bibliography

Alam, K., T. Blaschke, P. Madl, A. Mukhtar, M. Hussain, T. Trautmann, and S. Rahman. 2011. "Aerosol Size Distribution and Mass Concentration Measurements in Various Cities of Pakistan." *Journal of Environmental Monitoring* 13: 1944–52.

Ali, M., and A. Hasan. 2001. "Integrating Recycling and Disposal System for Solid Waste Management in Karachi." Fieldwork and technical support by Engr. Mansoor Raza and the Urban Resource Centre, Karachi.

Amjad, S. 2010. "Strategy for Industrial Waste Water and Pollution Control." *Pakistan Business Review* October: 601–06.

Awan, S. A. 2010. *Gender Dimensions of Bonded Labour in Brick Kilns in Punjab Province of Pakistan.* Lahore, Pakistan: Centre for the Improvement of Working Conditions and Environment (CIWCE).

CDGK (City District Government Karachi). 2007. *Karachi Strategic Development Plan 2020.* Karachi, Pakistan: Master Plan Group of Offices, City District Government Karachi.

Dawn. 2011. "Warning over Garbage Dumping, Burning." December 15. http://www
    .dawn.com/2011/12/15/warning-over-garbage-dumping-burning.html.

ECON. 2006. "Urban Air Pollution Control in Peru." Prepared for the Peru Environmental
    Analysis, World Bank, ECON Analysis, Oslo.

Express Tribune. 2011. "For the Cheapest of Building Materials, the Return of a Tax Opens
    New Window of Debate." June 13. http://tribune.com.pk/story/187759/for-the
    -cheapest-of-building-materials-the-return-of-a-tax-opens-new-window-on-debate.

FBS (Federal Bureau of Statistics). 2011. *Pakistan Statistical Yearbook 2011*. Pakistan:
    Federal Bureau of Statistics.

FFBL (Fauji Fertilizer Bin Qasim Ltd.). 2011. *Annual Report 2011*. http://www.ffbl.com.pk.

Hasan, A. 2007. "The Urban Resource Centre, Karachi." *Environment and Urbanization*
    19 (1): 275–92.

HDIP (Hydrocarbon Development Institute of Pakistan). 2009. *Pakistan Energy Yearbook
    2009*. Islamabad: Hydrocarbon Development Institute of Pakistan.

International Energy Agency. 2010. *2009 Energy Balance for Pakistan*. http://www.iea.org
    /stats/balancetable.asp?COUNTRY_CODE=PK.

KESC. 2011. *Annual Report* 2010–11. Karachi, Pakistan: Karachi Electric Supply Company.

Larsen, B. 2005. "Cost-Benefit Analysis of Environmental Protection in Colombia."
    Background paper prepared for the Colombia Country Environmental Analysis,
    Colombia: Mitigating Environmental Degradation to Foster Growth and Reduce
    Inequality, World Bank, Washington, DC.

———. 2007. "Cost-Benefit Analysis of Environmental Health Interventions in Urban
    Greater Dakar, Senegal." Paper prepared for the Senegal Country Environmental
    Analysis, prepared from ECON/Roche Canada, World Bank, Washington, DC.

MAC. 2006. Pre-Feasibility Study for Steel and Related Products. Prepared by the
    Management Advisory Center (MAC). Quality assured by National Management
    Consultants (Pvt) Ltd. Commissioned by Planning and Development Division,
    Government of Pakistan, Islamabad.

Mansha, M., B. Ghauri, S. Rahman, and A. Amman. 2011. "Characterization and Source
    Apportionment of Ambient Air Particulate Matter (PM$_{2.5}$) in Karachi." *Science of the
    Total Environment* 425: 176–83.

MIP (Ministry of Industry and Production). 2012. "Production Data of Selected Large
    Scale Manufacturing Items, July-Mar-2010–11." Ministry of Industry and Production,
    Government of Pakistan.

MoF (Ministry of Finance). 2011. *Pakistan Economic Survey 2010–11*. Islamabad: Ministry
    of Finance. http://finance.gov.pk/survey_1011.html.

NIPS (National Institute of Population Studies)/Macro. 2008. "Pakistan Demographic and
    Health Survey 2006–07." National Institute of Population Studies, and Macro
    International Inc., Islamabad.

Sajjad, S. H., N. Blond, A. Clappier, A. Raza, S. A. Shirazi, and K. Shakrullah. 2010. "The
    Preliminary Study of Urbanization, Fossil Fuels Consumptions and CO$_2$ Emission in
    Karachi." *African Journal of Biotechnology* 9 (13): 1941–48.

TurkPak. 1991. "Wood Use in the Brick Kiln Industry of Pakistan." Prepared by TurkPak
    International (Pvt) Limited under contract with Winrock International for the
    Government of Pakistan and USAID.

APPENDIX J

Particulate Matter Emission Factors

Particulate matter (PM) emission factors applied in this book are presented below, derived from various international sources. These emission factors can only be rough approximations of actual emission factors in Karachi, but they provide a basis for a first-round estimate of PM emissions in the city. Errors in a single or in a few of most of these emission factors have only a minor influence on the monetized health benefits per ton of particulate matter with a diameter of less than 10 microns (PM_{10})emission reductions estimated in this book. This is because each source of PM_{10} emissions (such as a particular type of road vehicle or industrial sector) identified in this book contributes only a relatively small share of total PM_{10} emissions responsible for the health effects. However, magnitude of error in a single emission factor does have a proportional impact on benefit-cost ratios for an intervention that is based on this emission factor. Thus, benefit-cost ratios can be adjusted if the emission factor applied is considered erroneous.

Road Vehicles

This book estimates that diesel vehicles, motorcycles, and rickshaws cause 97 percent of PM emissions from road vehicles in Karachi. Table J.1 presents fuel consumption and PM emission factors for these vehicles. The emission factors (grams of carbon dioxide per kilometer—g/km) combined with fuel consumption indicates a PM_{10} emission rate of 4.0–4.9 klilograms (kg) per ton of fuel for the four-wheel diesel vehicles. PM_{10} emissions per ton of fuel appear, however, to be substantially higher for two-stroke motorcycles and rickshaws even though these vehicles are gasoline fueled. The emission factors will depend on age, weight, and maintenance of vehicle, speed of driving, and other factors. The emission factors are therefore very rough estimates.

Fossil Fuel Combustion

Fuel oil and diesel are the main fuels used in Karachi that generate most of the PM emissions from fossil fuel combustion. Coal is almost exclusively used in brick kilns and cement plants, and PM emissions from these two sources are

Table J.1 Particulate Matter Emissions from Road Vehicles in Karachi

	Fuel consumption	PM_{10} emissions	
	Liter/10 km	g/km	kg/ton of fuel
Rickshaws (two-stroke)	0.45	0.35	10.9
Motorbikes (two-stroke)	0.2	0.25	17.6
Small trucks (vans and pickups) (diesel)	1.5	0.5	4.0
Minibuses (diesel)	2	0.7	4.2
Large buses (diesel)	2.8	1.1	4.7
Heavy-duty trucks (diesel)	3.6	1.5	4.9

Sources: Derived from ARAI (2008), COPERT 4 (2007), Meszler (2007), NAEI (2002), Nesamani (2009), and Shah and Harshadeep (2001).

estimated separately. The emission factor applied for high sulfur fuel oil used in boilers is 4.4 kg of PM per ton of fuel, of which 71 percent is PM_{10} and 55 percent is particulate matter with a diameter of less than 2.5 microns ($PM_{2.5}$). The estimate is based on the formula: $PM = 1.31*S + 0.47$ with the sulfur content (S) assumed to be 3 percent. The emission factor for the same fuel oil used in power plant turbines is 0.74 kg of PM_{10} per ton of fuel, of which 75 percent is $PM_{2.5}$. The emission factor for diesel used in large diesel engines is 2 kg of PM per ton of fuel, of which 75 percent is PM_{10} and 65 percent is $PM_{2.5}$. These emission factors are derived from USEPA (1995).

Brick Kilns

PM emissions from brick kilns vary greatly by kiln technology. Reported PM from a moving chimney Bull's Trench Kiln (BTK) is around 8 kg per 1,000 bricks while PM from a fixed chimney BTK and a vertical shaft brick kiln (VSBK) is around 1.7 kg and 0.55 kg per 1,000 bricks, respectively (Chaisson 2008). Emission factors for brick kilns in Pakistan are highly uncertain. Most kilns are BTK or similar kilns but the number of moving chimney versus fixed chimney kilns are uncertain. An emission factor of 2 kg of PM per 1,000 bricks is applied to estimate emissions in Karachi. The PM_{10}/PM and $PM_{2.5}$/PM ratios for coal-fired kilns are 78 percent and 48 percent, respectively (USEPA 1995).

Cement Industry

PM emissions from cement plants depend to some extent of production technology but more so on PM control technology. A plant with no control technology may emit on the order of 65–130 kg of PM per ton of clinker produced while a plant with electrostatic precipitators (ESP) or fabric filters may emit 0.2–0.6 kg per ton of clinker (USEPA 1995). Emissions also very much depends on the continuity or use, functioning quality, and operations and maintenance of the control technologies. Because PM emissions from the cement plant in Karachi are highly uncertain, this book applies a lower bound of 0.4 kg and an upper bound of 100 kg per ton of clinker. The PM_{10}/PM and $PM_{2.5}$/PM ratios for plants with PM control technology are on average about 78 percent and 48 percent, respectively, and 24 percent and 7 percent for plants with no control technology (USEPA 1995).

Oil Refineries

The main source of PM emissions from an oil refinery is from fuel consumed in the petroleum product refining process. A refinery will most often use the least valuable fraction of processed crude for production of refined petroleum products. This fraction usually has high sulfur content and PM emissions vary in relation to this content. Assuming 3 percent sulfur content, PM emissions are estimated at 4.4 kg per ton of fuel consumption. Fuel consumption by the refineries in Karachi is roughly estimated as the difference between process crude and petroleum product production.

Iron and Steel Industry

PM emissions from iron and steel plants and foundries are approximately 5–20 kg per ton of steel produced from processes with no PM control technology and 0.1–0.4 kg from processes with PM control technology (USEPA 1995). Annual steel production at the integrated iron and steel mill (Pak Steel) in Karachi is around 1 million tons. Annual production from numerous other foundries, mills, and smelters located in other areas of the city is uncertain. If production at these other plants is also 1 million tons, PM emissions from these plants may be around 5,000–10,000 tons per year if the plants have no PM control technology. Assuming that Pak Steel has well-functioning and well-operated and maintained PM control technology, PM emissions from this plant may be around 100 tons per year. In total, this would be around 4,300–6,100 tons of PM_{10} or 3,100–4,600 tons of $PM_{2.5}$ per year. In their PM apportionment study, Mansha and others (2011) estimate that the contribution to $PM_{2.5}$ ambient concentrations in Karachi from ferrous metal sources is 13.3 percent. On the basis of the emissions inventory estimated in this book a 13.3 percent contribution amounts to about 2,800–3,300 tons of $PM_{2.5}$ entering the urban air shed per year. Gross $PM_{2.5}$ emissions are higher because some emissions drift away from the city, depending on the location the emission source.

Solid Waste

An unknown amount of waste is burned in Karachi daily. For the emission inventory estimated in this book, it is assumed that 15–30 percent of 10,500 tons of waste generated daily is burned. The burnable fraction (organic waste) of this waste is around 55 percent (CDGK 2007), implying that burnt organic material amounts to about 865–1,730 tons per day. PM_{10} emissions are around 8 kg per ton of burnt material of which 90–95 percent is $PM_{2.5}$ (Countess 2003; Gaffney and Benjamin 2004; Scarborough, Clinton, and Gong 2002).

Solid Fuel Burning

Around 3 percent of households in Karachi use wood/biomass for cooking (NIPS/Macro 2008). Total wood/biomass consumption is thus around 96,000 tons per year if households on average use about 1.5 tons per year. PM_{10} emissions from wood burning are about 12 kg per ton of wood/biomass of which 92 percent is $PM_{2.5}$ (USEPA 1995).

Bibliography

ARAI (Automotive Research Association of India). 2008. "Emission Factor Development for Indian Vehicles." Prepared for the Air Quality Monitoring Project-Indian Clean Air Programme, Automotive Research Association of India, Pune, India.

CDGK (City District Government Karachi). 2007. *Karachi Strategic Development Plan 2020*. Master Plan Group of Offices, Karachi, Pakistan.

Chaisson, J. 2008. *Black Carbon from Brick Kilns*. Clean Air Task Force.

Countness, R. 2003. "Reconciling Fugitive Dust Emission Inventories with Ambient Measurements." Presented at the 12th International Emission Inventory Conference, San Diego, CA, April 29–May 1.

COPERT 4. 2007. *Computer Programme to Calculate Emissions from Road Transport*. LAT, Greece, and European Environment Agency.

Gaffney, P., and M. Benjamin. 2004. "Pune, India Regional Emissions Inventory Study." USEPA and the Indian Ministry of Environment and Forest.

Mansha, M., B. Ghauri, S. Rahman, and A. Amman. 2011. "Characterization and Source Apportionment of Ambient Air Particulate Matter (PM2.5) in Karachi." *Science of the Total Environment* 425: 176–83.

Meszler Engineering Services. 2007. "Air Emissions Issues Related to Two- and Three-Wheeled Motor Vehicles." Prepared for the International Council on Clean Transportation (ICCT).

NAEI (National Atmospheric Emissions Inventory). 2002. "Vehicle Speed Emission Factor Database Version 02/1." UK National Atmospheric Emissions Inventory, AEA Energy and Environment. http://www.naei.org.uk/emissions/selection.php.

Nesamani, K. S. 2009. "Estimation of Automobile Emissions and Control Strategies in India." Institute of Transportation Studies, University of California, Irvine, CA.

NIPS (National Institute of Population Studies)/Macro. 2008. "Pakistan Demographic and Health Survey 2006–07." National Institute of Population Studies, and Macro International Inc., Islamabad.

Scarborough, J., N. Clinton, and P. Gong. 2002. "Creating a Statewide Spatially and Temporally Allocated Agricultural Burning Emissions Inventory Using Consistent Emission Factors." Prepared for the Air Resources Board, California EPA.

Shah, J., and N. Harshadeep. 2001. "Urban Pollution from Two Stoke Engine Vehicles in Asia: Technical and Policy Options." Presentation at Regional Workshop on Reduction of Emissions from 2–3 Wheelers, Hanoi, September 5–7.

USEPA (United States Environmental Protection Agency). 1995. *Compilation of Air Pollutant Emission Factors*. AP-42 5th ed. Supplements, and Updates. Washington, DC: United States Environmental Protection Agency.

Benefits of Controlling Particulate Matter Emissions in Karachi

The estimated monetized health effects of particulate matter with a diameter of less than 2.5 microns ($PM_{2.5}$) and particulate matter with a diameter of less than 10 microns (PM_{10}) concentrations in Karachi amount to PRs 24–59 billion per year in 2009, or nearly 80 percent of estimated health effects in all cities with a population greater than 100,000 in Sindh province (see chapter 2 of part I of this book). Therefore, the benefits of a ton of PM_{10} emission reductions (B_{PM10}) are estimated at PRs 0.5–1.2 million (US\$6,300–15,600) as follows:

$$B_{PM10} = H/(PM_{10}^{A} + PM_{10}^{P} + \sum_{i=1}^{n} PM_{10}^{i}) \qquad (K.1)$$

where H is the monetized health effects and the denominator is annual PM_{10} in thousand tons from areawide sources, secondary particulates, and identified sources.[1]

The lower bound of monetized health effects and benefits per ton of PM_{10} emission reductions reflects valuation of mortality risk using the human capital approach—that is, estimated lost income from dying prematurely. The upper bound reflects valuation of morality risk using an estimate of the value of statistical life (VSL), which is based on individuals' willingness to pay (WTP) for a reduction in risk of death. The difference in valuation is large because most individuals dying from PM air pollution are at their late stage of working life or have completed their working life, thus lost income from premature death is relatively low. Because VSL is increasingly preferred over the human capital approach in studies valuing health effects of PM air pollution, the upper bound is applied in the benefit-cost analysis (CBA) in this book.

The health benefits of reducing PM_{10} emissions from a specific emission source depend on the location of the emission source and the $PM_{2.5}$ fraction of PM_{10}. The higher is the fraction of emissions ending up in the urban air shed,

Table K.1 Benefits of PM$_{10}$ Emissions Reductions in Karachi, 2009

	Benefits of PM$_{10}$ emissions reductions	
	PRs million/ton	US$ '000/ton
Road vehicles	2.12	27.1
Power plants	0.77	9.8
Cement plant	0.55	7.0
Industry (oil, gas consumption)	1.48	18.8
Ferrous metal sources	1.04	13.3
Brick kilns	0.32	4.1
Refineries	0.93	11.8
Other industry (PM from processes)	1.42	18.1
Domestic/public/commercial (oil, gas consumption)	1.97	25.1
Domestic (wood/biomass)	2.08	26.5
Secondary particulates (sulfates, nitrates)	2.12	27.1
Solid waste burning	1.49	18.9
PM from area wide sources	0.96	12.3
Average of all sources	1.22	15.6

Note: Benefits of reduced mortality risk is based on VSL.

and the higher is the PM$_{2.5}$ fraction of PM$_{10}$, the higher are the health benefits of PM$_{10}$ emission reductions.[2]

Benefits per ton of PM$_{10}$ emission reductions are estimated to be highest for emissions from road vehicles; oil and gas consumption in the domestic, public and commercial sectors; and domestic use of wood/biomass (table K.1). This is because almost all of the emissions from these sources end up in the urban air shed and the emissions have a very high PM$_{2.5}$ fraction. Benefits per ton of reductions are also high for PM$_{10}$ emissions from oil and gas consumption in industry, emissions from industrial processes ("other industry"), and burning of solid waste. Benefits per ton of reductions are lowest for emissions from brick kilns, cement, power plants, and refineries because of they are generally located somewhat away from the largest population centers in Karachi. These source-specific benefits are applied in the CBA when assessing the benefits and costs of a specific intervention. Reducing PM$_{10}$ emissions from one of the sources with low benefits per ton of emissions may still have high benefits relative to costs, if the cost of intervention is relatively low.

Notes

1. Health benefits include reduction in morbidity and reduced risk of mortality. Morbidity is estimated based on PM$_{10}$ and mortality based on PM$_{2.5}$. As a fraction of PM$_{10}$ is PM$_{2.5}$, benefits of PM$_{10}$ emission reductions include both a reduction in morbidity and reduced risk of mortality.
2. The PM$_{2.5}$ fraction of PM$_{10}$ relates to mortality benefits. The higher is the fraction the larger is the reduction in mortality risk (mortality benefits) per ton of PM$_{10}$ emission reduction.

Natural Resource Management Priorities for Sindh Province

Agricultural Losses Resulting from Salinity and Waterlogging

Salinity of water has long been a problem in Sindh. Agriculture relies mostly on surface water from the Sindh river basin because most groundwater is saline. At the same time, surface water is becoming scarce downstream in Indus River. Therefore, people are forced to spend resources and efforts trying to ensure sufficient water flow. Sindh has the most saline soils. The irrigation system built in the Sindh Province more than 80 years ago is deteriorating. Briscoe and Qamar (2005) report that a substantial part of the main irrigation canal leaks, with much of the water never reaching the crop zone. In addition, some water is wasted for irrigation purposes because of mixing with the saline ground water. This waste of irrigation water is causing waterlogging in head command areas as well as water deprivation at the far end of the canals. Salinity and waterlogging are still important problems for farmers in Sindh.

Table L.1 shows major characteristics of the agro-ecological zones in Sindh, as presented in the State of Environment in Sindh (IUCN Pakistan 2005). Salinity problems prevail in zones B and C. Zone B is the Indus River flood plain. Saline soils are identified in Sukkur and Ghotki districts in the Sukkur Division, (zone B1), and in Mirpurkhas and Sanghar districts in the Mirpurkhas Division (zone B2) (IUCN Pakistan 2005). Major Kharif crops in zone B are cotton and sugar cane, and wheat is the main Rabi[1] crop. Zone C is the zone of the Indus River delta. Saline and water logged areas are located in Badin and Thatta districts in the Hyderabad Division. Drainage is very difficult because of an absence of gradient. In addition, Thatta was negatively influences by polluted sewage from the Left Bank Outfall Drain Project. The main crops are rice and sugar cane in Kharif and wheat in Rabi.

Annual agricultural losses resulting from salinity and waterlogging in the six aforementioned districts are estimated using the difference between potential[2] crop yields in Pakistan and actual crops yields in the six districts. Table L.2

Table L.1 Agro-Ecological Zones in Sindh Province

| Factor | Agro-ecological zones in Sindh | | | | |
	A1	A2	B1	B2	C
Climate					
Mean annual rainfall, mm	75–100	75–100	75–120	120–230	180–250
Months with >20 mm rain	Jul–Aug	Jul–Aug	Jul–Aug	Jun–Sep	Jun–Sep
Annual evaporation, mm	150–175	150–175	175–200	200–225	150–225
Humidity	Low	Low	Low	Low–High	High
Water supply					
Perennial (%)	55	65	0	100	50
Irrigated area, thousand hectares	500	210	310	1,600	380
Tube well potential for drainage/Rabi water source	High	Low	High	High	Low
Soils					
Salinity (severe upper soils, %)	10	5	15	15–50	70
Cropping					
Main Kharif	Rice	Sorghum	Cotton	Cotton	Rice
Other Kharif		Rice, fallow	Rice	Sugarcane	Sugarcane, vegetables
Main Rabi	Wheat	Wheat	Wheat	Wheat	Sugarcane
Other Rabi	Fodder	Fallow	Fodder	Fodder, vegetables	Vegetables

Source: IUCN Pakistan 2005.

Table L.2 Potential and Actual Yields in Six Districts of Pakistan, 2009

	Rice	Wheat	Sugar cane	Cotton
Potential yield	4–4.5	3.6–5.2	59–84	1.2–2.8
Thatta	2.9	3.2	53	1.2
Badin	2.4	2.8	45	1.4
Ghotki	3.8	1.7	62	1.0
Sukkur	3.7	3.8	58	0.9
Sanghar	2.4	3.7	51	1.2
Mirpur khas	3.0	3.5	57	1.1

Sources: GoS 2010; Kahlown and others 1998.

presents potential yield for main crops (Kahlown and others 1998) and actual
yield in the six districts most affected by salinity and waterlogging in Sindh.

The Sindh Department of Agriculture reports farm gate prices of paddy rice
and cotton lint at PRs 40,000 per ton, wheat at about PRs 21,000 per ton, and
sugar cane at about PRs 3,250 per ton. The area under these four major crops is
2.5 million hectares.[3] At the aforementioned prices, the cost of crop yield losses
resulting from waterlogging and salinity is estimated at PRs 16–60 billion per
year (table L.2). This conservative estimate does not include effects of waterlogging and salinity on all crops and only analyses yield losses in the six most
affected districts in Sindh.

Table L.3 Annual Cost of Agricultural Crop Yield Losses Resulting from Waterlogging and Salinity in Sindh Province, 2010
Billion PRs

	Low	Midpoint	High
Rice	7	9	10
Wheat	4.5	11	16.5
Sugar cane	3	7	12
Cotton	1	12	22
Total	16	38	60

Figure L.1 Subsidy for Operation and Maintenance of Irrigation Systems in Sindh Province, 1993–2003

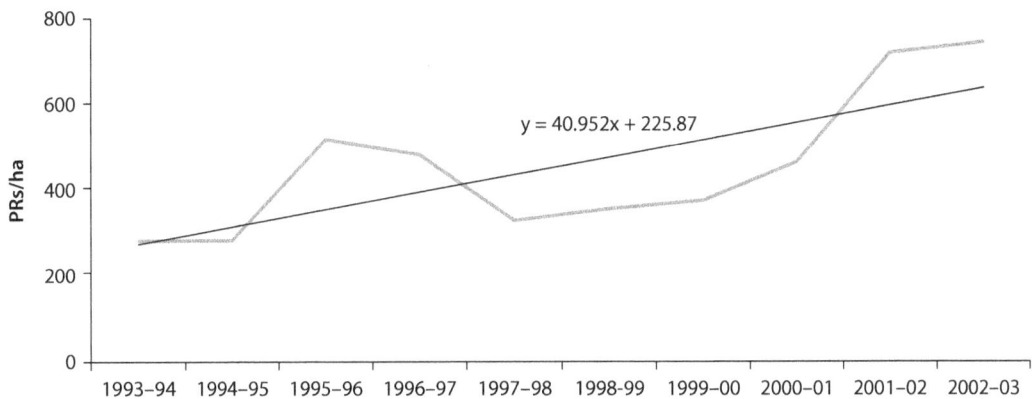

Source: Estimated from FAO (2003).

Annual losses from unused degraded croplands can also be included in the estimate of the economic cost of waterlogging and salinity by applying crop production profit margins as in table L.3. There are about 2 million hectares (ha) of fallow lands in Sindh. Assuming that 40–60 percent of these lands are out of use because of salinity and waterlogging problem, it is also a component of annual losses. Using the average cropping intensity of 1.36 in Sindh (GoS 2009) and the average gross profit margin of PRs 61,000 per hectare of productive lands estimated, the total cost of waterlogging and salinity of these lands is in the range of PRs 66–99 billion.

Total annual cost of waterlogging and salinity in Sindh is then estimated at about PRs 82–160 billion or 1.6–3.1 percent of Sindh's GDP in 2010.

An additional indicator of the high costs of agricultural land deterioration is the increase in the government of Sindh's budget allocation for operation and maintenance of the irrigation systems in the 1990s. As reflected in figure L.1, water-use subsidy increased in the past decade by about PRs 40 per year, which was far above the inflation level.

Over the past few years, availability of water resources and salinity have had opposite effects on agricultural productivity. While losses of water resources results in losses of irrigated lands, it also reduces waterlogging and salinity, enhancing productivity and increasing crop yields. Figure L.2 presents the trend in wheat

Figure L.2 Wheat and Rice Yield and Total Irrigated Area in Sindh Province, 1987–2008

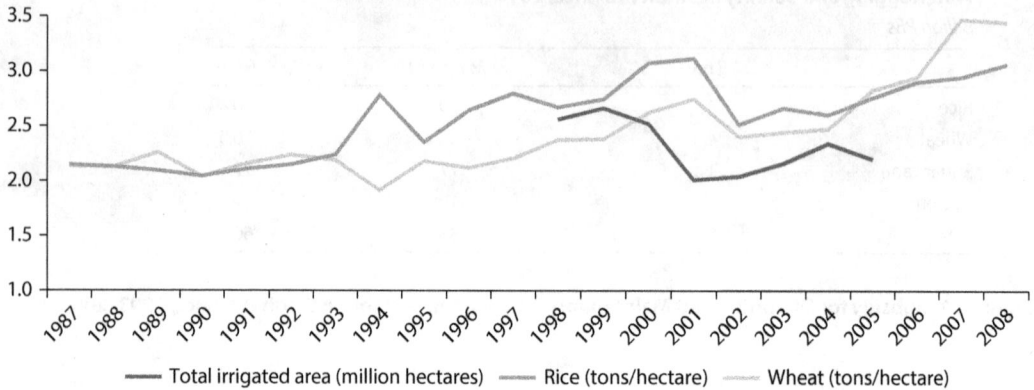

Total irrigated area (million hectares)   Rice (tons/hectare)   Wheat (tons/hectare)

Source: Estimated using data of Ministry of Food, Agriculture and Livestock, Agricultural Statistics of Pakistan (2004–05).

and rice yields in the past 20 years, as well as fluctuations in the total irrigated area in Sindh from 1997 to 2005. Data on total irrigated area demonstrates unreliable supply of water resources that is highly dependable on weather variability.

Irrigation is key for agricultural production in Sindh. Existing irrigation technologies are extremely water intensive. Water overuse leads to waterlogging and salinity. Since waterlogging and salinity reduces productivity, the positive effect of irrigation is partially offset. It explains relatively low productivity of crop production in Sindh compare to other countries (Tariq 2005). Although salinity levels were still high in 2005, waterlogging had declined slightly because of the general reduction of water flow (Briscoe and Qamar 2005). However, without drastic change of water use practice and underlying high salinity, crop yields will continue to deteriorate.

If irrigation provides reliable water supply, then productivity on irrigated lands is relatively stable and less vulnerable to droughts. There is a high risk of sequential droughts in Sindh, when available water resources are significantly less than those required for reliable water supply based on current irrigation practices. Climate change exacerbates weather variability and further increases risk of sequential droughts, as well as the frequency and severity of floods. Transition to water-efficient technologies will improve the reliability of the water supply. In addition, it will significantly mitigate waterlogging and salinity problems.

Losses from Natural Disasters (Floods)

Over time, siltation and narrow embankments has forced the rivers to flow within relatively narrow beds above the level of the land. Sedimentation of upstream reservoirs aggravates the flooding problem for Sindh. As Briscoe and Qamar (2005) note, over time, the likelihood of embankment-breaching increases, as do the problems of drainage from flooded lands. When this coincides with unfavorable tidal conditions, the consequences can be disastrous.

Therefore, elevation of riverbeds, sedimentation of reservoirs, together with glacier retreat and unstable monsoon precipitation, would likely increase the frequency of devastating floods.

High floods have occurred 16 times since 1940. The 2010 flood claimed the lives of more than 400 people, destroyed 350,000 houses, damaged more than 1 million houses, and displaced about 1.5 million people.

Financial costs of flooding include three assessment categories (ADB and World Bank 2010):

- *Direct costs* refers to the monetary value of the completely or partially destroyed assets, such as social, physical, and economic infrastructure immediately following a disaster.
- *Indirect costs* are income losses, and comprise both the change of flow of goods and services and other economic flows such as increased expenses, curtailed production, and diminished revenue, which arise from the direct damage to production capacity, and to social and economic infrastructure.
- *Reconstruction costs* measure the cost of rebuilding lost assets and restoring lost services. It is generally assessed as the replacement cost, with a premium added for building back smarter.

Economic cost includes only direct and indirect losses to avoid double counting.

The Asian Development Bank and the World Bank estimated total losses from the 2010 flood in Sindh as the highest among the provinces of Pakistan, at about PRs 250 billion of direct costs and PRs 120 billion of indirect costs. The cost of death of over 400 people can be added to this estimate. Applying a value of statistical life (VSL), the cost of deaths is estimated at about PRs 5 billion. Total cost of flood losses is then about PRs 375 billion or about US$4.4 billion (7.2 percent of Sindh's GDP in 2010). A major component of flood damage was damage to crops, which was more than 50 percent of the total damage cost.

The 2010 flood was an extraordinary event, but smaller floods occur more often than those the size of the 2010 event. Climate change studies indicate that, with monsoon rains, more severe flood events could happen more often, especially along the country's western rivers (the Indus River and Kabul). Flood periods are more prolonged, so floodwater damages both summer and winter crops. Climate change is expected to also contribute to more intensive rains and higher variability of precipitation in general. Higher temperatures also mean faster melting of Himalayan glaciers. As the melting season coincides with the monsoon season, any intensification of the monsoon is likely to contribute to flood disasters in the Himalayan catchment, where the Indus River belongs.

Precipitation already exhibits high variability and high frequency of extreme events, like droughts and floods. Droughts occurrence is more likely, they happen every 5–10 years (Khan 2001). Floods are relatively rare, but their impact is more devastating as it happened in 2010. Figure L.3 presents the distribution of annual precipitation in three cities of Sindh for 1961–2004.

Figure L.3 Distribution of Annual Precipitation of Three Cities in Sindh Province, 1961–2004

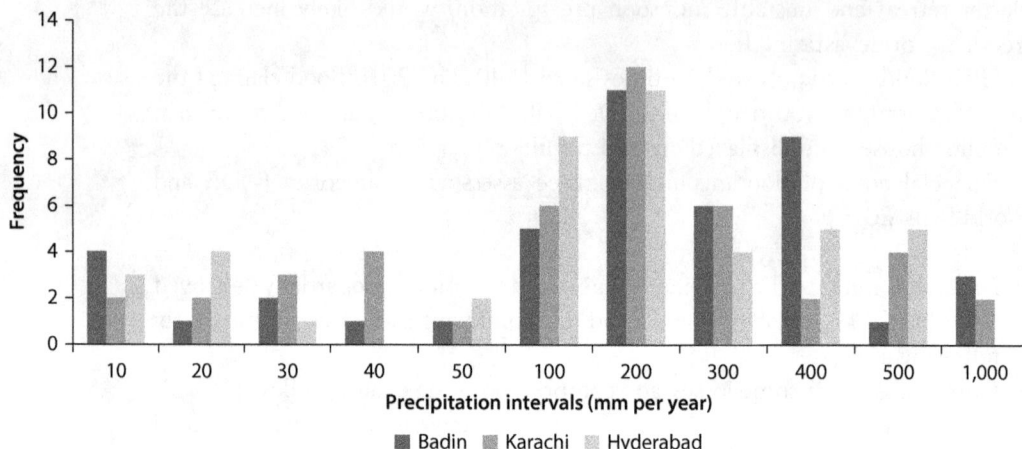

■ Badin ■ Karachi ▨ Hyderabad

Table L.4 Summary Statistics for Monte Carlo Simulations of the Drought Return for Three Cities in Sindh Province 1961–2004

Statistics	Badin	Hyderabad	Karachi
Trials	100,000	100,000	100,000
Mean	3.21	3.90	3.60
Median	3.00	4.00	4.00
Standard deviation	1.47	1.54	1.52
Variance	2.17	2.37	2.31
Skewness	0.25	0.14	0.19
Kurtosis	2.87	2.83	2.84

In all three cities, precipitation distribution demonstrates both right and left tails that determine relatively high risk of both droughts and flood. Precipitation places an important complementary role, especially between July and September. Insufficient summer precipitation would reduce the productivity of agriculture that relies on water extensive practices.

For purposes of illustration, we consider a 100-mm threshold and conduct a probabilistic analysis for the number of droughts that may occur during 10 years. A Monte Carlo simulation was applied, assuming the probability of drought return for each of 10 sequential years calculated based on 40 years of observations, 1961–2004. Table L.4 presents the results of these simulations.

All three regions are similarly exposed to risk of droughts. This risk is relatively higher in Hyderabad, and relatively lower in Badin, as shown in figure L.4, which presents the cumulative probability of flood distribution for all three regions. Table L.4 provides further details of the drought return probabilistic analysis.

In each region, the expected number of years with precipitation below 100 mm is between three and four. The standard deviation (SD) is about 40 percent. Excessive kurtosis is about 3. On the basis of these data, we can conclude that number of droughts is highly unpredictable. Then risk of exposure to drought is very high. The most reliable coping strategy would be to reduce

Figure L.4 Overlapping Cumulative Probability Function of Droughts for Three Selected Cities in Sindh Province

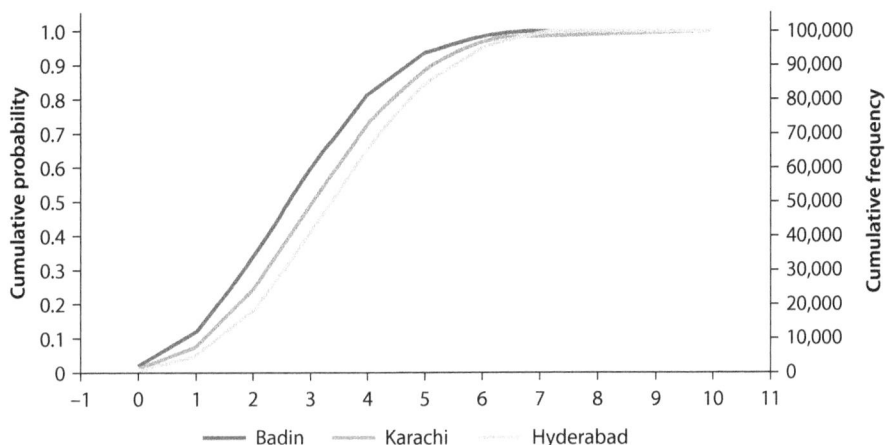

dependence on the water supply from irrigation. This conclusion contradicts the current trend in irrigation water demand, driven by water-intensive technologies with huge water losses.

Devastating floods are the other side of the coin. Torrential floodwaters could not be productively used by agriculture. On the contrary, they deteriorate productivity further, damaging irrigational infrastructure. Although in the north, the return period of the 2010 year flood is projected at 1,000 years (Tarbela), it is 86 years in the middle part of the Indus River (Taunsa). The magnitude of the event has a higher return period in the upper part of the catchment than in the middle part of the catchment (Straatsma, Ettema, and Krol 2010). This finding is consistent with the frequency of rain above 1,000 mm in the three Sindh regions estimated at the level below 2 percent.

A historic flood could be described as a catastrophic event with a relatively low probability of occurrence every year. Therefore, a conventional expected value approach may not be the best to characterize the actual cost of risks attributed to this event. Although historic flood events happen relatively rarely and it may take several years for the next records breaker to occur, other high-magnitude flood events happen regularly enough. The recent sequential high-magnitude floods in 2010 and 2011 confirm this.

Table L.5 describes major flood-event damages over the past 35 years. On the basis of these data, we calibrated a probabilistic model that takes into account the random frequency of flood events in Sindh and the probabilistic distribution of severity and exposure to these events. Distribution functions of flood severity and exposure were calibrated using data from table L.5. Population exposed to floods was selected as a primary variable to construct a probability density function (PDF) of exposure. Twenty-four time periods out of 35 have an assigned exposure equal to 0, and the other 11 time periods have an exposure estimated for the affected population and probability of occurrence 1/35.

Table L.5 Components of Damage from Floods in Sindh Province, 1976–2011

		Floods/rains				
	Lives lost	People affected (million)	Area affected (million acres)	Cropped area affected (million acres)	Houses damaged	Loss of cattle	Villages affected
1976	99	3,000	3,400	—	3,070,000	—	28,260
1977	280	0.300	0.320	—	51,145	20,139	—
1979	72	0.552	3.935	2.062	62,249	—	4,026
1992	232		—	—	578,000	67,104	—
1994	218	0.690	—	2.745	—	6,090	7,900
1995	172	1.025	1.423	0.085	—	6,547	1,370
2002		1.400	—	2.611	—	—	—
2003	519	4.100	—	—	307,464	37,250	5,200
2007	127	0.753	0.575	0.133	345,000	82	1,686
2010	414	7.274	7.238	2.5	1,073,847	263,589	7,507
2011	233	6	5.938	2.490	1,400,000	14,200	31,960

Sources: Estimated by the authors based on Disaster Risk Management Plan, Sindh Province. Provincial Disaster Management Authority (November 2008). http://www.pdma.pk/dn/LinkClick.aspx?fileticket=t0nKA3HvI98%3d&tabid=59; for 2010, Flood Situation Update 2010, http://www.pdma.pk/dn/Home/FloodSituationUpdate/tabid/120/Default.aspx; National Disaster Management Authority Summary of Losses/Damages due to Rain in Sindh—2011 (period covered: up to September 16, 2011). http://ndma.gov.pk/Documents/monsoon/Sindh/Losses_Damages_16Sep2011.pdf.
Note: — = not available.

The best available assessment of financial costs of flood event was conducted for the flood in 2010 (ADB and World Bank 2010). On the basis of that method, economic cost of flood event is modeled as a function of the affected population. The number of casualties was used to calibrate the slope of this function. R-squared was used to calibrate uncertainties for the function that translates the exposed population into economic damage. The model includes three independent sources of uncertainty:

- Probability of event occurrence at each year
- Magnitude of flood events (distribution of the exposed population)
- Risk coefficient: economic losses per exposed population.

Results of the Monte Carlo simulation are presented in table L.6 and illustrated in figures L.5–L.8

Figure L.5 presents a reversed cumulative distribution function (CDF) of economic damage per flood event. It characterizes the potential magnitude of an isolated shock (flood event) that may randomly happen in Sindh. Although the expected value of the flood event is about 2.3 percent of GDP, the tail risk is significant: risk may exceed 7 percent of GDP in 95 percent of the occurrences, which is a significant shock that may severely damage the regional economy. Because flood events happen randomly, it is important to understand the number of potential events that might occur over a limited time period. Thus, figure L.6 shows the modeled frequency of flood event return over a 10-year period.

Table L.6 Results of Monte Carlo Simulation for Flood Events in Sindh Province, 1976–2011

Statistics	Average annual losses associated with the event, % GDP	Number of events (next 10 years)	Total economic damage, % GDP (next 10 years)
Mean	0.71	2.83	6.43
Median	0.00	3.00	3.03
Standard deviation	1.69	1.40	8.19
Variance	2.87	1.95	67.04
Skewness	3.19	0.2696	2.40
Kurtosis	14.32	2.86	11.02
Percentile	Annual losses associated with the event	Number of events (next 10 years)	Total economic damage (next 10 years)
75	0.47	4.00	8.70
80	0.75	4.00	10.82
85	1.27	4.00	13.48
90	2.68	5.00	17.26
95	4.72	5.00	23.47

Figure L.5 Economic Damage per Flood Event in Sindh Province, 1976–2011

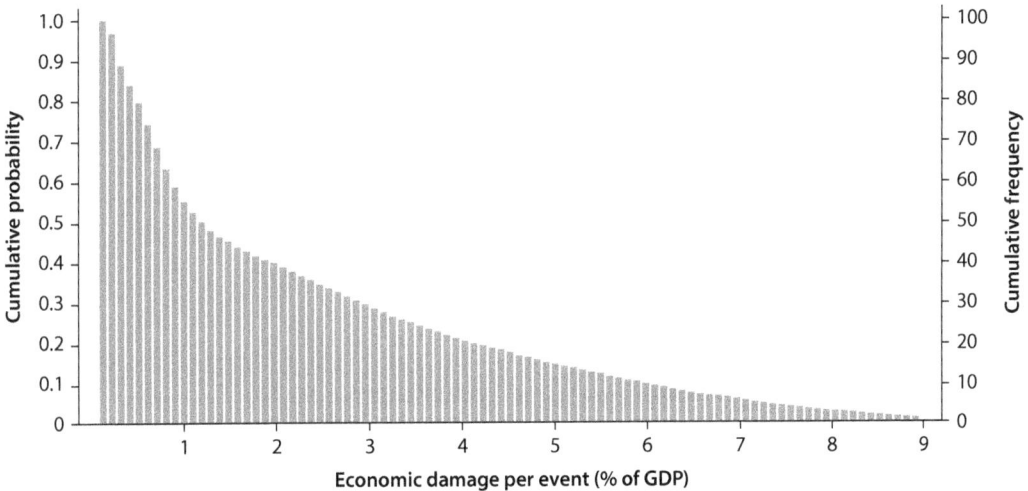

Since flood events do not happen every year, the annual average damage of floods than happen over the 10-year period appears less significant than 2.3 percent of GDP, with a mean value of economic cost that is slightly higher than 0.7 percent of GDP. However, in the 95th percentile, the estimated annual average damage of floods that happens over a 10-year period is slightly higher than 4.7 percent of GDP.

With a relatively low probability of 10 percent, five or more flood events could happen over a 10-year period. The total damage calculated for a given

Figure L.6 Frequency of Flood Event Return over a 10-Year Period in Sindh Province

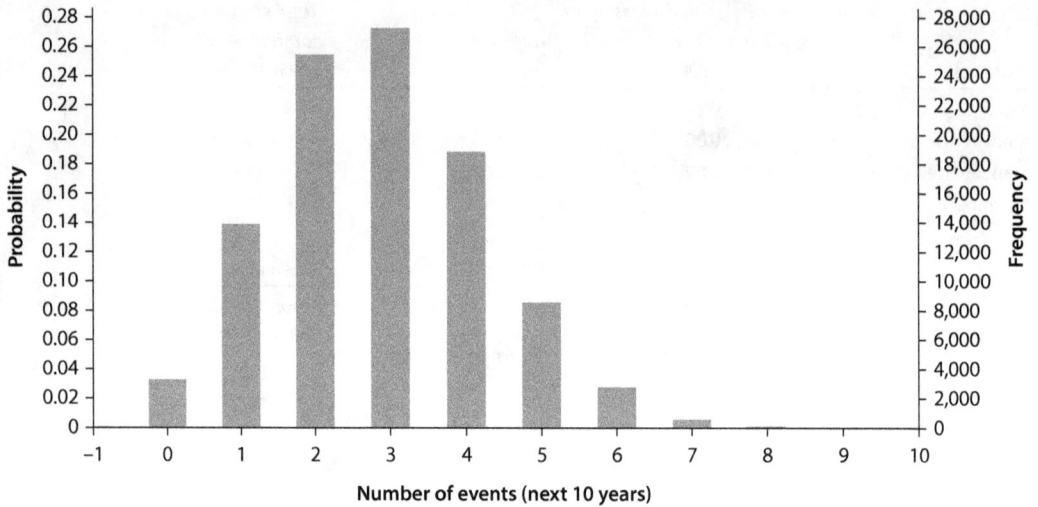

Figure L.7 Distribution of Total Economic Damage from Flooding over a 10-Year Period

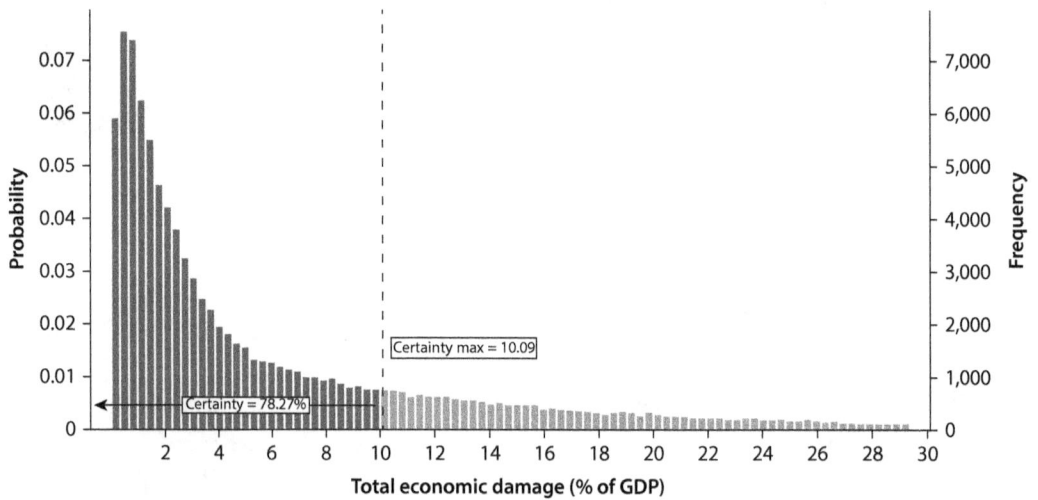

time period (10 years for flood return) provides a better indicator than the estimation of economic damage that that of independent random flood events. Figure L.7 presents the distribution of this parameter. With a probability of about 22 percent, total damage over a 10-year period exceeds 10 percent of Sindh's annual GDP.

Figure L.8 presents distribution of annual flood damage. This figure could be interpreted as a distribution of an annual contribution to a natural catastrophic events mitigation fund. As shown in table L.6, the mean annual contribution to the flood mitigation fund is 0.71 percent of GDP; however, to cope with

Figure L.8 Distribution of Annual Losses from Catastrophic Flooding in Sindh Province over a 10-Year Period

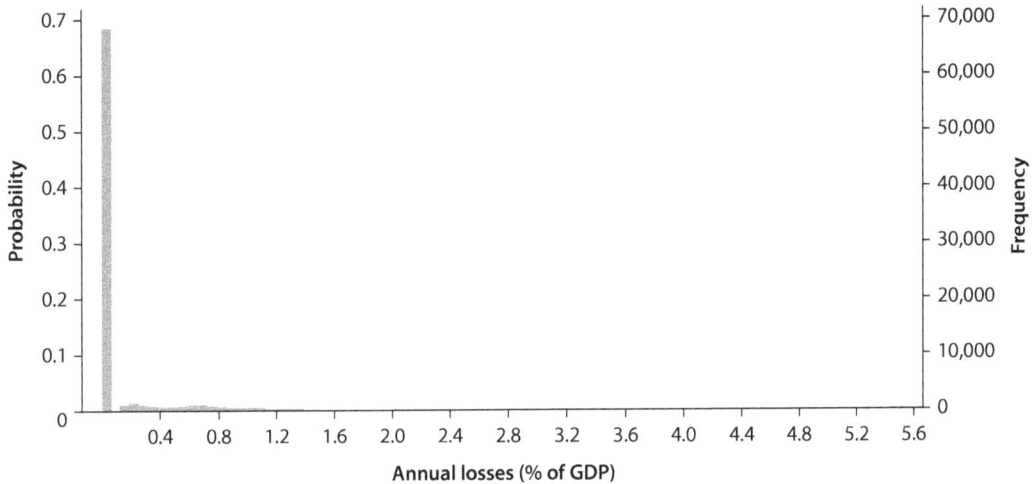

the consequences of catastrophic events with 90 percent confidence, the annual contribution should be at least 1.7 percent (17 percent for 10 years) of GDP.

To cover the cost of a catastrophic flood, the annual average contribution to the recovery fund (to take into account both an average expected cost any year and tail risk of a sequential occurrence of a catastrophic event) should be at least PRs 90 billion or 1.7 percent of Sindh's GDP. This amount was calculated assuming a confidence in adequate funds for a successful recovery with at least a 90 percent probability during a 10-year period.

Table L.6 demonstrates the significance of tail risk for catastrophic floods in Sindh. The additional premium reflects the risk from excessive damage resulting from the tail risk of magnitude and sequence of events over any 10-year period. The excessive contribution (about 1 percent of GDP) reflects the economic value of the risk of a catastrophic event or option value of alternative ways to mitigate these events.

Probabilistic analysis reveals an option value of alternative irrigation technologies and suggests a road map for gradual technological substitution that would minimize risk of exposure to droughts and floods given available resources. It could be estimated in the next stage of the analysis.

Notes

1. Kharif and Rabi are two major cropping seasons in Pakistan. In Kharif, sowing begins in April and harvest is between October and December. Rabi begins in October–December and ends in April–May. Rice, sugar cane, and cotton are mostly Kharif crops, while wheat is a Rabi crop (FAO 2003).

2. Established during field trials with agronomic recommendations as reported in Kahlown and others (1998).

3. http://www.sindhagri.gov.pk/estimate.html

Bibliography

ADB (Asian Development Bank) and World Bank. 2010. *Pakistan Floods 2010: Preliminary Damage and Needs Assessment*. Washington, DC: World Bank.

Briscoe, J., and U. Qamar. 2005. *Pakistan. Water Economy Running Dry*. World Bank, Oxford Press.

FAO (Food and Agriculture Organization of the United Nations). 2003. *Pakistan: Sindh Water Resource Management—Issues and Options*. Food and Agriculture Organization of the United Nations, Rome.

GoS (Government of Sindh). 2009. *Agricultural Data for 2008–09*. Unpublished report, Directorate General of Agriculture Extension, Hyderabad.

———. 2010. *All about Crops Website*. Agriculture, Supply & Prices Department. http://www.sindhagri.gov.pk/estimate.html.

IUCN Pakistan. 2005. "Mangroves of Pakistan. Status and Management." International Union for Conservation of Nature. http://www.iucn.org/.

Kahlown, M., M. Iqbal, M. Skogerboe, and G. V. ur Rehman. 1998. *Waterlogging, Salinity, and Crop Yield Relationships*. IMMI Report R-73. Lahore, Pakistan: International Irrigation Management Institute.

Khan, A. R. 2001. "Analysis of Hydro-Meteorological Time Series: Searching Evidence for Climatic Change in the Upper Indus Basin." IWMI Working Paper 23: International Water Management Institute, Lahore.

Straatsma, M., J. Ettema, and B. Krol. 2010. "Flooding and Pakistan: Causes, Impact and Risk Assessment." The Faculty of Geo-Information Science and Earth Observation (ITC) of the University of Twente. http://www.itc.nl/flooding-and-pakistan.

Tariq, S. 2005. "Water Productivity." Paper presented at the National Seminar on Integrated Water Resources Management, Islamabad.

Environmental Benefits Statement

The World Bank Group is committed to reducing its environmental footprint. In support of this commitment, the Publishing and Knowledge Division leverages electronic publishing options and print-on-demand technology, which is located in regional hubs worldwide. Together, these initiatives enable print runs to be lowered and shipping distances decreased, resulting in reduced paper consumption, chemical use, greenhouse gas emissions, and waste.

The Publishing and Knowledge Division follows the recommended standards for paper use set by the Green Press Initiative. Whenever possible, books are printed on 50 percent to 100 percent postconsumer recycled paper, and at least 50 percent of the fiber in our book paper is either unbleached or bleached using Totally Chlorine Free (TCF), Processed Chlorine Free (PCF), or Enhanced Elemental Chlorine Free (EECF) processes.

More information about the Bank's environmental philosophy can be found at http://crinfo.worldbank.org/wbcrinfo/node/4.

green press INITIATIVE

www.ingramcontent.com/pod-product-compliance
Lightning Source LLC
Chambersburg PA
CBHW080413270326
41929CB00018B/3009